LET'S STUDY ROMANS

In the same series:

LET'S STUDY MATTHEW by Mark E. Ross
LET'S STUDY MARK by Sinclair B. Ferguson
LET'S STUDY LUKE by Douglas J. W. Milne
LET'S STUDY JOHN by Mark G. Johnston
LET'S STUDY ACTS by Dennis E. Johnson
LET'S STUDY 1 CORINTHIANS by David Jackman
LET'S STUDY 2 CORINTHIANS by Derek Prime
LET'S STUDY GALATIANS by Derek Thomas
LET'S STUDY EPHESIANS by Sinclair B. Ferguson
LET'S STUDY PHILIPPIANS by Sinclair B. Ferguson
LET'S STUDY COLOSSIANS & PHILEMON by Mark G. Johnston
LET'S STUDY 1 & 2 THESSALONIANS by Andrew W. Young
LET'S STUDY 1 TIMOTHY by W. John Cook
LET'S STUDY JAMES by Sinclair B. Ferguson
LET'S STUDY HEBREWS by Hywel R. Jones
LET'S STUDY 1 PETER by William W. Harrell
LET'S STUDY 2 PETER & JUDE by Mark G. Johnston
LET'S STUDY THE LETTERS OF JOHN by Ian Hamilton
LET'S STUDY REVELATION by Derek Thomas

Series Editor: SINCLAIR B. FERGUSON

Let's Study ROMANS

Sinclair B. Ferguson

THE BANNER OF TRUTH TRUST

THE BANNER OF TRUTH TRUST

Head Office
3 Murrayfield Road
Edinburgh, EH12 6EL
UK

North America Office
610 Alexander Spring Road
Carlisle, PA 17015
USA

banneroftruth.org

First published 2025

ISBN
Print: 978 1 80040 500 4
Epub: 978 1 80040 501 1

*

*

Typeset in 11/12.5 pt Ehrhardt MT at
The Banner of Truth Trust,
Edinburgh

Printed in the USA by
Versa Press, Inc.,
East Peoria, IL

To

JOHN RAWLINSON

and

JONATHAN WATSON

Whose faithful commitment

to

Christian literature

has strengthened the church

to

the ends of the earth

Contents

Publisher's Preface

Let's Study Romans is part of a series of books which seek to explain and apply the message of Scripture. The series is designed to meet a specific and important need in the church. While not technical commentaries, the volumes comment on the text of a biblical book; and, without being merely lists of practical applications, they are concerned with the ways in which the teaching of Scripture can affect and transform our lives today. Understanding the Bible's message and applying its teaching are the aims.

Like other volumes in the series, *Let's Study Romans* seeks to combine explanation and application. Its concern is to be helpful to ordinary Christian people by encouraging them to understand the message of the Bible and apply it to their own lives. The reader in view is not the person who is interested in all the detailed questions which fascinate the scholar, although behind the writing of each study lies an appreciation for careful and detailed scholarship. The aim is exposition of Scripture written in the language of a friend, seated alongside you with an open Bible.

Let's Study Romans is designed to be used in various contexts. It can be used simply as an aid for individual Bible study. Some may find it helpful to use in their devotions with their husband or wife, or to read in the context of the whole family.

In order to make these studies more useful, not only for individual use but also for group study in Sunday School classes and home, church or college, study guide material will be found on pp. 401-425. Sometimes we come away frustrated rather than helped by group discussions. Frequently that is because we have been encouraged to discuss a passage of Scripture which we do not understand very well in the first place. Understanding must always be the foundation for enriching discussion and for thoughtful, practical application. Thus, in addition to the exposition of Romans, the additional material provides questions to encourage personal thought and study, or to be used as discussion starters. The Group Study Guide divides the material into twenty-six sections and provides direction for leading and participating in group study and discussion.

Outline of Romans

I. 1:1-17: INTRODUCTION

(i)	1:1-7	Greetings
(ii)	1:8-15	Explanations
(iii)	1:16-17	Theme: The Gospel is the Power of God for Salvation

II. 1:18-3:20: SALVATION NEEDED

(i)	1:18-32	Wrath towards Ungodliness and Unrighteousness
(ii)	2:1-16	God's Righteous Judgment
(iii)	2:17–3:8	Judgment on Jews
(iv)	3:9-20	All—Jews and Gentiles—under Sin

III. 3:21–5:21: SALVATION PROVIDED

(i)	3:21-26	Righteousness Manifested and Imputed
(ii)	3:27-31	Boasting Excluded, Law Upheld
(iii)	4:1-25	Righteousness Provided Always (and Only) by Faith
(iv)	5:1-11	Implications of Justification
(v)	5:12-21	The Deep Foundations of Sin and Salvation

IV. 6:1–8:39: SALVATION EXPERIENCED

(i)	6:1-14	Sin's Dominion Broken
(ii)	6:15-23	The Slavery of Perfect Freedom

Author's Preface

Let's Study Romans is intended to share the goals and the style of all the volumes in the *Let's Study* Series: to provide accessible commentary and exposition of the New Testament that will help individuals and small groups to understand and apply the Scriptures. Like all the other volumes in the series this one is deeply appreciative of and indebted to works of technical scholarship, but its goal has been to meet the needs of the church at large.

Thus, for example, these pages are relatively free of footnotes and aim at a fairly comfortable level of readability. Not all commentaries are designed for ease of reading. Rightly so, since some are works of technical scholarship that examine the ancient text and its context sentence by sentence, and even word by word. We tend to consult rather than read through them because they require us to move back and forwards between reading the text of the Scriptures and reading the pages of the commentary.

In keeping with the series style, the goal here has been different: to produce a study guide that can also be read in its own right; to explain and apply the text of the New Testament as though author and reader were sitting beside each other working their way through Paul's remarkable letter to the churches in Rome. The hope is that at the end readers will be able to turn back to the Scriptures for themselves and to 'read, mark, learn, and inwardly digest'[1] what they have studied.

Thus *Let's Study Romans* is not intended to be a word-by-word, line-by-line commentary, but an exposition with application sometimes stated, sometimes implied, that helps us feel that this letter is part of the living word of God to us today. Occasionally a more extended discussion is offered where a passage might

[1] From the collect for the second Sunday in Advent in Thomas Cranmer's *Book of Common Prayer*, 1549.

warrant special attention because of its doctrinal importance or contemporary relevance.

Romans pulsates with the logic of grace. In reading it we have the privilege of following Paul's thinking as the Spirit leads him to expound what he calls 'my gospel' (Rom. 2:16; 16:25). It is not only the longest, but also in places the most challenging of his letters. But any effort we make to grapple with its teaching will prove to be richly rewarding.

No letter in history has had a greater influence on the fortunes of the Christian church. And if by studying it we feel something of the impact other readers before us have felt then not a single hour of the time we have spent doing so will be fruitless. We may well echo the words of William Tyndale (*c*. 1490/94–1536), surely one of the greatest and most courageous of Englishmen, who wrote in 1526:

> 'Forasmuch as this epistle is the principal and most excellent part of the new Testament and most pure evangelion,' that is to say, glad tidings, and that we call gospel, and also is a light and a way unto the whole Scripture; I think it meet 'that every Christian man not only know it, by rote and without the book, but also exercise himself therein evermore continually, as with the daily bread of the soul. No man verily can read it too oft, or study it too well; for the more it is studied, the easier it is; the more it is chewed, the pleasanter it is; and the more groundly it is searched, the preciouser things are found in it,' so great treasure of spiritual things lieth hid therein.[1]

Tyndale himself was only echoing and indeed virtually quoting and expanding the words Martin Luther had written a few years before in his 1522 *Preface to the New Testament*:

> This epistle is in truth the chief part of the New Testament and the purest Gospel. It would be quite proper for a Christian, not only to know it by heart word for word, but also to study it daily, for it is the soul's daily bread. It can never be read or meditated too much and too well. The more thoroughly it is treated, the more precious it becomes, and the better it tastes.[2]

[1] William Tyndale, *A Prologue on the Epistle of St Paul to the Romans*, in *The Works of William Tyndale,* ed. Henry Walter (1848; repr. Edinburgh: Banner of Truth Trust, 2010), 1:484.

[2] *Martin Luther's Preface to the Epistle to the Romans* (Coromandel East, South Australia: New Creation Publications Inc., 1995), 1. The English translation is taken from the edition produced by Lutheran Publishing House, Adelaide, 1966.

This in turn was the very document that brought John Wesley to life when he heard it read in a never-to-be-forgotten meeting in Aldersgate Street, London on 24 May 1738. He famously described his experience in his journal:

> In the evening I went very unwillingly to a society in Aldersgate Street, where one was reading Luther's preface to the Epistle to the Romans. About a quarter before nine, while he was describing the change which God works in the heart through faith in Christ, I felt my heart strangely warmed. I felt I did trust in Christ, Christ alone for salvation: and an assurance was given me, that he had taken away my sins, even mine, and saved me from the law of sin and death.[1]

Reading these testimonies is surely reason enough to say *Let's Study Romans.*

Let's Study Romans is dedicated to John Rawlinson and Jonathan Watson, two men who have given their best energies and talents to leading the work of the publishers during the years in which the *Let's Study* series has been produced. Most of their work has been done in the background, where they have faithfully dedicated themselves to serve the Lord Jesus Christ through the work of Christian literature. They have shared Paul's desire to 'impart to you some spiritual gift to strengthen you' (Rom. 1:11). By God's grace the fruit of their years of service is now publicly evident throughout the world. Like many others, I am grateful for them.

SINCLAIR B. FERGUSON
October, 2024

[1] *The Works of John Wesley, Journals*, vol. 1 (New York: Eaton & Mains, no date), 74.

Introduction

We are about to embark on a study of the most important letter ever written. It has been read more frequently, studied more carefully, and influenced more people than any letter in the history of the world. Its author, once known to his fellow Jerusalem dwellers as 'Saul of Tarsus' and later by what was probably his Gentile 'given name,' as 'the apostle Paul,' experienced the most famous conversion in history. In turn his letter was instrumental in what have probably been the two most significant conversions since—that of Augustine of Hippo when he was resident in Milan, Italy, who will appear later in these pages, and a millennium later a monk of the Augustinian Order in Wittenberg, Germany, Martin Luther.

Most of us first meet Luther as a man with a reputation for deep piety, but suffering from a troubled conscience, who is engaged in a relentless quest to find a gracious God. He tells us how, in 1519, he was struggling with Paul's words about the righteousness of God in Romans 1:16-17. If God was indeed righteous then Martin Luther was surely condemned. He gave the world a first-person record of what happened:

> Though I lived as a monk without reproach, I felt that I was a sinner before God with an extremely disturbed conscience. I could not believe that he was placated by my satisfaction. I did not love, yes, I hated the righteous God who punishes sinners, and secretly, if not blasphemously, certainly murmuring greatly, I was angry with God …
>
> I raged with a fierce and troubled conscience. Nevertheless, I beat importunately upon Paul at that place, most ardently desiring to know what St Paul wanted. At last, by the mercy of God, meditating day and night, I gave heed to the context of the words, namely, 'In it the righteousness of God is revealed, as it is written, "He who through faith is righteous shall live."' There I began to understand that the righteousness of God is that by

> which the righteous lives by a gift of God, namely by faith. And this is the meaning: the righteousness of God is revealed by the gospel, namely, the passive righteousness with which merciful God justifies us by faith, as it is written, 'He who through faith is righteous shall live.' Here I felt that I was altogether born again and had entered paradise itself through open gates. ... [1]

Throughout the Christian centuries, readers of Romans have had similar experiences—usually much less dramatic, but no less real and life-transforming. They have discovered that to study and understand this one letter (as Luther came to see), is to be given a key to the whole Bible.

THE ROMANS

In the middle of the first century AD, when Paul's letter reached Rome the city stood at the epicentre of a world power whose territory stretched from the Middle East to Great Britain. The Roman Empire had been virtually all-conquering, and its dominance can still be seen in the roads, buildings, walls and artefacts in which archaeologists continue to uncover its remarkable accomplishments as well as its cruel deeds. But in the first century AD, in the capital city of that empire, a new kingdom was beginning to establish itself. Jesus Christ was fulfilling his promise to build his church (Matt. 16:18). The vision of the future that once disturbingly surfaced in King Nebuchadnezzar's dreams was coming to pass: a stone that 'was cut by no human hand' was beginning to become 'a great mountain' that would fill 'the whole earth' (Dan. 2:34-35).

But how did the church in Rome come to be?

On the Day of Pentecost, Luke tells us, 'there were dwelling in Jerusalem Jews, devout men from every nation under heaven' (Acts 2:5). Among these 'Jews and proselytes' who each heard the apostles 'speaking in his own language' were 'visitors from Rome' (Acts 2:6, 10). It seems likely that some of them were among the three thousand who were baptized that day (Acts 2:41). If so, the church in Rome was originally birthed in Jerusalem.

By the time Paul wrote to the Romans some two decades later there were several house churches in the city. Exactly how many is

[1] *Luther's Works,* vol. 34, ed. H. T Lehmann, *Career of the Reformer IV* (St Louis: Concordia Publishing House, 1960), 336-337.

difficult to determine. In his closing remarks he sends greetings to the church that met in the home of Prisca and Aquila, and also to two groups of friends and, in one case, 'the brothers who are with them,' and, in the other, 'all the saints who are with them' (Rom. 16:5, 14-15). There may have been other house church gatherings in the capital city. And if, as most scholars believe, Paul wrote his letter to the Philippians at the time of his later confinement in Rome (Acts 28:16-31), by the mid-50s AD there were believers even in Imperial service ('All the saints greet you, especially those of Caesar's household'—Phil. 4:22). What is also remarkable about the closing greetings in Romans 16 is the number of Christians in Rome who were already known to Paul, although he had never visited the city. He mentions no less than twenty-six by name and greets others of whom he had at least some knowledge.

It could not have been easy to be a follower of Jesus Christ in Rome. After all he had been 'crucified under Pontius Pilate'—onetime governor of the Roman Province of Palestine—as the 'Apostles' Creed' (that probably began life in the church in Rome) would later state. Those words must have served as a constant reminder that Christian faith was not only counter-cultural but also might prove costly.

Jesus had prophesied that 'the gates of hell' would attack the church he planned to build; but they would not prevail (Matt. 16:18). Those dark powers had already used more than one weapon of attack. If in Jerusalem intimidation failed to cower the apostles (Acts 4:18-22; 5:17-42), then either false ambition (as in the case of Ananias and his wife Sapphira in Acts 5:1-11), or internal division (as in the case of the complaints of the Hellenists against the Hebrews in Acts 6:1-6) might succeed.

While these tactics had failed to destroy the church in Jerusalem, Paul was conscious they would be used again. And we do not need to read far between the lines in his letter to the Romans to see that the churches there were under a similar attack.

PAUL

By the time Paul dictated his letter to Tertius (16:22), around 57 AD, he had been a follower of Christ for perhaps two decades. From the beginning of his Christian life he had been deeply conscious of the call of Christ and made profoundly aware that he had been set apart to be an apostle to the Gentiles—as doubtless Ananias had first relayed to him (see Acts 9:15; Gal. 1:15-16). Later, set apart with Barnabas by the church in Antioch (Acts 13:1-3) he had engaged in a series of missionary journeys throughout the Eastern Empire, planting churches, and thereafter encouraging new Christians both by his visits and his correspondence.

Now, at the time of writing, Paul was in the area of Corinth, hosted by Gaius, in whose home the Corinthian church probably met (16:23). He was *en route* to Jerusalem with the financial gift he had been collecting from the churches he had planted in order to give material assistance to the Jewish Christians in Jerusalem who had suffered persecution and privation of various kinds. Converted to Christ these Jewish Christians had probably been ostracized from family and social life; in addition, there had been periods of famine, so their need was considerable. In this practical gift (about which Paul had written at some length to the Corinthians—2 Cor. 8:1–9:15) the Gentile churches were expressing their love for, their sense of unity with, and indeed their indebtedness to, the church in Jerusalem (Rom. 15:25-27). It is not surprising then that even opponents of the Christian faith noticed that the followers of Christ seemed to love one another even before they met!

As the apostle made ready to leave Corinth for Jerusalem, a question uppermost in his mind was: 'What next?' He was a church planter, an apostle who laid foundations and nurtured them, rather than a long-term local pastor in one congregation (although he had ministered in Corinth for eighteen months and in Ephesus for almost three years). He felt that his work among the churches he had already planted and nurtured was drawing to a close. Now, he sensed, he should move further west. His plan was to go to Spain (15:28). The journey there would give him the opportunity to visit the believers in Rome. It was a natural as well as a spiritual ambition. After all, he was a Roman citizen. More important, he was an apostle to the Gentiles. He wanted to give his life for the blessing of the churches and the finding of the lost. Of course, he wanted to go to Rome. He had often hoped to visit; but thus far his hopes had never been realised (1:9-13). Now, surely, was the time.

But if Paul was sure he wanted to visit the church in Rome, could he be sure that all the Christians in Rome would want him to visit? And would they be willing to support his work in practical ways, as other churches had done? Presumably, his friends Prisca and Aquila would—he had, after all, lived with them for a while in Corinth (Acts 18:1-3) and at one time they had 'risked their necks' for him (16:4). Surely some of his other friends in the capital would also welcome and help him?

Nevertheless, Paul was conscious that not everyone was enamoured of his ministry. He had, after all, been a persecutor of the church. He was not one of the original apostles. And everywhere he went trouble seemed to erupt, especially among the Jewish population. Plus there were rumours about his teaching that had created some suspicion of him and his preaching of the gospel. It was even said that he believed we can 'do evil that good may come'—a charge he vigorously repudiated (3:8). When he visited Jerusalem shortly after sending *Romans*, James and some of the believers in Jerusalem had been sufficiently concerned about prejudice against his teaching on the law that they urged him to conform to certain Jewish practices while he was in the city (Acts 21:17-26).

Paul must have been conscious that rumours about him had almost certainly reached the ears of Christians in Rome—which, after all, was not a 'Pauline church.' He had not planted it, and most of its members had never heard his preaching and teaching. With all this in mind and having some sense of the situation in the house churches in Rome (perhaps from Prisca and Aquila), Paul now began to dictate to Tertius (16:22) the opening words of this his greatest letter: 'Paul, a servant of Jesus Christ ...'

THE LETTER

Romans is, in a sense, a letter of introduction. Paul's chief burden is to explain, expound, and defend what he twice calls 'my gospel' (2:16; 16:25). Of course, as he says elsewhere, there is only one gospel, not many (Gal. 1:6-9). But it is clear that each of the authors in the New Testament had his own approach to preaching it or writing about it. They all shared the same message about Jesus Christ, but the Spirit very clearly employed their distinctive personalities, experiences, gifts and ministry contexts as they composed the Gospels, the Acts of the Apostles, the Letters, and the Revelation. So, when Paul refers to the gospel he preached as 'my gospel' or 'our gospel' (2:16; 16:25; cf. 1 Thess. 1:5; 2 Tim. 2:8), he simply means the particular way he understood, preached, and applied the message of Jesus Christ, Son of God, Son of Man, crucified and risen Saviour and Lord.

So there were several reasons for writing *Romans*. Naturally, as the apostle to the Gentiles, Paul wanted to be in touch with the church in the capital city of the western world, the place of greatest influence, as well as the place where opposition to the gospel would become fiercest. As someone responsible under God for bringing the gospel to the Gentile world, Paul felt a responsibility for the Christians in Rome. No doubt the Christians there—as all believers do—needed instruction, encouragement, and direction. He knows his gospel will help them.

Then, as we have noted, Paul had also discovered, even before Simon Peter wrote about it (2 Pet. 3:15), that people were twisting his teaching. His understanding of the law of Moses was an ongoing issue. In fact it precipitated the events that led to him eventually arriving in Rome—as a prisoner (Acts 21:28)!

It was therefore especially important to him to show that his gospel was in complete harmony with the Scriptures of the Old Testament, and to demonstrate that he had been given divine insight into God's purposes through faith in the Lord Jesus. All this was vital if, as he hoped, the Roman Christians were to support his mission to Spain.

We will see these themes woven throughout the fabric of his letter. And we will also see Paul applying his gospel to situations he knew had arisen in the churches in Rome.

And so, with all this in view—and, behind him, two decades of experience of preaching the gospel—Paul now introduced himself to the church in Rome as Christ's servant and apostle (1:1), and began to dictate his letter. No doubt he made sure there was at least one copy of it. He then handed it to friends travelling to Rome and asked them to deliver it to the church there. He refers by name to one person almost certainly in that group, a woman called Phoebe, a faithful and generous member of the church in Cenchreae (the port of Corinth). She was a lady of means, travelling for undisclosed reasons to the capital of the Empire (16:1-2). Many commentators have assumed she was the bearer of the letter. Paul does not state this explicitly; but if she was it is certain she would not have been travelling on her own.

It would be several years before Paul would make his long-hoped-for journey along the *Via Appia* and arrive in Rome. He did not come in the way he had anticipated. But the Acts of the Apostles gives us a moving clue to the positive response his letter must have received: 'The brothers there [Rome], when they heard about us, came as far as the Forum of Appius and Three Taverns to meet us.' Given all that lay in the background to the writing of this letter it is not at all surprising that 'On seeing them, Paul thanked God and took courage' (Acts 28:15).

What Paul did at the sight of the Roman Christians we can surely do now as we begin to study the letter they had already read and absorbed! For in our hands is a doctrine-filled document that expounds 'the gospel of God'; a pastoral document that addresses some very real problems that continue to trouble the church; and a missiological document expressing Paul's burden to bring the gospel to places where it had never before been heard.

To Paul's *Letter to the Romans* then we now turn.

I

A Letter from Paul!

Paul, a servant of Christ Jesus, called to be an apostle, set apart
for the gospel of God, 2 which he promised beforehand through
his prophets in the holy Scriptures, 3 concerning his Son, who
was descended from David according to the flesh 4 and was
declared to be the Son of God in power according to the Spirit
of holiness by his resurrection from the dead, Jesus Christ our
Lord, 5 through whom we have received grace and apostleship
to bring about the obedience of faith for the sake of his name
among all the nations, 6 including you who are called to belong
to Jesus Christ, 7 To all those in Rome who are loved by God
and called to be saints: Grace to you and peace from God our
Father and the Lord Jesus Christ.

(Rom. 1:1-7)

It is not difficult to imagine the scene. Even in the great city of Rome word must have travelled fast among those who were known as 'Christians.' Perhaps the message was: 'Come to Priscilla and Aquila's home on the evening of the coming *Dies Dominicus* (the Lord's Day). A letter has arrived from the apostle Paul. Those who have already read it say he's hoping to visit us!'

They had never received a letter from Paul before, although a surprising number of them knew him (16:3-15). But as they made their way, perhaps to the home of Priscilla and Aquila, even those who knew him could hardly second-guess the contents of the letter. Little did they know that they were about to hear for the first time the most important letter ever written.

The New Testament contains thirteen of Paul's letters, written to various churches and individuals. Peter indicates that these letters were being collected in the churches and were already regarded as part of the new Scriptures that God was giving to his people (2 Pet. 3:15-16).

All of us have patterns of speech—characteristic ways of speaking or writing. Some of these patterns derive from the culture in which we live. Letters tend to have similar patterns. Paul's correspondence is no exception. In his culture letters sensibly began by the writer introducing himself, addressing the person or persons to whom he was writing, and expressing greetings.

Paul follows this pattern. But he also makes it his own. Or, more specifically, he fills out the pattern with the gospel—an illustration of the fact that for him faith in Jesus Christ affected every detail of his life.

Here he introduces himself (verse 1) and the letter's recipients (verse 7a) and greets them warmly (verse 7b). But he also develops his introduction of himself—after all, this is a letter written to a church he had never visited. Unlike the churches in (for example) Galatia and Corinth, Thessalonica and Philippi, it did not owe its origin to his ministry.

'Paul' (verse 1) was the name Saul of Tarsus used in the Gentile world from which he originally came, having been born in Tarsus in Cilicia (Acts 22:3). As in most of his other letters (those to Philippi and Thessalonica being exceptions) he introduces himself as an apostle. He is a man under authority—a 'sent one'—called by God (verse 1). He was not self-appointed. In fact he had been set apart initially before he was born and then called by Christ on the road to Damascus specifically to take the gospel to the Gentiles (Gal. 1:15; Acts 9:1-18). He was deeply conscious of his responsibility to care for all the Gentile churches (2 Cor. 11:28), and thus for the churches in Rome. So he was keen to minister to them (Rom. 1:11).

But, in addition, Paul is hoping to receive assistance from the believers in Rome as he envisages spreading the gospel further west into Spain (see 15:24). And he is very conscious that if he is to have the support and blessing of Christians who do not know him well, he needs to do two things: (1.) to lay before them his understanding of the gospel, and (2.) to clear up misunderstandings and false rumours that had been spreading about his teaching (something Simon Peter also knew had happened—2 Pet. 3:15-16).

SERVANT AND APOSTLE

This background to the letter perhaps explains the order of Paul's twofold self-description. He is first of all a 'servant [or *slave*] of Christ Jesus.' Ever since Christ had dramatically arrested him on the road to Damascus, he had called Jesus 'Lord' (Acts 9:5).

'Servant' (*doulos*, slave) conveys two aspects of Paul's self-understanding: (1.) His life was now entirely Christ's. As he says later, he had been set free from slavery to sin to become obedient to a new Master (6:17-18). But in addition (2.) Isaiah had used the term 'servant' when he announced the coming Saviour (Isa. 42:1; 49:5; 50:10; 52:13). He had taken 'the form of a servant' (Phil. 2:7). For Paul, therefore, no self-designation could bestow a higher honour on him. Perhaps there was an additional reason: numbers of early Christians were themselves slaves of human masters (Eph. 6:5-8; Col. 3:22-25)—possibly Paul was embracing both himself and them into the same category: they all served a higher Master, Jesus Christ.

The word 'apostle' is the Greek-derived equivalent of our Latin-derived word 'missionary'—someone who has been commissioned and sent. It has both a general and a special use in the New Testament. In a general sense it is used for individuals sent on a mission by their congregation. They were designated 'apostles' (messengers) of those churches (*e.g.* 2 Cor. 8:23; Phil. 2:25). But Paul usually employs the term as a reference to 'the twelve' and himself in the specialized sense to denote those who were set apart directly by Christ to be the foundation stones of the new covenant community (Eph. 4:11).

The apostles' many-sided calling and commission was to preach the gospel, to plant churches (Matt. 28:18-20), and to provide new Scriptures for the churches (our New Testament). With that in view, the Lord Jesus had promised that the Spirit would enable them to bear witness to him (John 15:26). He would bring to their mind all he had taught them, illumine for them the significance of his person and work, and unveil for them his purposes in the future (John 14:26; 16:12-15). As apostles directly commissioned by the risen Christ, their ministries were marked by 'the signs of a true apostle' (1 Cor. 9:1; 2 Cor. 12:12; cf. Rom. 15:19).

Fundamental then to Paul being 'a servant of Christ Jesus, called to be an apostle' was that he was 'set apart for the gospel of God' (cf. Gal. 1:15).

THE GOSPEL OF GOD

Paul here calls the gospel 'the gospel *of God.*' True, Christ stands at the centre of it, but he does so because he brings us salvation and the knowledge of God the Trinity—it is in and through the incarnate Son that we come to know both the Father and the Holy Spirit. To know Christ is to know the Father and to come to experience the Holy Spirit. We are baptized into this three-fold name. So to say, 'Christianity is Christ,' or 'Christ *is* the gospel' is true—but it is by no means the whole truth. The gospel that is given to us by God (it is 'the gospel *of* God' in that sense) is also *about* God, that is, God the Trinity. It is illuminating to read through Romans (especially chapters 5–8) to see the extent to which the united ministry of the three persons of the Trinity is woven into the very texture of the apostle's understanding of the gospel (*e.g.* 5:5-11; 8:9-11).

PAUL'S GOSPEL

It will soon become clear that Paul (i) has a real desire to visit Rome, (ii) is seeking the support of the church in Rome for further missionary work, and (iii) knows that twisted versions of his teaching may have already circulated in Rome. So in the way he frames his greetings to the believers he gives a brief summary of his understanding of 'the gospel of God' (what he later calls 'my gospel,' *i.e.* the gospel he preaches; 2:16; 16:25).

What follows is a remarkable 'confession of faith'—one worth committing to memory. It provides a summary of Paul's understanding of Christ and contains hints of themes Paul will develop as the letter progresses.

In essence this summary expresses several characteristics of the person of the Lord Jesus and his work, all of which are essential to a full understanding of the gospel.

1. The gospel is focussed on Jesus Christ. It is 'the gospel concerning his Son' (verse 3).

2. The gospel Paul preaches is not his own invention, or that of the apostles who accompanied Jesus during his earthly ministry. The prophets bore advance witness to it (verse 2). Hence Romans abounds in quotations from, and allusions to, the Old Testament.

As we will see, one of the questions raised by Paul's preaching (especially in the Jewish community) was whether his gospel was consistent with the teaching of the Old Testament. Paul believed that Jesus *fulfilled* the Old Testament, and in this simple statement he is already allaying any fears about his attitude to the Hebrew Bible.

3. The gospel began to be fully revealed in the incarnation. God's Son—a divine person with a divine nature—became incarnate. He was born of the seed of David (verse 3). Mary was not merely a conduit for a newly minted humanity unrelated to ours (cf. 9:5; Rev. 22:16). He came 'in the likeness of sinful flesh' (8:3). In the miracle of Christ's conception he remained the Son of God, yet, at the same time, by taking our human nature he was equipped to be our representative, substitute, and Saviour—what Paul elsewhere calls 'the second man' and 'last Adam' (1 Cor. 15:45-48). He will expound the significance of this later in 5:12-21.

4. Paul also describes Christ Jesus in terms of the resurrection in which he was 'declared to be the Son of God in power' (verse 4). Bible students have sometimes assumed that these words emphasize the *deity* of Christ, while verse 3 ('seed of David') had emphasized his *humanity*. But in fact he is thinking here not so much about his *two natures* but about his *two states.* The words in verse 3, 'descended from David according to the flesh' refer to the lowly condition in which the Son of God was born—to what theologians call his 'state of humiliation.' The words of verse 4 refer to his 'state of exaltation,' in which he, the incarnate One, was 'declared to be the Son-of-God-with-power' in the resurrection. In the incarnation God the Son humbles himself; in the resurrection God the Son, who humbled himself by taking our nature, is exalted.

5. This leads very naturally to the implications of the *reign* of the exalted Christ (cf. Matt. 28:18-20). In the light of Jesus' exaltation Paul has now received 'grace and apostleship to bring about the obedience of faith for the sake of his name among all the nations.' Paul's life has been caught up into the fulfilment of God's Old Testament promises (notice how the word 'nations' in Psa. 2:8 is echoed here in verse 5).

The significance of the preposition 'of' can be difficult to pin down. The expression 'the obedience *of faith*' is thus open to more than one interpretation. Does Paul mean 'the obedience that faith expresses' or that 'faith *is* obedience' because God commands it?

Perhaps his answer might be: 'Well, at the end of the day it is really both, isn't it?' When, for example, the Philippian jailer trusted in Christ he was (1.) being obedient to the command 'believe in the Lord Jesus Christ.' But (2.) his faith also gave rise to a life of obedience as he fulfilled the command to love his neighbour as himself by serving Paul and Silas (Acts 16:30-34). Later Paul describes coming to faith in Christ as becoming 'obedient from the heart ... [and becoming] slaves of righteousness' (6:17-18). There is no genuine faith that does not also prove itself by obedience.

6. Paul also hints at the *goal* of the gospel. It is to lead to the *international* honouring and glorifying of Christ (verse 5: 'among all the nations.' Cf. Luke 24:47). Paul, the servant of Christ Jesus, makes his name known so that through his ministry the incarnate, crucified, resurrected, and exalted Suffering Servant will 'sprinkle many nations ... kings will shut their mouths because of him' (Isa. 52:15; cf. Psa. 2:8). Before Paul concludes his letter he will tell us once again that he was deeply conscious he had been called to participate in that ministry (cf. 15:18-21).

Paul then brings the links in this wonderful chain of gospel grace to the point where it connects with the Roman Christians. His ministry to the Gentiles includes 'you who are called to belong to Jesus Christ. To all those in Rome ...' (verses 6-7). The gospel, designed in the heart of the eternal God, prophesied in the Old Testament Scriptures, realized in the life and ministry of Christ, preached among the nations so that Christ might be honoured, has now come to Rome, the epicentre of the ancient western world. God's purposes stretch from the world of eternity into the world of the contemporary. Every link in the chain has been secured by him. This, indeed, is 'the gospel of God'!

These wonderful, exultant words bring Paul to a simple greeting to the Romans.

GREETINGS

Different cultures tend to give greetings in diverse ways, usually in expressing hopes that the recipient is in good health, or that life is, generally speaking, stable, or that he or she is recovering from or coping with either sickness or sadness. Paul here enlarges on (i) his description of the Romans and (ii) his aspirations for them.

The believers in Rome are—like all Christians—'called to belong to Jesus Christ ... called to be saints' (or perhaps 'called saints'; 1:6-7). The reference is not only to some who were especially and distinctively 'saintly' but to all the believers. All of them had been set apart, 'sanctified' to God in that sense, reserved for him and for his purposes.

To this Paul adds a beautiful description of the Romans: they are 'loved by God.' He thus points them to what lies behind the unbreakable chain of God's purposes in verses 2-6 (cf. 8:35-39). At the root of everything, at the foundation of the plan of salvation, at the heart of the message of the gospel, lies the love of God for them. He will return to discuss this love later (5:8). But here, at the opening of a letter that will be filled with mind-stretching theology, he anchors his fellow believers in what is basic to his theology, namely the magnitude of what God had done and was continuing to do for them *because of his love*.

The apostle John described himself as 'the disciple whom Jesus loved' (John 13:23; 19:26; 20:2; 21:7, 20). His words are sometimes read as though he meant 'the disciple Jesus loved more than he loved anyone else.' But this cannot be his meaning. For Paul could also describe himself similarly. He spoke of 'the Son of God, who loved me ...' (Gal. 2:20). Were there, then, only two disciples especially loved? No. Paul hints here at this wonderful truth: every believer has the privilege of being able to say 'I am the disciple Jesus loved'—that was true of *every single believer* in each of the house-churches in Rome. He is reminding them that, whatever their differences, they belonged to the same family and shared the same DNA—they were 'loved by God.'

To 'all those in Rome' then, Paul wishes 'grace'—God's loving, faithful, merciful, condescension—and 'peace'—*shalom*, well-being, restoration of life to the way God originally intended it to be lived. Both are sourced in the heart of the loving Father, provided for us in his Son, Jesus Christ, and by implication (as Paul will show) brought into our lives by the Holy Spirit.

We have considered only the first seven verses of this letter, but already Paul's gospel has given us a theological 'work-out.' Yet he is also making it clear that its message is not merely a theoretical one designed to stretch the intellects of the best and brightest of the

Christians in Rome. No, this greeting is for every believer because the gospel of grace and peace is intended 'to bring about the obedience of faith for the sake of his name among all the nations ...' And that means what Paul says to the Romans he is also saying to every reader who belongs to Jesus Christ, wherever we are 'among the nations.'

2

Apostolic Attitudes

First, I thank my God through Jesus Christ for all of you,
because your faith is proclaimed in all the world. 9 *For God is*
my witness, whom I serve with my spirit in the gospel of his Son,
that without ceasing I mention you 10 *always in my prayers,*
asking that somehow by God's will I may now at last succeed
in coming to you. 11 *For I long to see you, that I may impart to*
you some spiritual gift to strengthen you— 12 *that is, that we*
may be mutually encouraged by each other's faith, both yours
and mine. 13 *I do not want you to be unaware, brothers, that*
I have often intended to come to you (but thus far have been
prevented), in order that I may reap some harvest among you as
well as among the rest of the Gentiles. 14 *I am under obligation*
both to Greeks and to barbarians, both to the wise and to the
foolish. 15 *So I am eager to preach the gospel to you also who*
are in Rome.

(Rom. 1:8-15)

The opening sections of Paul's letters often give us hints about what he will say later. On occasion we can almost 'read off' what is already on his mind and the themes to which he will return or the situations he will address. Here, at the outset of his letter he is expressing his bond of fellowship with the believers in Rome. For a surprising number of them with whom he seems to be familiar (see 16:3-16) this will simply confirm what they already know—namely that he cares deeply about them. But Paul also senses the importance of embracing those he has never met. So there is a pastoral wisdom underlying the fact that he leaves personal greetings to the end of the letter, lest he be suspected of favouritism. These individual expressions of affection to friends and colleagues are certainly legitimate; but first of all he wants to embrace each and every brother and sister in the church.

These verses also give us a glimpse—on Paul's part unself-conscious—into the way in which 'the gospel of God' (verse 1) had transformed this former Christ-hater's life. His verbs tell us a great deal about his heart.

He is thankful for the Romans—notice '*to* God' and '*through* Jesus Christ.' Like Gregory of Nazianzus three centuries later, Paul cannot think about one person of the Trinity without thinking of the others.

What stimulates his gratitude is the way the gospel that came from the heart of God has now reached the epicentre of the empire in Rome (verses 1-6). More than that, the fact that there are faith-filled Christians in Rome is now being 'proclaimed in all the world' (verse 8). Because of this, Paul embraces all of them ('all of you,' verse 8), just as his opening greetings had been addressed to them all. This comprehensive, loving embrace lays a good foundation for the way in which he will throughout the letter (and especially in chapters 11, 14 and 15) encourage Christians from differing backgrounds (Jew and Gentile) to welcome and embrace all their fellow believers.

Paul's uses 'world' (*kosmos*, verse 8) in a general sense here. He is not implying that every single human being has heard about the way people in Rome have come to faith. A similar general use is found elsewhere in Scripture (*e.g.* in John 12:19 when the Pharisees complain about the crowds following Jesus, 'Look, the world has gone after him'—as well as elsewhere).

THANKFULNESS AND PRAYERFULNESS

Elsewhere Paul encourages us not only to heed his teaching but to follow his example (Phil. 3:17). Here his sense of gratitude is an important challenge for us. What makes it particularly impressive is the way he is thankful for the work of grace in Rome. After all, the churches there were not the direct fruit of his own ministry. This is a striking indication of the extent to which Christ and his glory mean everything to him. His own success in ministry is fully subordinated to Christ's success. The litmus test of grace implied here is the ability to be thankful for the way God has prospered work that other believers have been engaged in without any contribution from ourselves.

Hand in glove with thankfulness is Paul's prayerfulness. It is one of his leading characteristics (*e.g.* Eph. 1:16; 1 Thess. 1:2; 2 Tim. 1:3). He was both preacher and prayer-warrior. Along with his unreserved submission to his Saviour—'God is my witness, whom I serve with my spirit in the gospel of his Son' (verse 9)—is his intercession ('I mention you always in my prayers' verses 9-10). As a servant or slave he is entirely dependent on his master to give every directive and to supply every need, both for himself and for others.

This mixture of thankfulness and prayerfulness had kindled in Paul a deep desire to visit these Christians in Rome. Whenever he prays for them he adds an extra personal petition: 'Lord, please let me visit the believers in Rome.' Even in the process of dictating this letter he was hoping it would be in the Lord's purposes for him to see them so that he might 'impart some spiritual gift to strengthen' them (verse 11).

It is fascinating to see that no sooner had Paul dictated these words to Tertius than he qualified them ('... that is ...,' verse 12). He is not withdrawing them as though they were in error—for these words too are part of God-beathed Scripture. They state quite plainly what Paul desired. But—perhaps sensitive to the fact that his critics (as critics do) pounced on anything they could twist (2 Pet. 3:15-16)—he explains that his desire here is not one-sided; his pastoral leadership is not pastoral 'control.' No, he hopes, indeed expects, to receive from them as well as give to them.

All ministry is two-sided like this. Paul had apostolic gifts none of the members of the churches in Rome possessed; but they too have gifts and graces to share with him. Later he would write to the Ephesians about the way the church is built up in love, not by one member alone, but when members of the body are all doing their work lovingly and using their gifts properly (Eph. 4:15-16). So Paul expects that, were he able to visit the Romans, his fellowship with them would be full of mutual encouragement.

When you think that these are the words of someone who belonged to a small (and in that sense 'elite') group of men, the apostles, this is a wonderful example of how gifts need to be coupled with grace; God-given abilities are meant to be embedded in a genuine humility coupled with a proper sense of the privilege and dignity these gifts bring. Paul does not deny the special apostolic authority and gifts present in his ministry. But nor does he demean or despise the blessing he receives from the ministry of others differently or even less gifted than himself. Jesus didn't either. Neither should we.

WHY THE DELAY?

These sentiments may well have raised a question for some of the Christians in Rome. All this sounded very sincere—this talk about prayer and thankfulness and a desire to see them. But if that was the case, why had he not already visited them? Were some of the rumours that circulated about him true?—for example, that he would sometimes make promises he failed to keep or say things he did not really mean. Perhaps the false rumours in Corinth had already reached Rome, that he had a habit of saying 'Yes, I'm coming' when he really meant 'No, you'll not be seeing me' (2 Cor. 1:16-22).

Paul is very insistent that he is hoping that 'at last' he can come ... and then he adds the apparently vague but actually prophetic words, '*somehow* by God's will' (verse 10). Each time he had resolved to go to Rome something had stymied him. He had similar experiences prior to his arrival in Philippi. In the preceding days, the Holy Spirit had prevented the apostolic band from preaching in the provinces of Asia and Bithynia (Acts 16:6-7). But in the case of his desire to visit Rome the delay had been long-term—and, unknown to the Romans, it would be even longer term yet.

Evangelistic work had preoccupied the apostle. But, as he later explains, all that now 'prevented' him from visiting Rome was his present task of taking to Jerusalem a love gift he had gathered from the Gentile churches he had founded. They had bonded together to help the needy Jewish saints in the Jerusalem church (see 15:18-29; he talks about it at length in 2 Cor. 8:1–9:15).

Paul went to Jerusalem fully conscious that his visit with this mercy gift would have serious repercussions (Acts 21:10-15). And these would eventually precipitate his trial in Rome. But in any event, his desire to visit Rome and preach there would be granted, if not in the way he had originally planned, or the Roman Christians expected, nevertheless 'somehow by God's will' (verse 10). But years were still to pass before he arrived.

The story of how Paul reached Rome ('somehow') contains a lesson well worth learning early in the Christian life. Our prayers do not control the way God answers them. He knows what he is doing, and why. The one thing Paul could be sure of was that if he did 'somehow' (verse 10) get to Rome it would be 'in order that I may reap some harvest among the Gentiles' (verse 13).

This sense of expectation of God's blessing on the ministry of the word of God (which is what Paul alludes to here and repeats later in Phil. 1:22) is admirable. It is also something we too should desire and pray for expectantly (either for ourselves if we are preachers, or for those who preach). God's word, preached in the power of God's Spirit, exalting God's Son, is what Paul has in view in visiting Rome. He has a deep conviction that if God allows him to make the journey, lasting fruit will be the result.

In Paul's view his (and our) spiritual gifts are not given for our personal aggrandizement but to give us hands and feet, eyes and ears by which we can minister to and bless others. No doubt we ourselves receive blessing as we minister; but the purpose of our gifts is primarily to bless others. It is a capital error to imagine that our gifts are intended to point people to our ability. They are instead to be exercised kneeling before others (at least in spirit) and saying, 'I am here to serve you' (cf. 2 Cor. 4:5).

OBLIGED BUT ALSO EAGER

Paul moves now from his desire to impart 'some spiritual gift to strengthen you' and to 'reap some harvest among you' (verses 11-12) to speak of his sense of obligation ('I am under obligation,' verse 14).

One of the challenging, but also potentially illuminating aspects of reading Paul's letters is trying to understand the workings of his great mind, directed as it was by the Holy Spirit. What is the theological, spiritual, and indeed logical connection between one statement and the next, one paragraph and the one that follows it? Asking that question can lead us into a better understanding of both the gospel and its outworking in our lives.

So why does Paul's mind move from his obvious assurance that a visit to Rome would bear spiritual fruit to a statement about his sense of obligation? It is a result of the principle: his spiritual gifts were given to him for others. Yes, without them he could not serve fruitfully. But fundamentally he saw his gifts as obliging him to love and serve others. Until he had discharged that responsibility he would not have used them properly. Later he will make this same point more generally: 'Having gifts that differ according to the grace given to us, let us use them' (12:6; cf. 13:8).

Paul saw himself as a man 'under obligation' (verse 14). He regarded himself as a debtor until he had discharged the debt he owed. Great gifts carry with them a commensurate responsibility to use them for the blessing of others. 'What we proclaim is not ourselves, but Jesus Christ as Lord, *with ourselves as your servants* for Jesus' sake' (2 Cor. 4:5).

The sphere of Paul's ministry was predominantly the Gentile world. It was to that world he had been called by God (Acts 9:15), separated by the Holy Spirit (Acts 13:2), sent by the church at Antioch (Acts 13:3) and recognized by the churches (Gal. 2:7-9). All the essential elements of a true call to ministry were present in his life.

But the intellectually gifted Paul did not limit his ministry to 'his own type of people,' namely the 'Jews,' the 'Greeks,' and the 'wise' (at least in their own eyes). His parish included the 'barbarian' and the 'foolish' (verse 14). The gospel is for all. That being the case, he was 'eager to preach the gospel' to the Christians in Rome, no matter what their ethnic background or social status.

Two features of this statement should be noted. One is that gifts should make us eager to use them. The other is that we are 'under obligation' to all to whom the Lord sends us. Thus, while there is immense joy in serving Christ, and especially when there is a harvest from the seeds of the gospel we have sown, there is also a burden that is only eased once the gifts have been used and the responsibility to use them has been discharged.

Wherever Paul travelled he went in the joy of the Lord. So joy and burden are not incompatible. But his words here remind us that those who preach to us carry an immense responsibility. They do not (and certainly should not) preach just because they know they have the natural capacity to speak, or because they love to teach, or to influence others, but because there is a divinely-given burden of love on their backs. Their gifts and their sense of compulsion both come from God. The burden can only be relieved when the gifts that have been given to us are fully used by us.

So we can imagine Paul's amanuensis now hearing him say: 'Tertius, write this now: "I am eager to preach the gospel to you also who are in Rome"' (verse 15).

A few verses later, Paul will provide another reason for his sense of obligation. He was also constrained to preach (2 Cor. 5:14) because he was conscious that those without Christ face the judgment and wrath of God (1:18-32; 2 Cor. 5:10). In the light of that, he recognized 'necessity is laid upon me. Woe to me if I do not preach the gospel' (1 Cor. 9:16).

As we continue to read Romans the implications of these words will become increasingly clear. Even before he is able to visit them Paul will seek to impart 'some spiritual gift to strengthen you.' This spiritual gift—much of which is probably expressed here in Romans, at least in summary form—undoubtedly strengthened the Roman believers in the mid-first century AD. More than that, it has instructed, challenged and encouraged Christians in every place and time since. For, like the rest of Scripture, Romans is 'profitable for teaching, for reproof, for correction, and for training in righteousness' (2 Tim. 3:16).

3

Unashamed of the Gospel

> *For I am not ashamed of the gospel, for it is the power of God for salvation to everyone who believes, to the Jew first and also to the Greek.* [17] *For in it the righteousness of God is revealed from faith for faith, as it is written, 'The righteous shall live by faith.'*
> (Rom. 1:16-17)

A helpful preliminary way to think about Paul's Letter to the Romans is that it contains—at least in part—the 'spiritual gift' he wanted to 'impart' to the church at the centre of the empire (verse 11). It is his own exposition of what he calls 'my gospel' (2:16; 16:25). It is not surprising therefore that it involves many chapters of rich exposition and close reasoning. But here in 1:16-17 he explains why he is eager to preach the gospel in Rome (notice the 'For' with which these verses begin). In addition, he states the theme—even the theme text—which he plans to expound.

There are many challenges in the Christian life. Sometimes people who oppose our faith (and ourselves) can seem like giants and by comparison we seem (and are made to feel) tiny. We are daunted. But Paul is like John Bunyan's Pilgrim—or more accurately, the Pilgrim is like Paul—'Hobgoblin nor foul fiend can daunt his spirit'! He is undaunted by the thought of preaching the gospel in Rome—despite the fact that it was the great metropolis of the ancient world, the seat of government and military power, and the home of the elites of the first century. And the reason for his disposition? 'I am not ashamed of the gospel' (verse 16).

UNASHAMED

But even if Paul is undaunted, we should not overlook the way he expresses it: 'not' is the first word in the Greek text: 'Not ashamed I am ...'). The elites of Rome expected Christians to be ashamed, just as the Greeks in Athens did (Acts 17:18). The world usually does.

At this stage Christianity was still viewed by the authorities as a Jewish sect (akin to the Pharisees and the Sadducees). To that extent it was a 'protected' religion (a *religio licita*). In addition at first sight it seemed to be a comparatively tiny, marginal, insignificant group. The few churches in Rome were 'house' churches, perhaps meeting in the tenement buildings of the city. But they were profoundly counter-cultural in lifestyle. They doubtless faced many of the same challenges the Corinthian Christians did in their culture, such as whether or not they should eat meat that had been offered to idols (1 Cor. 8:1-13), and the broader issue of how they were to respond to the cult of Caesar-worship.

But at the centre of everything stood Jesus. He had been executed for treason by the Roman authorities in Palestine; plus his death had been instigated by some of his own people. In addition even the man responsible in law for his execution, Pontius Pilate, was the disgraced former procurator of the small but troublesome Roman province of Judaea. He had died a decade earlier, and it was rumoured he had been forced to take his own life. Then to add to this whole wretched story was a fact that even the Christians did not hide and would soon state openly in their confession of faith: Jesus had 'suffered under Pontius Pilate' and was 'crucified.'[1] Cicero, one of Rome's greatest orators, spoke for many when he argued that the very word 'crucifixion' should never be found on the lips or heard by the ears of a Roman citizen.[2] In addition to all that, even mainstream Jews, themselves a demeaned minority, despised this new 'sect' of Jesus of Nazareth. Jewish-Christian tensions had already caused trouble in Rome (Acts 18:2). No wonder, then, if being a 'Christian' in Rome was a social shame.

Yet, despite this, Paul is 'not ashamed of the gospel.' Indeed he is 'eager' to preach it in Rome (verse 15).

Many Christians today live in cultures that are Romanesque in their deep-seated hostility to Christ and his teaching. For us then the question is pressing: 'Why was Paul not ashamed of the gospel?'

[1] *The Apostles' Creed.*

[2] Marcus Tullius Cicero, *Speech before Roman Citizens on Behalf of Gaius Rabirius*, 5.16.

How come he seems to have been unintimidated by the prospect of people seeking to 'shame' him? The question is a relevant one because Christians today can be and often are 'ashamed of the gospel.' And we know that while many early believers were, like Paul, 'unashamed,' there were others who weakened under the pressure of persecution and were ashamed. How, then, was Paul so consistently 'unashamed'?

The answer is not that he was naturally stubborn—although he may well have been! In fact he was profoundly conscious of his own frailty. He speaks about the 'weakness ... fear and much trembling' in which he came to Corinth (1 Cor. 2:3) and the 'fighting without and fear within' he experienced (2 Cor. 7:5). He was not Superman, nor was he a 'super-apostle' (2 Cor. 12:11). No, it was the greatness of the gospel that sustained him, not his own strong personality. What held him was the fact that the gospel had power far greater than Rome. It is 'the power of God for salvation to everyone who believes' (verse 16). Knowing and experiencing this enables the Christian believer to 'stand' (Eph. 6:14) in a world where the might of Rome (or Beijing, or Moscow, or Pyongyang, or Washington, or London) seems to dominate and permeate society.

ELUCIDATIONS

Before Paul goes on to explain what he means by the 'gospel' and 'salvation' he makes two elucidating statements:

(i) The first is that the gospel is God's saving power 'to everyone who believes.' It is to be preached to all. There are no prior qualifications, whether ethnic, social, intellectual, financial, geographical, or historical. None. The words the apostle spoke into the crisis in the Philippian jailer's life can be spoken to anyone, absolutely anyone: 'Believe in the Lord Jesus, and you will be saved' (Acts 16:31).

(ii) The second elucidation has sometimes been misunderstood: 'to the Jew first and also to the Greek.' This is not a *limitation* but a further *explanation*. Paul is reflecting the historical order of God's redemptive purposes: the promises and prophetic intimations of Christ's coming were first given to Abraham and his descendants, not simultaneously to the nations (although those promises always had in view the blessing of all nations, Gen. 12:1-3). Jesus himself had told a Samaritan woman, 'salvation is from the Jews' (John 4:22). And in his various missionary journeys, Paul's first port of call in a city was to the synagogue or Jewish place of prayer, to offer Christ to his own people. Only then (if his message was rejected) did he go to the Gentiles (*e.g.* Acts 9:20; 13:5, 13-14; 15:1). He would follow a similar pattern when he eventually came to Rome (Acts 28:17-28).

RIGHTEOUSNESS REVEALED

Paul spoke from experience when he said that the gospel is the saving power of God. He could affirm 'the saying is trustworthy' that 'Christ Jesus came into the world to save sinners' including himself as 'the foremost' (1 Tim. 1:15). That was neither false modesty nor hyperbole. He was possibly the only individual in the years immediately following the resurrection who had devoted himself to the entire destruction of the Christian church in its relative infancy (Acts 8:3; 9:1-2).

In this connection, it is interesting that Paul never once mentions the name of Stephen. But he must often have found himself hunted down by Satan whenever the memory of his martyrdom came to mind. We rarely think of the sense of shame the evil one must have imposed on him for approving his death and for his subsequent campaign to destroy both the testimony and the lives of Christian believers (Acts 8:1–9:2). Perhaps those memories lie behind his reference in 6:21 to past sins that cause present shame. But in Christ he had discovered the revelation of 'the righteousness of God' that secured his pardon and salvation.

This phrase 'the righteousness of God' takes us to the heart of Paul's letter and of his gospel.

THE RIGHTEOUSNESS OF GOD

What does Paul mean by 'the righteousness of God'? How is it 'revealed from faith for faith'? And why does he cite words from Habakkuk 2:4?

We are by no means the first Christians to ask what Paul means by 'the righteousness of God.' The expression caused Martin Luther more anguished heart-searching than any other in the entire Bible. He tells us he came to hate it. But then he discovered he had utterly misunderstood it.

In general terms, 'righteousness' conveys the idea of conformity to a norm. When it is used of God it expresses his consistency with himself, with his character, and therefore with the self-revelation he gave in his covenant bond with his people. When God's people responded to his promise in trust and obedience they experienced his covenant *blessing*. But if they were guilty of unbelief, of mistrust in God's promises, and of disobedience, they exposed themselves to his covenant *curse*.

This was vividly symbolized when the people entered the promised land and renewed the covenant. Half of them stood in front of Mount Gerazim and half of them in front of Mount Ebal as Joshua read out God's covenant provisions and prescriptions—'the blessing and the curse' (Josh. 8:33-34). It must have been a memorable day when one by one the curses and blessings recorded in Deuteronomy 27–28 were publicly affirmed and the people responded repeatedly with the single word, 'Amen'—so let it be!

The point is that God's righteousness could be revealed in different ways in different circumstances, in either blessing or cursing. But in either case he would be unfailingly righteous, unchangingly and unchangeably true to his character and his word.

But, for Martin Luther, God's righteousness meant only condemnation. That is why he came to hate the expression. No wonder if it spelled a lost eternity for him. He had come to realize

> *Could my zeal no respite know,*
> *Could my tears for ever flow*
> [and few men experienced so much of both];
> *All for sin could not atone:*
> *Thou must save, and Thou alone.*[1]

What Luther had failed to see is that here, in Romans 1:16-17, Paul was referring to the righteousness of God that is revealed *in the gospel*. God had devised a way of salvation in Christ by which *sinners* could be saved by a *righteous* God revealing his *righteousness* in a *righteous way* in order to count sinners as *righteous*! In the gospel we discover the righteous character of God, as well as of his acts—and, in addition, the fruit of that in the righteousness he counts to us.

How could this be?

[1] From the hymn 'Rock of Ages, cleft for me' by Augustus Toplady (1740–78).

Paul will return later to answer this question in detail (in 3:21-26). For the moment he is content simply to state that God has done this in the gospel (this is why it is *euangelion*—good news). It is a message of *salvation* not *condemnation.*

But the apostle makes clear that this good news has not only been revealed; it must also be received.

It is 'revealed from faith for faith' (verse 17). This somewhat enigmatic statement has been variously interpreted as meaning, 'from God's faithfulness to our faith response'; or 'from old covenant faith to new covenant faith,' or 'from faith from first to last.'

There is a similar (although not identical) expression in 2 Corinthians 3:18 that perhaps gives us a clue to Paul's meaning. There he speaks about believers being changed 'from glory to glory' (literally), that is, we are changed 'more and more into glory.' So perhaps his meaning here is that the righteousness revealed in the gospel is received by faith in God and his righteousness, only by faith, and always by faith, and is appreciated 'more and more' as we continue to trust in Christ.

When Paul speaks here about 'the righteousness of God' being revealed in the gospel he is thinking of the astonishing truth that the righteous God shows his righteousness to those who are unrighteous and under his just condemnation. But he has devised a way of doing this that both maintains his own perfect righteousness and yet also saves those who are unrighteous. By implication this answers the question, 'What must I do then to be saved by the righteous God?' Salvation is ours by faith, only by faith, by nothing but faith, and always by faith.

AS IT IS WRITTEN

Paul now confirms this from Scripture by quoting from Habakkuk 2:4: 'as it is written, "The righteous shall live by faith."' He had followed the same pattern in an earlier letter dealing with the way of salvation (Gal. 3:11), just as the author of Hebrews would also do (Heb. 10:37-38). He thus confirms the point made earlier in 1:2: his gospel is entirely in harmony with Old Testament prophecy and indeed with the whole Mosaic economy. Yes, the old covenant had regulations and stipulations Paul believed belonged to the old epoch. Some things had changed. But the way of salvation is a constant throughout redemptive history. To that extent 'faith' in the days of the old covenant speaks to 'faith' in the days of the new covenant. Salvation has always been by faith; and it has only been by faith; and it has been by faith alone.

Right from this introduction then, Paul makes clear that there are not two ways of salvation presented in the Bible, one by 'works' in the old covenant and another 'by faith' in the new. Nor are there two 'different Gods'—the angry one in the Old Testament and the kind one in the New—as is sometimes thought and taught. God has always been one and the same. And the salvation he provides has always been received by faith. For that reason some interpreters have thought that 'from faith to faith' also implies 'from start to finish, from old covenant to new covenant,' or as we might say 'from Genesis to Revelation.' Ultimately, therefore, there is only one people of God, not two. That which is 'for the Jew first and also to the Greek' is the same gospel offering the same salvation.

So the grand theme of Romans is 'the righteousness of God for salvation revealed in the gospel and applied by the gospel.' We can summarize the rest of the letter in terms of his exposition of various dimensions and applications of his theme statement and text. Thus, in the chapters that follow, Paul deals with:

1:18–3:20	The *lack* of God's righteousness in humanity
3:21–5:21	The *provision* of God's righteousness in Jesus Christ
5:21–8:39	The *implications* of God's righteousness for believers
9:1–11:36	The *vindication* of God's righteousness in history
12:1–16:27	The *application* of God's righteousness in the Christian life

The glory of the gospel is that in Christ the righteous God has righteously devised a way for sinners to be counted righteous in his sight although they are unrighteous in themselves. And then, by the power of that gospel he transforms them so that righteousness begins to be cultivated and expressed in their lives. And God has done this, and will continue to do this, in both Jews and Gentiles who come to faith in Christ, even though in themselves all are unrighteous, lost and condemned. Truly he can say, 'And there is no other god besides me, a righteous God and a Saviour; there is none besides me' (Isa. 45:21).

But first Paul will demonstrate why this salvation, this revelation of the righteousness of God, is necessary—because it is entirely and universally lacking in the human race. This he now embarks on proving in 1:18–3:20, a section climaxed by his words (in 3:10): 'None is righteous, no, not one.'

This brings us, in the following chapter, to the beginning of Paul's devastating exposure of the sinfulness of the human condition.

4

Wrath Revealed

For the wrath of God is revealed from heaven against all ungodliness and unrighteousness of men, who by their unrighteousness suppress the truth. [19] *For what can be known about God is plain to them, because God has shown it to them.* [20] *For his invisible attributes, namely, his eternal power and divine nature, have been clearly perceived, ever since the creation of the world, in the things that have been made. So they are without excuse.*
[21] *For although they knew God, they did not honour him as God or give thanks to him, but they became futile in their thinking, and their foolish hearts were darkened.* [22] *Claiming to be wise, they became fools,* [23] *and exchanged the glory of the immortal God for images resembling mortal man and birds and animals and creeping things.*

(Rom. 1:18-23)

These verses constitute one of the most sobering passages in the whole of the New Testament, but they are by no means unique. They are paralleled for example in Galatians 5:19-20; Ephesians 4:17-19; and 2 Timothy 3:1-7. Here they form the opening movement in Paul's dark symphony on human sin in its various and often subtle forms. It extends from 1:18 through to 3:20 before he allows us to breathe out a sigh of relief at his declaration 'But now ...' (3:21). When studying Romans it is a valuable spiritual exercise to pause at the end of each of its 'sections' and to read it as a whole in one sitting. Doing so with this section will lead to a profound sense of gratitude when we eventually discover how God has intervened to save us.

In 1:16-17 Paul had explained that the gospel is God's saving power because in it his righteousness is revealed. As Martin Luther eventually discovered—God reveals his righteousness in the way he acts for our salvation.

But why is *salvation* necessary? Because we are unrighteous and therefore unacceptable to a righteous God. But from what do we need to be saved? The answer is sobering: God's wrath. In fact it is even more sobering. At the end of the day it is not a 'from *what*?' that we need to be saved. It is a 'from *whom*?' God's wrath is not something that can be separated from him. It is his disposition, his attitude—it is God himself in action toward us. We need to be saved from God himself! It is a 'fearful thing to fall into the hands of the living God' who 'is a consuming fire' (Heb. 10:31; 12:29).

Here again we notice the connecting links in Paul's 'joined-up thinking.' The revelation of God's saving righteousness (verse 17) has been given in the gospel because of ('for,' verse 18) another revelation—the revelation of his wrath (the verb is the same in both statements). The same God who reveals his righteousness in salvation is the One whose righteous wrath is already being manifested (notice the present tense).

God's wrath is the expression of his settled opposition and antagonism towards sin in every form. The psalmist provides us a pre-summary of Paul's entire argument in 1:18–3:20: 'If you, O Lord, should mark iniquities, O Lord, who could stand?' (Psa. 130:3).

REVELATION AND SUPPRESSION

God's wrath is 'revealed against all ungodliness and unrighteousness of men, who by their unrighteousness suppress the truth' (1:18). The importance of Paul's teaching here can scarcely be overestimated.

First, we should notice that there is a logical and theological reason for the order: ungodliness leads to unrighteousness; breaches of the first four commandments (those related directly to God) lead inexorably to breaches of the commands that follow (relating to our neighbours). Fail to love the Lord with heart, soul, and strength, and we will inevitably fail to love our neighbour as ourselves.

Then, second, Paul indicates the effect sin has on us: it leads us to 'suppress the truth' (verse 18). Paul may even mean '*repress* the truth,' that is, not only resist it and its impact on our consciences ('suppress') but deny it and drive the consciousness of it underground as it were. Thus a person may so resist God that they profess to have no awareness of him or his law. But *repressed* truth is not *destroyed* truth. There is in fact no escape from God, even if we were 'to take the wings of the morning and dwell in the uttermost parts of the sea' (Psa. 139:9). There is no hiding place where we are secure from his self-revelation.

What Paul says here is immensely important for our Christian witness: Christians know something about unbelievers that they deny about themselves. The apostle affirms that God has made himself clearly known in his creation (verses 19-20). They deny that. Are we then to assume that it is simply one person's opinion against another's? No, says Paul, we need to remember that sin deceives, and sinners engage in self-deceit. Sinners deny what 'deep down' they know to be true. We must not lose our nerve.

'Truth will out'—and in this case it usually emerges in the inconsistencies between what a person professes in theory and how he or she speaks and acts in practice. Thus, for example, the atheist suddenly catapulted into a crisis may cry out 'O God!'—this time not as a curse word but as a cry for help. Their instincts give the lie to what they profess.

There is a further important nuance here. We are accustomed to the biblical teaching that sin deserves judgment and condemnation, and that God's wrath will be revealed on the *final* 'day of wrath' (2:5). But here Paul's verb is in the present tense ('the wrath of God *is* revealed,' verse 18). Just as there is a present and a future tense to God's salvation, the same is true of his wrath. God's wrath is *already* being revealed.

Our culture demeans, despises and even ridicules the idea of God's wrath. After all, it is said, 'We openly and freely do what Paul condemns here in Romans 1:18-32. But where are the lightning bolts of his judgment? There are none. And there are none because there is no wrath of God!'

Paul gives the lie to such easy arrogance. In fact he does it in a threefold way. In verses 24-25, 26-27, and 28-32 he provides three separate catalogues of human sin. And on each occasion he introduces the ungodliness and unrighteousness described with similar wording:

- verse 24: Therefore *God gave them up* ...

- verse 26: For this reason *God gave them up …*
- verse 28: And since they did not see fit to acknowledge God, *God gave them up …*

The verb here (*paradidōmi*) is regularly used in the New Testament to express a judicial action, a handing over to judgment (*e.g.* Matt. 4:12; 5:25). It is used of the (illicit) judicial process in which Jesus was tried, condemned, and crucified (Matt. 17:22; 20:18-19; 26:2).

Paul uses the same verb later in 8:32 when he speaks about God's judicial 'giving up' his Son to the cross for our sake. There he is describing the wonderful exchange that lies at the heart of the gospel (the Father 'handed over' Jesus to the judgment we deserve). But here he is talking about the way God hands sinners over in judgment to their sin.

People say, 'Look, we are flaunting God's laws to our hearts' content, and there is no sign of the wrath of God.' Paul's response is: 'But *that* is precisely the judgment of God. He has handed you over to your sin. That is how he ordinarily reveals his wrath in the present time. The very abandonment to sinful practices that you view as proof that there is no wrath is actually a manifestation of it. Alas, you are self-deceived and too blind spiritually to see or understand.' Sobering indeed.

THE BITTER FRUITS

There is more detail, of course, in what Paul says, but this is the overall pattern of Romans 1:18-32. When God is no longer in our thoughts (Psa. 10:4) godliness evaporates.

Rome was the centre of the pre-Christian world when Paul wrote this letter. We read it today in a post-Christian world. When a society has received but then rejected the gospel it is often assumed that people will 'return' to being the basically good human beings they were before the culture was invaded, sidetracked, and even 'colonialized' by the distinctives of the Christian faith. But what Paul describes here *is that pre-Christian culture.* Before the gospel came, outside of God's covenant revelation, our societies were in fact pagan. To that condition, albeit with centuries of increased sophistication, God-rejecting societies inexorably return. That we are basically good underneath is a myth Paul here explodes.

The reasoning embedded in this whole section is the notion that when God is rejected it inevitably follows that the biblical view of man as the image of God (male and female, Gen. 1:26-28) also inevitably disintegrates (*i.e.* lose God, and the image of God is lost to us). Consequently a true ethic dissolves, and we no longer understand or appreciate our true identity as humans. Alienation from God leads to alienation not only from any transcendent meaning to life but also from self-understanding, as well as from absolute norms, and ultimately from lasting hope. This was Paul's world before the gospel came; it is our world when the gospel has been rejected.

All this results from the suppression of the truth (verse 18). People suffer from the self-delusion that they are truth-seekers when in fact they are truth-repressors. Just at this point Paul's gospel pulls from us the most common security blanket to which we cling: the assumption that we have a 'neutral' view of the world, we 'see things as they really are' without presuppositions. That world-view (despite the history of philosophy that has so often questioned it) is the miasma of our times. In Romans 1:18-22 Paul penetrates it and exposes it with the truth of God.

THE TRUTH

The 'neutral' says that 'If only God had made himself clearer I would, of course, believe. The problem is (of course) that he has not made himself clear—for if he had (of course) I would believe.'

Paul's response is a straightforward contradiction of this claim. God's being and his character ('what can be known about God') are plain for all to see for one simple reason: God has made himself known in his work of creation. Everything that is part of his creation bears his autograph (verse 19).

But what, exactly, can be known about God from creation? A surprising amount. Paul's analysis gives us an impressive list of divine attributes that are expressed in the created order. God is 'the invisible God' (cf. Col. 1:15; 1 Tim. 1:17; Heb. 11:27); no one has ever seen him (John 1:18); but he is not 'the unknown God' (cf. Paul's speech to the Athenians in Acts 17:22-31).

As John Calvin suggested, in and through the created order God, as it were, puts on 'outdoor clothing' to make his 'invisible attributes' known: 'his eternal power and divine nature have been clearly perceived since the creation of the world' (verse 20). But we have 'exchanged the glory of the immortal God for images' (verse 23).

Paul is not giving us here an exhaustive list of divine attributes, but nevertheless it is an impressive one: invisibility, eternity, power, divinity, creative ability, glory, immortality are all not only ascribed to God but made 'plain to them,' because 'God has shown it to them' (verse 19). These attributes are 'clearly perceived' (verse 20). And indeed they should evoke both 'honour' and 'thanks' (verse 21).

Paul draws several conclusions from the clarity of divine revelation, and the sufficiency of it as a basis for our honouring God and thanking him:

(i) The knowledge of God revealed in creation is clear. It is not obscure, indeed the very reverse.

(ii) Therefore men 'knew God' (verse 21).

How is this conclusion to be reconciled to Paul's teaching elsewhere that by nature we do not know God (Gal. 4:8; 1 Thess. 4:5)—and that he is 'the unknown God' (Acts 17:23)?

The apostle is not implying here that God is known in the sense of faith-knowledge, covenant-knowledge, communion-knowledge, saving-knowledge. He means that surrounded by God's revelation (and invaded by it, since man is the image of God) we cannot escape from knowledge of him. It is impossible for those who have been created as the image of God not to be aware of the God whose existence their own being reflects—even if that knowledge is hated and suppressed.

(iii) Since this is so, people who reject the revelation God has given are 'without excuse' (verse 20). Unbelievers are *anapologētos*—without an apologetic, as it were. Created to honour and thank God, they dishonour and despise the revealed God to whom they owe their very existence.

(iv) Consequently, when we reject our divinely-created inbuilt purpose—to glorify God and enjoy him forever—our entire life is thrown into a kind of reverse gear. Our thinking becomes 'futile' (verse 21). Of course it does, because life ceases to have any transcendent meaning; its history is without design, and we are incapable of finding any ultimate significance beyond ourselves.

In addition our 'foolish hearts were darkened' in the sense that we now think of ourselves as 'wise' and yet have abandoned ourselves to the basic folly of a life with no inherent meaning and purpose. Ultimately we are in a universe with no inherent rationale.

Paul expresses the nadir when he says that we have made the tragic exchange. We have swapped 'the glory of the immortal God for images resembling mortal man and birds and animals and creeping things' (verse 23). When all that is left to us is ourselves and Planet Earth, inevitably these become our gods. For them we live, to them we become devoted, for them we offer our little sacrifices. But, as Augustine discovered, since God made us for himself our hearts will remain restless until they find their rest in him.[1]

Underlying Paul's thinking here is his understanding of Genesis 1:26-28. Man was made as the image of God, male and female, in order to 'reign in life' (Paul's use of this phrase when he speaks about the restorative effect of Christ's work in 5:17 is significant). Adam's world was a miniature of the cosmos over which his Creator and Father was King. As such he was created as God's 'likeness,' able to know him, fashioned for fellowship with him, invited to share his wisdom, and live as a reflection of his glory. He was created with a unique capacity to enjoy intelligent communication and communion with his Creator. No wonder Paul sees the present human condition as one of tragic folly. Esau-like, we have exchanged our inheritance for a 'mess of pottage' (Gen. 25:29-34, KJV).

This, then, is the human condition and situation, under the wrath of God. In what follows Paul plans to give a more detailed account of the effects.

We appreciate the wonder of salvation in direct proportion to our awareness of what it is we have been saved *from*. So, before we continue, we should pause and consider what Anselm (1033–1109), the mediaeval archbishop of Canterbury, called 'the greatness of the weight of sin.'[2]

[1] These, probably his most famous words, come from the opening paragraph of his *Confessions*.

[2] Anselm, *Cur Deus Homo*, Book 1, chapter 21.

5

Handed Over

Therefore God gave them up in the lusts of their hearts to impurity, to the dishonouring of their bodies among themselves,
25 because they exchanged the truth about God for a lie and worshipped and served the creature rather than the Creator, who is blessed forever! Amen.
26 For this reason God gave them up to dishonourable passions. For their women exchanged natural relations for those that are contrary to nature;
27 and the men likewise gave up natural relations with women and were consumed with passion for one another, men committing shameless acts with men and receiving in themselves the due penalty for their error.
28 And since they did not see fit to acknowledge God, God gave them up to a debased mind to do what ought not to be done.
29 They were filled with all manner of unrighteousness, evil, covetousness, malice. They are full of envy, murder, strife, deceit, maliciousness. They are gossips,
30 slanderers, haters of God, insolent, haughty, boastful, inventors of evil, disobedient to parents,
31 foolish, faithless, heartless, ruthless.
32 Though they know God's righteous decree that those who practise such things deserve to die, they not only do them but give approval to those who practise them.

(Rom. 1:24-32)

In the previous section Paul had emphasized the character of God's revelation of himself in the created order. In summary he had stressed four of its characteristics:

(i) Clarity—what can be known about God is clearly seen in his creation. Just as an art expert can recognize the brushwork of a particular artist, so man, created as God's image, is constituted with the capacity to recognize the autograph of God on everything he has made.

(ii) Sufficiency—God's self-revelation is altogether adequate to lead human beings to thank and adore him for who he is and what he has made.

(iii) Universality—this revelation is not limited to only some. Neither ethnicity nor ability disqualifies an individual from being confronted with the being and character of the Creator in his creation.

(iv) Inexcusability—the point to which all this is leading is that given these characteristics of God's revelation those who reject it, and him, render themselves inexcusable. They are never in a position of being able to say, 'You didn't make yourself clear.' The reverse is true. The reality is that sinners have suppressed the truth; the darkness is within.

The divine response is to give us exactly what we want—a point made with striking eloquence in the parable of 'the prodigal son' (Luke 15:11-32). He hands us over to it.

FATAL EXCHANGES, FAITHFUL JUDGMENTS

Sinful humanity has made a tragic exchange which increasingly reverses our created purposes:

(i) We have exchanged the glory of the immortal God for images resembling mortal man (verse 23). Man is made as the image of God to reflect him but instead worships the image as his god.

(ii) We have exchanged the truth about God for a lie (verse 25). Man rejects the true knowledge of God and therefore believes the lie about him.

(iii) We have exchanged natural relations for unnatural ones (verse 26). Made as the image of God, and for God, men and women turn in on themselves and begin to invert the God-ordained use of their bodies in the most intimate relations of life. The result is a disordering, distorting, and ultimately perverting of the natural order of things.

In response to this, God's ways are perfect and his judgments are both just and appropriate. The present expression of his wrath is a handing over of sinners to their sin. They become like the objects of their devotion, their equivalent of the ancient gods (Psa. 115:8).

God's judgment involves removing the restraints of common grace on sinful actions and on what they lead to.

Paul details the consequences. The image of God is blurred, and therefore also obscured is the conviction that we have been created to express that image in specifically 'male and female' forms. Thus women exchange natural relations with men; men also abandon natural relations (verses 24, 26-27). The effect of disordering the basic instinct of the image of God to reflect and worship him leads to the perversion of other instincts and the distortion of their proper function.

It is important to notice here that the biblical opposition to homosexual acts (as in Lev. 18:22; 21:13) is not rooted in prejudice but in an exalted view of who we are as human beings, made in God's image both male and female. When we reject God's design for the body this leads, in various forms and to varying degrees, to the self-destroying effects of the worship of the body. The entail of this process is its eventual degradation (verse 24), domination by lust, the disintegration of what is truly natural (verse 26), and bondage to uncontrollable passions (verse 27). Instead of being 'free' (as is often claimed) we become prisoners. For our gods must be reverenced and satisfied. Clearly for Paul *what is* and *what ought to be* are by no means the same.

In verse 25, Paul penetrates to the heart of this terrible reversal of our relationships with the Creator and his creation, with ourselves and with others. At the root of our fallen condition is that we have 'exchanged the truth about God for a lie.' The result is that we worship and serve created reality rather than its Creator.

Although omitted in the ESV (following the Revised Standard Version translation) in Paul's Greek text 'lie' has the definite article ('*the* lie'). *The* truth is exchanged for *the* lie. It is not surprising then if humanity develops an inbuilt bias in favour of lies about God, since one lie tends to lead to (and usually requires) another.

But what is this lie? Paul is possibly thinking here in very broad terms (meaning simply a generally mistaken view of God instead of a biblical one). But there may well be more to it than this. Behind Romans 1:18-32 lies the shadow of Genesis 3:1-7. There the satanic serpent perpetrated the great lie. It was multi-layered. He cast doubt on the reliability and truth of God's word but also on his character and specifically on his goodness, kindness, and generosity. He questioned what God had said, but he also planted doubts in Eve's mind and affections as to whether God was really as good and generous as he made out. 'Did he put you in this magnificent garden, full of trees laden with beautiful and delicious-looking fruit, and then tell you none of it was for you? What kind of God is that? He surely wants to make you a slave and to deprive you of all pleasure and joy. Do not trust him! You cannot trust him!' (Gen. 3:1-5).

And so was injected into the human bloodstream 'the lie about God'—that he takes rather than gives; that he spoils our enjoyment of the world rather than enhances it; that there is, perhaps, malice towards us lurking deep down in his character; that he cannot be trusted unreservedly if at all; that therefore his design for life, and his directives, constitute a bondage against which we need to rebel if we are to be set free for ourselves. The long-term effect is that people live believing 'the lie.' The entail is that we eventually regard as good activities that are sinful. God then gives us over to ourselves (verse 24).

DISORDERED HUMANITY

In verses 26-28 Paul develops his argument further. Now he becomes more specific. He traces the progress of the exchange that has been made and focusses on a breach in the created order.

God made man male and female. He gave Eve to Adam as his best created gift. That was how it was in the beginning and, as Jesus taught, was always to remain (Matt. 19:4-6—verses that make clear Jesus did address the question of human sexuality, contrary to what is asserted by some media 'elites'). But in rebellion against God people make a bad choice, the giving up of natural relations. That choice in turn leads to the enslavement of the affections (they are 'consumed with lust') and in due course to distorted lifestyles ('shameless acts with men') which eventually lead to people 'receiving in themselves the due penalty for their error' (verse 27).

Paul is not specific here. He draws a veil over the tragic result. We do not break God's commandments so much as break ourselves against them. We come to a point where we say, 'I can sin to my heart's content.' And we do—except (as Augustine famously discovered) our heart is never content. Sin cannot bring lasting joy, even if it brings momentary pleasure (Heb. 11:25). Instead sinners become subject to forces they cannot control: they receive back as a matter of justice what is appropriate to their crime against God.

Clearly Paul is speaking here about the kind of sexual behaviour which today is claimed to be 'natural' ('This is who I am'). But he affirms that the biblical starting place is quite different: we are no longer what we were created to be; what 'is' is not what was 'meant to be.' As he goes on to indicate forcefully in verses 29-31, disorder in sexual relations is by no means the only form of distortion. But to fail to recognize the way sin creates distortion and disorder—to regard it as 'natural' and 'normal'—is to be adrift on the ruthless high seas of relativism.

Verses 24-27 are set in the context of a description of 'all ungodliness and unrighteousness.'

(i) Verse 18 suggested that when such behaviour is regarded as 'natural' a suppression of the truth is taking place, driven by the ungodliness that leads to unrighteousness.

(ii) Verses 21-22 provide a further analysis: such thinking is 'futile' and an expression of the fact that 'foolish hearts were darkened.' Futile—because they 'exchanged natural relations for those that are contrary to nature' (verse 26). Scripture teaches that men and women are not only biologically and psychologically *different from* each other but are thus *created for* each other. So the 'exchange' means what we were created to gain is now lost.

(iii) Verses 24-27 describe the nature of such behaviour patterns as 'impurity,' 'dishonouring of their bodies' (verse 24), and worshipping the creature rather than the Creator (verse 25). They involve 'shameless acts,' are the fruit of 'dishonourable passions' (verse 26), and involve being 'consumed with passion' (verse 27).

To say this lifestyle is 'natural' or 'normal' then not only denies the reality of our fallen and sinful condition, but it also makes us the norm and sole interpreter of the universe. Paul sees this as self-deception. When at the core of our being we have believed 'the lie about God' everything becomes distorted. The behaviour described here is not to be thought of as 'normal' or 'natural' but as a twisting of the Creator's design. Again, although Paul devotes particular attention to sexual disorder here, we need to remember that this is by no means the *only* distortion—as verses 29-31 make clear.

In a striking (and illuminating) comment at the end of the passage, Paul adds that those who engage in these acts 'not only do them but give approval to those who practise them' (verse 32). They are driven to justify their lifestyle as 'normal' and therefore by an internal necessity are further compelled to encourage others to behave like themselves. What was presented as merely the individual's freedom of choice will inevitably turn out to be much more than that. Ostensibly what was asked for was 'equality' or 'personal freedom.' The almost universal mantra was 'this will not affect other people in any way.' But it is not long before the opposite is true. Everyone's life is affected. As has become clear in the early twenty-first century, even little children's lives are impacted, and indeed invaded.

We have a saying, 'misery *loves* company' but it is also true that sin *demands* it. And it has an inbuilt tendency to seek to silence contrary voices. The reality is that when living for the glory of God is rejected, distortion reigns. And the entail is that rather than dispense with the category of 'sin' it is redefined. No longer is 'sin' seen as rebellion against and transgression of God's law, but the holding, and the acting upon views contrary to the new social norms. Forces are released that demand the elimination of biblical teaching.

HIGHWAY TO DISASTER

Paul's pattern of God's 'giving up' is illuminating. Its climax is evident in the way he 'gave them up' not only to impurity (verse 24) and 'dishonourable passions' (verse 26) but also 'to a debased mind to do what ought not to be done' (verse 28). The moral dam of God's law, built to protect humanity, has been breached. Now the land begins to be flooded. The 'debased mind' sees biblical righteousness as the new social sinfulness. God's ways are abandoned (verses 29-31). The rejection of the principles of the Ten Commandments inexorably drives governments to create or revise an ever-increasing number of laws in order to try to close the Pandora's box that has been opened.[1] But law never works grace. In

[1] For example, the language in traditional wedding services explaining that 'society' can be 'strong only where the marriage bond is held in honour'—meaning the marriage of a man and a woman—in many countries today has been made to sound almost revolutionary and incendiary. Few politicians are prepared to attribute some of the deepest-seated ills of Western society to the breakdown of

this context too, it can be said that 'the law came in to increase the trespass' (Rom. 5:20). But governments can offer no corresponding word of hope that even begins to compare with the glorious truth the gospel proclaims that 'where sin increased, grace abounded all the more' (5:20).

Paul's words in this passage are as illuminating as they are sobering. Men (and women) may loudly demean and despise all talk about God's judgment. There is much bravado: 'You threatened us with the judgment of God if we lived this way; but we are living this way to our heart's content! Where is your God of wrath and judgment now?' Paul's answer is devastating: God's wrath 'is revealed against all ungodliness and unrighteousness of men who by their unrighteousness suppress the truth … God gave them up … God gave them up … God gave them up'—to their own heart's desires. *That* is the judgment.

There is no peace along the road on which the self-deceived travel. And yet underneath it all there is a reality from which they cannot escape. 'They know God's righteous decree that those who practise such things deserve to die' (verse 32). It is often scarcely-repressed anger about this inescapable reality that comes to expression in the frenzied insistence on the right to live life 'my way' rather than God's way.

Appearances of 'joy' and claims to belong to a 'community' cannot mask the loneliness before the judgment of God that seared consciences experience. That is why those who sin brazenly must influence others to do likewise: 'they not only do them but give approval to those who practise them' (verse 32b). The only way to persuade yourself you are safe from the wrath of God is to make your actions not only 'normal' but 'normative'—the canon by which all behaviour is to be assessed.

Paul's words teach us how important it is for Christians not to be deceived by the voices of viewpoints and lifestyles that reject God and his word and claim they are only seeking space for 'diversity' and 'equality.' It is never so. Rejection of God's ways must always seek dominion. The mantra 'this will not affect your life' is always

---

the stability of the biblical view (and practice) of marriage and family life. The result is that more laws need to be created in order to try to cope with the effects of the rejection of God's ten basic ones.

a lie. Only the gospel that restores God's image rather than distorts it can produce a society in which genuine diversity and equality function in true harmony and to the benefit of all. It is this that the church family is called to illustrate.

PAUL AND SINFUL BEHAVIOUR

Since these verses contain the apostle Paul's powerful statement on homosexual behaviour two comments are necessary.

The *first* is that he makes it clear that sexual sin is not the only sin. He (and we after him) speak of it only necessarily because in a culture without God it is characteristically here that distortion manifests itself. Idolatry or paganism has always gone hand in hand with sexual deviation. But we must not lose sight of the way Paul indicates that sin has many faces: envy, deceit, malice, gossip, slander, boasting, lying, despising parents, ruthless behaviour (verses 29-31)—each and all are manifestations of a life that has dethroned God, distorted human nature, and is in deep spiritual danger. Boasting and ruthless behaviour make us just as much liable to the wrath of God as sexual disorder.

The *second* important comment is that Paul's searing analysis of human sin and his sobering words about the judgment and wrath of God are intended in part to prompt the question: 'Is there no hope?' Elsewhere he provides a twofold answer: 'No' if a person persists in sin and rebellion against God. But 'yes,' if they repent and believe in Jesus Christ (see 1 Cor. 6:1-10, and 11).

Soon, as Paul develops his exposition of the gospel, we will encounter something wonderful—not only the possibility of faith and repentance but the assurance that God's kindness can lead us to that repentance (2:4). The question we need to ask is: Where is that kindness to be found?

Paul's answer is that it can be found in what the reformers called 'the wonderful exchange.' Three times in this passage he has used the verb 'to hand over/to give over' (*paradidōmi*) with its judicial overtones to describe the judgment of God. We will find him using it again later to explain the mercy of God. The first *Greek-speaking hearers* of Romans would have been more sensitive to this than we *English readers* are. This mirror image use of the same verb underlines how God in his grace has made provision for sinners: a saving exchange has been made in Christ that can reverse the damning exchange we have made:

- Romans 4:25: Jesus our Lord … was *delivered up* ('handed over') for our trespasses.
- Romans 8:32: He … did not spare his own Son but *gave him up* ('handed him over') for us all.

But it will be some time before this relief takes centre stage. We must first become more deeply conscious of our need if we are to appreciate the nature of God's superabundant grace. And so the next section in Romans continues the exposure of human sinfulness.

Thus Paul begins his exposé of human sin and spreads the dark backcloth against which the gospel will shine like a diamond. But his analysis is based on the whole story of his Hebrew Bible. It was taught in the Law and the Prophets. And the writings of the Psalms bore witness to the same pattern of sin and grace that this letter expounds so thoroughly and magnificently:

> They made a calf in Horeb
> and worshipped a metal image.
> They exchanged the glory of God
> for the image of an ox that eats grass.
> They forgot God, their Saviour,
> who had done great things in Egypt,
> wondrous works in the land of Ham,
> and awesome deeds by the Red Sea.
> Therefore he said he would destroy them—
> had not Moses, his chosen one,
> stood in the breach before him,
> to turn away his wrath from destroying them.
> (Psa. 106:19-23)

Thanks be to God that a greater than Moses has come to stand in the breach!

6

Righteous Judgment

Therefore you have no excuse, O man, every one of you who
judges. For in passing judgment on another you condemn yourself,
because you, the judge, practise the very same things. 2 *We know*
that the judgment of God rightly falls on those who practise
such things. 3 *Do you suppose, O man—you who judge those*
who practise such things and yet do them yourself—that you
will escape the judgment of God? 4 *Or do you presume on the*
riches of his kindness and forbearance and patience, not knowing
that God's kindness is meant to lead you to repentance? 5 *But*
because of your hard and impenitent heart you are storing up
wrath for yourself on the day of wrath when God's righteous
judgment will be revealed.

6 *He will render to each one according to his works:* 7 *to those*
who by patience in well-doing seek for glory and honour and
immortality, he will give eternal life; 8 *but for those who are*
self-seeking and do not obey the truth, but obey unrighteousness,
there will be wrath and fury. 9 *There will be tribulation and*
distress for every human being who does evil, the Jew first and
also the Greek, 10 *but glory and honour and peace for everyone*
who does good, the Jew first and also the Greek. 11 *For God*
shows no partiality.

(Rom. 2:1-11)

Of all Paul's letters, *Romans* reads most like a sermon. We feel as though he is not only *dictating* a letter to Tertius (16:22) but *preaching* it. We can imagine him in the room in Corinth, visualizing himself transported to a gathering of all the Christians in Rome and preaching to them. In that connection the change in his choice of pronouns is interesting: in 1:18-32 he speaks of people in the third person ('they,' 'their,' 'them'), but the language now becomes more direct.

Now the apostle is not only describing people, he is addressing them: '*you* have no excuse, O man, every one of *you* ... *you* condemn yourself ...' (verse 1). In verses 1-5 alone Paul uses 'you' ten times, 'yourself' three times, and 'your' once. His style echoes Nathan's radical exposure of David. He first draws out a judgmental response on those he described in 1:18-32 and then points an accusing finger, 'You are the man' (2 Sam. 12:1-7). The second-person address (*you*, *yourself*, *your*) sounds like a drumbeat. There is an apostolic relentlessness here, in the interests of bringing us to see the true nature of our position before God.

We have no way of knowing whether in dictating his letter Paul spoke slowly and deliberately, or whether Tertius used some form of shorthand and could keep up with the occasional rapid-fire speech of Paul's argument. If so he would have written out the letter later in longhand. But in either case it is not difficult to imagine Paul's emphatic pronunciation. There is a sign of it in verse 1: 'You have no excuse, O man, every one of you who judges ...'

These are not the gentle words of an intimate letter to friends (although he had a number in Rome; see 16:3-15). Probably Tertius and the others with Paul had heard him say the same things, make the same emphases (perhaps with different kinds of application), when he had preached in Corinth. As he develops his argument, he turns now from describing the condition of humanity in general to address a more specific group of people.

These people belong to a category: 'every one of you who judges' (verse 1). Later on (verse 17) he specifically mentions Jews ('But if you call yourself a Jew ...'). It is not clear whether these words are retrospective (the 'you' in verse 1 being the same as the 'you' in verse 17). If so Paul has his kinsmen in mind from the beginning of the chapter. Commentators are not agreed. But in either case what is clear is that he is now addressing people who not only distance themselves from those he had described in 1:18-32, but also condemn them. Their reaction to God's wrath being revealed against the sins Paul has described is a hearty 'Quite right! Amen!' They are in complete agreement with both Paul and God! But Paul will demonstrate, they are making a fatal mistake in assuming that this renders them immune from God's judgment. In fact they too need to repent (verse 4), and in failing to do so they are storing up wrath for themselves (verse 5).

If Paul *already* has his own Jewish kinsmen in mind from verse 1, he would have been conscious that this presumption of safety from judgment was also shared by others in the first century, just as it is today. There were, and are, many people who possess a serious moral code who assume that, while not claiming to be perfect, they are not themselves 'sinners' in any significant sense. They are, therefore, sufficiently secure in their own righteousness to judge and even condemn others—after all, *they* (those others) deserve it!

WITHOUT EXCUSE

But in fact those who pass judgment in this way 'have no excuse.' Paul once again uses the word *anapologētos* (cf. 1:20), the negative form of the Greek word from which 'apologetics' is derived—that is, the explanation and defence of the faith. Those who act as judges have nothing to plead in their own defence that will stand up to divine scrutiny. Thus the apostle unmasks those who agree with his exposition of divine wrath in 1:18-32 but assume they are safe from it. In fact they 'practise the very same things.' Their self-assured judgment of others is in effect also a self-condemnation (verse 1).

Whoever Paul has in mind here, they share the conviction that the sins on which he has majored in chapter 1 should be divinely judged and condemned: 'We know that the judgment of God rightly falls on those who practise such things' (verse 2). For that judgment is based on the truth, the reality of the situation—not merely on appearances. But such judges are also self-deceived, for they 'practise the very same things' (verse 1). They will not escape divine judgment (verse 3).

Paul's charge here is that those who are casting the first stones are not without their own sin. In fact, written into his catalogue of sin in 1:29-31 are sins that occur among people who profess the highest standards of respectability ('covetousness, malice ... envy ... strife, deceit ... They are ... foolish, faithless, heartless, ruthless ...').

How is it possible to be so mistaken? Paul's answer is given in verse 4: (i) they 'presume on the riches of his [God's] kindness and patience.' (ii) they ignore the fact that 'God's kindness is meant to lead you to repentance.'

PRINCIPLES OF JUDGMENT

Paul's words here are reminiscent of the way Jesus exposed the attitude of some of his Jewish contemporaries—for example in his parable of the Pharisee and the Tax Collector (Luke 18:9-14).

We should note that if Paul has his own people in mind in this passage (as he certainly does later), there is no anti-Semitism here in Paul or in Jesus. Both were Jews; both deeply loved the Jewish people (cf. Matt. 23:37; Rom. 9:1-3). In fact the principles in this section surely had a broad application to Gentiles as well, which may explain why Paul does not specify his own Jewish people until verse 17.

The tragic error in view here is the assumption that, for whatever reason—for example the assumption that God is 'kind'—we are 'OK' before him, even if we occasionally (in our own view) fall short of his standards. But Paul points out the fallacy of the logic here: 'God's kindness *is meant to lead you to repentance*' (verse 4). In fact rather than embracing God's grace they were despising it; they were building a dam against its influence rather than allowing grace to overflow into their hearts and lives and thus master and transform them.

The fallacy has a modern version:

- When God's love finds me he accepts me the way I am;
- Therefore I can remain the way he found me.

Whereas the truth is:

- God's love *finds me despite the way I am*;
- God's love *never leaves me the way he found me.*

Here we encounter a principle that will reappear in various parts of Romans: the more profound the exposition of God's grace, the more all-embracing and all-demanding is the summons to a life of repentance and obedience. Ignore that principle, Paul is indicating, and instead of being authentic recipients of divine kindness, we are demeaning it and 'storing up wrath ... on the day of wrath.' For then 'God's righteous judgment will be revealed' (verse 5).

Paul has now underlined two important principles in God's judgment:

(i) 'We know the judgment of God rightly falls …' (verse 2). More literally translated Paul says that God's judgment is 'according to truth,' or 'according to reality.'

(ii) It is also a *righteous-judgment* (one word in Paul's Greek). It is made according to a fixed norm—and that norm is the righteous character of God expressed in his revelation.

Well might we now hold our breath at hearing anyone say they were confident that they could stand before God with equanimity. For Paul that is a thoughtless and reckless assumption. It presumes a disastrously mistaken conclusion from the premise that God is rich in kindness (verse 4). It is also a symptom of a heart that has been hardened rather than melted by the truth that God is kind (verse 5). The psalmist knew better. If our sins were counted and exposed, none of us could stand. God's forgiveness results in 'fear,' or reverent and loving awe, admiration, and worship, not self-satisfaction and pride (Psa. 130:3-4).

There is such a thing as compound judgment. Those Paul has in mind assume they are, as it were, 'storing up brownie points' as they condemn others. But in fact they are 'storing up wrath' that will be revealed 'on the day of wrath' when God's judgment will become clear. Like Chorazin and Bethsaida, towns that had witnessed the grace of the Lord Jesus Christ and his mighty works of restoration, they will be brought down low (cf. Luke 10:13).

Paul has already hinted at two principles of divine judgment: (i) it is based on reality, not appearances; (ii) its standard is always God's own righteous character. His grace and kindness do not dilute his holiness. Now he introduces a further principle: (iii) 'He will render to each one *according to his works*' (verse 6). The divine assessment that is according to both reality and righteousness is also made on the basis of what a person has actually been and done.

The whole Bible teaches us that there are, at bottom, only two ways to live—the broad way or the narrow way; against God or for God; in unbelief or in faith; outside of Christ or in Christ; foolishly or wisely. So here: ongoing faithfulness, doing what pleases God and serves his glory, is the pathway to eternal life; but love of self, rejection of the truth and righteousness is the high road to condemnation (verses 7-8). The end? 'Wrath and fury … tribulation and distress' for those who do evil (verses 8-9). There are no exceptions—whether

Jew or Gentile ('Greek,' verse 9). But for anyone who faithfully seeks to do 'good'—(that is, what is pleasing to God and conforms to his will as did the original 'good' creation)—the pathway leads to 'glory and honour and peace' (verse 10). Again, there are no exceptions (whether Jew or Gentile, verse 11).

God does not show partiality as though what really matters with him is where we were born or what we have inherited. He judges us fairly and equally as men and women made in his image, created to love, serve and enjoy him, and as those to whom he has sufficiently revealed himself in the world so that we would seek him (Acts 14:15-17).

Does Paul sound as though he is teaching that it is possible to be saved by our own goodness and merit? He will more fully express his negative answer in due course. Here his point is simply to emphasize that God's judgment is related to the reality of our individual lives. As he will indicate, he is not denying that salvation is a gift of grace, not something we merit (cf. 5:15, 17; 6:23). It is clear in his general teaching that it is only by grace that we seek 'glory and honour and immortality' (verse 7). Without Christ we will remain self-seeking (verse 8), not God-honouring.

For Paul there is a basic twin principle: (i) salvation is by grace; (ii) God's assessment of our lives will be related to what we have been and done, that is, to our 'works' (cf. 2 Cor. 5:10). In this connection, the Scottish theologian James Buchanan (1804–70) recorded an instructive axiom his friend and colleague Thomas Chalmers (1780–1847) shared with him: 'I would have every preacher insist strenuously on these two doctrines—a present justification by grace, through faith alone, and a future judgment according to works.'[1]

So Paul does not here compromise his teaching that, apart from the pardoning grace of God through the work of Christ, only one verdict on our lives is possible for both Jew and Gentile—condemnation. It is important to bear this in mind lest we misinterpret Paul's words. But for the moment all this hangs in the air. Paul will not prescribe the remedy until he has shown us that we have a fatal disease.

[1] James Buchanan, *The Doctrine of Justification* (1867, repr. Edinburgh: Banner of Truth Trust, 2016), 222.

IMPARTIALITY

There is a fourth principle of divine judgment: 'God shows no partiality' (verse 11). Our standing before God is not a matter of ethnicity, wealth, intelligence, or any such distinctions. There is no distinction in us that grounds a partiality in God towards any individual or group among humanity. That had already been made clear in the pages of the Old Testament (Deut. 7:7; Amos 3:2) and would be repeated in the New (cf. Rom. 9:6-13; Gal. 6:15).

Paul's words here echo those of the apostle Peter when the Roman centurion Cornelius invited him to speak to the gathering of Gentiles in his house: 'Truly I understand that God shows no partiality …' (Acts 10:34).

The fact that God's word came 'to the Jew first' (1:16) should not be misunderstood to mean that this privilege exculpated them from all responsibility to respond in repentance and faith to God's overtures of grace. Paul makes that clear: the 'tribulation and distress' of divine judgment is also 'for … the Jew first and also the Greek' (verse 9). Indeed the greater the privilege of the revelation received, the greater the responsibility to respond to it in faith and obedience.

These again are sobering words. Every human being will stand before the judgment seat of Christ (2 Cor. 5:10). That is the consistent testimony of Scripture. What happens now, what we do, how we live—in faith or unbelief—matters. How we live has eternal consequences that are, on the one hand, fearful ('tribulation and distress,' verse 9), or, on the other hand, wonderful beyond our imagination ('glory and honour and peace,' verse 10).

Paul points us to a principle of spiritual life that runs through Scripture: we will experience the consequences of what we seek; we will reap what we sow (Gal. 6:7). Unbelief and rejection inexorably lead to a world without faith or hope or love; trusting and obeying constitute the pathway that leads to glory. In this sense we get what we really want. Later Paul will show us how only God's grace in Christ can transform what we actually want.

These are the only two ways God sets before us. There is a broad way—the way that seems right to a man—that leads to death and destruction (Prov. 14:12). But there is also a narrow way and those who are on it find life; they 'trust and obey' knowing that 'there is no other way to be happy in Jesus.'[1] That way has only one entry point: the saving grace of God in Jesus Christ. He alone is the way to life.

The purpose of Paul's sobering exposition is simple. He sets before us the reality of God's judgment—just as Moses had done in his great covenant sermon recorded in the book of Deuteronomy. But he has already set these words within the context of the way of salvation in the fulfilment of God's covenant in Jesus and the gospel (1:16-17). Romans as a whole therefore echoes Moses' exhortation given so long beforehand: 'I call heaven and earth to witness … I have set before you life and death, blessing and curse. Therefore choose life …' (Deut. 30:19).

Before Paul expounds how this is so, he has more to say about our sinful condition and its consequences. We should remember that he speaks here as a spiritual physician. He must give us his diagnosis before he gives us the hope of a cure or writes a prescription for the soul-medicine that God has dispensed in the gospel.

[1] From the hymn 'When we walk with the Lord' by John Henry Sammis (1846–1919).

7

A Law to Themselves

For all who have sinned without the law will also perish without the law, and all who have sinned under the law will be judged by the law. [13] *For it is not the hearers of the law who are righteous before God, but the doers of the law who will be justified.* [14] *For when Gentiles, who do not have the law, by nature do what the law requires, they are a law to themselves, even though they do not have the law.* [15] *They show that the work of the law is written on their hearts, while their conscience also bears witness, and their conflicting thoughts accuse or even excuse them* [16] *on that day when, according to my gospel, God judges the secrets of men by Christ Jesus.*

(Rom. 2:12-16)

'God shows no partiality' (verse 11). Our natural (and sinful) instinct is to prefer to think, or even assume, that he does—at least in our own case, although not in the case of those we condemn. But the person who thus condemns others is as self-condemned as King David was when he responded to Nathan's parable (2 Sam. 12:1-14). Thus 'in passing judgment ... you, the judge, practise the same things' (verse 1).

In verse 17 Paul will fix the cross-hairs of his argument on his own Jewish people. But in verses 1-11 they were probably already in his mind. The same is true in verses 12-16. Here he spells out in specific terms what God's impartial judgment actually implies: those who have never had the law (*i.e.* the Law of Moses, the Ten Commandments) but who sin will perish. This is *not* because they did not have the law but because they did not live righteously in the light of God's general revelation. On the other hand, those who have the law (Paul and his kinsmen), yet sin, will be judged according to the law—the implication being that they too will be condemned.

Paul knew from his own experience that the natural instinct of the self-defensive Jew was to appeal to the fact that (unlike the Gentile) he possessed the revelation of the law to Moses. God had been gracious in giving that law to his ancient people. They were, therefore, surely a 'special case.' Does this not imply that in this one instance God does show a kind of favouritism (verse 11)?

The role of the law is a major theme in Romans. Here, in his first discussion of it, Paul lays down the principle that what pleases God is not knowledge of the law (being 'hearers' of it) but obedience to the will of God revealed in it (verse 13). Privilege always brings responsibility, and to fail in responsibility is to despise privilege.

Paul is developing an argument here: verses 12, 13, and 14 all begin with the connective word 'for' (typically the second word in a sentence in Greek). It signals the fact that verse 12 is logically connected to verse 11, verse 13 to verse 12, and verse 14 to verse 13. But tracing the connections in Paul's thinking can require some thought. It is not unusual (as here) for interpreters to differ in the way they trace his theological logic.

The 'For' in verse 12 introduces a proof of the fact that 'God shows no partiality'—sin will be judged, and people will perish for it, whether they have had the law or not. It is not the law that causes sin!

The 'For' in verse 13 introduces an explanation for the fact that all who sin (whether with or without the law) will face judgment and condemnation. Having the law is not the issue; keeping the law is.

But what is the force of the 'For' in verse 14? In verses 14-16 Paul appears to be explaining the righteousness of God in his judgment of those who have not had the revealed law of God (*i.e.* 'Gentiles'). After all he will later say 'where there is no law there is no transgression' (4:15).

The explanation sheds light on his understanding of the theology of the whole Bible.

WHICH GENTILES?

A major question of interpretation arises in understanding verses 14-16: about whom is Paul speaking here? What he seems to be saying is in essence as follows (we will consider some of the details in due course):

> When Gentiles (who do not have the revealed law of God) 'by nature do what the law requires' they are 'a law to themselves.'
>
> This doing 'by nature' indicates that 'the work of the law,' while not revealed to them in propositional form (in the written text of the Ten Commandments), is nevertheless written somewhere else, namely 'on their hearts.'
>
> Their consciences are then, apparently to some degree, calibrated to this law, with the result that their consciences either accuse or excuse them before the judgment of God.

The general direction of Paul's thought is clear enough. But who are these Gentiles? Here interpreters are not agreed.

Some draw the conclusion he must be thinking about Gentiles who have come to faith in Christ. Surely they alone can be described as doing what the law requires (verse 14)? In them the prophecy of the new covenant is fulfilled: 'I will put my law within them, and I will write it on their hearts ...' (Jer. 31:33). Paul's words, therefore, are a description of a sub-category of Gentiles—those who have become Christians.

The alternative view is that Paul is speaking about Gentiles in general. All Gentiles are sinners—after all, universal sinfulness is the fundamental point he is establishing from 1:18–3:20: 'None is righteous, no, not one' (3:10). Nevertheless there are occasions when their behaviour patterns conform to the requirements of the Ten Commandments (not everyone lives in adultery, steals, murders, etc.). This, then, is an indication that Gentiles do have an awareness of the commandments set out in the law; 'the work of the law is written on their hearts.' It cannot be otherwise if the law reflects God's character. Although distorted, they remain the image of God (as Scripture indicates—Gen. 9:5-6; James 3:9). As a result, in the light of their knowledge of the judgment of God (1:32), their consciences will accuse them—or perhaps on occasion even excuse them—even if those consciences are not always reliable, nor are they the final judge of behaviour.

These two different interpretations can be traced throughout the history of the church. Augustine, for example, held the first view.[1] John Calvin held the second: 'the Gentiles had the natural light of righteousness which supplied the place of the law by which the Jews are taught, so that they were a law unto themselves.'[2]

Several considerations tend to support the second view over the first. Paul is speaking here about Gentiles in general.

(i) The point of his argument here is to establish the righteousness of God in his judgment of Gentiles.

If it was Israel alone, not the Gentiles, who were given the law, and the Gentiles had no knowledge of God's standards, how then could he judge them in their ignorance? Verses 14-16 provide the answer: they are not ignorant. In fact, 'when Gentiles, who do not have the law, by nature do what the law requires ... They show that the work of the law is written on their hearts.'

There has been considerable debate about where our English translations should place the comma in verse 14.[3] Should it be after the word 'law' (so that Gentiles 'by nature do the works of the law' or after the word 'nature' (so that although Gentiles do not naturally have the law, they do what it requires to a certain extent)? But in either case the main point indicates that a reflection of God's law is present in their lives.

(ii) Paul further describes these Gentiles as having conflicting thoughts before God's judgment throne—about their guilt and innocence. This hardly seems consistent with the experience promised to believers by Jeremiah that 'they shall all know me ... For I will forgive their iniquity, and I will remember their sin no more' (Jer. 31:34). Nor is it consistent with the assurance enjoyed by believers (including Gentiles!) Paul later describes in 5:1-11. The persons described in 2:14-16 lack that assurance; they are conflicted. In sharp contrast, the persons described in 5:1-11 (and thereafter) are already exulting!

[1] Augustine, *The Spirit and the Letter*, 26:43–28:49.

[2] John Calvin, *The Epistles of Paul the Apostle to the Romans and to the Thessalonians*, tr. Ross Mackenzie, ed., D. W. & T. F. Torrance (Edinburgh: Oliver & Boyd, 1961), 48.

[3] It will be remembered that Paul *dictated* his letter to the Romans rather than wrote it himself (his scribe was Tertius: 16:22), and also that the punctuation in ancient Greek manuscripts is sparse by comparison with modern English.

(iii) Strictly speaking, Paul (unlike Jeremiah) does not refer here to *the law itself* being 'written on the heart' but to '*the work* of the law.' The distinction may appear to be subtle, but it is, surely, not accidental. Paul appears to highlight that he is referring here to something different from the promise of the new covenant in Jeremiah 31.

(iv) Then, fourthly, Paul describes these Gentiles as being 'a law to themselves,' and states that they 'do not have the law.' But this would be a strange, and indeed inaccurate, way of describing Gentile Christians. As believers they would be quite familiar with the Decalogue. Paul's copious references to the Old Testament throughout his letters assumes such knowledge.

This interpretation both illumines and harmonizes with Paul's whole-Bible theology.

WHOLE-BIBLE THEOLOGY

We are all, 'by nature' created as the 'image and likeness' of God (Gen. 1:26-28). Adam did not have the tablets of the law. But he reflected instinctively ('by nature') what pleased God. In that sense it could be said of Adam and Eve in Eden that 'the work of the law is written in their hearts' (verse 15).

It is also clear that when our first parents fell what Paul says in 2:15-16 was also true of them. When God confronts them in judgment, 'their conflicting thoughts accuse or even excuse them'! Their consciences, though fallen, accuse them and lead them to cover their nakedness and hide. At the same time, their excusing themselves is recorded in Genesis 3:12-13. For Eve, it was the serpent who was to blame; for Adam it was the woman (and perhaps also the Lord himself since it was he who gave her to him!).

Here, then, as elsewhere in Romans, there are echoes of the Garden of Eden, of Adam and Eve's creation, and of their fall.

When Adam fell, although tragic distortions took place in his life, he remained the image of God. In addition to Genesis 9:6 and James 3:9, Jesus alludes to this in Matthew 22:20-21: if we are to 'render to Caesar' what is his because his image is on the coin of the realm, we should likewise render to God whatever bears his image, namely ourselves.

Thus, because they remain the image of God—yes distorted, no longer obedient, and with a sinful will and a confused mind—'the work of the law' is still written on Gentile hearts. This, in the Bible, is the explanation for a universal moral consciousness in the human race, for the activity of conscience, and also for the universal deep-down awareness of the judgment of God (1:32).

In a word, therefore, the divine standard of judgment was written on tablets of stone at Sinai; but that was not its first 'writing.' It had been inscribed on the human heart on the day man was created as the image and likeness of his Maker. While that writing is no longer clear, it still remains.

Paul thus explains in verses 12-16 how it is that God can righteously judge those who have never had access to the Law given at Sinai.

We should notice, (i) He is not saying the Gentiles are justified by obedience to the law. (ii) He is not saying Gentiles either consistently or perfectly keep the law. But (iii) He is saying that since men and women, even apart from special revelation, remain the image of God, they will function as such, however inconsistently. And as he has already said in 1:32, they cannot escape their sense of moral norms and divine judgment. Conscience will react to their behaviour, even although it is in itself fallible.

MORE PRINCIPLES OF JUDGMENT

To summarize: Paul has laid out several principles of God's judgment: it is made 'rightly,' *i.e.* it is made according to the truth and reality of the situation. It is also made in accordance with what we have done ('each according to his works,' verse 6). In addition, it is without partiality (verse 11).

Verses 12-16 added further dimensions to this righteous judgment. It is made, as is often said, 'according to, and on the basis of, the light we have received.' Those who have received the law will be assessed in accordance with the clear revelation God graciously gave to Israel at Sinai. But Gentiles, who have not had access to the Sinaitic law, will also be assessed by the revelation they have received—'the work of the law' inscribed on their hearts, even if their grasp of it is distorted.

This principle has sometimes been misapplied, as though it implies that since Gentiles have had little revelation the judgment on them will be incidental. On the contrary, Paul was at pains in 1:18-32 to indicate that 'the wrath of God is revealed from heaven against all ungodliness and unrighteousness ...' (1:18). The clarity and the sufficiency of the revelation that surrounds and even invades us grounds this righteous condemnation. Paul makes it clear that 'all who have sinned without the law will also perish without the law' (2:12).

To these principles of judgment the apostle now adds two more, both in verse 16. The *first* is that the judgment of God will reach to 'the secrets of men.' The word Paul uses here (*krupta*) means the 'hidden things'—almost certainly in this context implying things we would prefer to remain hidden (it is used in this sense in 2 Cor. 4:2). But there is nothing hidden from God: 'For the word of God is living and active, sharper than any two-edged sword, piercing to the division of soul and spirit, of joints and of marrow, and discerning the thoughts and intentions of the heart. And no creature is hidden from his sight, but all are naked and exposed to him to whom we must give account' (Heb. 4:12-13).

Furthermore, Paul states that God will judge these secrets 'by Christ Jesus.' This standard is the ultimate guarantee of the righteousness of his judgment.

(i) These words echo the teaching of Jesus in John's Gospel that the Father has committed all judgment into his hands (John 5:22); that he has this authority as the Son of Man (John 5:27); that his judgment is just, since he always seeks the will of the Father who sent him (John 5:30); and that his judgment is true because he judges in concert with his Father (John 8:16).

(ii) This teaching also carries profound implications for Paul's understanding of Jesus. For Paul as a Jew, the judge of all the earth is Yahweh. That Christ is not only associated with him in this judgment but has that judgment committed to him by his Father indicates that in Paul's view Jesus shares divine prerogatives because as God's Son he shares the divine nature.

(iii) These words imply that we can never argue that God's standard of judgment is inappropriate or that his understanding of the human condition is imperfect or inadequate. The standard of judgment is the incarnate Christ, who was tempted in every way we are (Heb. 4:15). We will never be able to say on the Day of Judgment,

'You set the bar too high; you didn't have any idea what it is like to be human'—not when the judgment seat before we appear is that of the incarnate Lord Jesus.

All this, Paul suggests, is part and parcel of the gospel he preaches ('my gospel,' verse 16).

In the verses that follow (verses 17-29) Paul turns directly to address Jewish people ('But if you call yourself a Jew ...'). But it is already clear, even although his words in 2:1-16 are broadly applicable to all, that his argument is especially applicable to them. They are already familiar with Scripture's teaching on the righteous judgment of God (verse 2). Those same Scriptures had taught them never to repeat the mistake of presuming on 'the riches of his [God's] kindness and forbearance and patience' (verse 4).

In what follows, Paul's words—as the word of God—will be 'sharper than any two-edged sword' (Heb. 4:12). He has not yet come to the end of his sobering exposé of sin.

The question is: will his kinsmen—and will we—receive his word 'not as the word of men but as what it really is, the word of God' (1 Thess. 2:13)?

8

Call Yourself a Jew?

But if you call yourself a Jew and rely on the law and boast in
God [18] *and know his will and approve what is excellent, because*
you are instructed from the law; [19] *and if you are sure that*
you yourself are a guide to the blind, a light to those who are in
darkness, [20] *an instructor of the foolish, a teacher of children,*
having in the law the embodiment of knowledge and truth—
[21] *you then who teach others, do you not teach yourself? While*
you preach against stealing, do you steal? [22] *You who say that*
one must not commit adultery, do you commit adultery? You
who abhor idols, do you rob temples? [23] *You who boast in the law*
dishonour God by breaking the law. [24] *For, as it is written, 'The*
name of God is blasphemed among the Gentiles because of you.'
[25] *For circumcision indeed is of value if you obey the law, but*
if you break the law, your circumcision becomes uncircumcision.
[26] *So, if a man who is uncircumcised keeps the precepts of the*
law, will not his uncircumcision be regarded as circumcision?
[27] *Then he who is physically uncircumcised but keeps the law*
will condemn you who have the written code and circumcision
but break the law. [28] *For no one is a Jew who is merely one*
outwardly, nor is circumcision outward and physical. [29] *But a*
Jew is one inwardly, and circumcision is a matter of the heart,
by the Spirit, not by the letter. His praise is not from man but
from God.

(Rom. 2:17-29)

Paul now specifically addresses Jews directly for the first time in the letter. His style of speech indicates that he is increasingly moving from exposition to application. The passage abounds in direct address. Verses 17-23 are punctuated by relentless 'finger-jabbing' rhetorical statements ('you' occurs thirteen times, 'yourself' a further three times). Paul has shifted gears and is now in full preaching mode.

He first works his way through areas of life where the Jews typically thought of themselves as superior to Gentiles (verses 17-20). Then he points out the commandments that are being egregiously breached among them (verses 21-24). This leads (verses 25-29) to answering an objection (or at least a question) about his teaching, namely that it sounds as though he is dismissing circumcision out of hand and regards it as valueless. How can he say what he does about circumcision without demeaning the 'sacrament' that God had given to Abraham and his seed to be observed throughout the generations (Gen. 17:10-14)?

PRIVILEGE BRINGS RESPONSIBILITY

In verses 17-20 Paul provides a catalogue of qualities and abilities by which a Jew might self-identify. They are self-explanatory—and, if true, profoundly impressive. The Jew has superior knowledge (verses 17-18) and a superior position (verses 19-20). Paul does not deny these privileges (as he makes clear in 3:1; 9:4-5). But the profession of privileges is not the same as the possession of the righteousness of justification.

In distinction from a Gentile, a Jew had the clearly-articulated law of God given to Moses. What could be more reliable than that? Jews possessed the Ten Commandments, Gentiles did not. God had revealed himself exclusively to Israel at Sinai. The Jew could boast in this. The Gentile could not. After all God had told the Jews that they belonged to the only family on earth Yahweh had chosen (Amos 3:2). They could 'boast in God' (verse 17). They had access to his revealed will in the Hebrew Bible with all its promises, prescriptions and examples. The Jew approved God's excellent way because he was 'instructed in the law.' It did not seem to him surprising therefore if he was an 'instructor of the foolish, a teacher of children' because what the Jew possessed in the law of Moses was 'the embodiment of knowledge and truth' (verse 20).

What then is the problem? Did the Jew not belong to God's chosen people? Was he not therefore a 'special case,' standing in special favour with God by contrast with the Gentile?

Paul answers: the issue before God is not the Jew's possession of privileges *per se.* It is how he responds to God in the light of them. For it is a basic biblical principle that the gifts of God summon us to be faithful to him, to choose the way of trust and obedience rather than faithlessness and disobedience. It is one thing to have the law, to know the law, and to teach others the law. But the bigger issue is: are you teaching yourself to trust the Law-Giver and obey his law (verse 21)? Paul presses home the issue by challenging objectors not about whether they *know* the law, but whether they *obey* the law they know. It has not escaped the notice of psychologists and psychiatrists, or for that matter the media, that people sometimes condemn the very activities in which they themselves engage; or condemn others in order to mask their own moral failures.

Here the apostle mentions specific commandments (stealing, committing adultery). But then he asks, 'You who abhor idols, do you rob temples?' This rather obscure question may refer to the view that since pagan temples were idolatrous their contents were 'fair game' to rob—the general principle being that 'if it is done in the name of God, it's OK!' It is possible, however, that Paul is alluding to the accusations Malachi levelled against his contemporaries (Mal. 3:6-15)—although the use of the plural 'temples' would seem, if anything, to favour the first view. In any event there lay a deep hypocrisy in the action.

Paul is driving home a simple point by way of these illustrations: to boast about having the law without seeking to love the Lord of the law himself with heart and soul and strength by obeying it, is to dishonour the God who gave it in the first place. It is to despise the whole purpose of the law. And the result is horrific: 'The name of God is blasphemed among the Gentiles because of you' (verse 24).

These last words are cited from Isaiah 52:5. The biblical principle is that we become like whatever we worship (Psa. 115:8). If this was the lifestyle of the worshippers then it was hardly surprising that the object of their worship was despised. The principle holds good today too: the name of God is too often and too easily blasphemed among those who make no profession of Christian faith because of the lives of those who do.

Could there be a more shameful denunciation? Called to be a light to the nations, God's chosen people were causing them to turn away from him. Paul is making it plain that there is no security in possessing privileges that do not lead to practice. If anything those privileges only add to condemnation.

CAN CIRCUMCISION SAVE?

In verses 25-29 Paul moves from a general catalogue of the privileges and special identity markers of God's people to the oldest and most basic of them all—circumcision. It had marked the entry point for Abraham's male descendants since time immemorial. For a male not to be circumcised was to be outside of the covenant community (Gen. 17:14). But just as in the Christian church it has too often been assumed that the water of baptism secures salvation, a similar false assumption was often present in relation to circumcision.

Paul has been deconstructing the notion that divinely given privileges in and of themselves are fail-safe guarantees of divine acceptance. Then, as now, a faithless response to marks of privilege turns them into marks of judgment (cf. 1 Cor. 11:29).

Since circumcision was a sign of God's covenant, its significance depended on the nature of his covenant-making. His covenants were made unconditionally and unilaterally. They were not negotiated settlements between two parties, but a sovereign commitment on God's part given to his people to be received and acted on by them. But while unilateral and unconditional in their *creation*, they were bilateral and carefully conditioned in their *application*. They called for a response of faith and repentance on the part of the recipients if they were to enjoy the promised blessings. Otherwise they would expose themselves to God's judgment curse.

This being the case, unbelief and disobedience to God's covenant pledge did not destroy the way circumcision signified God's covenant promise. Instead it transposed its effect. Although its blessings were rejected in unbelief, circumcision still pointed to God's faithfulness to his covenant. But now it highlighted his promised judgment. It signified not being 'cut off' *for* God but being 'cut off' *from* God. The covenant-rejecting individual had in fact exposed himself to the covenant curse and in effect rejected the covenant blessing. To be circumcised yet not be faithful to God and his ways was to place oneself under divine judgment. It was in this sense that circumcision became 'uncircumcision' (verse 25).

Thus Paul argues that circumcision had the value placed on it by the Jews only when the reality it symbolized was realized.

What Paul is making clear here is that Scripture taught that the power and value of circumcision did not lie in the rite itself but in the God whose covenant it signified and sealed (4:11). If that was the case, then an uncircumcised person who 'keeps the law will condemn you who have the written code and circumcision but break the law' (verse 27). If someone lived the lifestyle of repentance and faith without having the sign that summoned them to it, they already experienced the reality to which the sign was the summons. In fact—although Scripture nowhere expresses it this way—this was surely true of every believing wife of a circumcised Israelite!

Ultimately, then, as Paul says later (4:11), circumcision functioned as a sign and seal; it was not the reality itself. What mattered, as was already clear in the Mosaic period, was not the sign on its own, *per se*, but experiencing the reality to which it pointed: divine renewal that led to law-loving (Deut. 30:6), repentance, and a new life of consecration to the Lord (Deut. 10:16; Jer. 4:4). It was *never* appropriate to think that a circumcised *body* substituted for a circumcised *heart* (Jer. 9:26). Sign and reality belong together.

This leads to Paul's foundational point in verses 28-29: being a (true) Jew is never merely a matter of externals. It is in the heart and life that the true distinguishing markers exist. This is 'a matter of the heart by the Spirit,' not of externals ('by the letter') unaccompanied by the reality of repentance, faith and new life.

The ESV rightly capitalizes the word Spirit (*pneuma*) in verse 29. Being a Jew was never intended to be merely a matter of external conformity to externals, *e.g.* in circumcision. It was always a matter of the renewal and obedience of the heart effected by the Spirit of God. The old covenant people had been taught by Moses that circumcision contained a call to repentance and new life: 'circumcise the foreskin *of your heart*' (Deut. 10:16). But he knew that this could be accomplished only by an inward divine work ('The Lord your God will circumcise your heart and the hearts of your offspring, so that you will love the Lord your God with all your heart and with all your soul, that you may live'; Deut. 30:6). This is why Nicodemus should have been able to 'understand these things' when Jesus spoke to him about the need for renewal from above (John 3:1-10).

There are two important implications of this. *First*, the reality enshrined in circumcision was never intended to be merely external and physical but internal and spiritual. And *second*, these words underline the teaching of the Old Testament itself that the Spirit was already engaged in the personal renewal of God's children between the time of Abraham and Jesus. He alone could effect the reality to which the sign of circumcision pointed. That was why the truly circumcised man looked to God in faith, not to man for praise (verse 29c).

The charge Paul levels against his kinsmen here, that they were 'uncircumcised in heart,' had at one time enraged him. It was one reason he had approved of the stoning of Stephen (Acts 7:51-54). How wonderful that he now realized that it was the unvarnished truth of God and was now preaching it himself! Over his eyes too, there had once been a veil whenever he read or heard the law of Moses (2 Cor. 3:14-16). But now he could see.

This clears up a misunderstanding Christians sometimes have about circumcision. While it was given in the context of the promise of land, it never pointed only or dominantly to physical privileges. Nor did it mark the automatic granting of grace—*ex opere operato,* as theologians say, *i.e.* simply by the act of being circumcised. It was *never* acceptable in Yahweh's sight to be circumcised but not to trust in him. The prophets had taught as Paul now does, that this had never been the case. Being a (true) Jew always required a circumcised heart (Jer. 6:10; 9:26).

Jesus had implied this in his teaching. John records (John 8:31-47) how our Lord's (circumcised) opponents argued, 'Abraham is our father.' But their lives demonstrated to the Saviour that their hearts were uncircumcised. 'You,' he said in response, 'are of your father the devil'; they were not 'of God' (John 8:44, 47). To have received the 'sacrament' of circumcision but not to live the circumcised life was to be uncircumcised, and ultimately to be excommunicated from the presence of God.

So we should never lose sight of the axiom that every spiritual privilege calls us to respond in repentance, faith, and obedience. This is as true for God's people in the new covenant as it was for those in the old covenant. We must learn to,

Trust and obey!
For there's no other way
To be happy in Jesus
But to trust and obey.[1]

A REPEATED MISTAKE

The misstep Paul's contemporaries made is always a danger. Christians too can very subtly focus on, and then rely on, externals as the ground for their acceptance with God. We can receive baptism and the Lord's Supper too—and substitute these things for faith and new obedience. And, sadly, that error is all the more likely to delude us when our lives no longer match our profession. It leads us to have what Paul calls 'the form of godliness' without its 'power' (2 Tim. 3:5)—being baptized, but not living the baptized life; receiving communion, but not living in communion with the Lord Jesus.

This searching teaching gets under our skin. When Jesus taught this distinction between external privilege and internal reality the reaction was one of physical violence: 'they picked up stones to throw at him' (John 8:59).

Paul too experienced a variety of violent reactions when he preached the same truth. One was marked by a kind of verbal violence, as here: 'Are you saying that there is no advantage in being a Jew and no value in circumcision? How dare you! Heretic!'

Well, was there any 'advantage' in being a Jew? To this question Paul now turns. We can perhaps guess his answer. But before we try to do that we should ponder whether in our own lives profession is matched by possession and sign matched by reality.

[1] From the hymn by John Henry Sammis (1846–1919), 'When we walk with the Lord.'

9

None Righteous, No, Not One

Then what advantage has the Jew? Or what is the value of
circumcision? [2] Much in every way. To begin with, the Jews
were entrusted with the oracles of God. [3] What if some were
unfaithful? Does their faithlessness nullify the faithfulness of
God? [4] By no means! Let God be true though every one were
a liar, as it is written,

> *'That you may be justified in your words,*
> *and prevail when you are judged.'*

[5] But if our unrighteousness serves to show the righteousness of
God, what shall we say? That God is unrighteous to inflict wrath
on us? (I speak in a human way.) [6] By no means! For then how
could God judge the world? [7] But if through my lie God's truth
abounds to his glory, why am I still being condemned as a sinner?
[8] And why not do evil that good may come?—as some people
slanderously charge us with saying. Their condemnation is just.
[9] What then? Are we Jews any better off? No, not at all. For
we have already charged that all, both Jews and Greeks, are
under sin, [10] as it is written:

> *'None is righteous, no, not one;*
> *[11] no one understands;*
> *no one seeks for God.*
> *[12] All have turned aside; together they have become worthless;*
> *no one does good,*
> *not even one.'*
> *[13] 'Their throat is an open grave;*
> *they use their tongues to deceive.'*
> *'The venom of asps is under their lips.'*

[14] *'Their mouth is full of curses and bitterness.'*
[15] *'Their feet are swift to shed blood;*
[16] *in their paths are ruin and misery,*
[17] *and the way of peace they have not known.'*
[18] *'There is no fear of God before their eyes.'*

[19] *Now we know that whatever the law says it speaks to those who are under the law, so that every mouth may be stopped, and the whole world may be held accountable to God.*
[20] *For by works of the law no human being will be justified in his sight, since through the law comes knowledge of sin.*

(Rom. 3:1-20)

Paul now draws to a conclusion the first main section of his letter (1:18–3:20). He has been engaged in an extended and appropriately relentless argument exposing the universal guilt and lost condition of humanity. By the time he has reached 3:20 he will have silenced every protest.

No doubt when Paul preached on the themes he has been expounding here he experienced a variety of reactions—ranging perhaps from a simple 'Please explain what you are saying' to outright and even violent hostility. The number of question marks in 3:1-9 is indicative of this. There are nine of them in verses 1-8, and as we read them we can sense in the background an air of hostility towards Paul's teaching.

ADVANTAGE JEW?

In the previous verses (2:25-29) the apostle had argued that the physical rite of circumcision in effect becomes uncircumcision if it is not accompanied by faith that issues in a covenant-keeping life. Not only so, but he had stated that an uncircumcised individual who trusted in the Lord could belong to him without ever being circumcised. Inevitably, to someone who placed high value on the external physical rite, at the very least Paul's teaching cried out for an explanation. It raised fundamental questions: 'Then what advantage has the Jew? Or what is the value of circumcision?' (verse 1).

Perhaps some of Paul's hearers asked these questions in a spirit of honest enquiry; but doubtless others spat them out in bitter hostility ('How dare you imply we Jews have received no advantages from God when we are his chosen people?').

There is a calmness and tranquillity in Paul's answer. He replies that in fact there are considerable advantages in being a Jew and real value in receiving the sign of circumcision. The first is that 'the Jews were entrusted with the oracles of God' (verse 2, 'oracle' being a synonym for God's revelation, *e.g.* 2 Sam. 23:1; Hab. 1:1; Heb. 5:12; 1 Pet. 4:11). God gave his people a physical sign, but he did not leave them to their own intelligence or imagination to interpret either it or his will for their lives. He gave them his word of interpretation and wisdom. And in addition, those 'oracles' contained the record of his watch-care over them and the guidance they needed to help them to live for his glory. Here, in shorthand form, is the same view of Scripture the apostle would later express to Timothy. It is 'God-breathed'; it comes from the mouth of God as his oracles; and as such it is useful for teaching, reproof, correction (or transformation), and training in the life of righteousness (2 Tim. 3:16).

THE FOLLOW-UP QUESTIONS

A follow-up question arises. 'What if *some* were unfaithful?' Paul's language is full of tact here; the fact was that *most* seemed to have rejected the oracles of God with respect to Jesus the Messiah. Does the unfaithfulness of God's people imply that God himself was no longer faithful to his word?

Here, as elsewhere, Paul gives an immediate brief answer to which he will return later in greater depth (in chapters 9–11): God is faithful to his every word. He never falsifies or fails. Even if everyone else becomes a liar God remains true (verse 4). The Old Testament affirmed this, as Paul's quotation from Psalm 51:4 indicates.[1] God's chosen people may become faithless, but God remains righteous. With respect to his consistency with his covenant promises he is 'justified.'

More questions follow in quick succession. Their spirit is clearly argumentative and illustrates the fact that hostile questioning often twists the truth under the guise of seeking it: 'But if you claim that our unrighteousness simply shows how righteous God is, he would be unrighteous to condemn us for it!' Here the questioner is not

[1] Paul quotes from the Septuagint, the Greek version of the Old Testament.

sympathetically asking Paul for an explanation, but drawing false conclusions from his teaching in order to contradict him.

Paul clearly has a distaste for even repeating such words: 'I speak in a human way' (ver. 5), he adds. His response in verse 6 is a simple denial: 'By no means!' (the same expression he used in verse 4 and will use several times hereafter). He continues: 'If that were the case I could not have argued as I have (from 1:18 onwards) that God will judge the world' (which he takes to be an agreed first principle).

But the questioner will not leave things there and persists, responding with a 'Yes, *but* ...': 'But you are saying that—for example—my lie becomes the occasion for God's truthfulness to be highlighted and thus to display his glory. If that's what happens, how can he righteously condemn me as "a sinner" when in fact I'm serving his glory? Don't you see the logic of your view is that our faithlessness simply highlights God's faithfulness? If that's true, then, "Why not do evil that good may come?"' (verse 8).

Paul's response is instructive. First, he acknowledges that this is not the only time such an accusation has been levelled against his teaching. But he rebuts it immediately. It is slanderous.

Later he will deal with similar questions arising from his teaching that where sin abounds grace superabounds (in 5:20–6:2) and explain in detail how the gospel works. Here his answer is short and simple: 'Their condemnation is just' (verse 8).

There are points in Paul's letters where he declines to enter into further debate. The suggestion that one should sin in order to promote God's glory (verse 8) is manifestly false and indeed perverse. There is no more to be said. Only a conversion involving a complete paradigm shift will correct both the presuppositions and the antagonism of the objector.

There is a lesson for us here. There are times when unless and until the deep foundations of the gospel are welcomed a right understanding of it will never be reached.

IT IS WRITTEN

This section began with the question whether the Jews had any advantage, for example, in the gift of circumcision. Paul indicated that God had indeed given them privileges. But now the question returns in verse 9, yet differently nuanced. The Jews had been given privileges, but were they in fact 'better off'? For those privileges called for a response of repentance, faith, and obedience on their part. God's covenant was freely and graciously made with the people; but it called for an appropriate response. Without that an individual forfeited the privileges. Indeed they were transformed into grounds for divine judgment and condemnation.

So the Jew who fails to respond to God's covenant mercy in repentance and faith is no better off than the Gentile unbeliever, 'No, not at all' (verse 9). Both Jews and Greeks are 'under sin.' In Charles Wesley's words, we are all 'fast bound in sin and nature's night.'[1] This, as Paul now demonstrates, is the testimony of the Jews' own Hebrew Bible. The words 'as it is written' settle the issue. The oracles of God are the final authority (1:17; 3:3).

The selection of quotations that follows in verses 10-18 is a tapestry woven from various sections of Scripture, mainly from the Psalms but also from Proverbs and Isaiah. They give a vivid analysis of universal human sinfulness.

The words cited in 3:10-12 while not a precise quote are derived from Psalm 14:1-3. As sometimes happens when preachers refer to Scripture, Paul brings out and applies the relevant sense of the passage while quoting only part of it with precision.

We do not know if Paul owned his own copy of the Hebrew Bible.[2] Doubtless he knew much of it by heart. But he does not seem to have paused to say to Tertius, 'Wait a minute while I look up the texts I want to quote here!' He is probably always quoting from memory (a memory much more retentive than ours tend to be today).

There is again a relentless beat in Paul's rhetoric here. He uses the same negative expression ('there is not,' *ouk estin*) five times: 'There is none righteous'; 'there is none understands'; 'there is none seeks God'; 'there is none does good'; 'there is none—not even one.' The beat is insistent. The universal depravity of the human race is underlined. Not only so, but Paul has in view here what theologians have called 'total depravity.' It is not that human depravity is as

[1] From the hymn 'And can it be?' by Charles Wesley (1707–88).

[2] He perhaps refers to his own copies of parts of Scripture in 2 Tim. 4:13.

complete as it might be—thanks to God's common grace—but no aspect of our lives is left untouched by sin.

This is expressed by quotations from Psalm 14:2 (verse 11); Psalm 14:3 (verse 12); Psalm 5:9 and Psalm 140:3 (verse 13); Psalm 10:7 (verse 14), and Isaiah 59:7-8 (verses 15-17):

- our understanding is deficient (verse 11a);
- our aspirations are not God-centred (verse 11b);
- our sense of direction is confused and pointless (verse 12a);
- our actions are never truly good (verse 12b);
- our speech is carried on the breath of death (verse 13a);
- our words are deceptive (verse 13b) and poisonous (verse 13c);
- our language is foul and full of hatred (verse 14);
- our attitude to others is hostile (verse 15);
- our lives have an effect that is destructive (verse 16);
- and our sin prevents us from finding peace (verse 17).

For Paul, all this is summed up in Psalm 36:1, in a statement that is both explanatory and climactic:

- 'There is no fear of God before their eyes.'

THE FEAR OF GOD

The fear of God is the heartbeat of faith. Scripture does not present it as craven terror but as the effect on our spirit of having a proper sense of who God is as Creator, Sustainer, Redeemer, and Lord, and of his character, his mighty works, and especially of his saving grace. There is an appropriate sense of being overwhelmed by the wonder of his being. Indeed not to fear him in this way would be to fail to appreciate who he really is and also who we really are. Such fear of God, as the wise father was encouraged to teach his son, is the beginning of both knowledge and wisdom (Prov. 1:7; 9:10). Psalm 19:9 states that it is 'clean'—the Hebrew word (*tahor*) is used of 'clean' animals and of the 'pure' gold with which various temple objects were overlaid (Exod. 25:11-39).

Thus the fear of God involves an unalloyed devotion to him. When it is 'before' our eyes everything else is viewed and evaluated in the light of who he is, what he is like, what he has done, and what he says. To 'fear God' is so to live that his smile of approval is everything to us but his frown is our sorrow.

This last citation points to the root cause of all the elements in Paul's portrayal of total depravity. When we live before God in a spirit of awe-filled faith, loving obedience will permeate our lives. Live without it and moral and spiritual disintegration results. The tragedy of the human condition is not only that we are condemned by the law; it is that life ceases to be what it was meant to be when lived lovingly before the face of God. In our sin we have lost our original righteousness in God's sight, and as Paul points out a few verses later, we have also forfeited the destiny for which we were created in God's image. We have, alas, fallen short of glory (3:23).

Verses 19 and 20 round off the argument Paul has been developing from 2:1 onwards. Condemning others for their sin may be a form of self-justification, but it cannot effect our justification before God. We are all sinners. Not one of us is righteous. God's judgment has no inbuilt partiality or favouritism. He judges according to truth. And since his law—including those passages Paul has just cited—addresses the Jewish people who possessed it, they cannot exclude themselves from its judgment and condemnation (verse 19).

THE CONCLUSION OF THE MATTER

And so the apostle reaches his conclusion (verses 19-20). If none is righteous, not even one, then every single human being stands condemned before the judgment seat of God. We may have rehearsed our speeches of self-vindication, or excuses, or devised our special pleading. But Paul's incisive, biblical reasoning has silenced them. He envisages the whole of humanity standing before God's throne at the Last Assize and bids us listen. Silence reigns ('*every mouth ... stopped*,' verse 19).

The word 'stopped' (*phragē*) is derived from a verb meaning to block, bar, or shut. Self-justifications, excuses, self-created imagination of being a special case, or different, or at least 'OK,' may spring up within fallen hearts and minds. But when God himself arises in judgment in Christ Jesus the only words that self-justifying sinners will be able to speak will be echoes of those John records in the Book of Revelation:

> When he opened the sixth seal, I looked, and behold, there was a great earthquake, and the sun became black as sackcloth, the full moon became like blood, and the stars of the sky fell to the earth as the fig tree sheds its winter fruit when shaken by a gale. The sky vanished like a scroll that is being rolled up, and every mountain and island was removed from its place. Then the kings of the earth and the great ones and the generals and the rich and the powerful, and everyone, slave and free, hid themselves in the caves and among the rocks of the mountains, calling to the mountains and rocks, 'Fall on us and hide us from the face of him who is seated on the throne, and from the wrath of the Lamb, for the great day of their wrath has come, and who can stand?' (Rev. 6:12-17).

A NEW PERSPECTIVE?

Paul's conclusion, that 'by works of the law no human being will be justified in his sight, since through the law comes knowledge of sin' (verse 20) has been much discussed. That no human being will be justified is precisely the point he has argued from 1:18 to 3:19. But what does he mean by 'the works of the law'?

Traditionally the expression has been interpreted as another way of saying 'by our own efforts to obey the law.' Some of the early fathers in the church restricted it to the ceremonial works of the law.

This view has been adopted by some scholars today. They have maintained that since Judaism was a religion of grace, it never envisaged a person being justified on the basis of good deeds or personal merits. So 'the works of the law' to which Paul refers here must be ceremonial identity markers such as circumcision. Thus what was controversial in Paul's teaching was *not* that we are justified 'by grace' rather than 'by works,' but that this can be true of Gentiles as well as Jews. According to this view Paul's 'conversion' was not the Luther-like conversion of someone who once sought justification on the basis of his own good works but now discovered it can be received only by grace through faith. Rather it was the realization that Jesus was the promised Messiah and that he was so for Gentile as well as Jew.

It is not possible to discuss this view at length here. It is true that the Old Testament never taught that justification is by our works, but by grace through faith in God's covenant promise and provision. Salvation has always been by grace.

But our own experience teaches us that despite the New Testament's teaching on justification by grace through faith there have been many people in Christian churches who have believed that they will be saved by doing their best and by God's acceptance of their good works (whether actual or ceremonial). Personal convictions do not always match orthodox confessions of grace. Something similar was true in biblical times. In addition, both 'ceremonial' and 'moral' works of the law can mistakenly be regarded as grounds for our justification. Paul himself describes his own works in terms of 'having a righteousness of my own that comes from the law' (see Phil. 3:4b-9).

So it is important to distinguish here between what the Old Testament Scriptures taught and what people actually believed. There seems to have been plenty of 'works righteousness' around in the days of Jesus and the apostles!

THE MAIN POINT

But the larger point to be made here is that Paul's argument in Romans 1:18 to 3:20 is demonstrating that the whole world, both Jew and Gentile, and every individual in it, stands guilty before God. We are all subject to his wrath. In a later letter, Paul includes himself, a Jew, in the category 'by nature children of wrath' (Eph. 2:3). Neither possessing Jewish identity markers nor relying on them as marks of justification can grant an exception. None of us can establish 'a righteousness of my own that comes from the law' (Phil. 3:9)—whether by sacraments or by our own good works. To rely on them for justification will leave us spiritually bankrupt. What is needed is the conviction that we are sinners who cannot save ourselves, and a turning in faith (conversion) to Christ.

This is not to say that the New Testament lays down a detailed pattern of conversion experience. There is rich variety in the ways God brings us to faith in Christ. But in Paul's own case, he confessed that he could not attain a justifying righteousness through the law, that is by his own obedience to it; he needed a Saviour who would clothe him in his righteousness (Phil. 3:9). He learned that his circumcision was not the same as his justification. As he emphasizes later (7:7-13) whatever efforts he made to keep the law of God were doomed to failure. None is righteous, no not one—not only 'no Gentile' but also 'no Jew,' however formally a member of the covenant community. All have sinned; all need to be convicted of their sin. All need the same Saviour. This is what Paul is arguing.

As Paul saw, ultimately the issue for both Jews and Gentiles was the same. All needed to consider 'the greatness of the weight of sin' (Anselm). In Romans 1:18–3:20 he is pressing that weight down on to the shoulders of every human being. But he does so only to prepare us to see what God has done to remove that weight.

Never were the words 'But now …' more welcome.

10

But Now

But now the righteousness of God has been manifested apart from the law, although the Law and the Prophets bear witness to it— [22] *the righteousness of God through faith in Jesus Christ for all who believe: For there is no distinction:* [23] *for all have sinned and fall short of the glory of God,* [24] *and are justified by his grace as a gift, through the redemption that is in Christ Jesus,* [25] *whom God put forward as a propitiation by his blood, to be received by faith.*

(Rom. 3:21-25)

Paul's words 'But now ...' open a new section in his letter and signal perhaps the greatest relief moment in the whole Bible. It has precursors, such as the great turning point in the penitential Psalm 130: 'If you, O Lord, should mark iniquities, O Lord, who could stand? *But with you there is forgiveness*, that you may be feared' (Psa. 130:3-4—these last words take on a special significance in the light of the words Paul cited in 3:18 that 'there is no fear of God before their eyes'). What makes the statement here even greater is that Paul now patiently explains *how* God provides forgiveness. It is not merely by divine *fiat*. The wonder of the gospel is that the God who is righteous has provided a righteous way to justify those who are not.

Paul never employs rhetoric simply for effect; he rejected 'lofty speech and [worldly-] wisdom.' He believed that the truth and logic of 'Jesus Christ and him crucified' (1 Cor. 2:1-2) should govern the way he presented the gospel. But who can deny that his gospel created an eloquence of its own?

Here (in verse 21) we have an illustration of this eloquence. He picks up the idea he had introduced in 1:18, that the righteous wrath of God has been revealed (*apokaluptein*, to unveil) against sin. Although using a different verb (*phaneroō*, to manifest, make visible) he now draws a parallel and a contrast: now the righteousness, not the wrath of God stands revealed, and the result (verse 24) is the justification of sinners, not their condemnation. Once again Paul's words are like the sound of an army marching in time to a single drumbeat—but now the sound is 'upbeat' in contrast to verses 10-12. In verses 21-26 he uses the same word root in a variety of forms no less than seven times ('righteousness,' 'just,' 'justify,' 'justifier'). Righteousness and justification are now ours through faith!

Here we arrive at what has often been referred to as 'the heart of the gospel' or 'a Bible within the Bible.' These are words every Christian should seek to understand and preferably also memorize. In a style that is almost hymn-like the apostle describes the way of salvation in Christ.

THE DETAILS

While all Scripture is equally God-breathed (2 Tim. 3:16), not all Scripture is equally significant. Some passages invite greater study and meditation than others. This is one of them. Among the significant points Paul makes are the following:

(i) He had stressed that 'by works of the law no human being will be justified, since through the law comes knowledge of sin' (3:20). 'But now' (3:21) something new has been introduced.

The word 'now' here is not incidental. Paul argues throughout Romans that the gospel stands in continuity with the promises of the Old Testament. But 'now' something unprecedented has taken place in Christ—although Paul keeps us in suspense to the next verse (verse 22) before he explains exactly what has happened.

Elsewhere the New Testament indicates that this 'now' means that the long-awaited 'last days' have begun; the new age has been inaugurated. This is the 'now' that separates BC (Before Christ) from AD (In the year of our Lord). With Jesus' death, burial, resurrection, and ascension, and his sending of the Spirit on the Day of Pentecost, the 'end of the ages has come' (1 Cor. 10:11). We are now living in 'the last days' (Acts 2:17; 2 Tim. 3:1; Heb. 1:2; 2 Pet. 3:3). What God has done is that significant.

(ii) This righteousness—which Paul announced earlier (in 1:16-17) lies at the heart of the gospel—has been revealed 'apart from [the] law.' In the Greek text there is no definite article before 'law.' But whether Paul refers here to the law of Moses or to law in general makes no difference to his point. This must have sounded revolutionary to Jewish ears since virtually the whole of the Old Testament, and the life of every Jew, was governed by the law of Moses. Was it not in the law that God revealed his righteousness? How, then, can Paul claim that God is now revealing it 'apart from the law'? The idea is, surely, unthinkable! But (and at this point we do not yet know exactly how this 'but' is going to be explained) if this is true, it changes everything!

(iii) Paul realizes that some people will immediately draw the wrong conclusion from what he has just said. Inevitably so if their whole thinking is law-shaped rather than grace-leading-to-law-shaped. He expects a 'knee-jerk' reaction. And so, just as he had done in 1:16-17 by vindicating his words with reference to the Old Testament Scriptures ('as it is written ...'), here he affirms that this manifestation of righteousness '*apart from* the law' is not *contrary to* the law or a repudiation of it. In fact 'the Law and the Prophets bear witness to it' (verse 21).

Once again Paul states his position without elaboration. Perhaps he had planned an outline of his letter in advance, but doubtless he was employing patterns of thought he had already followed in sermons, discussions, and debates. He already knew that he would soon take up this point and explain it in detail (as he does in chapter 4).

(iv) The question then is 'How has this righteousness of God (to which the Old Testament Scriptures bear witness) been manifested?' Paul's answer echoes and further elaborates his theme statement in 1:16-17. It is 'through faith in Christ for all who believe.'

What follows explains this affirmation.

This righteousness is 'through faith' (verse 22). It is not acquired on the basis of our obedience. Nor is it bestowed only on those who stand in the line of the covenant promise given to Abraham. It is 'for *all* who believe.' In addition, as he later indicates, it is the *only* way of righteousness, 'for *all* have sinned and fall short of the glory of God' (verse 23). There are no distinctions; there is no partiality; there are no alternatives; there is no exception.

(v) Paul's choice of language here is illuminating. We, perhaps, would have instinctively said 'all have sinned and broken the law of God' or 'rebelled against God.' That would be true. It would also be in keeping with Paul's argument thus far. But here again his words seem to reflect an earlier statement.

In 1:23 he had described the effect of sin: we have 'exchanged the glory of God ...' The *wickedness* of sin is expressed in rebellion against God and his word, by the transgression of his law. But there is also *tragedy* in sin. It disqualifies us from the destiny for which God created humankind: to admire, reflect, express, and ultimately enter into the presence of the glory of God. We have been created for this now-unimaginable privilege, but have 'fallen short.' Made originally for glory, now sin covers us in shame. There is no more exalted creature on earth than a human being; but there is no more tragic figure. Significantly, perhaps the most common New Testament word for 'sin' is *hamartia*—which in classical Greek carries the nuance of 'falling short' or 'being deprived of' something. Ultimately that 'something' is glory.

This perspective is a clue to Paul's (and Jesus') compassion for sinners. Sin is evil. But the tragedy of sin, what Jonah described as forsaking the hope of God's steadfast love (Jon. 2:8), the privileges that sin forfeits, elicits sorrow and compassion. Later, in 9:1-5, Paul will give moving expression to this.

So these words remind us that Christians should never be guilty of the kind of metallic judgmental spirit Paul condemns in 2:1. There is a difference between assessing human sinfulness with a hard heart and doing so with a broken heart. The broken heart shares the sadness of the Lord Jesus (and of Paul) over the tragedy of human sin as well as recognizing its evil.

RIGHTEOUSNESS MANIFESTED

Against the background of the manifestation of God's wrath (1:18), God has now manifested his righteousness (3:21). But how?

This question has played in the background of the letter since 1:16-17 when Paul had announced his theme. The densely packed words that follow bring us to his answer and to the very heart of this section of Romans. Several 'big words' of the Bible are here: *justify*, *grace*, *gift*, *redemption*, *propitiation*, *faith*, and *righteousness*.

Sinners are '*justified* by his *grace* as a *gift*, through the *redemption* that is in Christ Jesus, whom God put forward as a *propitiation* by his blood, to be received by *faith*. This was to show God's *righteousness*, because in his divine forbearance he had passed over former sins. It was to show his *righteousness* at the present time, so that he might be *just and the justifier* of the one who has *faith* in Jesus' (3:24-25).

We have seen that to be 'righteous' in God's sight means to be rightly related to him in his covenant, experiencing his grace, living a life centred in God, faithful to his word, and loving him with heart, soul, and strength (Deut. 6:5). What is remarkable in the Old Testament is that although God frequently finds his people in a state of sin and failure—*i.e.* under his judgment—the revelation of his righteousness is seen not only in his judgment but also in his saving mercy and grace.

The great prayer recorded in Daniel 9:3-19 (especially verses 16-19) illustrates this. On the one hand God's righteousness leads to judgment:

> To you, O Lord, belongs righteousness, but to us open shame ... the curse and oath that are written in the Law of Moses the servant of God have been poured out upon us, because we have sinned against him ... As it is written in the Law of Moses, all this calamity has come upon us ... for the Lord our God is righteous ... (Dan. 9:7-8, 11, 13-14).

But precisely within the context of God's *covenant* righteousness, Daniel is able to appeal to him for mercy and salvation:

> To the Lord our God belong mercy and forgiveness, for we have rebelled against him ... O Lord, according to your righteous acts, let your anger and your wrath turn away from your city Jerusalem, your holy hill ... For we do not present our pleas before you because of our righteousness, but because of your great mercy (Dan. 9:9, 16, 18).

Daniel does not ask God to forget his righteousness and show mercy *instead*, but rather to do the latter *because of* the former.

So we find already enshrined in the Old Testament that while people are condemned for their sin because of the covenant Lord's righteousness, the same righteous God, in exercising his righteousness, shows mercy. Nor is this simply 'how things are,' and taken for granted. It is a cause of wonder and praise. Grace has always been amazing. According to his promise of mercy in his covenant bond and promise, God 'passes over' sin (3:25), and counts those who have sinned as 'righteous' in his sight.

LEGAL OR RELATIONAL?

The question is sometimes asked: since this is the work of the *covenant* God, should we see justification, being counted righteous in God's sight, as a *forensic* or *legal* matter, or as a *personal* and *relational* matter. But these are not mutually exclusive ideas. It is God himself who is Law-Giver, Judge *and* the Covenant Redeemer (as Daniel emphasizes by using God's covenant name, the Lord [Yahweh] and referring to him as the one 'who keeps covenant and steadfast love ...,' Dan. 9:4).

Thus justification is not merely a legal pronouncement; it is also a personal engagement precisely because the law is an expression of the personal character of God and our person-to-person relationship to him. Indeed, as the Old Testament theologian Geerhardus Vos pointed out, to separate the law of God from the person of God is to fall into legalism, which is 'a peculiar kind of submission to law, something that no longer feels the personal divine touch in the rule it submits to.'[1]

But this Old Testament teaching left a question lingering in the air down through the centuries. It is one thing to have God's promise that he will do this, but how can he do it *righteously*?

The Lord gave his old covenant people *symbolic answers* to that question by means of the tabernacle and temple liturgy in the sacrifices of substitutes.

He gave *prophetic, personal answers* in the promise of a Prophet like Moses (Deut. 18:15), a King like David (Psa. 72), a Priest like Melchizedek (Psa. 110:4), in the coming Son of Man (Dan. 7:13-14), and supremely in the figure of the Suffering Servant who would be led as a lamb to the slaughter, where he would be wounded, bruised, chastised, and experience 'dispeace' for the sins of his people (Isa. 53:5). But only 'now ... at the present time' has the reality to which these divinely-given hints pointed become clear. These were not

[1] Geerhardus Vos, *The Self-Disclosure of Jesus*, edited and revised by J. G. Vos (1926; Nutley, NJ: Presbyterian & Reformed, 1953), 17.

prophecies of several different individuals but of one, the Lord Jesus Christ.

In Jesus Christ, then, God has demonstrated his righteousness 'at the present time' (the equivalent of his earlier 'now'). In the previous epoch, in his forbearance God 'passed over' sins (verse 25). He did not bring upon them the final judgment they deserved. But now he has decisively dealt with them in Christ—as Paul will explain. Moreover, he has done so in a way that preserves his own righteousness (he is just) and at the same time justifies the ungodly through faith (verse 26).

Paul's turn of phrase here underlines a massively important truth. Put negatively: he does *not* say that God justifies the ungodly through faith *despite the fact that he is righteous.* The marvel of his plan of salvation is that in devising and accomplishing it he remains righteous! God did not put aside his righteousness. Nor was the cross an illustration of God's grace or love *overcoming* his righteousness (although it is sometimes portrayed that way). No, he saves sinners righteously. Rather than compromise his righteousness the cross displays it. It is 'the trysting place where heaven's love and heaven's justice meet.'[1] And how he displays it is, as we will see, a reason for wonder, love, and praise. 'He is faithful *and just* (*dikaios*) to forgive us our sins' (1 John 1:9).

Who is a God like our God who in perfect righteousness counts as righteous those who have no righteousness of their own? No wonder Micah exclaimed: 'Who is a God like you, pardoning iniquity and passing over transgression for the remnant of his inheritance? He does not retain his anger forever, because he delights in *steadfast love* [*ḥeseḏ*—another covenant-saturated expression]' (Mic. 7:18).

[1] From the hymn 'Beneath the cross of Jesus' by Elizabeth Clephane (1830–69).

11

Redemption Provided, Boasting Excluded

For all have sinned and fall short of the glory of God, 24 *and*
are justified by his grace as a gift, through the redemption that
is in Christ Jesus, 25 *whom God put forward as a propitiation*
by his blood, to be received by faith. This was to show God's
righteousness, because in his divine forbearance he had passed
over former sins. 26 *It was to show his righteousness at the present*
time, so that he might be just and the justifier of the one who
has faith in Jesus.
27 *Then what becomes of our boasting? It is excluded. By what*
kind of law? By a law of works? No, but by the law of faith.
28 *For we hold that one is justified by faith apart from works of*
the law. 29 *Or is God the God of Jews only? Is he not the God of*
Gentiles also? Yes, of Gentiles also, 30 *since God is one—who will*
justify the circumcised by faith and the uncircumcised through
faith. 31 *Do we then overthrow the law by this faith? By no*
means! On the contrary, we uphold the law.

(Rom. 3:23-31)

As Paul continues his exposition of the heart of the gospel we should not misunderstand the words of verses 23-24 that '*all* ... are justified by his grace ...' He is not a universalist. The 'all' here refers back to those who experience 'the righteousness of God through faith' (verse 22). It is *all who have faith* who are 'justified by his grace ...'

The logic of Paul's words (which is not identical to the order of his statements here) is as follows:

- God put Christ forward as a propitiation by his blood;
- As a result there is redemption in him;

- The propitiation effected in Christ that provides redemption is received by faith;
- Those who thus believe are justified;
- Thus justification becomes ours by God's grace as a gift.

Here we will concentrate on Paul's 'big words': 'propitiation,' 'redemption,' and 'justification.'

PROPITIATION

The word 'propitiation' (*hilastērion*) has been much discussed by scholars, for two reasons.

(i) Some have objected to the translation 'propitiation' because it carries the nuance of satisfying or averting someone's anger. It is objected that an 'angry God' is a distortion of the biblical view of a God who is gracious. This view dilutes the significance of the revelation of the 'wrath of God' (1:18) to a kind of impersonal force in the created order, the inexorable outworking of the consequences of our sin—not the personal hostility of God against us.

The Revised Standard Version, under this influence, translated *hilastērion* as 'expiation' rather than 'propitiation.' Expiation cleanses away our sins, and of course Christ does this. But 'expiation' does not convey the idea of averting or 'satisfying' (in the sense of bearing the whole weight of) the righteous wrath of God.

Apart from other considerations, this view of wrath represents poor psychology, as though (in distinction from 'bad temper') anger is itself immoral. There are occasions when anger is surely the only morally appropriate response to a situation; to fail to have it would be a moral deficiency in us, suggesting indifference to evil and wickedness. When Scripture speaks of God's wrath against our sin, it refers to the righteous and pure recoil of his whole being and his opposition to sin as both rebellion against himself and the cause of the destruction of our lives and our world.

(ii) There is a further question about the translation 'propitiation.' Paul's term (*hilastērion*) was translated by the courageous William Tyndale as 'mercy seat'—referring to the gold-plated covering over the ark of the covenant on which the high priest offered sacrificial blood on the Day of Atonement (Lev. 16:15). Some of the early fathers in the church, as well as Martin Luther and John Calvin in the sixteenth century, and a variety of scholars since, have understood the term in this way: Christ himself is the 'mercy seat' where (in the offering of his shed blood on the cross) propitiation was made for our sin. One strong argument for this is that in the Greek translation of the Old Testament used by Paul (usually referred to as the *Septuagint*) the Hebrew word 'mercy seat' (*kappōreṯ*) was translated *hilastērion*. It would be natural therefore to assume this is what Paul meant by using the term here. But by no means all interpreters have agreed, and many believe that the better translation is 'propitiation' or 'propitiatory sacrifice.' After all, the current meaning of a word is not always identical to or wholly determined by its past use. We are all familiar with words that have changed their meaning (sometimes radically).

In either case, the precise translation aside, the 'mercy seat' does present us with a vivid picture of the work of Christ. He fulfils the symbolism of the ritual of the Day of Atonement. The wrath of God was focussed on him as both High Priest and Victim when, 'made sin for us' (2 Cor. 5:21) on the cross, he entered the holy presence of God bearing our guilt and became 'a curse for us' (Gal. 3:13). Our Lord Jesus bore the full weight of divine wrath against our 'ungodliness and unrighteousness' (Rom. 1:18).

At Calvary, all kinds and conditions of men and women witnessed the death of Jesus—enemies, soldiers, passers-by, dearest friends, and his mother. There he, as it were, passed through the veil of the temple and offered himself on the altar of the cross for our salvation. But only by the eye of faith did any of them come to 'see' what took place hidden from mortal eyes:

> *Bearing shame and scoffing rude,*
> *In my place condemned he stood;*
> *Sealed my pardon with his blood:*
> *Hallelujah! What a Saviour!*[1]

One further comment should be made here about 'propitiation.' The idea has been rejected by more recent critics on the grounds that had God directed his wrath towards his Son, it would have been an act of 'cosmic child abuse.'

In view of the long history of Christian teaching there is something offensive about such a statement. It loses sight of the

[1] From the hymn 'Man of Sorrows!' by Philip P. Bliss (1838–76).

biblical teaching that the cross, in all its horror—yes, a horror that made the Lord Jesus shrink from its implications (Mark 14:32-42)—was borne *willingly* by him and was in perfect accord with the plan devised and shared with the Father and the Holy Spirit in their trinitarian love for sinners. Christ bore the wrath of God out of love for his Father as well as out of compassion for sinners.

In addition this 'cosmic child abuse' view falls under the criticism of Anselm of Canterbury cited earlier: it fails to take account of the greatness of the weight of sin; it assumes we do not merit God's wrath and rejects the biblical teaching that our only hope of being saved from it is if someone takes our place.

In fact our Lord was conscious that the hour of his atoning sacrifice, when he bore the wrath of God, would also be the hour when his Father's love for him would reach its high point: 'For this reason the Father loves me, because I lay down my life ... No one takes it from me, but I lay it down of my own accord ... This charge I have received from my Father' (John 10:17-18).

Whether *hilastērion* is translated 'propitiation' or 'mercy seat,' in either case the reference is to the way Christ took our place and in his death for us absorbed the wrath of God against our sin.

REDEMPTION

Paul further develops his exposition of the saving work of Christ by referring to 'the redemption that is in Christ Jesus' (verse 24) as a result of the shedding of his sacrificial blood. From his childhood Paul was familiar with the idea of redemption. His parents, his teachers in synagogue school in Tarsus, and Gamaliel his theology professor in Jerusalem, would all have taught him its meaning. Every year at Passover its significance would be reinforced as he celebrated the way God had redeemed his people from their bondage in Egypt by the shedding of the blood of a blemish-free lamb (Exod. 6:6).

While the Exodus was a real and dramatic historical event, it was also a 'type,' a kind of advance working model of what Christ would accomplish. Later, on the Mount of Transfiguration, Moses and Elijah discussed with Jesus the 'departure' (literally the *exodus*) he would accomplish in Jerusalem (Luke 9:30-31). He himself said he had come to give his life a 'ransom' for many (Matt. 20:28; cf. 1 Tim. 2:6). He died to redeem us (Gal. 3:13; Titus 2:14; 1 Pet. 1:18;

Rev. 5:9). Thus his propitiatory sacrifice was the high price our Lord paid to bring about a spiritual exodus and deliver us from bondage. On the cross he not only dealt with our alienation from God but also the fact that we are by nature slaves of sin and oppressed by Satan (Eph. 2:1-3).

Paul's words here express more than the simple fact that Christ paid our ransom price. The redemption price was not something *external* to him. He *is* the redemption price. Paul speaks about 'the redemption *that is in Christ Jesus.*' The significance of this is well captured in a profound comment by Professor John Murray:

> It should be noted ... that the apostle conceives of this redemption as something that has its permanent and abiding tenancy in Christ; it is 'the redemption that is in Christ Jesus.' The redemption is not simply that which we have in Christ (Eph. 1:7) but it is the redemption of which Christ is the embodiment. Redemption has not only been wrought by Christ but in the Redeemer this redemption resides in its unabbreviated virtue and efficacy.[1]

These words help correct the false perspective that on the cross Christ purchased redemption and now passes it on to us as though it were a commodity. Redemption is ours only *in Christ*. In that sense, we never 'possess' or 'own' redemption as a commodity. It resides in Christ and is ours only as we reside in him through faith. This is a principle that is embedded in the foundations of Paul's theology. We have 'every spiritual blessing' *only in Christ* (Eph. 1:3-14). He is the one '*in whom* we have redemption' (Eph. 1:7).

Understanding this saves us from depersonalising redemption, and indeed any of the various facets of our salvation, or detaching them from Jesus Christ himself. And the good news is that when we are 'in Christ' *every* spiritual blessing is ours (Eph. 1:3). What we need is Christ himself, 'clothed with his gospel.'[2] We do not possess these blessings apart from him. They are not given to us without us receiving him. And when we are united to him all of the blessings are ours.

Thus when we receive him we receive everything that is embodied in him for our sake. This includes *justification*.

[1] John Murray, *The Epistle to the Romans* (London: Marshall, Morgan and Scott, 1967), vol. 1:116.

[2] John Calvin, *Institutes of the Christian Religion*, tr. by F. L. Battles, ed. by J. T. McNeill (Philadelphia: Westminster Press, 1960), III.ii.6.

JUSTIFICATION

What is justification? asks *The Shorter Catechism*, and answers:

> Justification is an act of God's free grace, wherein he pardoneth all our sins, and accepteth us as righteous in his sight, only for the righteousness of Christ, imputed to us, and received by faith alone.[1]

There are two dimensions then to justification. We have sinned, are guilty before God, and need to be pardoned. Since it is against God we have sinned, he alone can pardon us. That pardon is granted because Christ has paid the penalty we deserve.

But if that were the sum total of Christ's accomplishment, while our past sins would be forgiven, the net effect would be only to bring us 'back to square one' as it were, to try again where Adam failed. If that were the case the gospel would not, and indeed could not, provide the assurance of final salvation Paul later articulates: 'those whom he justified he also glorified' (8:30). What we need is not only the pardon of our past sins through the death of Christ, but also being counted *fully* and *finally* righteous before God through the life of Christ (cf. 4:23-25). As Horatius Bonar put it, with childlike simplicity:

> *Upon a Life I have not lived,*
> *Upon a Death I did not die,*
> *Another's Life; Another's Death,*
> *I stake my whole eternity.*[2]

This is the justification which is counted to us in Christ. And as Paul will later explain (*e.g.* in 5:1-11), when this dawns on us we begin to rejoice in the privileges of the gospel. For now we realize that 'Christ Jesus ... became to us ... righteousness and ... redemption.' Therefore, 'as it is written, "Let the one who boasts, boast in the Lord"' (1 Cor. 1:30-31).

THE WHOLE PICTURE

Before we leave this important section, we should stand back from its details to notice what it is that 'God put forward' (verse 25). When we take in the picture Paul has painted as a whole we see that he

[1] *The Shorter Catechism*, Question 33.

[2] The first verse of the hymn by that name written by Horatius Bonar (1808–89).

expresses the 'multivalent' character of the atonement (in the sense that there are multiple dimensions to Christ's work).

Theologians have often written about what they call 'theories of the atonement,' sometimes claiming that one or another is dominant, at other times playing one off against another. But 'theories of the atonement' is misleading language. The various ways in which Christ's work is expounded in Scripture are not 'theories.' And they are certainly not competitors. Paul is simply expressing the whole of the gospel in the light of its various dimensions. And it takes all of the dimensions mentioned in Romans 3:21-26 to express the multivalent character of what God has done for us in Christ. And this is so because our need is multivalent: our sin involves transgression, rebellion, falling short of glory, bondage to sin and Satan, and shame. Christ saves us from them all.

Further, we should notice the consistent emphasis in Romans on the freeness of the gospel. Here Paul highlights this by what at first sight is a redundant use of language. We are 'justified *by his grace as a gift*.' To say we are justified by his 'grace' already implies that it is a 'gift.' Why then this apparent redundancy? Surely to emphasize that while our salvation was costly to God, it is free to us. God calls 'everyone who thirsts' to 'come to the waters; and he who has no money, come buy and eat' (Isa. 55:1).

Here again we should remind ourselves that the 'gift' of 'grace' is not the transfer of a commodity, packaged by God and then handed over to us. Strictly speaking then we do not 'get grace'—a concept whose roots lie in mediaeval Catholicism and its sacramental theology rather than in Scripture. We may also need to be careful that we are not misled by the expression 'means of grace.' Grace is the graciousness of God the Father expressed in his Son, Jesus Christ, whom we experience through the tender ministry of the Holy Spirit. When we see this, our eyes are protected from the tendency to stray from a proper focus on Christ himself to a mistaken focus on ourselves and what we possess in our own experience.

The tendency of mediaeval theology was to focus on the sacraments as 'means of grace' and to lose sight of the person of Christ to whom the sacraments were intended to point. Faith then became a matter of the right and regular employment of these sacraments. As a result people lost sight of the Lord Jesus, and therefore also of Paul's teaching here that our justification is found only in union and communion with him (and therefore not by the reception of physical objects).

It is important also to notice here that while we need God's gracious working within us to bring us to faith in the Lord Jesus, we are not justified on the basis of anything God does *in us*, but only on the basis of what he has done *outside of us* and *for us* in Christ. God's gracious disposition towards us in him is therefore both the source and the atmosphere of our justification. Yes, faith is necessary if we are to be justified in Christ—but our faith contributes nothing to what Christ has done. Faith looks away from itself and receives everything in him. We are, indeed, justified by God's grace in Christ as a gift!

DIFFICULTIES CLEARED

This whole section in Romans breathes the atmosphere of Paul's preaching. He announced a text (in 1:16-17); he then began to expound what our spiritual forefathers called its 'doctrine' and 'uses'—explanation and application of its teaching. In addition he engages in what (again) those forefathers described as 'clearing difficulties.' In this context that means showing how justifying righteousness comes 'apart from the law, although the Law and the Prophets bear witness to it' (3:21).

Paul's gospel (2:16; 16:25) is consistent with the teaching of the Old Testament in general. But this consistency can also be shown from the lives of its greatest figures in particular—two of whom, Abraham and David, will be discussed in chapter 4.

But before he comes to that, having exposed universal human sinfulness, silenced all excuses, and explained the gracious way God has provided deliverance from guilt, wrath, and bondage in Jesus Christ, he comes to a conscience-piercing application: 'Then what becomes of our boasting?' (verse 27).

Since Paul has already silenced 'every mouth' (3:19), we can anticipate his answer: 'It is excluded' (verse 27). But then he asks a further question: 'By what kind of law' (or principle) is our boasting excluded? And here his answer is surely a surprise. He seems to anticipate that we will instinctively reply, 'By a law of works' (verse 27). 'Yes,' surely. After all, he has just demonstrated that what the law does is expose our sin and condemn us. It silences us (verse 19) because we have no works that can justify us. The 'law of works' therefore excludes all our boasting.

That is true, surely? But Paul replies, 'No ...'! That is not an absolute 'No.' We could paraphrase what he means by saying, 'That is a good answer, but it is not the one I am thinking about here.' In a sense he had already given that answer—answer part one, we might say—rooted in our sin and guilt. But part two, the additional part of the answer, is related to the gospel itself. Yes, it is true that boasting is excluded because in our sinfulness we fail to keep God's law. But it is also excluded because of the nature of the gospel itself. Justification is by grace as a gift. It comes through faith, which is receptive, not contributory. Thus, *in the very nature of the case, because of the character of the gospel itself, there is no room for boasting.*

Theoretically, if we did keep the law, we could say 'I have accomplished my righteousness'—and so we could 'boast' or 'exult' in our own achievements. But when salvation is accomplished by God's grace in Christ and received by us in the empty hands of faith, *in the nature of the case* there can be no boasting about our contribution to our justification. It is excluded not simply because of our failure, but by the very logic of the situation itself. The gospel-way, the faith-way, by definition excludes boasting (verse 27).

Paul's point is logically devastating; but it is also personally liberating. For—as we will discover in chapter 5—the gospel that silences all my boasting then gives faith something really worth boasting about. Here (3:27) Paul uses the noun *kauchēsis* (boasting, exulting); later, in chapter 5, he will use its verbal form (*kauchaomai*—5:2-3, 11). When I 'hold that one is justified by faith apart from works of the law' (verse 28) then 'I pour contempt on all my pride,'[1] because I now begin to glory in the cross!

Paul drives his point home with a further question: 'Or is God the God of Jews only? Is he not the God of Gentiles also?' (verse 29). The answers are (by implication) 'No' and (by affirmation) 'Yes, of Gentiles also, since God is one—who will justify the circumcised by faith and the uncircumcised through faith' (verses 29-30). God is not restricted to being 'the God of Jews only' because his way of salvation, of redemption and justification, is not based

[1] From the hymn 'When I survey the wondrous cross' by Isaac Watts (1674–1748).

on the Abrahamic rite of circumcision or the Law of Moses, but on his grace in Jesus Christ. It is received not by the external rite of circumcision—otherwise God would be the God of Jews only. It is received by faith. In fact this always has been the case, as the apostle will demonstrate in chapter 4.

These words are the final nail in the coffin of all claims to Jewish exclusiveness when it comes to favour with God. There is no partiality with him. Although the message of righteousness did in one sense come first to the Jew[1] this was not a matter of partiality; it was not that they had any qualification for special treatment. It was a matter of the sovereign divine plan of redemption. Moses had long ago emphasized this: 'It was not because you were more in number than any other people that the Lord set his love on you and chose you, for you were the fewest of all peoples, but it is because the Lord loves you ... (Deut. 7:7-8).

God's choice was entirely unconditioned and sovereign. From the beginning he called his people to be (what they failed to be) a blessing to the nations, not just to themselves (Gen. 12:1-3). God was always God for both Jews and Gentiles. Now the full revelation of the way of righteousness by grace, apart from law, through faith in Christ, makes clear that salvation is not the exclusive property of the Jews; it is to be offered to all, whether Jew or Gentile. If salvation does not depend on keeping the requirements of the law specially revealed to Israel at Sinai (or for that matter written on the heart), but comes through faith, then God is not only a Saviour for Jews but for Gentiles also—indeed for *all who believe*.

What then of the mark of circumcision that distinguishes Jew from Gentile? And what about the Law of Moses?

Paul teaches that justification does not come on the basis of circumcision. There has always been only one way of salvation for any and all—the way of faith. There is one God (the foundation of the *Shema*, the great Jewish confession of Deuteronomy 6:4-5), who 'will justify the circumcised by faith and the uncircumcised through faith.' It is by faith that the righteous live (1:16-17)!

[1] It should be remembered that it was God's word of promise, not the identity, character, or quality of the recipients that created the people of God in the first place. After all, Abraham was living in post-Babel, pagan Ur of the Chaldees when God began to move in his life. He was not a 'Jew' when he was called.

OBJECTION!

As Paul continues his teaching he patiently answers our questions about the relationship between grace and law, and between the law and the gospel. But at this stage, one final issue remains. He anticipates an objection to his teaching that he must have heard frequently in the synagogues of the empire: 'Your teaching about justification by grace through faith is overthrowing the law of God!' The verb 'overthrow' (*katargeō*) is used regularly in the New Testament to convey disintegration, destruction in that sense.

It must have been discouraging for Paul to hear this objection repeatedly. It was a radical (and at times deliberate) misunderstanding and distortion of what he actually taught. But it would certainly not have surprised him. The same objection was raised against the teaching of his Saviour. Indeed the Sermon on the Mount seems to have been structured in such a way that it specifically answered a similar question: 'You are telling us that it is by the coming of the kingdom of heaven that God's covenant blessings are experienced and we become "the light of the world" (Matt. 5:2-12). But that involves overthrowing the law!' On the contrary, our Lord responds that he had come not to destroy the law but to fulfil it, and then to apply it properly (Matt. 5:17-48).

Paul's point is essentially the same: 'Do we then overthrow the law by this faith? By no means! On the contrary, we uphold the law' (3:31). It is only by faith that the law is truly upheld.

Once again Paul does not pause to explain this. He will do so later as he further expounds his gospel (*e.g.* in 8:3-4). For the moment he presses on to vindicate his teaching on justification by grace not on the basis of works but by faith. He does this by showing how it is written large in the lives of Abraham and David (4:1-25). He will return later to show why it is that the law is impotent to accomplish its own goals, but they are in fact fulfilled through faith in Christ. Rather than overthrow the law, only the gospel can uphold it!

In what follows, the three answers Paul has given to the questions of 3:27-30 are now further illustrated and developed. But already the conclusions to be drawn are clear: Boasting is excluded; salvation is freely available in Christ for all who will believe, whether Jew or

Gentile; and it is God's grace, not the law itself, that establishes God's law.

This is truly an amazing gospel! It is simultaneously consistent with God's righteous character, and yet meets sinners' deepest and most desperate need for salvation. It reveals God's amazing grace in Christ and provides a justification that is full and free; and yet at the same time it 'establishes' the law.

Truly we can sing in response:

Great is the gospel of our glorious God,
Where mercy met the anger of God's rod;
A penalty was paid, and pardon bought,
And sinners lost at last to Him were brought:

O let the praises of my heart be Thine,
For Christ has died that I may call Him mine,
That I may sing with those who dwell above,
Adoring, praising Jesus, King of love.[1]

[1] From the hymn 'Great is the gospel of our glorious God' by W. Vernon Higham (1926–2016).

12

Exhibits A and D

What then shall we say was gained by Abraham, our fore-
father according to the flesh? 2 For if Abraham was justified
by works, he has something to boast about, but not before God.
3 For what does the Scripture say? 'Abraham believed God, and
it was counted to him as righteousness.' 4 Now to the one who
works, his wages are not counted as a gift but as his due. 5 And
to the one who does not work but believes in him who justifies
the ungodly, his faith is counted as righteousness, 6 just as David
also speaks of the blessing of the one to whom God counts right-
eousness apart from works:

> *7 'Blessed are those whose lawless deeds are forgiven,*
> *and whose sins are covered;*
> *8 blessed is the man against whom the Lord*
> *will not count his sin.'*

9 Is this blessing then only for the circumcised, or also for the
uncircumcised? For we say that faith was counted to Abraham
as righteousness. 10 How then was it counted to him? Was it
before or after he had been circumcised? It was not after, but
before he was circumcised. 11 He received the sign of circumcision
as a seal of the righteousness that he had by faith while he was
still uncircumcised. The purpose was to make him the father of
all who believe without being circumcised, so that righteousness
would be counted to them as well, 12 and to make him the father
of the circumcised who are not merely circumcised but who also
walk in the footsteps of the faith that our father Abraham had
before he was circumcised.

(Rom. 4:1-12)

The *Letter to the Romans* provides a *summary* of what Paul calls 'my gospel.' It is also an *exposition* of it because he senses the need to present his 'credentials' to the church in Rome before he visits them, as he hopes to do. It is also an *explanation* of what he teaches, in view of the fact that he has been accused of distorting biblical teaching, especially in relationship to the law of Moses.

In addition, throughout the letter the apostle is preparing its first readers and hearers in Rome for his later *application* of the gospel to their specific circumstances. The churches in Rome, once a mixture of believers of Jewish and of Gentile backgrounds, had become largely if not exclusively Gentile in character when Claudius Caesar had expelled Jews from Rome around AD 50.[1] No doubt when they were able to return perhaps four or five years later, as Priscilla and Aquila had done (16:3; cf. Acts 18:2), the culture of the churches had changed. Much can happen in five years of a church's life. The Roman house churches had almost certainly become 'Gentile' in atmosphere and practice. It was almost inevitable that tensions would arise when Jewish Christians were able to return—as chapters 14 and 15 make clear they did.

IF IT WAS GOOD ENOUGH FOR ABRAHAM ...

Romans chapter 4 serves a double function. On the one hand, we can well imagine a Jewish-background critic who heard Paul's teaching saying, 'I am deeply troubled by what your teaching implies about the great figures of the old covenant like Abraham and David. They were circumcised men, righteous men, and they were Jews. You are demeaning them!'

Paul responds to such complaints, and in doing so he begins to lay foundations for encouraging harmonious church fellowship between believers from Jewish and Gentile backgrounds. He does so by showing that they have all experienced what both Abraham and David did—forgiveness and justification by faith.

[1] The Latin author Suetonius (AD 69–122) records that the reason for Claudius's action was that 'the Jews constantly made disturbances at the instigation of Chrestus.' 'Chrestus' is usually understood to be a reference to Jesus, and an indication of conflict within the Jewish community because some of their own number had come to faith in Christ. Suetonius, *Lives of the Caesars*: Divus Claudius, 25. Scholars of antiquity have debated how strictly the edict was applied, but certainly it affected Priscilla and Aquila and others.

Here, then, in chapter 4, Paul confirms by these examples that justification has always been by faith (either in the promise of Christ or in the Christ who has now become incarnate). This being the case, his teaching of justification by grace through faith is entirely consistent with, and vindicated by, the Old Testament Scriptures.

We can follow his exposition in stages.

First of all Paul establishes that Abraham was justified by faith, not by law works (verses 1-8).

He 'gained' nothing 'according to the flesh'—that is, by his ancestry, circumcision, or action. If he had been 'justified by works he has something to boast about, but not before God' (verse 2). The very points he had established in 3:19 (every mouth shut) and 3:27 (boasting excluded) had universal reference and therefore included Abraham.

Here the apostle picks up the theme of boasting or glorying in personal accomplishments (cf. 2:17, 23; 3:19, 27). If 'father' Abraham had been 'justified by works' then he would have been able to boast. But the Scriptures make clear that in fact he had nothing to boast about before God (verse 2) because he was not justified by working but by believing. Work is recompensed by wages earned, not by gifts graciously given. Faith is different: 'to the one who does not work but believes in him who justifies the ungodly, his faith is counted as righteousness' (verse 5). And this is what Scripture says about Abraham: 'Abraham believed ... and it was counted to him as righteousness' (verse 3; cf. Gen. 15:6). It was not by his works but through his faith that Abraham was justified. And that is exactly what Paul has been teaching!

DETAILS MATTER

Two details should be noted here:

(i) Throughout the rest of the chapter Paul repeats the idea of righteousness being 'counted' (verses 3-7, 9, 20-24). The verb 'to count' (*logizomai*) in this context means to take into account, to reckon, to consider something to be the case. It can mean to count something either for or against someone. Here Paul understands Genesis 15:6 to mean: in the matter of righteousness, what God took into account in Abraham's case was *his believing his promise*, not *works he had done*—in other words, 'faith.'

(ii) The way Paul expresses himself here: '*it* [*i.e.* the faith by which 'he believed God'] was counted to him as righteousness' (verse 3) is clarified by his teaching as a whole. He is not saying that faith itself is the basis, and in that sense the cause, of justification—as though God was now adopting a different (and lower) standard so that now instead of works God had decided to substitute faith. Faith is not the ground of justification, but the means by which we receive Christ (the object of that faith). Paul has already argued that the grounds for justification are found in Jesus Christ (3:21-24), not in us or in our faith. As he will say at the end of this chapter, our Saviour was 'delivered up for our trespasses and raised for our justification' (4:25).

Lest this be thought to be special pleading—since, after all, the text does say it was his faith that was counted as righteousness—we should remember that Paul had earlier used the word 'faith' in a similar 'shorthand' way in Galatians 3:23. There he described the whole old covenant epoch as a time 'before faith came.' He is not denying that faith was present in the old covenant era. Rather, 'faith' (in Gal. 3:23 and here in Rom. 4:3) is shorthand for 'faith in the now incarnate, crucified, risen, ascended, and reigning Lord Jesus Christ—who is the ground of our justification.'

Faith, then, is what theologians call the 'instrumental cause' (how we receive) not the 'material cause' (the ultimate basis) for justification. Another way of saying this would be that faith never looks to itself in order to be justified; it always looks only to Christ. It is 'Christ Jesus [not faith] … who became to us … righteousness …' (1 Cor. 1:30).

The significance of this was memorably expressed by the American theologian Benjamin B. Warfield:

> The *saving power* of faith resides thus not in itself, but in the Almighty Saviour on whom it rests … It is not, strictly speaking, even faith in Christ that saves, but Christ that saves through faith. The saving power resides exclusively, not in the act of faith or the attitude of faith or the nature of faith, but in the object of faith; and in this the whole biblical representation centres, so that we could not more radically misconceive it than by transferring to faith even the smallest fraction of that saving energy which is attributed in the Scriptures solely to Christ himself.[1]

[1] B. B. Warfield, *Biblical Doctrines* (1929; repr. Edinburgh: Banner of Truth Trust, 1988), 504.

Thus justification comes to the one who believes, receptively—not to the one who works, actively. And this means, as our spiritual forefathers sometimes said, that weak faith gets the same saving Christ as strong faith.

DAVID TOO

Paul further confirms his interpretation of Genesis 15:6 and the experience of Abraham by appealing to the words of the other towering figure of the old covenant, King David: 'Blessed are those whose lawless deeds are forgiven, and whose sins are covered. Blessed is the man against whom the Lord counts no iniquity' (Psa. 32:1-2).

What makes these words all the more impressive is that they come from one of the traditional penitential psalms (6, 32, 38, 51, 102, 130, 142). True, the Genesis account of Abraham's life did not air-brush his failings. But David's sins were eventually clear for all to see; they were beyond being air-brushed. Scripture records them in upper case letters, as it were, for all to read—adultery and conspiracy to murder. He sinned 'with a high hand' (Num. 15:28-31; ESV 'intentionally'). There was no sacrificial provision made in the law for David-like sin! And yet when he pleads with God for mercy he finds it. His lawless deeds were forgiven, and his sins were covered.

David had no right or title to pardon; he recognized that he had no grounds for it in his law-keeping. His justification needed to be *counted to him* not *earned by him.* The same is true for us. Something is counted to us (righteousness) that is not accomplished by us but by Christ. By faith we embrace him in whom our righteousness is found. Faith thus receives everything from Christ and contributes nothing to what he has accomplished.

Having (i) appealed to Genesis 15:6 to demonstrate the biblical nature of his teaching that the way of justification by faith excludes all boasting, and (ii) having confirmed it from David's testimony in Psalm 32:1-2, Paul now returns to the Abraham narrative and develops a second stage in his argument.

BUT WHAT ABOUT CIRCUMCISION?

In verse 9 Paul raises another question—one that he had no doubt frequently encountered. 'Is this blessing then only for the circumcised, or also for the uncircumcised?' (verse 9).

Hidden behind the question lies the objection: 'Yes, but even granted Abraham and David were justified by faith, *both of them were Israelites—they were Jews*, not *Gentiles*!'

We can well imagine this reaction from a Jew, perhaps even a Jewish Christian already uncomfortable with the way Paul seemed to put both Jews and Gentiles (the circumcised and the uncircumcised) on the same level ground. 'Yes, Paul, it is fine to appeal to Abraham (and even for that matter to David). But even if Abraham was justified by faith and not by works, *he was circumcised*. So all you have shown us is that Jews who have been circumcised like Abraham, or those Gentiles prepared to be circumcised, can be justified.'

Anyone who objected in these terms had failed to follow the teaching Paul had already given. But they were also walking into a biblical trap! The apostle's response is devastating. We can express it in the form of a conversation:

> *Objector*: So, suppose I grant you that Abraham, and yes, David too, were justified by faith. But they were both circumcised. So that proves only that the circumcised can be justified, surely?
>
> *Paul*: Have you thought much about Abraham's justification?
>
> *Objector*: What do you mean?
>
> *Paul*: I mean—*when* was Abraham counted righteous?
>
> *Objector*: I'm not following your argument
>
> *Paul*: Well, was he justified *after* he was circumcised, or *before*?
>
> *Objector*: Oh!

Do you see Paul's point? Abraham was justified 'not after, but before he was circumcised' (verse 10). The implication is as unavoidable as it is devastating: Abraham—the very same Abraham to whom God gave the command of circumcision—is an example of someone who was justified although he had not been circumcised!

There is no reference to circumcision in the Abraham narrative until Genesis 17:9-14, that is two chapters *after* the record of his justification in Genesis 15:6. Paul's point is as overwhelming as it is simple: the circumcision of Abraham, the father of the faithful, took place *after* he was accounted righteous by faith. Justified Abraham was uncircumcised Abraham! Circumcision, therefore, cannot be the *sine qua non* of justification if Abraham 'received the sign of circumcision as a seal of the righteousness that he had by faith *while he was still uncircumcised*' (verse 11).

Point taken?

SIGN AND SEAL OF WHAT?

The apostle's description of circumcision as a 'sign and seal' also deserves our careful attention.

Notice what he is *not* teaching. He does not say that circumcision was a sign and seal of Abraham's *faith*. Rather it was a 'sign and seal *of the righteousness* that Abraham had by faith' (verse 11). Circumcision did not in the first instance point to Abraham's faith (*i.e.* his response to God's promise), but to God's gracious provision of righteousness. It was a sign and seal of grace—God's grace—not a sign of Abraham's response—his faith.

This is confirmed by (and indeed required by) the fact that the sign and seal was to be given not only to Abraham but to his infant male offspring throughout the generations. If circumcision had been given as a sign *of faith*, how could God command that it be given to eight-day-old boys (Gen. 17:12)? But because it was a sign of God's covenant promise and provision of righteousness it could be given to a little boy only a week after he had emerged from his mother's womb. Thus Abraham's male descendants were to be circumcised with a view to their future confession of faith in the covenant Lord. In fact circumcision was given to them as a sign and seal of God's covenant promise, and a summons to respond to it. By it they were summoned to trust in the covenant-keeping Lord and to 'circumcise' their hearts in lives marked by ongoing and lifelong repentance and faith (Deut. 10:16).

This is a pattern we can trace in all the visible ordinances or sacraments in Scripture, including those in the new covenant. They do not in the first instance signify and seal our faith; rather they point to, and proclaim, the Lord Jesus Christ whose gospel grace they signify and seal. They are not given to us as reminders of what we have done. These signs point us away from ourselves to who he is, to what he has done for us, and what we will find in him. And thus they summon us to respond in faith and repentance.

When we see this, even if we differ in our convictions about other aspects of baptism or the Lord's Supper, we will benefit increasingly from these Christ-ordained ordinances. Thus, for example, we will appreciate what Paul later teaches in Romans 6:1-14, that baptism is meant to have an ongoing impact on our lives; it is not merely a reminder of something we did yesterday. And in the Supper we will be lifted beyond reflecting on our own spiritual condition to catch a glimpse of Christ crucified, risen, reigning, returning, and present with us in holy communion.

So there is much we can learn from what Paul says here about the particular 'sacrament' of circumcision. But his overall point is as powerful as it is simple. Since Abraham was justified before he was circumcised he is 'the father of all who believe without being circumcised' (verse 11). And because he was later circumcised, he is also the father of those who are circumcised—that is, not merely physically circumcised but also so spiritually transformed that they walk by faith in his footsteps—the same faith he had *before* he was circumcised (verse 12).

So Paul is indicating there is more to Abraham than meets the eye. Or to be more exact, he shows his objectors what they ought to have seen in Scripture, but apparently never did. The patriarch was both the father of those who believe without being circumcised, and of those who are circumcised and believe. He is 'the father of all who believe'—whether Jew or Gentile.

Although it is not yet obvious (since at this stage in Romans we do not know that in chapters 14 and 15 Paul will discuss relationships between Jewish and Gentile believers), he is already laying a solid foundation for both groups to understand how and why they belong together.

There is more to be said about Abraham. But before we turn to it in the second half of chapter 4, we ought to emphasize again Paul's basic lesson. When it comes to justification—and to the signs and seals of it—it is a mistake to look within ourselves to see its cause and foundation. Rather we need to look away from ourselves to the One in whom alone justification is to be found—the One to whom these signs and seals point, Jesus Christ himself.

13

It All Depends on Faith

For the promise to Abraham and his offspring that he would be
heir of the world did not come through the law but through the
righteousness of faith. 14 For if it is the adherents of the law
who are to be the heirs, faith is null and the promise is void.
15 For the law brings wrath, but where there is no law there is
no transgression.

16 That is why it depends on faith, in order that the promise
may rest on grace and be guaranteed to all his offspring—not
only to the adherent of the law but also to the one who shares
the faith of Abraham, who is the father of us all,— 17 as it is
written, 'I have made you the father of many nations'—in the
presence of the God in whom he believed, who gives life to the
dead and calls into existence the things that do not exist. 18 In
hope he believed against hope, that he should become the father of
many nations, as he had been told, 'So shall your offspring be.'
19 He did not weaken in faith when he considered his own body,
which was as good as dead (since he was about a hundred years
old), or when he considered the barrenness of Sarah's womb.
20 No unbelief made him waver concerning the promise of
God, but he grew strong in his faith as he gave glory to God,
21 fully convinced that God was able to do what he had promised.
22 That is why his faith was 'counted to him as righteousness.'
23 But the words 'it was counted to him' were not written for
his sake alone, 24 but for ours also. It will be counted to us
who believe in him who raised from the dead Jesus our Lord,
25 who was delivered up for our trespasses and raised for our
justification.

(Rom. 4:13-25)

In Romans 4 Paul is building up his argument in explaining and defending his teaching on justification by faith.

Stage one demonstrated that Abraham—the great father-figure of the Jews—was:

- *not justified by works,*
- *had nothing therefore to boast about,*
- *and was in fact justified by faith.*

This, Paul has pointed out, is further confirmed by David's words in Psalm 32:1-2.

In stage two he had gone on to show that Abraham was

- *not justified on the grounds of circumcision,*
- *but was in fact counted righteous* before *he was circumcised,*
- *and so is the father of both the uncircumcised and circumcised who share his faith.*

Paul now moves on to a further stage in his argument: while justification is *not* received on the basis of circumcision, neither is it received on the basis of the law.

REMEMBER YOUR HISTORY!

Paul's argument here is reminiscent of, but not identical to, one he had employed in his letter to the Galatians. There he had appealed to the fact that the promise Abraham believed, and that led to him being counted righteous, was given 430 years *before* the law was given at Sinai. It operated before, and therefore 'apart from the law' (Gal. 3:17-18). Here in Romans he is content simply to say that 'the promise to Abraham ... did not come through the law but through the righteousness of faith' (verse 13). If so, then justification does not come to us because we have been circumcised (the point already established in the case of Abraham). Nor does it come by a 'law-way' but by a 'faith-way.' Thus, in a few sentences Paul has demolished the ideas that either or both circumcision and the law were ever the operative agents in relation to justification. Prove this in the case of Abraham and the issue is settled. If the father of the faithful, the great prototype of justification, was not justified on the grounds of circumcision or on the basis of law-keeping, then surely nobody is!

Imagine yourself in the position of a Jew hearing this, or perhaps even a Jewish Christian with remnants of the old instincts still remaining in your thinking. Can you sense the unsettling, even deeply disturbing impact it must have had? What was important to the typical Jew? It was Abraham and circumcision and Moses and the law. They were a unique and distinct people with special boundary markers that distinguished them from Gentiles. These spoke of their unique relationship with, and status before, Yahweh (3:1-2; 9:4). That was what made them 'different,' and special to God. These (at least in their own eyes) were the essential ingredients in their right standing with God. So what Paul is now saying is devastating. Not only is circumcision *not* essential to justification, since Abraham was justified *before* his circumcision; in addition, law-obedience is not the pathway to justification either! It was not for Abraham. It is not for us.

No surprise then if Paul was sometimes accused of ignoring the law and teaching others to do the same. But in that misunderstanding he was simply being treated as the Lord Jesus and Stephen had been before him.

Paul's response is once again to appeal to Scripture. How did the promise given to Abraham come to pass? It was not by Abraham obtaining righteousness through law-obedience; it came through the faith-way-of-righteousness (verse 13).

LAW-WAY OR FAITH-WAY?

The law-way and the faith-way are antithetical to each other. To drive this home, Paul puts his point the other way round (verse 14). If inheriting this promise comes by the law-way, then the faith-way is cancelled out—and vice-versa.

He now adds a further counter-argument (verse 15). The law-way can bring only wrath, since no one is able to keep the law—that was the conclusion he had reached in his argument from 1:18–3:20. As far as righteousness and justification are concerned the law-way proved to be null and void. All that comes through the law, because of our proven inability to keep it, is the knowledge of sin and the reality of condemnation.

Paul further explains: 'but where there is no law there is no transgression' (verse 15b). That is to say: when we bring the law into the picture, we also bring our transgression of it into view. And when we do that the wrath of God also inevitably comes into the picture. In other words, since we all transgress the law, and are thereby exposed to God's wrath, what the law-way of bringing justification reveals is only that we desperately need a different way if we are to be accepted by God. When it comes to the justification of the ungodly, only the faith-way actually works!

This, then, brings us to the summation of his argument that justification has always been by the way of faith. And this in turn leads Paul to comment on the nature of such faith (4:16ff.).

THE FAITH-WAY IS THE GRACE-WAY

Paul's summation is arrestingly worded: 'That is why it [*i.e.* being counted righteous] depends on faith, in order that the promise may rest on grace and be guaranteed to all his [Abraham's] offspring—not only to the adherent of the law but also to the one who shares the faith of Abraham [but is not an adherent of the law, *i.e.* not a Jew]' (verse 16).

This is probably not the way most of us would have anticipated Paul would speak.

We might have anticipated he would say:

- Being counted righteous depends on grace so that it comes by faith.

But instead he puts things the other way round:

- Being counted righteous is by faith so that it might be by grace and guaranteed.

The point is that justification by faith 'safeguards' grace. It gives expression to the genius of the divinely ordained way of justification. Faith is our activity; we (not God) are the ones who believe. True, faith is a gift of God (Eph. 2:8-10). But like suffering, it is 'granted' to us (Phil. 1:29). Just as *we* are the ones who suffer (God does not suffer instead of us), *we* are also the ones who believe (God does not believe instead of us). Faith is, therefore, *our* activity. Yet, while this is true, in the nature of the case it is non-contributory with respect to what it receives.

Thus human responsibility and activity are well-married to divine grace. The divine way of justification involves our activity but not our contribution. Faith 'locks on' to grace, works never do; in faith we look away from ourselves and what we do, and look to God and what he has done in Christ. Thus the promise is both given in grace and received by faith. The way of justification is the faith-way, not the law-way, or the works-way, so that it might be the grace-way.

Moreover because the promise is 'by grace' it can be 'guaranteed' to Abraham's offspring. Were it dependent on law-works it would necessarily depend on us, and therefore could never be guaranteed.

Paul quickly adds an explanation of what he means by saying 'guaranteed *to Abraham's offspring*.' Is he now retracting his earlier emphasis on the gospel being for both Gentile and Jew? He explains: when he refers to 'Abraham's offspring' he means 'not only ... the adherent of the law [*i.e.* the Jew] but also ... the one who shares the faith of Abraham.' Thus Abraham is 'the father of us all' (verse 16). All who believe, whether Jew or Gentile, are included in the family. This was already envisaged in God's call of Abraham (Gen. 12:1-3), and later confirmed in his promise to him: 'I have made you the father of many nations' (Gen. 17:5).

Here again Paul makes clear that his gospel is not only *consistent with* the Old Testament Scriptures but in fact is an *exposition of them*. It is not some novel teaching that contradicts the true 'tradition' of the old covenant. For, as he later wrote to Timothy, when rightly understood 'the sacred writings' (*i.e.* the Old Testament Scriptures) were 'able to make ... wise for salvation *through faith* in Christ Jesus' (2 Tim. 3:15).

The words that follow here in 4:17, '... in the presence of the God in whom he believed ...,' at first sight seem to hang in the air. How are they connected to what precedes them? They probably refer back to Paul's comment that Abraham is 'the father of us all.' They lead us into the next stage in Paul's argument, in which he moves on from confirming that justification is by faith to a further discussion of the nature of this faith (verses 17-22). For, if Abraham is the prototype of justification by faith, he is also the prototype of the nature of the faith that justifies.

Faith—as is evident here—is not an abstract commodity. It is not to be thought of as a kind of super-added substance given to us by God. Rather it is the new disposition of relying on the Lord Jesus Christ as our Saviour and Lord. It is not an isolated component in our lives, but the heartfelt response of the person who, like Abraham, in the presence of God entrusts himself or herself to the God 'who gives life to the dead and calls into existence the things that do not exist' (verse 17).

TO WAVER OR NOT TO WAVER?

These last words in verse 17 are sometimes taken to echo two of the great moments recorded in Genesis: Abraham's willingness to sacrifice Isaac, the son of the promise ('life from the dead'—Gen. 22) and behind that the creation of the universe (calling into existence things that do not exist—Gen. 1).

It has been argued that if this were the case the order would have been reversed. So perhaps the reference is to the way the birth of Isaac was a gift of life to 'the dead' Abraham (a hundred years old) and Sarah (a lifelong barren woman) by which God called 'the things that do not exist as existing.' But the order is not necessarily decisive for the meaning. In either case what is in view is God's ability to do all his holy will; what seems impossible to us is possible for him (Mark 10:27). The faith that 'locks on' to the grace of God also 'locks on' to the God of resurrection power and new creation, the God of complete sovereignty.

If Abraham had rested his hopes either on his own body or on Sarah's womb he would have been staring at death. In fact Paul refers literally to 'the death [*nekrōsis*, ESV *barrenness*] of the womb of Sarah' (verse 19). In themselves this elderly couple had no reason to hope that together they would have a son. But faith does not rest on anything in us. It finds its strength in the promise and character of God. Hence Paul's marvellous statement: 'In hope he believed against hope' (verse 18). And so it came to pass: Isaac, the son of the promise was born.

These words help us put Paul's further statement in verse 19 into their appropriate context: 'He did not weaken in faith.' He is not implying that Abraham had 'perfect' faith but he did have determined faith.

When Abraham was told that he and Sarah would have a son together: he 'fell on his face and laughed and said to himself, "Shall a child be born to a man who is a hundred years old? Shall Sarah, who is ninety years old, bear a child?"' (Gen. 17:17). The idea was, in fact, laughable. But perhaps this is the point of Paul's words 'In hope he believed against hope' (verse 18). Having faith does not mean pretending that what philosophers call 'counter-factuals,' contradictory considerations, do not exist. We sometimes have to battle spiritually and mentally to believe what God says over against such 'counter-factuals.'

This fits well with the words in verse 20: 'No unbelief made him [Abraham] waver concerning the promise of God' (verse 20). When he considered his own age and Sarah's barrenness, there was no reason to believe that they could have a son together; in fact, the reverse was the case. These 'counter-factuals' were solid grounds for unbelief. But living faith does not rest on our capabilities or circumstances; it looks to and rests in God, his character, and his promises. What settled the issue for Abraham was not any natural reasons for hope but the fact that 'he had been told' (verse 18).

Thus faith rests in God's word; it hopes in that word, where necessary over against human hopes (Psa. 119:81, 114, 147). That is how Abraham 'grew strong in faith as he gave glory to God' (verse 20).

The Westminster Divines might well have used this as a 'proof text' to establish their answer to Question 2 in *The Shorter Catechism*:

> Q. What rule hath God given to direct us how we may glorify and enjoy him?
> A. The word of God … is the only rule to direct us how we may glorify and enjoy him.

Charles Wesley (1707–88) did in fact use it as a 'proof text' for a hymn:

> *Faith, mighty Faith the promise sees,*
> *And looks to that alone;*
> *Laughs at impossibilities,*
> *And cries, 'It shall be done!'*

In faith we believe God and his word. That was the character of the faith that led to Abraham being counted righteous. But now Paul affirms that the same is true for us: 'The words "it was counted to him" were not written for his sake alone, but for ours also' (verses 23-24). How so? Because we believe in the same Lord God as Abraham did. Not only so, but we can now see in full measure that he not only 'gives life to the dead' in the way he did for Abraham and Sarah. He has now done so in the resurrection of the crucified Jesus (verse 24).

DYING FOR SIN, RISING FOR JUSTIFICATION

In the course of this entire chapter on justification by faith Paul makes no direct reference to the Lord Jesus until the closing two verses. But in doing so now he brings to a climax the entire argument he has been developing on the sinfulness of humanity, the provision of redemption, and the vindication from Scripture that justification was, is, and always will be by faith. Now, in the fullness of time, righteousness is 'counted to us who believe in him who raised from the dead Jesus our Lord, who was delivered up for our trespasses and raised for our justification' (verses 24-25). Justification is anchored in Christ crucified and risen.

These words have a rhythmic ring to them; it is not surprising that some scholars have wondered if they were originally part of an early Christian confession. Verse 25 in particular contains rich biblical theology in concentrated form.

Paul says that Christ was 'delivered up for our trespasses.' This is not the first time in Romans he has used this verb (*paradidōmi*). In 1:24, 26, 28 he spoke of God 'giving up' sinners to their sin. There, as here, it had the same judicial nuance that is present in its use in the Gospel accounts of Jesus' trial and passion. He was repeatedly 'handed over' (*e.g.* in John 18:2, 5, 30, 35-36; 19:11, 16, 30—and similarly in the other Gospels).

We could call this 'The Great Exchange Verb.' Under God's wrath we are judicially handed over to the implications and consequences of our sin (1:24, 26, 28). But in God's mercy, he has 'handed over' his Son, our Lord Jesus, to bear the judgment we deserve (4:25; cf. 8:32). On him, instead of on us, 'the Lord has laid … the iniquity of us all' (Isa. 53:6). He was 'numbered with the transgressors … bore the sin of many …' (Isa. 53:12).

The Saviour who 'was delivered up for our trespasses' was also 'raised for our justification' (verse 25). The words are in the form of a Hebrew parallelism in which two statements, standing in parallel to each other, develop a whole thought—in this case by the second statement adding to the first.[1] Thus in a few memorable words Paul climaxes his exposition so far by affirming that through Christ's death believers' trespasses have been dealt with and through his resurrection they are justified.

But why does Paul connect justification with the *resurrection* of Christ? Earlier he had spoken of the way we are 'justified ... through the redemption that is in Christ Jesus, whom God put forward as a propitiation by his blood' (3:24-25).

The answer is that, for Paul, the death and resurrection of Christ belong together. He is not suggesting that it is only through the *resurrection* of Christ (*i.e.* not his *death*) that we are justified. For him these are two 'moments' in the same event. He is employing a 'synthetic parallelism' in which one idea is developed and filled out by two statements. So here two aspects of a single salvation are accomplished by two aspects of the single work of Christ in his death and resurrection: our sins are forgiven, and in addition we are positively accounted righteous. Just as Christ's death and resurrection are two aspects of the one reality, so are our being forgiven and being accounted positively righteous.

This way of expressing the heart of the gospel is illuminating in two ways:

(i) The first is, as we saw hinted earlier in Romans, that the forgiveness of our trespasses is not the whole of our justification. Forgiveness, while wonderful in itself, would only bring us back to square one to begin again. We need more than forgiveness—we also need to be positively *accounted righteous* in God's sight.

So in this synthetic parallelism Paul is teaching us that full salvation is provided for us in Christ, crucified and risen.

(ii) But in addition, saying that Christ was raised *for* (or on account of) *our justification* helps us grasp more fully what this involves. Elsewhere Paul teaches that in his death Christ was made sin for us—'In my place, condemned, He stood.'[2]

[1] Other parallelisms accomplish this by contrasting lines.

[2] From the hymn 'Man of sorrows' by Philip P. Bliss (1838–76).

But in his resurrection the Son of God, who had been treated as a sinner on the cross, was declared by God to be righteous in his sight. He was 'vindicated [*justified*] by the Spirit' (1 Tim. 3:16). His death was his condemnation in our place, his resurrection was his justification on our behalf.

Paul says that Christ was raised 'for' or 'on account of' our *justification*. This could mean either (i) 'on account of our justification being accomplished' or (ii) 'with a view to our justification taking place.' Commentators differ. But in a sense *both* are true. For in Christ the justification of all who belong to him is guaranteed since he is their representative; and through Christ we come to experience the reality of it.

If our justification resides in his justification, certain implications follow—implications that, in his usual style, Paul will develop later in his letter.

- If our justification is in Christ, then it is already complete and perfect. We may be more or less sanctified; but we cannot be more or less justified.
- If our justification resides in Christ then no believer can be less or more justified than any of his or her fellow believers.

Furthermore,

- If our justification is found in the risen Christ, it is irreversible. Indeed it is as irreversible as Christ's resurrection (later in 6:9 Paul says that 'We know that Christ, being raised from the dead, will never die again').

And in addition,

- If our present justification is in the risen Christ, the final judgment of the Last Day has already been pronounced on us—we are fully, irreversibly and also finally justified!

Think for a moment of one major implication of this. We do not need to try to add to our justification. Indeed we cannot! For the most mature Christian we know is no more justified than the newest Christian in our church family. Let that permeate the way we think about ourselves and it will bring both relief and joy. And let it permeate the way we think about other members of our church, and it will transform our fellowship.

Surely here at the end of Romans chapter 4, Tertius's fingers were probably already sore from taking down Paul's exposition—perhaps in shorthand, to be written out in full later. Did he wonder if anything more wonderful than this could be said?

If so, he was about to discover much more glorious gospel truth!

14

Justified!

Therefore, since we have been justified by faith, we have peace
with God through our Lord Jesus Christ. [2] *Through him we*
have also obtained access by faith into this grace in which we
stand, and we rejoice in hope of the glory of God. [3] *Not only*
that, but we rejoice in our sufferings, knowing that suffering
produces endurance, [4] *and endurance produces character, and*
character produces hope, [5] *and hope does not put us to shame,*
because God's love has been poured into our hearts through the
Holy Spirit who has been given to us.

(Rom. 5:1-5)

In distinction from our English translations of Romans 5:1, 'therefore' is not the first word in the Greek text (typically it comes second in a Greek sentence). So here a grammatical rule has the effect of highlighting Paul's single-worded glorious and triumphant announcement: 'Justified!'

In technical terms the word is a masculine plural passive participle in the aorist tense. We might capture Paul's joy by translating 'Justified is what we have been and now are!' It expresses the emotional relief and joy someone accused of a crime carrying the death penalty would feel when the chairman of the jury announced the verdict 'Not Guilty!' and the judge said, 'You are free to go …'—only more so, because what is at stake here is not merely a verdict and a sentence against which we might appeal, but an eternal destiny from which no appeal is possible.

AN INTRIGUING STRUCTURE

Commentators typically 'divide' books of the Bible into sections.[1]

[1] As has been done often, see pp. xi-xiii above.

Often Romans 5:1 is seen as the beginning of a major new section in the letter which then continues on until 8:39. Paul has sealed his argument about justification by faith in his appeal to Scripture in chapter 4. In a sense the case is now closed. In addition 5:1-11 and 8:18-39 seem to belong to a ring of teaching, beginning and ending on similar triumphant notes. And it could be argued that having appealed to Habakkuk 2:4 (in 1:16-17)—'the righteous shall live by faith,' Paul has in 1:18–4:25 expounded what it means to be 'righteous' or 'justified,' and now in 5:1–8:39 he goes on to expound what it means to 'live.'

But it is helpful to think about the structure of Romans in a more organic way, like the growth of a tree or the blossoming of a flower, rather than as a straight-line development of one discrete section followed by another, followed by another. If this is the case, then chapter 5:1-11 represents not a break between two sections but a further exposition of justification in terms of its effects. This makes sense then of the teaching of 5:12-21. Its function is to dig down into the roots that undergird 1:18–5:11 and then to serve as the foundation for what follows in 6:1–8:39.

Here we will follow this second approach.

We have been justified by faith—'So what?'

The answer is that 'The Great Exchange' that has taken place in Christ now leaves an answering imprint on our lives—a 'great exchange' in our experience. Justification in Christ produces a reversal of condemnation—not only the verdict pronounced on our lives but what follows it.

Thus:

3:17	We did not know the way of peace	5:1	But now we have peace with God
3:20	We stood guilty before God	5:2	But now we stand in grace
3:19	Our sinful mouths were shut	5:2-3	But now we express open rejoicing
3:23	We fell short of the glory of God	5:2	But now we rejoice in hope of the glory of God

2:9	Eternal tribulation was our destiny	5:3	But now we rejoice in present tribulation
1:18	We were under God's wrath	5:11	But now we rejoice in God himself

DO WE HAVE IT?

We do not have the original manuscript of Romans (or of any book in the Bible). Our versions are translated from ancient copies. Before the invention of the printing press these were made by hand, often by a process of dictation. Sometimes that led to small discrepancies in the copies. Most modern translations indicate in a footnote that there is one such discrepancy here in 5:1. Did Paul say (i) 'Since we have been justified by faith, *we have* peace with God' or (ii) 'Since we have been justified by faith, *let us have* peace with God'?

The difference in the underlying Greek text is between a short *o* and a long *ō*! Perhaps during dictation of the verse one person heard and wrote a 'short *o*' (the letter *omicron*): '*we have* peace'; while another heard and wrote a 'long *ō*' (the letter *omega*): '*let us have* peace.' A Scotsman saying, 'You're a bonnie laddie' might easily be understood by a non-Scot (or even by a Scot!) as saying 'You're a bony laddie'—but there is a difference between being handsome ('bonnie') and being skinny ('bony')!

Scholars often solve these minor differences by asking diagnostic questions that will suggest which text is original—such as 'which makes better sense in the context?' Here most have been persuaded that the flow of Paul's argument suggests he would have said ' Being justified by faith *we have* peace'; enmity is ended; there is *shalom.*

If, however, Paul said '*Let us have* peace' he was clearly not urging the Romans to make peace with God, but saying, 'Since we are justified, then let's "have" the peace God has given us. Let's enjoy what we have.' If at a family picnic someone opens a food hamper and says, 'Let's have lunch,' they don't mean 'We don't have any food, so let's go to a restaurant,' but 'Let's enjoy what we have here.'

A similar issue arises again in verse 3.

So, what—in either case—do we experience when we are justified?

PEACE, PERFECT PEACE

The foundational blessing of justification is 'peace with God.'

Think back to the picture behind the wording of 3:25 (Christ as the 'propitiation' or 'mercy seat'). Jesus' death fulfils the significance of the ritual of the Day of Atonement. Once a year, the high priest sprinkled sacrificial blood on 'the mercy seat' over the ark of the covenant. Picture him now emerging to face the people. Imagine him raising his hands toward them, and pronouncing 'the Aaronic blessing' of Numbers 6:24-26: 'The Lord bless you ... lift up his countenance upon you *and give you peace.*' The judgment curse on their sinfulness had been symbolically removed. Now the blessing was theirs and the relief of divinely-provided pardon was proclaimed. The people heard God's word to them: *shalom.*

Now, in Christ's fulfilment of that old covenant picture, we enjoy *shalom.* We are no longer God's enemies—peace reigns. But we also enjoy what only the high priest experienced, on that one day in the year: access into the very presence of the God of grace.

We now have 'access by faith into this grace in which we stand' (verse 2)—access into the holy of holies, the very presence of our God. Just as King Ahasuerus held out the golden sceptre to Esther and granted her access to stand in his presence (Esther 5:2), Christ has become the 'golden sceptre' of the King of Heaven. As Esther 'approached and touched the tip of the sceptre' so we, 'touching' Christ by faith, are given access to God—knowing that our sins are permanently forgiven, and that 'we have peace with God through our Lord Jesus Christ.' We can now 'stand' in God's presence! The kind of fear expressed in Psalm 130:3 ('If you, O Lord, should mark iniquities, O Lord, who could stand?') is banished. Now the filial fear the psalmist then describes becomes ours because 'with you there is forgiveness, that you may be feared' (Psa. 130:4).

SOMETHING TO BOAST ABOUT?

This, in turn, is the introduction to a further breathtaking blessing. In addition to peace, access, and a right standing before God, we now 'rejoice in hope of the glory of God' (verse 2).

The verb Paul uses here ('rejoice,' *kauchaomai*) must have arrested the attention of his scribe Tertius, as well as any others who may have been in the room as he spoke. It certainly would have had that impact on the Christians in Rome when the letter was first read. It means to boast in the sense of exulting in something. The reason it would have arrested attention is that Paul had earlier used words related to it when he spoke of false boasting. In 4:2 he had denied that Abraham had any ground for boasting (*kauchēma*) before God. Even earlier he had used it of Jews who boasted in their position (2:17, 23). And most memorably, in 3:27 he had pronounced the pride-devastating words: 'Then what becomes of our boasting (*kauchēsis*)? It is excluded.'

But now, because of the great exchange Christ has effected, a reversal takes place. Paul can use the verb three times in a wonderfully positive sense. Verses 2, 3 and 11 form the backbone of this section. Believers 'rejoice in hope of the glory of God' (verse 2). 'Not only that, but we rejoice in our sufferings' (verse 3). And finally, 'More than that, we also rejoice in God through our Lord Jesus Christ' (verse 11). Christians—whose mouths were once shut before the judgment seat of God, and had nothing to boast about in themselves, and no reason to rejoice—are now justified in Christ. We now have much to boast about, to rejoice in and exult over. The 'Great Exchange' accomplished for us, outside of us, in Christ, now effects a 'great exchange' in our experience!

Paul outlines this in three stages, two of which are found in verses 1-5.

REJOICING—STAGE ONE

We rejoice or boast 'in hope of the glory of God.' We tend to use the word 'hope' as the equivalent of wishful thinking. We 'hope' we will make our appointment, or our flight connection (although we are doubtful if not completely pessimistic!). But in the New Testament 'hope' is confidence in something assured but not yet fully realized. A young woman when asked, 'Are you dating anybody?' might hold out her left hand to show an engagement ring and say, with a smile, 'I am hoping to be married this summer.' Her 'hope' is not a state of anxiety or doubt; it is an assurance of something that has not yet been fully realized.

But what creates this hope of glory?

Answer: the nature of our justification. It is complete in the resurrection of Jesus Christ and, as we have seen, it is also final and irreversible. The verdict on us has already been pronounced on him—and we are 'in him.' The glory of God is our certain destiny—although not yet fully experienced by us. But of this we are sure: 'those whom he justified he also glorified' (8:30; notice the tense).

Here again we see the outworking in our lives of the 'Great Exchange.' We were created as the image of God (Gen. 1:26-28), to reflect the glory of God (1 Cor. 11:7). But, alas, we exchanged the glory of God (1:23). As a result of our sin we all 'fall short of the glory of God' (3:23). But the Son of God, who is the 'radiance of the glory of God' (Heb. 1:3), became one of us, in our flesh, in order to bear our sin and shame, and as a result to be 'marred, beyond human semblance' (Isa. 52:14). But now, on our behalf, he has been resurrected, 'justified' and indeed 'glorified' (cf. John 17:24), in order that in him we might be transformed into his likeness, 'from one degree of glory to another' (2 Cor. 3:18). This, then, is our destiny as Christians (8:29; 1 Cor. 15:49; Phil. 3:20-21). The author of Hebrews concurs. Christ was made 'perfect through suffering' in order to bring 'many sons to glory' (Heb. 2:10).

Justification by grace through faith in Christ therefore raises us up from the dust and brings us the assured hope of glory to come.

But then, Paul says, 'Not only that, but …' (verse 3).

We may be inclined to respond, 'You mean there is more?'

REJOICING—STAGE TWO

'Not only that, but we rejoice in our sufferings' (verse 3). The reason for the language ('Not only that, but …') is obvious. Rejoicing in hope of the glory of God is a breathtaking reversal of our condemnation. It is also an enviable condition. And perhaps even a sympathetic non-Christian could say 'Your joyful sense of assurance is wonderful. I wish I had it.' But rejoicing in sufferings is more than *enviable*; it is *remarkable.* It is wholly counter-intuitive to our ordinary ways of thinking. This truly is a case of 'more than that.'

But how can Paul say this? Was he masochistic? Did he enjoy suffering? By no means. He appreciated having Dr Luke with him on his journeys; he was surely appreciative of the newly-converted Philippian jailer washing his wounds (Acts 16:33); he advised

Timothy to drink a little wine rather than water, for 'the sake of [his] stomach and [his] frequent ailments' (1 Tim. 5:23). He believed in employing all appropriate means to relieve human suffering. So the apostle is *not* saying that Christians should rejoice in pain or suffering for its own sake.

What then? The key here lies in the verb Paul uses. Suffering '*produces* ...' It is an intensive compound form of the verb 'to work' (*katergazomai*). God intends his children's suffering not to destroy them but to be productive in them and then through them. We do not rejoice in suffering as such but in the process of transformation it can effect: 'suffering produces endurance, and endurance produces character, and character produces hope' (verses 3-4).

The word endurance (*hupomonē*) suggests the picture of someone who is able to 'remain under' pressure. Think of an Olympic Games weightlifter, his body trembling under the intense pressure of the weight he is lifting. How is it that he can successfully hold it above his head for the requisite time before letting it down with a platform-shaking thud? Only because of the weeks, months, and years of muscle-building, strength-producing (and pain-experiencing) training he has undergone. He did not simply get off the couch from which he was watching the Olympics on TV and win the gold medal!

There is a deep spiritual logic here: only what is antithetical to our comfort can produce endurance. And in due course, this builds 'character' that is stable and reliable because it has been well tested ('character' translates the word *dokimē,* which is derived from the verb *dokimazō,* to test or prove). We cannot develop 'tested' Christian character without being 'tested.' None of us develops the strength of patience we need without being placed in situations that test and try our patience!

Paul now adds that 'character produces hope'—that is 'the hope of glory.'

Notice the parallel here between verses 2 and 3.

In verse 2 it is the *theology* of the 'Grand Reversal' in justification that leads us to rejoice in the hope of glory. Doctrine is joy-producing! Now, in verses 3 and 4, it is the *experience* of the 'Grand Reversal' in us that causes rejoicing. So we have here in verses 1-4 a powerful illustration of Paul's understanding of the marriage of doctrine and experience. What our minds grasp theologically and what our lives experience existentially belong together. There is no tension or contradiction.

HOPE THAT DOES NOT LET US DOWN

Paul anticipates that what he has said is almost bound to raise a 'Yes, *but* ...' question: 'But how can I be sure this hope will not prove to be a disappointment and leave me feeling let down and ashamed?' Many of us have had high hopes only to be left disappointed and perhaps even feeling ashamed. How is this hope any different? The answer stretches from verse 5 through to verse 10. Paul's concluding words—we 'shall be saved by his [Christ's] life'—exude confidence. But that is the conclusion of his carefully thought-out theology.

Verses 1-4 spoke of rejoicing in the hope of glory on the basis of both doctrine and experience. What follows also speaks about assurance in these terms too. But now Paul reverses the order. First he speaks about the believer's experience and then about the doctrine that lies behind it.

The experience is outlined in verse 5: 'and hope does not put us to shame, because God's love has been poured into our hearts through the Holy Spirit who has been given to us.' These words echo his statement in 1:16-17 (he is 'not ashamed of the gospel'—he uses the same verbal root in both places). But they also reflect Joel 2:26 where, immediately preceding the Pentecost-fulfilled prophecy of the outpouring of the Spirit, God says that his people 'shall never again be put to shame.'

Paul talks first about the *subjective* aspect of our confidence: 'God's love [*i.e.* his love for us] has been poured into our hearts through the Holy Spirit given to us' (verse 5). This is what we experience through the ministry of the Spirit who is 'poured out on us richly' (Titus 3:6).

Why does this assure us? Because our present experience of God's love—the realization that we are loved by him—is a foretaste of the glory that is assured us. It represents its firstfruits.

In 1738 Jonathan Edwards preached a now famous series of sermons on 1 Corinthians 13, later published as *Charity and its Fruits.* The final sermon (on 1 Cor. 13:8-10) is entitled 'Heaven, A World of Charity or Love.'[1] That description helps us here. For Paul

[1] Jonathan Edwards, *Charity and its Fruits* (1852, repr. London: Banner of Truth

is suggesting that the Spirit of the Father and the Son brings down the atmosphere of the heavenly world into our hearts. Here and now the believer experiences—although not yet fully—that heavenly love. We enjoy assurance of heaven because we already experience a degree of its atmosphere of perfect love (yes, even while we live in the polluted atmosphere of the present age).

The fact that God loves us is a fundamental truth of the gospel (*e.g.* John 3:16). Experience this love and we will enjoy assurance.

It may come as a surprise to realize that this is only the second reference in Romans to the love of God (the first was in 1:7). Only now does Paul more fully explain what lies behind the justifying activity of God in Christ—his love for us. It is perhaps therefore not a surprise that he pauses here to expound its wonder.

But before we turn to follow Paul's teaching on its full wonder, we should ask ourselves if we can echo his words and say that 'God's love has been poured into our hearts through the Holy Spirit who has been given to us.' If not, let us read and re-read Romans 5:1-5, praying that the experience these verses describe will become ours through faith in Christ.

Trust, 1969), 323-368.

15

All the Proof We Need

> *For while we were still weak, at the right time Christ died for*
> *the ungodly. [7] For one will scarcely die for a righteous per-*
> *son—though perhaps for a good person one would dare even*
> *to die— [8] but God shows his love for us in that while we were*
> *still sinners, Christ died for us. [9] Since, therefore, we have now*
> *been justified by his blood, much more shall we be saved by him*
> *from the wrath of God. [10] For if while we were enemies we were*
> *reconciled to God by the death of his Son, much more, now that*
> *we are reconciled, shall we be saved by his life. [11] More than*
> *that, we also rejoice in God through our Lord Jesus Christ,*
> *through whom we have now received reconciliation.*
>
> (Rom. 5:6-11)

At the end of the previous section (verses 1-5) Paul had spoken about the assurance the Christian believer enjoys (our 'hope [of glory] does not put us to shame'). The specific reason he gives is that we already enjoy a foretaste of glory in the way 'God's love has been poured into our hearts through the Holy Spirit who has been given to us.'

Two questions almost inevitably arise here:

QUESTIONS WITH ANSWERS

(1) *What is this experience of the outpouring of the love of God?*

It is, perhaps, best described in Paul's own words in his prayer recorded in Ephesians 3:14-19:

> I bow my knees before the Father, from whom every family in heaven and on earth is named, that according to the riches of his glory he may grant you to be strengthened with power through

> his Spirit in your inner being, so that Christ may dwell in your hearts through faith—that you, being rooted and grounded in love, may have strength to comprehend with all the saints what is the breadth and length and height and depth, and to know the love of Christ that surpasses knowledge, that you may be filled with all the fullness of God.

In a word, the experience of the love of God being 'poured into our hearts' is a consciousness of the magnitude of his love for us in Christ. Paul says it 'surpasses knowledge'—our language points to it and describes it, but we cannot fully express it or grasp it. It is after all the infinite love of the infinitely great God for finite sinners. Furthermore, the reason for this love lies in him, not in us. Nevertheless we experience what we cannot fully understand or explain.

This is the point of what Paul says in verses 6-8. Then, in verses 9-10, he draws out the implications. Finally, in verse 11, he builds on all he has said and brings this magnificent sub-section of his letter to a conclusion in climactic rejoicing.

(2) *How then are we to think about, and take in, the grandeur of this divine love?*

In Ephesians 3:18 Paul describes its dimensions. Here he does the same thing but in a different way.

We measure love in a variety of ways:

(i) By the dignity and greatness of the person who loves.
(ii) By the difference between the person who loves and the person who is loved.
(iii) By the unworthiness of the person who is loved to receive that love.
(iv) By what the lover is prepared to sacrifice for the loved one.
(v) By the gifts the lover bestows on the loved one.

By these measurements, the love of God poured into our hearts is breathtakingly great. For this is:

(i) The love of the Triune Divine Creator and Sustainer of all things.

(ii) A love that is directed towards tiny creatures made from the dust of the earth.

(iii) A love of which the recipients are altogether unworthy since they are: weak (verse 6), ungodly (verse 6), sinners (verse 8), and enemies of God (verse 10).

(iv) A love that is expressed in the fact that the Divine Lover was willing to die for those he loved.

The verb 'to die' sounds like a drumbeat through verses 6-8. That was even more obvious when the Greek text of the letter was read to the gathered Christians in Rome than it is in our English translations. For there the verb 'die' is consistently in an emphatic position at the end of each statement:

- For while we were still weak, at the right time for the ungodly Christ *died* (verse 6).
- For one will scarcely for a righteous person *die* (verse 7a).
- Perhaps for a good person one would dare even to *die* (verse 7b).
- But God shows his love for us in that while we were still sinners, for us Christ *died* (verse 8).

In this sense 'death'—*that is, Christ's death*—does have the last word—but only in order to highlight the greatness of the sacrifice the Divine Lover was prepared to make for those he loves.

And then, in addition, love is expressed by a further consideration:

(v) The gifts the Heavenly Lover gives in order to benefit the loved one: reconciliation by his death, and salvation from wrath by his resurrection life: 'For if while we were enemies we were reconciled to God by the death of his Son, much more, now that we are reconciled, shall we be saved by his life' (verse 10).

GOD IS IN THE DETAILS

Three details of Paul's words here are noteworthy.

(i) The first is their rhythmic quality:

- enemies—reconciled—death of Christ
- reconciled—saved—(resurrection) life of Christ

As we have seen, this Hebraic style of speaking—in parallelisms—was one to which Paul was naturally attracted. Scripture abounds in it, and we find it throughout the apostle's writings (*e.g.* in 2 Cor. 4:10-12; Phil. 3:10-11). When we were still God's enemies he reconciled us by Christ's death. This is good news indeed. But there is even more blessing in Christ, indeed 'much more' (verse 9). For now that we are reconciled (and therefore no longer enemies but, by implication, friends) we will be saved by Christ's risen life—and this involves not only justification—it includes adoption, sanctification, and ultimately glorification.

What did Paul mean by saying we are *reconciled* by Christ's death and *saved* by his life?

Several answers have been suggested, but perhaps the most likely is that he is simply wanting to bring out both the fullness of Christ's work and the completeness and certainty of our salvation. Thus 'death' here is a reference to his *finished* work (cf. 1 Pet. 3:18), while 'life' is a reference to his *ongoing* work as our resurrected, ascended, and reigning Saviour. Thus reconciliation means present peace, salvation means final transformation.

(ii) Once again we should notice Paul's appreciation of the deep logic of the gospel. His language signals this (verse 10: 'For if … much more …'). We often think of the apostle as a deeply logical thinker. But Paul did not *invent* or *create* the logic of the gospel. Rather, he *recognized* and *received* it in the very nature of the gospel itself.

Romans 5:1-11 demonstrates to us the way the internal logic of Paul's gospel points to the superabundance of God's grace in Christ. The flow of thought is impressive:

- verse 3: 'More than that …'
- verse 8: 'but God shows his love in this …'

- verse 9: 'much more ...'
- verse 11: 'More than that ...'

It continues into the next section:

- verse 15: 'For if ...'
- verse 17: 'For if ... much more ...'

And all of this leads to his comment—

- verse 20: 'where sin increased, grace abounded *all the more.*'

(iii) Christ's death also took place, Paul notes, 'at the right time' (verse 6).

Two words are used for 'time' in the New Testament: *chronos*, what we might call 'clock time'; and *kairos,* which refers to a specific, significant moment or critical point in time. Paul uses the latter term here.

The incarnation took place 'at the critical moment' in world history. Perhaps even more accurately, the incarnation *created* the critical moment both in world history and for our personal history. It took place exactly where and how God had planned it, at precisely the moment he had decreed. In addition it fulfilled all of the Old Testament prophecies that pointed to it. Moreover, from our point of view, it was when we desperately needed him that Christ came: it was 'when we were weak ...while we were still sinners ... enemies' that 'Christ died for the ungodly' (verses 6-10).

God's love was, then, revealed in a substitutionary sacrifice that surpasses all human measure.

Paul underlines this in verse 7. We are reluctant to sacrifice our lives for others—even for someone who is 'righteous.' Paul may mean this in the sense of a moral-living individual. But he then adds that 'for a good' man someone might be willing to make the ultimate sacrifice. The early church father Origen of Alexandria (c. 185–c. 253) intriguingly suggested that the reference here (to 'a good man') was to the Lord Jesus, the only truly 'good man.'[1] If that is the case, then it is moving to think that within a decade perhaps some of the first readers and hearers of this letter (even some of those Paul

[1] Origen, *Commentary on the Epistle to the Romans*, 2 vols, tr. Thomas Scheck (Washington D.C.: Catholic University of America Press, 2001, 2002), 1:293-294.

mentions in chapter 16) might have been numbered among those who did 'dare even to die' for the one truly 'good man' during the Emperor Nero's persecution.

But most commentators have understood 'good' here to refer to someone who is not only morally 'righteous' (although perhaps somewhat 'metallic' in their righteousness) but is truly 'good' in the sense of being kind, attractive, approachable, loving, and generous. But whatever the intended nuance, Paul's chief point is that God's love in Christ surpasses every measure of human love because it is bestowed not on those who are 'righteous' or even 'good' but on those who are 'weak' (verse 6), 'ungodly' (verse 6), 'sinners' (verse 8), and his 'enemies' (verse 10).

REJOICING—STAGE THREE

Paul has now brought us to the climactic stage of our rejoicing. If as enemies we were reconciled to God by Christ's death, much more will we be saved by Christ's life (verse 10). The One who died for us will not let us go now that he is risen from the dead. Salvation has tenses: we *have been saved* by Christ; we *are being saved* by him; we *shall be fully and finally saved* by him.

What then is the third rung on Paul's ladder of exultation? We rejoice in hope of the glory of God; we rejoice even in our suffering; but now, '*More than that*, we also rejoice in God through our Lord Jesus Christ' (verse 11).

Rejoicing in our assurance of the hope of glory is something non-believers might find admirable and even enviable; rejoicing in sufferings is, surely, remarkable to them. If so, then they will find this third stage of rejoicing—*in God himself*—incomprehensible. For they are enemies of God (verse 10). To them he is never 'God my exceeding joy' (Psa. 43:4).

Doubtless there are non-Christians who will vigorously deny the biblical idea that they are at enmity with God. Some, with little self-knowledge, may even deny it while in the same breath cursing him. But the evidence that they are at enmity is enshrined in this verse, for they do not rejoice or exult in God who created man, male and female, with the capacity and purpose of knowing, trusting, loving and glorifying him. True, if they believe there is a God, they will almost certainly affirm that he is a 'God of love.' It is the one attribute most people seem to *insist* that he must have. But their reasoning is self-absorbed, not God-centred. It has nothing to do with who God is and everything to do with them—they are, in their own eyes, someone God is required to love! But they do not respond to him as though they really believed it.

But the litmus test of believing that God loves us is that we rejoice in him and are happy to yield our lives to him. Or, in the time-honoured words of the *Shorter Catechism*, we want both 'to glorify God, and to enjoy him for ever.' And so in these verses Paul invites us to climb the gospel's ladder of the logic of grace. The steps seem counter-intuitive. Only when we trust Christ and understand the nature of our sinful condition and the wonder of the gospel do they begin to make sense.

Step 3: *We rejoice in God himself* (verse 11).
Step 2: *We rejoice even in our sufferings* (verse 3).
Step 1: *We rejoice in the hope of glory* (verse 2).

We have seen that one reason for thinking that 5:1-11 is not so much the beginning of a new section in Romans, but the climax of the exposition thus far, is the way in which these words mark a reversal of Romans 1:19-25:

- 1:18: Ungodliness now gives way to God-centredness.
- 1:18: Suppression of the truth about God now gives way to embracing that truth.
- 1:21: Not honouring God as God now gives way to yielding entirely to him.
- 1:21: Not giving thanks to God now gives way to rejoicing in him.
- 1:23: Exchanging the glory of God now gives way to glorifying him.
- 1:25: Exchanging the truth about God for a lie gives way to exchanging the lie for the truth.
- 1:25: Substituting the worship of the creature for the worship of God gives way to rejoicing in God.
- 1:28: Not seeing fit to acknowledge God gives way to recognizing his Lordship over us.

- 1:30: Being haters of God gives way to being reconciled and devoted servants and friends.

Now we rejoice in God himself, embraced in his superabundant love in Jesus Christ, poured out into our hearts by the Holy Spirit. This is the 'grace in which we stand' (verse 2).

What will Paul say next? His answer may come as a surprise, but it enables us to penetrate even further down into the deep logic of his gospel.

16

Two Men—A Pattern Reversed

Therefore, just as sin came into the world through one man, and
death through sin, and so death spread to all men because all
sinned— 13 for sin indeed was in the world before the law was
given, but sin is not counted where there is no law. 14 Yet death
reigned from Adam to Moses, even over those whose sinning
was not like the transgression of Adam, who was a type of the
one who was to come.

15 But the free gift is not like the trespass. For if many died
through one man's trespass, much more have the grace of God
and the free gift by the grace of that one man Jesus Christ
abounded for many. 16 And the free gift is not like the result
of that one man's sin. For the judgment following one trespass
brought condemnation, but the free gift following many trespasses
brought justification. 17 For if, because of one man's trespass,
death reigned through that one man, much more will those who
receive the abundance of grace and the free gift of righteousness
reign in life through the one man Jesus Christ.

18 Therefore, as one trespass led to condemnation for all men, so
one act of righteousness leads to justification and life for all men.
19 For as by the one man's disobedience the many were made
sinners, so by the one man's obedience the many will be made
righteous. 20 Now the law came in to increase the trespass, but
where sin increased, grace abounded all the more, 21 so that, as
sin reigned in death, grace also might reign through righteousness
leading to eternal life through Jesus Christ our Lord.

(Rom. 5:12-21)

We are now familiar with Paul's use of the logical connective 'therefore' (verse 12). But we could hardly anticipate the teaching that now follows his climactic statement that we rejoice in God himself (5:11).

Paul could perhaps have moved on immediately from 5:11 to 8:31-39, from rejoicing in God because of our reconciliation in Christ (verse 11) to confidently declaring that nothing can separate us from God's love in Christ (8:39). Why then do we now have one of the most complex passages in his letters as he works his way through this extended comparison and contrast between Adam and Christ?

FOUNDATIONS

In fact in these verses Paul is digging down into the foundations of the gospel. His exposition of the roles of Adam and Christ turns out to be fundamental to both what has *preceded* and also to what *follows* in the next three chapters.

First of all, 5:12-21 undergirds the two elements of sin and grace in 1:18–5:11. He indicates that the ultimate roots of universal human sinfulness are found in the fall of Adam ('sin came into the world through one man,' verse 12). 1:18-32 especially is full of echoes of that tragic event.

On the other hand, 5:12-21 also points us to the deep roots of our justification in Jesus Christ ('by the one man's obedience the many will be made righteous,' verse 18).

But then, 5:12-21 also undergirds what Paul will go on to say about the nature of the Christian life. Our lives, formerly dominated by the implications of Adam's sin, are now transformed by the implications of Christ's obedience. We are part of a 'new creation' (2 Cor. 5:17). Nevertheless we are still living in the ruins that Adam created. We are 'recovering Adamites,' 'rehabilitated sin-addicts' who continue to battle with 'withdrawal symptoms' in relation to our old life. Thus, as we will see, chapters 6, 7, and 8 all give expression to the tension created in believers between what we are *already* in Christ and what we are *not yet*.

Thus Paul's 'therefore' (verse 12) is partly retrospective (looking back to 1:18–5:11) and also partly prospective (looking forward to 6:1–8:39). The whole section (5:12-21) is designed to help us better understand humanity's sinfulness and plight, but especially the gospel's greater grace (expressed in the 'much more' of verses 15 and 17) and our ongoing Christian experience.

For many contemporary Christians these verses present a new and unaccustomed way of thinking about the gospel. Like wearing a new pair of spectacles, it can take a little time for our vision to adjust. Perhaps, therefore, the most helpful way to explore them is to look first at the big picture—the pattern of teaching.

THE PATTERN

Paul is positioning believers within the context of 'the grand narrative' of world history. He paints a picture of two men, Adam and Jesus. The key to understanding his thinking is in verse 14: 'Adam ... was a type [*tupos*] of the one who was to come [Jesus].'

A 'type' is a pattern or model (Paul uses it in this sense in Phil. 3:17). A *type*writer works by the shape of a letter impressing itself on paper. So here Paul is indicating that in certain respects the work of Christ is patterned after the life of Adam. They had somewhat similar or analogous roles in history. Both were individuals, but they were also appointed by God as representative figures so that what each of them did had profound implications for all those they represented—the whole of humanity in the case of Adam, and all believers in the case of Christ. But, as the passage explains, Adam and Christ engaged in radically contrasting acts that have had dramatically different implications and consequences.

We are familiar with this concept of one person being a representative of others from the ministry of the high priest in the Old Testament. He was, of course, a particular individual. But in his ministry he acted on behalf of the people. What he did was treated as though they had all done it. His representative role was symbolized by the jewels on his breastplate and shoulders on which the names of the tribes of Israel were engraved (Exod. 28:6-30).

In a similar way Adam, the first man, was appointed by God to represent us. He was, in that sense, the high priest of all humanity. And Jesus was similarly appointed to act on our behalf. In both cases what they did carried profound implications for all those they represented. This is why Paul elsewhere calls Adam 'the first man' and the Lord Jesus 'the second man' and 'the last Adam' (1 Cor. 15:45-47). There is no similar figure in history between Adam and Christ (he is 'the second man'), and no other will be needed after him (he is 'the last Adam').

So the first man Adam was appointed to be not only the root of all humanity but also its representative. His decisions and actions carried implications not only for himself but for all those he represented, all those who were 'in Adam' (1 Cor.15:22). In the same way, Jesus Christ was the representative of those who are 'in Christ' so that what he has done carries implications also for them. And for Paul, we are all by nature 'in Adam'; only by grace are we 'in Christ.'

This way of thinking is basic to Paul's biblical perspective. But it is less familiar to us in the profoundly individualistic way of thinking of our times, and is too often neglected. A helpful starting place is to notice how the ESV divides the passage into three paragraphs: verses 12-14, verses 15-17, and verses 18-21.

'JUST AS' BUT NO 'SO ALSO'

Paul begins by introducing a comparison: 'Therefore, *just as* sin came into the world through one man, and death through sin, and so death spread to all men because all sinned …'

The words 'just as …' lead us to expect that the sentence will continue '… so also …' But instead the comparison is broken off. In fact there is no 'so also …' until verse 18 ('Therefore as … so …').

Paul plans to tell us something about the analogy between Adam and Christ—just as one thing has happened through one man (Adam), so something similar (so also …) has happened through another man (Christ). Why then does he stop so suddenly without completing the comparison?

Two reasons could be noted:

The *first* is that Paul feels that before continuing he needs to answer a possible objection to his statement. His argument has been:

- One man (Adam) brought sin into the world
- That one man's sin then brought death into the world
- That one man's sin brought death to the world, resulting in death spreading to all men
- The one man's sin-bringing-death led to death spreading to all '*because all sinned*'

But this raises a question: How can Paul speak about 'sin' being in the world before the law was given? After all, 'sin is not counted where there is no law' (verse 13).

'Counted' here expresses the idea of an account being presented so that a bill can be settled. Paul uses the word later when he tells his friend Philemon that if he has suffered financial loss because of his runaway-but-now-converted slave Onesimus, 'charge that to my account' (Philem. 18). In other words, 'Send the bill to me and I will settle it myself!'

So the question is: how can Paul speak about the presence of 'sin' in a period (between Adam and Moses) when there was no way of identifying or measuring it?

In answering the question, Paul reasons:

- Death came through sin.
- Death reigned between Adam and Moses (the law-giver) 'even over those whose sinning was not like the transgression of Adam.'
- Therefore: Sin must have been in the world before the law was given.

There is a *second* reason for breaking off the comparison. The direction in which it is heading could give the wrong impression.

Since the first part of the comparison is:

- Just as one man's sin brought death into the world and resulted in all dying 'because all sinned ...'

it might seem that the second part of the comparison should be:

- So also one man's obedience brought life into the world and resulted in all living 'because all were obedient.'

But that would contradict Paul's own gospel. And so he breaks off the sentence and presses the pause button in order to state *first of all* the radical contrasts and differences that exist within the analogy between Adam and Christ before restating it clearly.

Once we have followed the general pattern of his teaching we can return to consider what exactly he meant when he said that 'death spread to all men *because all sinned*' even if their 'sinning was not like the transgression of Adam, who was a type of the one who was to come' (verses 13-14).

CONTRASTS WITHIN A SIMILARITY

Having introduced the typological relationship between Adam and Christ ('just as in Adam ... so also in Christ ...') but broken it off immediately, Paul now explains that there are sharp *contrasts* within the parallel between the two men; their actions and the consequences of them are radically different:

Contrast 1: verse 15:

(1) Through Adam's *trespass* many *died*;

(1a) The *grace of God* in Christ abounds to many *for life.*

Contrast 2: verse 16:

(2) The *judgment* following Adam's (*one*) *trespass* brought *condemnation*;

(2a) The *free gift* in Christ following *many trespasses* brings *justification.*

Contrast 3: Verse 17:

(3) Because of Adam's *trespass, Death reigned*;

(3a) Because of *Christ, his abundance of grace and the free gift of righteousness, we reign in life.*

Having explained the contrasts, Paul is now able to return in verses 18-19 to the analogy, the similarities between Adam and Christ, set now within the context of these contrasts.

PARALLELS WITH A DIFFERENCE

Parallel 1: verse 18:

Just as: *One* trespass led to condemnation;

So also: *One* act of righteousness leads to justification.

Parallel 2: verse 19:

Just as: *One man's* disobedience made many sinners;

So also: *One man's* obedience makes many righteous.

This then leads Paul in verses 20-21 to his conclusions.

CONTRASTING CONCLUSIONS

In verse 20 the apostle now clarifies his earlier comment on the relationship between the law and sin. Rather than sin being present only when it could be identified by the law, he explains:

The coming of the law only increased the trespass.

By contrast, where the trespass increased grace abounded all the more.

Then in verse 21, he concludes:

Through Adam: Sin reigned in death.

Through Christ: Grace reigns through righteousness to eternal life.

Perhaps the simplest way to express this is in diagrammatic form:

TWO MEN:	**ADAM**	**CHRIST**
Engaging in:		
TWO ACTS	SIN / TRANSGRESSION	OBEDIENCE / RIGHTEOUSNESS
Leading to:		
TWO VERDICTS	CONDEMNATION	JUSTIFICATION
Resulting in:		
TWO EFFECTS	DEATH REIGNS OVER US	WE REIGN IN LIFE

A KEY ISSUE

Throughout the centuries elements of this passage have challenged the best theological minds in the history of the church. But even before we examine it in more detail we should pause to feel the burden of what Paul is saying:

- The enemy Death reigns over human life. It has spread to us—there have been only two exceptions (Enoch and Elijah).
- This enemy entered the world in one way—'through sin.'
- The source of sin and death are found in one man—Adam.

There is no escape hatch or get-out clause from the consequences of Adam's transgression. We are all members of the Adam family.

But what Paul wants us to see by means of his contrasts in these verses is that while Adam and Christ have analogous roles, and while their actions and effects are opposite to each other, the contrast between them is not 'equal and opposite.' The work of Christ is greater.

In this way the gospel is the saving power of God: by it believers have been transferred from the family of Adam, with its genetic code of sin, condemnation, and death, to the family of Jesus Christ to share in righteousness, justification, and eternal life. Seeing and understanding the depth of our need because of Adam's sin is the dark backcloth against which the grace and glory of our salvation in Christ shines like a priceless diamond. This is always the way. As we see the depth of our need on the one hand we will be able more fully to appreciate the grace of God in Jesus Christ on the other.

But an important question remains: What is the precise relationship between Paul's words, 'sin came into the world through one man, so death spread to all,' and his explanation, '*because all men sinned*'? The answer takes us down into the foundations of Paul's gospel, to what undergirds all he has thus far said about sin (1:18–3:20) and salvation (3:21–5:11), and all he is about to say about the Christian life (6:1–8:39).

A more detailed examination of this must wait for the next chapter. But for now we should allow the sobering reality of what Paul says to sink in: since the time of Adam all men and women have died because of the entrance of sin. That is the greatest tragedy that has overtaken the human race.

Thank God that by the end of this chapter Paul has taught us that where 'sin reigned in death' grace has now come to 'reign through righteousness leading to eternal life through Jesus Christ our Lord' (5:21).

So if this passage tells the bleakest story in the whole Bible, it also highlights the good news, indeed the best news we could ever hear: where sin abounded, grace has super-abounded. There is salvation for us in Jesus Christ!

17

Sin and Grace

Therefore, just as sin came into the world through one man, and
death through sin, and so death spread to all men because all
sinned— 13 for sin indeed was in the world before the law was
given, but sin is not counted where there is no law. 14 Yet death
reigned from Adam to Moses, even over those whose sinning
was not like the transgression of Adam, who was a type of the
one who was to come.
15 But the free gift is not like the trespass. For if many died
through one man's trespass, much more have the grace of God
and the free gift by the grace of that one man Jesus Christ
abounded for many. 16 And the free gift is not like the result
of that one man's sin. For the judgment following one trespass
brought condemnation, but the free gift following many trespasses
brought justification. 17 For if, because of one man's trespass,
death reigned through that one man, much more will those who
receive the abundance of grace and the free gift of righteousness
reign in life through the one man Jesus Christ.
18 Therefore, as one trespass led to condemnation for all men, so
one act of righteousness leads to justification and life for all men.
19 For as by the one man's disobedience the many were made
sinners, so by the one man's obedience the many will be made
righteous. 20 Now the law came in to increase the trespass, but
where sin increased, grace abounded all the more, 21 so that, as
sin reigned in death, grace also might reign through righteousness
leading to eternal life through Jesus Christ our Lord.

(Rom. 5:12-21)

We have seen that in Romans 5:12-21 Paul exposes the roots of our sin and our salvation. He had expounded both in 1:18–3:20

(universal sin) and 3:20–5:11 (salvation in Christ alone). Now he is showing us what lies underneath the surface, as it were. In doing so he helps us to see our lives within the context of the 'grand narrative' of God's dealing with the world throughout human history.

Although this seems a complex passage we have seen that it has a key. Adam was a 'type' of Christ (verse 14). Both men were individuals, but they also functioned as representatives of others—of all humanity in Adam's case, and of all who believe in him in Christ's case.

This principle—illustrated in the role of the high priest in Israel—can also be seen in one of the most famous stories in the Old Testament—the conflict between David and Goliath in 1 Samuel 17. Both David and Goliath were the 'champions' of their people, individuals who fulfilled a representative role. When David slew Goliath he secured victory not only for himself but for all Israel; when Goliath fell, the Philistines fell with him and fled.

In the same way, Paul sees Adam and Christ as representatives. When Adam 'fell' we fell with him; when Christ brought salvation that salvation was won for us. This whole passage, 5:12-21, then presents the contrast between the actions of Adam and Christ (sin–obedience), their consequences (condemnation–justification; death–life), and also the magnitude of them (one sin–many sins; sin abounds–grace superabounds).

As Paul works this out in detail in verses 15-21 it becomes clear that there are important depths to his opening statement that 'death spread to all men *because all sinned*' (verse 12). This is perhaps clearest in verses 18-19. Here he returns to his original 'just as …' (in Adam) and, having underlined the contrast between Adam and Christ, he now explains the 'so also …' (in Christ). He says:

- *Just as*: By one man's disobedience many were 'made' sinners,
- *So also*: By one man's obedience many will be 'made' righteous (verse 19).

The connection between Adam's sin and us and Christ's obedience and us is that in both cases the action of the one man 'made' us either 'sinners' or 'righteous.'

Our English word 'made' is rather general. Paul has something more precise in mind. The verb he uses (*kathistēmi*) means 'to set something down' or 'put something in place.' It refers in the first instance to a change in status or position.

'IN ADAM'S FALL WE SINNÈD ALL'[1]

Earlier Paul had affirmed that '*all sinned*' (3:23). There he was speaking about the acts of individuals—each of us sins.

But in the light of his exposition in 5:12-21, when he said that 'death spread to all *because all sinned*' (verse 12), he seems to have something different in mind, namely that our personal sin (as in 3:23) is rooted in the original sin of Adam. Since he was our representative, his sin has implications not only for himself but for us.

This comes to the surface throughout the passage in Paul's repeated emphasis on *the one sin of the one man* bringing the whole human race into jeopardy.

- *The sin* (singular) of the *one man* Adam brought death to all (verse 12).
- Many died through *the trespass* (singular) of *one man* (verse 15).
- The judgment following *one trespass* (singular) brought condemnation to all (verse 16).
- Because of *the trespass* (singular) of the *one man* death reigned (verse 17).
- *The trespass* (singular) of *one man* led to condemnation for all (verse 18).
- By *the disobedience* (singular) of the *one man* the many were constituted sinners (verse 19).

These statements stress the effects of the one man, Adam (verses 12, 15, 17-19). But they also place an emphasis on a single act on his part—'sin' not 'sins,' 'one trespass' not 'trespasses,' 'disobedience' not 'acts of disobedience' (verses 12, 15-18). Paul's repeated emphasis is on the effect of the 'one trespass.' There is a causal connection between Adam's one sin and our subsequent situation.

Paul is not indicating merely that Adam was a bad example and that we all 'become our own Adam' (although he was probably

[1] The words are from the *New England Primer*.

familiar with that view). Adam and Christ are not presented in this passage as *exemplars* but *representatives.*

Nor is he indicating that we are 'constituted sinners' because we inherit Adam's sinful nature (although it is true that we do). The relation between Adam's sin and our fallen condition is that because Adam was the representative of the whole human race, when he sinned we all sinned in him.

We have seen that the ultimate reason for the *analogy* running through this passage is not only to highlight our desperate situation, but to underline that we have another and better representative, Jesus Christ. What he has done for us, as our representative, is counted to us! And what he has accomplished for us outweighs what Adam did.

Thus the action of these two representative men determines the status of those who are 'in' them. 'In Adam' we sinned; 'in Christ' we become righteous. Thus Paul says in verse 19:

- Adam's single act of 'disobedience' led to the result: many were 'made sinners.'
- Christ's whole life of 'obedience' led to the result: many were 'made righteous.'

Thus Paul excavates his earlier statement that 'all sinned.' And this further explains why he broke off his opening 'just as … so also' statement. Only by explaining the significance of the one sin of the first man, Adam—that in his sin and fall we all sinned and fell—will it become clear that there is a glorious but radically contrasting analogy in Christ: in his righteous obedience he was not acting as an isolated individual for himself, nor as an example to be followed, but as our substitute and representative. In him, the second representative man, is found our righteousness and justification. And so Paul uncovers not only the connection between Adam's sin and our sinful status, but also and more importantly (thank God!) the connection between Christ's righteous obedience and our status as justified (cf. 3:21-24).

TWO VIEWS

Theologians have tended to give two different answers (with individual variations) to the question: How are we 'made [*i.e.* constituted as] sinners' (verse 19)? Either:

(i) We inherit a sinful nature from Adam because he was the root of the human race. In this view we have become sinners because of the *impartation* of Adam's sinfulness. Or:

(ii) We sinned 'in Adam' as our representative. Therefore his sin is counted to us. In this view we are sinners because of the *imputation* of Adam's sin (although it is also true that since Adam was the root of humanity we also experience the *impartation* of his sinful nature).

The undergirding analogy, or typology (verse 14) throughout these verses requires this second interpretation. We are not justified on the basis of the *impartation* of Christ's righteousness to us, but by its *imputation* to us. We are not justified on the basis of his righteousness being worked into us (in sanctification) but by it being accounted to us (in justification).

Thus while the acts and effects of Adam and Christ stand in sharp contrast, what they have in common is that they 'make' or constitute 'the many' they represent either 'sinners' or 'righteous.'

This, then, is what lies behind both Romans 1:18–3:20 and also Romans 3:21–5:11. We were constituted sinners in Adam our representative. And since he is also our 'root' we inherit his sinful nature. We are constituted righteous in Christ and we also then inherit in and from him 'every spiritual blessing' (Eph. 1:3).

DO NOT LOSE SIGHT OF THE MAIN POINT

This teaching of the imputation of Adam's sin can overwhelm us—not only because we struggle to grasp this new way of thinking about ourselves, but also because it exposes in a profound way the deep and desperate nature of our lost condition. So we must make sure we do not lose sight of Paul's main point: *there is more grace for us in Christ than all that Adam lost for us*. The ultimate point of the analogy is to show us the magnitude of the saving work of Jesus, the second man (1 Cor. 15:47). This is why he is called 'the *last* Adam.' Not only has there been no representative man like Adam until the Lord Jesus (that is why Paul specifically calls him the 'second' man), but there is no need for another like Adam! For Jesus has been obedient where Adam was disobedient; he has succeeded where Adam failed. And through faith in him, in his representative role and substitutionary work on our behalf, we are constituted righteous in the sight of a holy God.

Thus, against the dark backcloth of our being constituted sinners in Adam, there is good news: Christ has taken our place. Where our first representative, Adam, failed us by his disobedience and brought death, our new representative, Jesus Christ, has obeyed on our behalf, taken the death-judgment on our sin, risen again for our justification, and is now the One in whom we 'receive the abundance of grace' (verse 17) as his sacrifice pays for our sins and his obedience clothes us in his righteousness.

Truly, then 'grace ... abounded' (verse 15); indeed, 'where sin abounded, grace abounded all the more' (verse 20). And therefore we rejoice in God (5:11). Jesus Christ provides a glorious 'much more.'

In Him the tribes of Adam boast
More blessings than their father lost.[1]

IN HIS LIGHT WE SEE LIGHT

All readers of Romans recognize that 5:12-21 is a complex passage. It may puzzle us why Paul would write the way he does. It may be helpful to reflect on some of the reasons for this.

1. When Simon Peter wrote about Paul's letters that 'there are some things in them that are hard to understand' (2 Pet. 3:16), he was neither being critical nor trying to be funny. Rather he was acknowledging that profound truths are not necessarily easy to understand. We cannot grasp and appreciate them without serious thought. And Paul's teaching here is profound. It is radical in the basic sense of the word—it takes us to the roots of human history; it explains the human condition; it puts our lives in context; it shows us that there is a grand narrative into which our lives fit; it helps us to see our place in history; it tells us the story of tragedy and triumph. In the light of Paul's teaching we see in a new light both the depths of the gospel and the wonder of our salvation.

2. We also find this teaching challenging because we do not naturally think in these terms or in this way. And we can perhaps understand why those who preach and teach do not often draw our attention to these verses. If most of us have to work hard to understand what Paul is saying here, we can appreciate why they are by no means simple to preach about!

[1] From the hymn 'Jesus shall reign where'er the sun' by Isaac Watts (1674–1748).

But Paul's teaching is important not only because of its exaltation of Christ, but because of the way it calls for a change in our individualistic thinking.

Western culture over the past two centuries and more has become increasingly dominated by individualism. Even if we are Christians we may not be conscious of the extent to which our world has squeezed both our thinking and our instincts into its mould and shaped our view of ourselves. So these new lenses of our union with the first Adam and then with Christ the Last Adam require getting used to. But as we adjust to them everything becomes clearer. Now we have better depth perception on the *bad news.* But we can also see just what *good news* the gospel really is.

This, as we have seen, is Paul's ultimate goal in these verses—to show us the greatness of the salvation in Christ he had earlier expounded in 3:21-24, and to help us grasp the 'much more' of God's grace. This is why we are able to rejoice in the hope of the glory of God, and rejoice even in our sufferings, and to (amazingly!) rejoice in God himself because of how 'much more ... the grace of God ... [has] abounded for many' (verse 15); and because of the wonder of the 'much more [of] ... the abundance of grace' (verse 17). For now 'as sin reigned in death, grace also might reign through righteousness leading to eternal life through Jesus Christ our Lord' (verse 21).

3. A third reason we may find these verses challenging is because we feel there is mystery attached to *why* God has constituted the human race not only as individuals but in this corporate way as a family.

When we think about the ways of God we should always remember such verses as Deuteronomy 29:29 and Psalm 131:1. The things that are revealed belong to us and our children; but the hidden things belong to God—and we are not God. We learn to be at peace therefore by exploring the limits of God's revelation and knowing when we have reached them. We are not capable of understanding all his ways, or indeed any of his ways fully.

However, there is, perhaps, a clue to help us here. God seems to have created the 'two branches' of his created family—men and angels—in a different way. Some—indeed many—angels seem to have rebelled against God. Thankfully by no means all!

But those who sinned and fell did so individually. Satan may have been the leader whose example they followed; but he was not their representative head. The angels did not fall 'in Satan.' By contrast, God constituted us 'in Adam the First.' 'In Adam's fall we sinnèd all.' We are so constituted that in his sin all humanity fell. We fell in the person of the first man, Adam. We cannot recover ourselves. But the good news is that in our case, just as we fell in one man we may be recovered by a second man—if a 'last Adam' could become our representative.

Were we created as the angels were, the Lord Jesus Christ would have been able to represent only one individual at a time. Thus, even if he were willing, he could save only only one person at a time. If he were to save 'many' he would need to become incarnate, live, die and rise again repeatedly—as many times as there were individuals he planned to save. How marvellous therefore to know that if 'one trespass led to condemnation for all men, so one act of righteousness—an act that involved a whole life, death, and resurrection of righteousness—leads to justification and life for all …,' that is, for all who are 'in Christ' (5:18).

Truly there are deep and wonderful mysteries in the gospel, to which we can react in different ways. We can respond angrily because we do not understand why God does things the way he does—and behind that be angry that we are not God. Or we can respond in faith and worship, and sing:

'Tis mystery all! the Immortal dies!
Who can explore His strange design?
In vain the firstborn seraph tries
To sound the depths of love Divine!
'Tis mercy all! let earth adore,
Let angel minds inquire no more.[1]

One sin of one man has resulted in universal human tragedy. But undoing it required an entire lifetime of perfect obedience on the part of our Lord Jesus, climaxing in his becoming 'obedient to the point of death, even death on a cross' (Phil. 2:8). Thanks be to God that his Son not only did what Adam failed to do and bore the divine judgment on that failure, but that he also lived a life of perfect obedience that could be counted to all those who are 'in Christ.'

[1] From the hymn 'And can it be' by Charles Wesley (1707–88).

ONCE MORE—THE LAW

Paul now brings this profound passage to a triumphant conclusion. And perhaps because of his deep sensitivity to the Jewish Christians in Rome, and also to guard against distortions of his teaching on the law, he now further explains his earlier comment on its relationship to sin (verse 13): 'the law came in [not to justify us—that was never its God-given purpose—but] to increase the trespass' (verse 20).

The giving of the law was not the foundation of man's relationship to God. It 'entered in' to the story of God's dealings with us, not to save us, but to reveal sin to us. And its effect was not to justify us but 'to increase the trespass' (verse 20). So we dare not rely on the law for our justification.

If the entrance of the law has not brought us salvation but only increased the trespass by making its nature crystal clear and causing it to abound, then the good news is that grace has 'abounded all the more' (verse 20). But—we should never forget—grace reigns *through righteousness* (verse 21).

Once again Paul hints at something he will later explain further (in 8:1-4). Grace does not abolish 'the righteous requirement of the law.' Instead it reigns through righteousness—through Christ's righteousness, of course; but then he reproduces his righteousness in our lives too. For those to whom Christ's righteousness is imputed discover that personal righteousness begins to be worked into them by the Spirit (8:3-4). Thus grace reigns and leads to 'eternal life through Jesus Christ our Lord' (verse 21). For our great Saviour is 'more full of grace than I of sin.'[1]

ALL IN CHRIST

Grace reigns 'through Jesus Christ our Lord' (verse 21). The language of salvation 'in' or 'through' Christ runs like a refrain throughout these chapters. Paul had used it earlier when he spoke of the righteousness of God that is 'through faith in Jesus Christ' (3:22), and of the justification that comes 'through the redemption that is in Christ Jesus' (3:24). In addition, he had concluded the previous section (5:1-11) by saying that we rejoice in God 'through our Lord Jesus Christ' (verse 11). When we are 'in Christ,' united to

[1] From the hymn 'Weary of wandering from my God' by Charles Wesley (1707–88).

him by faith, all that he has done for us becomes ours. Truly, God 'has blessed us with every spiritual blessing in Christ' (Eph. 1:3).

In 5:12-21 Paul has now laid the groundwork for our union with Christ against the background of our natural union with Adam. Now we are no longer united to Adam. We must therefore learn to see ourselves in terms of our union with Christ. That theme will reappear repeatedly in what follows:

- in 6:3 we are reminded that we have been 'baptized into Christ Jesus';
- in 6:11 we are urged to consider ourselves 'dead to sin and alive to God in Christ Jesus';
- in 6:23 the free gift of God is 'eternal life in Christ Jesus our Lord';
- in 7:25 deliverance from the body of death comes 'through Jesus Christ our Lord';
- in 8:1 there is no condemnation 'for those who are in Christ Jesus';

and then,

- in 8:39 we are given the assurance that nothing will be able to separate us from the love of God 'in Christ Jesus our Lord.'

Thus 5:12-21 has taken us down into the foundations of all that Paul has said in 1:18–5:11. It now leads on to what follows in 6:1–8:39. The ultimate origin of our status and condition as condemned sinners is our union with the first Adam in whom we sinned and fell. The ultimate foundation for the justification that we now experience is found in the last Adam, Jesus Christ, in whose obedience and blood we are constituted righteous.

In chapters 6, 7, and 8, Paul will work out in detail the implications of this union. He will show us what it means no longer to be 'in Adam' and now to be 'in Christ' even while we are still living in a world that has inherited the poisoned fruit of Adam's fall.

We are now 'in Christ' and no longer 'in Adam.' We enjoy 'much more'; but we are not yet in glory. We still live in the same territory and in the same bodies we did when we were 'in Adam.' The effect of his sin and ours continues to invade and surround us. Paul therefore wants to teach us how to live faithfully in the present age until the day dawns when we will be 'saved to sin no more.'[1]

Paul's message is wonderful: 'Where sin increased grace abounded all the more' (verse 20).

'But,' someone might say: 'You are implying that we can continue in sin because the result will be the promotion of grace!' In fact someone—perhaps many—did say that to Paul. So to that question Paul now turns—and we will follow him in the next chapter.

[1] From the hymn 'There is a fountain filled with blood' by William Cowper. (1731–1800).

18

Dead and Alive

What shall we say then? Are we to continue in sin that grace
may abound? 2 By no means! How can we who died to sin
still live in it? 3 Do you not know that all of us who have been
baptized into Christ Jesus were baptized into his death? 4 We
were buried therefore with him by baptism into death, in order
that, just as Christ was raised from the dead by the glory of the
Father, we too might walk in newness of life.
5 For if we have been united with him in a death like his, we
shall certainly be united with him in a resurrection like his.
6 We know that our old self was crucified with him in order that
the body of sin might be brought to nothing, so that we would
no longer be enslaved to sin. 7 For one who has died has been
set free from sin. 8 Now if we have died with Christ, we believe
that we will also live with him. 9 We know that Christ, being
raised from the dead, will never die again; death no longer has
dominion over him. 10 For the death he died he died to sin, once
for all, but the life he lives he lives to God. 11 So you also must
consider yourselves dead to sin and alive to God in Christ Jesus.
12 Let not sin therefore reign in your mortal body, to make
you obey its passions. 13 Do not present your members to sin as
instruments for unrighteousness, but present yourselves to God
as those who have been brought from death to life, and your
members to God as instruments for righteousness. 14 For sin
will have no dominion over you, since you are not under law
but under grace.

(Rom. 6:1-14)

When the author of Hebrews introduces a quotation from Psalm 8 by writing, 'it has been testified somewhere …,' he had not forgotten where to find the verses; nor did he know he was writing Hebrews chapter 2 verse 6! Dividing the text of Scripture into chapters and verses did not become really important to most Christians until after the invention of the printing press when individuals could afford to purchase their own Bible.

These divisions are extremely helpful. We find them essential. But it is worth reminding ourselves that Paul did not dictate Romans in chapters and verses. It can therefore be helpful to think of Romans in a different way—like the flow of a river, gathering from various tributaries and growing as it makes its way to the sea; or like a tree with roots, branches, and foliage.

Here, for example, Romans 6:1-14 grows out of what Paul has said in 5:12-21, and especially his words in verse 20: 'where sin increased, grace abounded all the more.' That statement almost inevitably raises a question, if not an objection: If the increase of sin leads to a superabundance of grace, surely this implies that the more we sin, the more grace is displayed. Does Paul's gospel imply we can go on sinning—because there will always be more grace? (6:1).

It is just possible to read this question as a relatively neutral one, sympathetically asked by someone puzzled by what seems to be the application of what Paul has said. But the sharpness of the answer 'By no means!' suggests otherwise. The question was probably either:

(i) what is called a *reductio ad absurdum* argument, in which a viewpoint is rejected because its implications are obviously false and therefore it cannot be correct. If this was the logical conclusion of what Paul was teaching then obviously his gospel must be false. Or,

(ii) an antinomian-style response: 'Great, we can sin to our heart's content and experience all the grace we will ever need.' It seems that Paul was accused of teaching something like this, as he indicated back in 3:8 when he responded to the accusation that he taught we can safely ignore the law (and thus by implication, he was opening the door to ungodly living).

Since Paul was presenting his gospel ('my gospel') to the Romans it was essential for him to correct misapprehensions and false accusations. He characteristically turns this situation into a 'teaching moment' and demonstrates that the superabundance of grace has the opposite effect—it leads to holiness.

'GOD FORBID!'

'What shall we say then? Are we to continue in sin that grace may abound? By no means!' (verses 1-2). Paul's response is typical (see 3:4; 3:6; and later in 6:15 and 7:13). He is here faced with a doctrinal issue that has grave practical implications. But his immediate response seems to be instinctive and emotional rather than (as we might expect from him) theological. The Authorised (King James) Version offered the emotive translation: 'God forbid.'

Paul placed considerable emphasis on the use of the mind and on thinking theologically. It would be natural therefore to wonder why here he seems to *emote* first and to *think* afterwards. Is he encouraging us to live the Christian life on the basis of our feelings and our emotional reactions? No. In fact this response illustrates the extent to which Paul's instincts have been trained by his theology. He 'reacts first, thinks second' only because his instinctive and intuitive reactions have already been shaped and informed by his understanding of the gospel.

There is an important lesson to learn here. The Christian life is not lived on the basis of our emotions or intuitions, but on the basis of biblical teaching. But we should expect to see our emotional reactions and our intuitions increasingly cleansed, shaped, informed, disciplined, and clarified by that teaching so that they are recalibrated and aligned to the gospel.

Thus here—without pausing to think about it or consult a manual—Paul instinctively realizes that to suggest we continue in sin so that grace may abound contradicts his gospel. And that reaction is the kind of fruit the contents of *Romans* ('my gospel') produced in him—and will also produce in us as we absorb its teaching.

But this *reaction* is immediately followed by an *explanation* of the theological reasoning that lies behind it (in 6:2b-14). The strength of Paul's 'gut-reaction' is in direct proportion to the strength of his doctrine and has been informed by the logic of the gospel. The Christian does not go on living in sin for the simple reason that he or she has 'died to sin' (verse 2). We cannot live in that to which we have died. To do so would be an inherent contradiction. More, it would be an *ontological* contradiction—a contradiction of who we now are—people who are no longer in Adam but in Christ.

WE ARE THE PEOPLE

When Paul says 'How can we who died to sin live in it?' (verse 2) he uses a distinctive form of the relative pronoun [*hoitines*, a plural of *hostis*[1]]. It denotes people who belong to a category.

Christians belong to the category 'those who died to sin.' This is our new identity in Christ. When Paul reflects on what it means to be a believer, this is his answer: 'We are those who in Adam were dead *in* sin; but now in Christ we have died *to* sin and have been raised to new life (verse 4). That is what defines us and explains who we are as Christians.' To go on living in the sin to which we have died would therefore be a contradiction of who we are.

This, then, is our new identity in Christ. We have 'died to sin' and are now 'alive to God in Christ Jesus' (verse 2; verse 11). In Adam we died *because of sin*; in Christ we have *died to sin*. What follows in verses 3-10 forms the basis for Paul's important instruction: Since this is who you now are in Christ, you must learn to think about yourself this way ('you also must consider yourselves dead to sin and alive to God in Christ Jesus,' verse 11).

In verse 3, Paul further implies that if we understood the significance of our baptism we would realize this. We were baptized 'into Christ Jesus.' In the naming ceremony of baptism we received a new family name with a new identity. It may take an individual—a new bride, or an adopted son—some time to adjust to a new name. So here; but it is our new identity that will determine the character of our new lifestyle.

When we were 'in Adam,' we participated in all that he did as our representative. But now that we are 'in Christ' we participate in what he has done for us. In union with him we died to sin (verse 2) and have been raised again 'to walk in newness of life' (verse 4). For if we are united to him in a death like his and share in its significance, it follows that we must also be united to him in a resurrection like his and share in his life (verse 5).

Paul's theological logic is clear. And judging by his question (verse 3, 'Do you not know ...?'), he believed its implications should

[1] This form of *hostis* is used 'qualitatively—a. to indicate that persons (or things) belong to a certain class (such a one).' W. F. Arndt, E. W. Gingrich trs., W. Bauer, *A Greek-English Lexicon of the New Testament* (Chicago: University of Chicago Press, 1957), 591.

have been common knowledge to the Christians in Rome. They should have understood the message their baptism 'preached' to them was about union with Christ in his death with a view to sharing in his resurrection and living a new life characterized (as Christ's was) by living for God (verse 10). As a 'visible word' baptism points to our new identity in Christ. It preaches this message: 'In Christ you died to sin; in Christ you have been raised to walk in a new way altogether; therefore live a baptized life.'

This way of thinking can be challenging to grasp when we first hear it. We do not think this way naturally, either about ourselves or about our baptism. But its effect can be wonderfully life-transforming. It reminds us that the most fundamental truth about us as Christians is that we are 'in Christ.' If we miss this, and the implication that in him we have died to sin and been raised into newness of life, we are missing the point of our baptism. And we are also depriving ourselves of the powerful impetus to live a new life in Christ we are meant to find in our baptism.

Paul adds that in baptism those who have thus died with Christ have also been 'buried … with him' (verse 4; cf. Col. 2:12) with a view to living a new life patterned after the risen life of Christ. We are no longer 'in Adam' but 'in Christ.' We belong to the new creation (2 Cor. 5:17).

The logic is both simple and powerful. And it is also life-changing. But what exactly does Paul mean by saying that believers have 'died to sin'?

DIED TO SIN

Paul explains in two stages, verses 6-7 and verses 8-10.

Verses 6-7 are tightly packed with ideas: 'We know that our *old self was crucified with him* in order that *the body of sin* might be *brought to nothing* so that we would no longer be *enslaved to sin*. For one who has died has been *set free from sin*.' These expressions—'old self,' 'crucified with him,' 'body of sin,' 'brought to nothing,' 'set free from sin'—cry out for explanation.

(i) *'The old self'* (literally, old man or person). What is 'our old self' ('our old man')? It is sometimes taken to mean 'the person I was before I was converted.' While that is certainly involved, it is only part of the meaning.

The expression is set against the background of our once being 'in Adam' and now being 'in Christ' (5:12-21). Paul not only means 'the first part of my biography' (BC as it were—Before I met Christ). Against the background of 5:12-21, the 'old man' refers to all that I was *in Adam.* Similarly when Paul speaks elsewhere about the 'new man' he is not merely thinking about our biography part two, but about who we now are *in Christ.*

The situation for that 'old man' in Adam was that 'sin reigned in death' over him (5:21). But now, united to Christ in his death ('crucified with him,' verse 6) and resurrection ('raised with him'), 'grace reigns through righteousness to eternal life,' and we too reign. Sin no longer has dominion over us (cf. 6:14).

While we are still the same person, we are no longer the 'old man.' In Christ we have died *to sin*—now its dominion over us has been brought to an end. We have now been raised into newness of life, into the new creation, and given a new identity.

(ii) '*The body of sin.*' The result of the 'old self' having been 'crucified with him' is that 'the body of sin might be brought to nothing.' Paul uses the expression 'body of sin' only once in his letters—here. So we cannot discover its significance by comparing other examples of its use. It has been variously understood. Some commentators have held that he is thinking of sin itself as a 'body' or 'mass.' But a helpful clue lies in the similar expression used in 7:24: the 'body of death.' There Paul is referring to our physical body dominated by and destined for death. So probably here he also has in view our physical body, dominated by death because it is dominated by sin. It is 'the body of death' because it is the 'body of sin.'

(iii) '*Brought to nothing.*' In union with Christ 'the body of sin' is 'brought to nothing.' Paul is not suggesting the body itself is destroyed. But now that we are 'in Christ' our body is no longer dominated by sin. It is no longer the natural soil in which sin flourishes, as was formerly the case. In fact our bodies are now temples of the Holy Spirit, consecrated to the nurturing of holiness (1 Cor. 6:19).

(iv) '*No longer enslaved to sin.*' Formerly we were sin's slaves. Throughout this whole section (5:12–6:14 and beyond) Paul personifies sin as a reigning power and a slave master—he constantly uses the definite article (*hē hamartia, the* sin). But now we are in union with Christ (signified in baptism), 'King Sin' no longer reigns over us. Sin was once a vicious slave-master; now in union with Christ in his death to the reign of sin, we are 'no longer … enslaved to sin. For one who has died has been set free from sin' (verses 6-7).

(v) '*Set free from sin.*' In what sense are Christians now 'set free from sin'? Not, surely, in the sense expressed in J. B. Phillips's (usually excellent) translation: 'for a dead man can safely be said to be immune to the power of sin.'[1] It 'can safely be said' that we are *not* 'immune' to sin's power!

How then have those who 'died to sin' been 'set free from sin'?

Commentators have struggled with Paul's meaning here partly because the verb he uses (translated 'set free') is usually translated 'justify' (*dikaioō*). Some therefore hold that Paul is talking here about the freedom that justification brings *from the guilt of sin.* They usually appeal to what is said about Christ in 6:10, 'the death he died he died to sin,' and argue that since Christ was never 'alive' to sin, the only sense in which he could have 'died to sin' is that he died *for* sin. What Paul must have in view in verse 7 is the believer's freedom from sin's guilt in justification. But is this the case?

JUSTIFIED OR SET FREE?

It is certainly true that Christ died *for* the guilt of our sins. Nevertheless there are reasons why the majority of English translations continue to translate Paul's words 'set free from' rather than 'justified from':

(1.) The verb *dikaioō* has a range of meaning, including the idea of deliverance.

(2.) Paul uses the verb here in the context of deliverance from the dominion of sin (not the guilt of sin).

In Romans 5:12–7:25 Paul consistently uses the singular noun 'sin' (typically with the definite article). He is therefore not speaking about specific sins and our need for justification, but about sin (singular) as a power exercising dominion over us.

(3.) Furthermore, throughout this section Paul is addressing the reign of sin, not its guilt. He had already dealt with the theme of

[1] J. B. Phillips, *The New Testament in Modern English* (London: Geoffrey Bles, 1980), 319-20.

justification. His argument is *not*: 'We do not continue in sin because justification motivates us not to sin.' Instead he appeals to our new identity as those who in Christ have died to sin's dominion and been set free from its mastery or reign over our lives.

(4.) This perspective is illustrated in the way Paul speaks about 'sin' in 5:12–6:23. He virtually personifies it. He signals this by his descriptions of it: it is a king who reigns (5:21; 6:14); a vicious slave-owner who mistreats us (6:6, 17); even, perhaps, a general whose weapons we have become ('instruments,' *hopla*, used twice in verse 13 could be translated 'weapons'); it is an employer who pays wages—death (6:23).

(5.) Later in this chapter Paul is discussing bondage or slavery to sin's dominion rather than its guilt (verses 16, 18-20, 22). More specifically in verse 18 (a statement parallel to verse 7), he speaks about believers 'having been *set free* from sin.' Here he employs the standard verb for liberation from bondage (*eleutheroō*). In Adam we were slaves; but now we are Christ's freedmen.

TRUTH AND CONSEQUENCES

Verses 8-10 further develop the significance of union with Christ and underline the inherent contradiction between being a baptized Christian and continuing to live in sin.

As Christians we are united to the Lord Jesus Christ. If we have died with him it follows that we will also be raised with him (verses 5, 8). And since death's dominion over him was permanently vanquished by his resurrection (he will never die again, verse 9)—our new life in union with him will be as permanent as his resurrection.

Not only so, but while 'the death he [Christ] died he died to sin,' his new life of resurrection is lived to God. There is, therefore, a double reason we do not go on living in sin (verse 1): we have both died to its dominion and been raised to live new life devoted to God.

With all this in view, it would be an intolerable contradiction of our new identity in Christ if we were 'to continue in sin.' After all, Christ died and rose so that 'as sin reigned in death, grace might reign through righteousness leading to eternal life through Jesus Christ our Lord' (5:21).

To recap: We have died to sin in the death of Christ because he died to sin (verse 10). We are united to him in his death to sin's reign (verse 10) and have been set free from its dominion (verses 3, 5, 6). In fact, if Christ did not die *to sin* as dominion and reign, then neither have we. If all Paul meant here was that Christ died for the guilt of our sin to bring us justification, that might provide a *motivation* for no longer living in sin, but not a real *liberation* from sin's dominion. But *liberation* is Paul's whole focus in this chapter. Moreover, if Paul had been thinking about justification he would surely have said that Christ 'died *for* sin,' and not this distinctive expression 'died *to* sin.'

Furthermore, Jesus did in fact 'die to sin' in terms of its dominion. When he took our place on the cross, he was 'made sin for us.' If 'sin reigned in death' (5:21), and Jesus died, then for a brief season sin did 'reign in death' over him. But because it was also true that 'he knew no sin' (2 Cor. 5:21) 'it was not possible for him to be held by it [death]' (Acts 2:24). And in that mystery of our Lord's death *to* sin is found our deliverance from sin's dominion.

A further consideration is sometimes brought forward and seen to clinch the argument that Paul is speaking here only of freedom from the guilt of sin: if he had meant that believers are free from sin's reign he would not have said (as he does in verse 12), 'Let not sin therefore reign in your mortal bodies.'

But sometimes we say to teenagers 'Don't be a baby' precisely because they no longer are babies. In the same vein there is no logical objection to saying to someone who has died to sin in Christ 'Don't let sin reign.' We are to live out the new identity we already possess. We are *not* to live as we formerly did because 'in Christ' we no longer have the identity we formerly had when we were 'in Adam.'

Paul's whole point here is that since we are already free from sin's dominion, but not yet free from its presence and influence, the summons not to let sin reign is a necessary one.

THE IMPERATIVE LIFE

Now, for the first time in the letter, imperatives begin to flow freely, one after another. There is good reason for their vigour and rigour. For while we have died to sin, it has not yet finally died out in us. This is why we need the imperatives of 6:11-14. And Paul is teaching us that God's grace enables us to respond to them.

(i) Verse 12: Since sin no longer reigns over you—don't let it reign at all! Here we are being urged to act in a manner consistent with who and what we now are.

(ii) Verse 13: If we are to resist sin, then we need to engage in *detailed* consecration and make sure that we present our 'members' (eyes, ears, hands, feet, mouth, mind) to the Lord, in a manner that reverses their past submission to our sinful instincts. Here again Paul excels in simple practical counsel: 'Remember who you now are—someone who has been brought from death to life!'

These are all-demanding exhortations. But they are grounded in the all-sufficiency of God's grace, in our new identity in Christ, and in our new-found freedom from sin's dominion (verse 14). Thus Paul reminds us of a great truth, lest we have forgotten it, or doubted it: 'Sin will have no dominion over you, since you are not under law ...' (verse 14). For law increases the trespass (5:20), but grace in Christ delivers us from bondage to sin.

Now Christ reigns! Grace reigns! And therefore we also reign in life through Christ Jesus our Lord. Sin no longer has dominion over us. For we are 'not under law but under grace.'

This last statement hangs in the air. It is both natural and inevitable that we should ask what it means. As Paul continues his letter the answer to that question will become clear.

19

Before and After

What then? Are we to sin because we are not under law but under grace? By no means! [16] *Do you not know that if you present yourselves to anyone as obedient slaves, you are slaves of the one whom you obey, either of sin, which leads to death, or of obedience, which leads to righteousness?* [17] *But thanks be to God, that you who were once slaves of sin have become obedient from the heart to the standard of teaching to which you were committed,* [18] *and, having been set free from sin, have become slaves of righteousness.* [19] *I am speaking in human terms, because of your natural limitations. For just as you once presented your members as slaves to impurity and to lawlessness leading to more lawlessness, so now present your members as slaves to righteousness leading to sanctification.*

[20] *For when you were slaves of sin, you were free in regard to righteousness.* [21] *But what fruit were you getting at that time from the things of which you are now ashamed? For the end of those things is death.* [22] *But now that you have been set free from sin and have become slaves of God, the fruit you get leads to sanctification and its end, eternal life.* [23] *For the wages of sin is death, but the free gift of God is eternal life in Christ Jesus our Lord.*

(Rom. 6:15-23)

Romans 6 began with a question prompted by Paul's statement in 5:20. If grace superabounds where sin abounds, why not sin so that it may superabound? His response to that perverse suggestion ended with a ringing affirmation: 'Sin will have no dominion over you.' But then he had added, '*since you are not under law but under grace*' (6:14).

'Not under law'? This raises another question which Paul immediately addresses. It belongs to the same world of truth-twisting as the question in verse 1. The error has been expressed in the ditty,

> *Free from the Law,*
> *O blessed condition;*
> *I can sin as I please,*
> *And still have remission.*

Paul's response is identical to verse 1. 'Never!' And his explanation begins in the same way: 'Do you not know ...?' We have noticed before that for Paul knowledge and understanding are vital in the Christian life and yet being a Christian is not merely an intellectual matter. Mindset and lifestyle are intimately related to each other.

The principle undergirding Paul's teaching here is that those who are 'in Christ' are united to him in all that he has accomplished for them. So there is no receiving Christ for justification without receiving him for sanctification. Faith receives a person and he is not divisible in that way. As John Calvin wrote on a number of occasions, to think that we can have Christ for justification without having him for sanctification is to think that Christ can be 'torn into parts.'[1]

We are not saved as 'a result of works' but by grace; but we are now 'God's workmanship, created in Christ Jesus *for good works*' (Eph. 2:8-10). There is no room for moral carelessness under the reign of grace. We have 'died to sin' and therefore cannot continue to live in it. In addition, since 'grace reigns through righteousness' (5:21), freedom *from* the reign of sin takes place within the context of freedom *for* Jesus Christ and leads to a life of righteousness. We are now bondservants of the Lord Jesus, pledged to be obedient to him 'whose service is perfect freedom' (to borrow the language of the Collect for Peace in the *Book of Common Prayer*).

So, once again Paul is at pains to point out the internal logic of the gospel and its implications for believers: 'Do you not know that if you present yourselves to anyone as obedient slaves, you are slaves of the one whom you obey, either of sin, which leads to death, or of obedience, which leads to righteousness?' (verse 16). The grace that releases us from the dominion of sin involves redemption (3:24). We are redeemed from Sin the slave-owner by the blood of Christ in

[1] *E.g.* Calvin, *Institutes*, III.xi.6.

order to belong to him as our new and gracious Master. Our new-found freedom involves serving and obeying him. He has redeemed us for holiness, not for licentiousness. We have been 'bought with a price' and are therefore to 'glorify God' in our bodily existence now as well as hereafter (1 Cor. 6:20; cf. Rom. 7:23; 12:1-2).

Our thinking is often clarified by the use of comparisons. Paul employs that principle here in verses 17-23.

SLAVES YET FREE

Once we were slaves, now we are free; once we were in bondage to sin, now we are slaves of righteousness. The 'members' (*i.e.* of our physical body) that were formerly slaves of impurity leading to increasing lawlessness are now servants of righteousness leading to holiness (verses 17-19).

The lesson here is a fundamental one. It is easy for us to lose sight of the magnitude of the transformation that has taken place in our lives. We may be conscious of how little progress we seem to have made in grace; we feel we are far from being what we are called to be. But Paul reminds us here that we are no longer what we once were. Our progress may seem to be slow and even inconsistent. But as wise spiritual guides teach us, our true progress is not measured by where we seem to have arrived but by the distance we have travelled from where we began, and the obstacles we have overcome to get where we now are. That is the real measure of our spiritual growth.

Paul thanks God that those who were slaves of sin have become 'obedient from the heart to the standard of teaching to which [they] were committed' (6:17). This language marries together divine activity ('were committed' is in the passive voice, suggesting that God was the agent) and human responsiveness (they became 'obedient from the heart'). Thus Paul gives thanks to God for what has happened—it is *his* doing. At the same time, his work in them has produced *their* heart-obedience to him. We are not automatons (cf. Phil. 2:12-13).

The object of this commitment is described as 'the *standard* of teaching.' Here 'standard' translates the Greek word *tupos* (used earlier in 5:14 of Adam as a 'type' of Christ). It refers not to a standard in the sense of a 'benchmark' (a Creed, or a Confession of Faith, for example) but the pattern or shape the doctrine of the gospel produces in our lives.

This is a suggestive choice of words. In coming to faith we commit ourselves to the person of the Lord Jesus, to be conformed to his likeness. That involves being shaped by the doctrine in the Scriptures by which he is made known to us. As our minds are renewed by its teaching our lives are transformed (12:1-2). We hear and see Christ revealed in his word and are 'transformed into this same image' (2 Cor. 3:18).

A further detail worth reflecting on here is in verse 19: 'I am speaking in human terms because of your natural limitations.' Paul was sensitive to using slave language in speaking about the gospel since at least some of those to whom he was writing were themselves slaves.[1] There was a wide discrepancy in the way slaves were treated in the Roman Empire—some were well-treated while others were abused. He wants his readers to filter out the sinister connotations of the metaphor when he applies it to their relationship to Christ. For he is the kindest, wisest, and gentlest Master. His yoke is easy, and his burden is light (Matt.11:30). Paul is not only an expert theologian; he is a wise and sensitive pastor. Those who appreciate the former, and love to study his teaching, must never overlook the latter. Like him we need to be mindful of the fact that 'the aim of our charge is love …' (1 Tim. 1:5).

In the structure of the closing verses of the chapter (For … But … For … But … But … For …verses 20-23) Paul couples the *emotion* with which he had responded to the suggestion in verse 15 and his *explanation* of the new life in Christ, with *motivation* for living as those over whom 'sin will have no dominion' (verse 14).

PAST AND PRESENT

Before his readers became Christians, when they were 'slaves of sin,' they had been 'free in regard to righteousness' (verse 20), that is, 'under no sense of obligation to live righteously.' They saw themselves as self-determining individuals, lords of their own lives, doing whatever pleased them and promoting their own happiness.

[1] Some of those he greets in 16:3-16 have common slave names. Estimates of the slave population in Rome vary but it is possible the total number reached several hundred thousand.

The motivational contrast Paul is now using is between 'before' and 'after.' The advertising industry appeals to this instinct in us in the way it promotes products as diverse as washing-up liquid, anti-ageing creams, hair restorer, and dental implants. 'Look at the difference between before and after!' it says—it is obvious which is better and more desirable. So here Paul makes spiritual application of this natural instinct by asking the simple question: 'How did that old lifestyle benefit you spiritually?' 'You were planting, nurturing, and harvesting—what?—Death!' (verses 20-21).

Paul is illustrating here how God's word works. In order to be 'profitable ... for training in righteousness' it must first be profitable 'for teaching, reproof, correction ...' (2 Tim. 3:16). Here we find an example of 'reproof' and 'correction.' His question ('what fruit were you getting ...?') touches both the memory and the emotions. It evokes a godly shame as we reflect on our former lifestyle: 'you once presented your members as slaves to impurity and to lawlessness leading to more lawlessness' (verse 19). What lasting effect did that have? What lasting profit did you gain? Now compare that with the effects of the gospel in your life!

Looking back on our pre-Christian life the words 'I am sorry, Lord' may instinctively come to our lips and a sense of shame may rise in our hearts. 'Remember not the sins of my youth,' cried David (Psa. 25:7). Many a Christian has said, with Samuel Rutherford, 'The *old ashes* of the *sins* of *my* youth are *new fire* of sorrow to me.'[1] Many biblical passages encourage us to look back at the past to provide motivation for the present.

Paul reminds us here that the new lifestyle of grace not only begins but continues with repentance. As the first of Martin Luther's *Ninety-Five Theses* stated, 'When our Lord Jesus Christ said "Repent," he meant that the whole Christian life should be repentance.' By grace we see our past life in its true colours, *coram Deo* (in the presence of God), and we are ashamed. 'For the end of those things is death.' 'But now ...,' adds Paul, in a blessed contrast, 'But now that you have been set free from sin and have become

[1] Andrew A. Bonar, ed., *Letters of Samuel Rutherford* (1891; repr. Edinburgh: Banner of Truth Trust, 1984), 349. The letter was written to William Gordon of Earlston who in later life was met by a party of English soldiers after the defeat of the Scottish Covenanters at the Battle of Bothwell Bridge in 1679, and killed on the spot.

slaves of God, the fruit you get leads to sanctification and its end, eternal life' (verse 22).

Earlier in this chapter Paul affirmed that 'we have been *united with him* [Christ] in a death like his … [and] we shall certainly be *united with him* in a resurrection like his' (verse 5). The word translated as 'united with' (*sumphutos*) is very suggestive. It comes from a verb (*sumphuō*) which means 'to grow up together with,' 'innate.' When we are united to Christ, the fruit of Christ's death and resurrection is built into our new spiritual DNA. What has been thus planted in us begins to manifest itself in the new fruit of grace in 'sanctification'—Christlikeness (Rom. 8:29). The harvest now is not death but eternal life (verse 22).

Christians often think about their conversion to Christ mainly in terms of *what they did* when they first trusted in Christ ('my faith,' 'my decision for Jesus'). But it is an essential element in Christian growth to understand *what God did*. Our response was 'the tip of the iceberg.' Underneath, hidden away, and yet fundamental to our Christian life is *what God did*, drawing us to himself, regenerating us, and uniting us to Christ in his death and resurrection with all the implications that follow.

Paul saw this with tremendous clarity. What happened when we came to trust in Christ? Our way of describing it might be 'I made a decision to follow Jesus.' Paul does not doubt that is true. But something far bigger happened. For 'If any—in Christ—new creation' (2 Cor. 5:17, literal translation). Becoming a Christian introduces us to a far greater reality than we imagined—a new creation. That involves becoming someone who, in Christ, died to sin and has been raised into newness of life.

When we begin to understand what a deep and radical thing it is to trust in Christ and grasp the reality of our union with him, the teaching of Romans 6 will shape and fashion our whole view of the Christian life.

UNPLEASANT—BUT MEDICINAL

The questions raised in Romans 6:1 and 15 are expressions of a sick theology. And in much of the chapter Paul is serving as a spiritual physician prescribing medicine. In these latter verses he has been reflecting with us on our past. Our instinct may be to avoid doing that because it is unpleasant and embarrassing; it makes us feel 'ashamed' (verse 21). We naturally want to move on from, rather than reflect on, past failure. But Paul counsels us not to move on impatiently lest like false prophets we heal our wounds too easily and superficially by saying to ourselves '"Peace, peace" when there is no peace' (Jer. 6:14). We must not seek or rest content with only superficial healing rather than deep-down, lasting transformation and *shalom*. We must learn to face up to the reality of the sin, the shame, and the spiritual famine that marks life without Christ if we are to appreciate the rich privileges, the transformation, the new identity and the wonderful destiny that have become ours in Christ.

Paradoxically it is only when we do this that we realize what may seem at first to be an outrageous thought: *the Lord Jesus is more interested in us than he is in our sin; he is more concerned to change us than to blame us.* After all, he died and rose in order that we might die to sin and be raised into a new life of transforming fellowship with him. His interest in our sin is only to deliver us from its guilt, to enable us to overcome it, and to transform us into his likeness.

And so Paul comes to his 'bottom line': 'The wages of sin is death, but the free gift of God is eternal life in Christ Jesus our Lord' (verse 23). Once more 'sin' ('the Sin') is personified. The apostle is once again talking about its power, not its guilt. Sin is a slave-master, but it is also a wage-paying employer. And the wages are paid in exact accord with the wage structure posted beside the tree of the knowledge of good and evil in the Garden of Eden: 'In the day that you eat of it you shall surely die' (Gen. 2:17). In biblical Hebrew emphasis is expressed not by italics or underlining but by repetition, and the divine wage structure in Eden was posted in heavily emphasized words: 'Dying you shall die!' Sin's final salary is 'death'—in all its dimensions: separation from God; separation from others; separation of body from soul; separation from our true destiny in glory; outer darkness, weeping and gnashing of teeth.

Paul is now bidding us not only to look back to the past days of our old lifestyle, or to consider our present transformation. He challenges us to look forward to the last day and to consider the final 'pay day.' Jesus Christ holds out a wonderful prospect to us in the gospel. While 'Sin' paid the 'wages' of 'death,' we are no longer its employees. We now belong to Christ; we are now destined for 'eternal life.' And what we are receiving is not 'wages' but 'the free gift of God.'

What motivation this is for us to meditate long and deep on Paul's teaching in this chapter, and to live as those who have died to sin and been raised to new life in Christ. We are under grace and not law; our lives are now marked by progress in holiness. We are already enjoying the beginnings of eternal life in Christ!

No wonder the great nineteenth-century Scottish church leader Thomas Chalmers thought that with respect to the transformation the gospel brings, Romans 6 is the most interesting chapter in the whole Bible!

20

Free from the Law

Or do you not know, brothers—for I am speaking to those who know the law—that the law is binding on a person only as long as he lives? 2 For a married woman is bound by law to her husband while he lives, but if her husband dies she is released from the law of marriage. 3 Accordingly, she will be called an adulteress if she lives with another man while her husband is alive. But if her husband dies, she is free from that law, and if she marries another man she is not an adulteress.

4 Likewise, my brothers, you also have died to the law through the body of Christ, so that you may belong to another, to him who has been raised from the dead, in order that we may bear fruit for God. 5 For while we were living in the flesh, our sinful passions, aroused by the law, were at work in our members to bear fruit for death. 6 But now we are released from the law, having died to that which held us captive, so that we serve in the new way of the Spirit and not in the old way of the written code.

7 What then shall we say? That the law is sin? By no means! Yet if it had not been for the law, I would not have known sin. For I would not have known what it is to covet if the law had not said, 'You shall not covet.' 8 But sin, seizing an opportunity through the commandment, produced in me all kinds of covetousness. For apart from the law, sin lies dead. 9 I was once alive apart from the law, but when the commandment came, sin came alive and I died. 10 The very commandment that promised life proved to be death to me. 11 For sin, seizing an opportunity through the commandment, deceived me and through it killed me. 12 So the law is holy, and the commandment is holy and righteous and good.

(Rom. 7:1-12)

Paul's words 'you are not under law but under grace' (6:14) may well have shaken some of the believers in Rome when they first heard his letter read to the church. Having defended his teaching on the law from criticism, was the apostle now deliberately inviting it? He was well aware that many Jewish Christians were already suspicious of his teaching. So what possessed him to say, 'you are not under law' (verse 14)?

Now he returns to address the question of the law more fully. The connection back to chapter 6 is signalled by the introductory 'Or.' This is not a new topic altogether, but a development and explanation of what he had already said. He is continuing to explain the implications for all believers, Jew or Gentile, of now being 'in Christ' and no longer being 'in Adam.'

Earlier he had claimed that rather than denigrate the law the gospel established it (3:31). In the early verses of the next chapter (8:1-4) he will return to that theme and demonstrate how his gospel does in fact 'uphold the law' (3:31). It is only in Christ and by the Spirit that the law is established.

But first he develops in detail what it means (and what it does not mean!) that believers are no longer 'under the law' (6:14).

MARRIAGE LAWS—NATURAL AND SPIRITUAL

Paul assumes that the Roman Christians are familiar with law and how it functions: 'the law is binding on a person only as long as he lives' (verse 1). This is a truism. Laws govern living human relationships; a person's death brings the law's authority over them to an end.

In verses 2-3 this principle is illustrated in the marriage relationship. When one partner dies, the legal bond of marriage ends. In the case of a married woman, for example, if her husband dies, she is now 'released from the law of marriage' (verse 2). While her husband is alive she is not 'free' (verse 3) to marry another man—that would constitute adultery. She is 'bound by law to her husband' (verse 2). But, if her husband dies, and 'she marries another man she is not an adulteress' (verse 3). She has been 'released from the law of marriage' to her first husband. The law neither binds her to the first husband nor condemns her for marrying the second husband.

All this is straightforward. But Paul's *application* of his illustration has caused many readers to take a second look (and perhaps a third!) at what he is saying.

The application is as follows: 'Likewise, my brothers, *you also have died to the law* through the body of Christ, *so that you may belong to another*, to him who has been raised from the dead, in order that we may bear fruit for God' (verse 4).

The problem? *In the illustration* it is the person who does not die (the wife) who is free to marry another. But *in the application* it seems to be the person who dies who is free to marry another 'likewise you have died to the law … that you may belong to another' (verse 4).

At this point interpreters have tended to adopt one of several views of what Paul is doing here:

(i) Unsympathetic readers of Paul have suggested that his illustration is at best awkward or at worst simply inept and a little confused. That, however, would be very unlike Paul. In addition, Tertius, his amanuensis (16:22), was listening to him very carefully; along with Timothy and others who may have been with them (16:21, 23). If they felt that Paul was confusing the issue they would surely have suggested he clarify his teaching.

(ii) Other readers, sympathetic to Paul, have taken the view that the illustration is not meant to be read as though it were an allegory with a point by point correspondence. The only point he is illustrating is that death ends the marriage bond.

(iii) Yet other readers have felt that it would be odd for Paul to make this point in such a complicated way if all he meant to say was that the binding character of the law on believers has come to an end. So there is a third possibility. Against the background of 5:12-21 perhaps his illustration should be applied in this way:

Illustration: In natural marriage:

- A woman's first husband dies
- Therefore: The woman is now free to marry another husband.

Application:

Formerly:

- By nature I was united to Adam (my 'first marriage'):
- But I died in Christ's death and my (marriage) union with Adam ended.

Therefore:

- In Christ, the 'law of marriage' to Adam is ended.

Now:

- But now, raised to life in Christ, I am free to marry again—the risen Christ has proposed to me, and I am now married to him.

Whether interpretation (ii) or (iii) is correct, in any event, chapter 7 displays a similar inner theological logic and application to chapter 6:

Principle:

In Christ we died and have been raised.

Outworking:

(i) Chapter 6: we died to sin
(ii) Chapter 7: we died to the law.

In chapter 6: By nature (*in Adam*) we were slaves of the Adamic master and sin reigned over us. But *in Christ* a death blow has been dealt to that old master (Adam) and we are delivered from the reign of sin to serve God in righteousness

In chapter 7: By nature (*in Adam*) we were 'under the law,' caught in an Adamic (and abusive) marriage from which we could not escape. But our union with Christ in his death was the death blow to that Adamic marriage. Now, raised into a new life in Christ, we are 'free' to enjoy a fruitful second marriage (verse 4)—to the same loving Christ who is now risen.

In our union with Adam we were 'in an abusive relationship.' Not now! The death of Christ took our first husband to the grave. As surely as he left behind his burial clothes, Christ left our first husband in the tomb and came forth in the resurrection to propose marriage to us.

There was a time when some British women referred to their husband colloquially as 'my old man'—the same expression Paul uses in 6:6 when he says that our 'old man ['self' ESV] was crucified with Christ'! In ourselves we had neither right nor power to escape from him. But dying in Christ we were delivered from that 'old man.' Now Christ has married us himself! Formerly in an 'abusive relationship,' now in Christ we 'bear fruit for God' (7:4)—a phrase that echoes Paul's earlier question in 6:21 ('what fruit were you getting at that time from the things of which you are now ashamed?').

In verse 5, Paul further explains the dynamics of this transition. In Adam, we were living in the flesh. Our marriage to him had an atmosphere dominated by the fall and corrupted by sin. The law 'bound us'; it had no power to release us. In fact it simply 'aroused' our sinful passions to produce death (verse 5). When 'Thou shalt not' meets 'Nobody tells me what to do!' this is the inevitable result. But now, no longer 'under the law' that held us 'captive,' no longer condemned to abuse in our former marriage to Adam, a wonderful transformation has taken place. Now 'we serve in the new way of the Spirit and not in the old way of the written code [*i.e.* the law]' (verse 6). For—as Paul will explain more fully in 8:9-11, to be 'in Christ' and to be indwelt by the Spirit are simply two ways of describing the same wonderful reality.

Woven into these words is a principle that Paul will later develop (in 8:3-4). Only in this 'new way of the Spirit' will the goals of the law be fulfilled—just as only in the second marriage envisaged are the goals of marriage fulfilled—harmony of companionship, satisfaction in union, and fertility in life.

NO MORE ABUSIVE MARRIAGE

Paul's marriage metaphor resonates with our contemporary culture. We are too familiar with stories—usually but not exclusively—of women 'locked' in abusive marriage relationships. This analogy to our spiritual condition is apt, as Paul goes on to show. Now in our second marriage we discover that the Lord Jesus is the most loving of all husbands. Yet, just as in the natural order, the impact, perhaps even the scars of our earlier abusive marriage may well remain with us until glory brings final healing. We need constantly to refresh ourselves in the knowledge that we are united to Christ and are in a new marriage bond with the gentlest and kindest of husbands. In this relationship we share one Spirit with him—Jesus' own Spirit (8:8-9). Participation in the new creation (2 Cor. 5:17) leads to a new way of life. The 'new way' of the Spirit stands in stark contrast with the 'old way.'

Yet the spectre of the past continues. Our first husband may be dead, but the impact of our former marriage to him lingers on. Increasingly, however, our new husband brings healing.

IS THE LAW SIN?

Under law, because of our union with Adam, we were in an abusive relationship. But does the fact that the law held us in that old marriage relationship mean that 'the law is sin' (verse 7)?

Paul repeats his now familiar emotive response: 'By no means!' (verse 7; cf. 6:2; 6:15). The idea that the law that forbids sin is itself sinful is self-contradictory. In fact 'the law is holy, and the commandment is holy and righteous and good' (verse 12). It is 'spiritual' (verse 14). He could hardly have put it more strongly.

But while not *causing* sin or being responsible for our sins, the law *reveals* what is sinful in us: 'if it had not been for the law, I would not have known sin.' For example, the law *against* coveting *reveals* coveting (verse 7); instead of destroying coveting its effect on my sinful heart may well be to produce more coveting (verse 8)!

The law functions like the sign 'Keep off the grass' might to a naughty eight-year-old boy. Had there been no sign he might not have been stimulated to walk on the grass in defiance of the sign. Similarly 'apart from the law, sin lies dead' (verse 8). It is dormant. Before we became Christians we were not deeply troubled by our sinfulness; we assumed our goodness compensated for it and perhaps even cancelled it. Paul himself understands this: 'I was alive ... but when the commandment came, sin came alive and I died' (verse 9).

To continue the illustration, when the little boy actually notices the sign (that was meant to prevent him from walking on the grass) instead of filling him with a desire to fulfil its purpose he does the exact opposite—he walks on the grass! In a similar way, the law promised 'life' but brought 'death' (verse 10). My perverse and sinful heart saw the sign 'Thou shalt not ...' and was deceived into thinking that 'But I will ...' was the way to satisfy myself. Thus 'the commandment that promised life' instead 'proved to be death.' What deception!—I lost what would have given ultimate pleasure (glorifying and enjoying God) by my determination to fulfil my own sinful pleasure. 'For sin, seizing an opportunity through the commandment, deceived me and through it killed me' (verse 11).

The situation then is this: it was not the good law that brought death. It was the sin embedded in my rebellious heart. The law in itself is good; but my sin, rebelling against the law, brought about death. Thus my sin is revealed for what it really is ('sin might be shown to be sin,' verse 13) and simply goes from bad to worse ('sinful beyond measure,' verse 13). It is not difficult to hear the echo of Genesis chapters 3, 4, and 5 in these words. The taking of the forbidden fruit eventually led to marital conflict, family alienation, and societal disintegration.

The conclusion of the matter—to this point—is that rather than being sinful, 'the law is holy, and the commandment is holy and righteous and good' (verse 12). There is no rejection of the law here!

Paul's explanation of his answer to the question 'Is the law sin?' has been quite straightforward. The law is 'by no means' sinful, 'Yet if it had not been for the law, I would not have known sin' (verse 7). The law has a catalytic effect on sinners while it remains pure and holy.

But Paul's explanation of this simple statement (in verses 7-13) brings us to one of the most debated issues in his letters.

At verse 7 there is a very marked transition from the use of the first person *plural* ('we' and 'our' in verses 5-6) to the first person *singular*. In the ESV translation of verses 7-24 there are some thirty references to 'I,' ten references to 'me,' and another seven to 'my.'

No other passage in Paul's correspondence is so densely 'first person singular.' Yet paradoxically the question frequently asked of this passage is: Who is this 'I'? Is the apostle thinking of himself here? Are we hearing the 'voice' of Paul the Jew, or Paul the Christian (and if so, what is his spiritual state?), or is he not talking about himself as an individual at all?

Nor is the question merely theoretical. The answer we give can have an important bearing on our understanding of the Christian life. But finding the answer is made more difficult because over the centuries interpreters equally committed to the inspiration and authority of Scripture have held differing interpretations.

THE PUZZLE OF THE 'I'

Older commentators on Romans 7:7-25 tended to adopt views based on specific statements in the passage that lent support to them.

Surveying interpretations, the most commonly held in the history of the church have been:

(i) Paul is speaking in dramatic form in the present tense about *his past experience as a non-Christian*—only a non-Christian would, for example, say that he was 'sold under sin' (verse 14). Only a non-regenerate person would confess, 'I know that nothing good dwells in me' (verse 18) and cry out 'wretched man that I am!' (verse 24).

(ii) Paul is speaking in the present tense about the experience of a 'backslidden' or 'carnal' Christian ('I am of the flesh' ['carnal,' KJV]) . Whether this was Paul himself or not, such a Christian (as used to be said) needs to 'get out of Romans 7 and into Romans 8!'

(iii) Paul is describing Christian experience with all the struggles for holiness it involves.

During the past hundred years probably the majority of scholarly commentators have tended to adopt a different approach to the passage:

(iv) Paul is not speaking directly about his own experience but adopting a 'voice' that represents a theological analysis. That said, there has not been universal agreement about exactly what 'voice' he is using. Perhaps the 'I' represents the story of Adam in Eden, or the story of redemption expressed in a personified way, or the experience of a Jew under the law, seen from the vantage point of the coming of the gospel. In any event, it is argued, Paul is not giving us a transcript of his own experience as a Christian.

Against the older standard Reformed interpretation of the passage that Paul is speaking as Christian believer, it is characteristically argued that he has just claimed Christians have been set free from sin (chapter 6), while here he says he is 'sold under sin' (verse 14). In addition it is said that he makes other statements that contrast too sharply with—indeed contradict—the picture of the Christian life painted in the surrounding chapters: 'I am of the flesh, sold under sin' (verse 14); 'I do the very thing I hate' (verse 15); 'I know that nothing good dwells in me' (verse 18); 'Wretched man that I am! Who will deliver me from this body of death?' (verse 24) are (it is argued) hardly the words of someone who has been 'set free from sin' (6:18) or is among those who have become 'more than conquerors through him who loved us' (8:37).

A further impetus for these more recent views has been the argument that the New Testament nowhere indicates that Paul himself experienced the Martin Luther-like, or John Bunyan-like conviction of sin described in 7:7-12. His claim that 'as to righteousness under the law' he was 'blameless' (Phil. 3:6) is often cited as absolute proof of this. So when he says here, 'I was once alive apart from the law, but when the commandment came, sin came alive and I died' (7:9), this cannot have been his personal testimony. His 'I' here must be some kind of 'theological I' representing a theological perspective rather than Pauline experience.

It is beyond our scope to discuss these views in great detail here.[1] Although various forms of the 'modern' interpretation have been fashionable (although not universal) in much scholarly literature on Romans, there are considerations that favour the 'classical reformed view' (that Paul is in important respects describing his own experience). These include: Christians in Rome might well understand that when Paul uses the first person singular ('I') he is not necessarily referring to himself *alone*. But would they have instinctively realized that he was *not speaking about himself at all* here? Is it likely that they would immediately have seen what it has taken readers of Romans almost two thousand years to discover?

The view adopted here can best be expressed by a series of affirmations, as follows.

- Paul is in fact describing experience which includes his own experience as a Christian.
- But he is also thinking *theologically* about himself from one particular perspective.
- Perhaps the best way to interpret Romans 7:14-25 is that what is said here is *true* of Paul, but it is not the *whole truth* about him.

We will consider these verses in two stages, the first in the present chapter:

[1] Different views are represented in the commentaries listed in the section 'For Further Reading' at the end of this volume. Versions of the more 'modern' view can be found in the works of William Hendricksen and John R. W. Stott. A version of the 'classical' Augustinian view is expounded in the commentary by John Murray.

STAGE ONE

In 7:7-13 Paul appears to be speaking about his own past experience—although it is by no means unique. It is often claimed that the Paul who describes himself prior to his conversion in these terms: 'as to righteousness under the law, blameless' (Phil. 3:6) could not also have described himself in the words of Romans 7:7-13.

But the Rich Young Ruler who asked Jesus what he needed to do to have eternal life (Mark 10:17-22) could probably have written Philippians 3:6 as well as Romans 7:6-13. Neither he nor Paul regarded himself as sinlessly perfect. But like many commandment-honouring religious people they nevertheless thought of themselves as 'blameless' (Phil. 3:6)—not wretched sinners but basically good people, who had never strayed from God's commandments. The Rich Young Ruler believed he had kept them from his youth (Mark 10:20).

But if either the Young Ruler or Saul of Tarsus were to come to faith they needed to be disabused of this superficial view of themselves—or in the language of our fathers, be 'convicted of sin.' Jesus performed that ministry himself in the case of the Young Ruler. Paul is describing his own version of a similar experience.

According to 7:7-8 it seems the Spirit used the same commandment (against coveting) in Saul as Jesus had employed to convict the Rich Young Ruler of the sinfulness of his heart by telling him to sell everything and give the proceeds to the poor. The young man discovered that he had, after all, *not* kept that commandment from his youth (Mark 10:20). He was 'disheartened' and 'went away sorrowful' (Mark 10:20-22). It seems he was *convicted*; but he was not *converted*.

The experience of Saul of Tarsus may seem to be less obvious, but what is striking is that the confession in verses 7-11 indicates that the same commandment also challenged his own view of himself. That is not to say that he necessarily analyzed his experience in this way *at the time.* Most of us reflect on the shape of our conversion only in retrospect. But Paul's words here suggest that there was more to his conversion than the crisis event on the Damascus Road.

It is worthwhile exploring this a little.

CLUES TO CONVERSION?

Several clues embedded in the New Testament help us to piece together what may be behind these words in Romans 7.

As a young man Saul of Tarsus was not only religiously self-sufficient, but superior. In fact Philippians 3:4-6 suggests this was his goal, as does Galatians 1:14 where Paul says 'I was advancing in Judaism beyond many of my own age among my people' (Gal. 1:14). 'Many' may well indicate Paul's embarrassment as a Christian at the memory of days when he was seeking to advance beyond *everyone* his own age! But then Saul of Tarsus encountered Stephen. He was 'full of the Spirit and of wisdom ... full of faith and of the Holy Spirit ... full of grace and power' (Acts 6:3, 5, 8)—the very *antithesis* of Saul, and a living model of the grace that Saul lacked.

One particular Jerusalem synagogue (or synagogue group) took it upon itself to lead the opposition against Stephen. Those who did so, 'belonged to the synagogue of the Freedmen ... and of the Cyrenians, and of the Alexandrians, and of those from Cilicia and Asia.' They soon discovered that 'they could not withstand the wisdom and the Spirit with which he was speaking' (Acts 6:9-10).

The details of this 'ethnic congregation' may cause our eyes to glaze over. But the reference to 'Cilicia' is, surely, significant. For Saul came from *Tarsus*; and Tarsus was in Cilicia. Since it is in this context he makes his first appearance in Acts (Acts 7:58), this was almost certainly the synagogue to which he would have belonged from the early days when he was first 'brought up in this city [Jerusalem]' and 'educated at the feet of Gamaliel according to the strict manner of the law of our fathers, zealous for God ...' (Acts 22:3).

The story of Stephen ends with his lifeless stone-broken body lying on the ground. Saul stands nearby:

> And the witnesses laid down their garments at the feet of a young man named Saul. And as they were stoning Stephen, he called out, 'Lord Jesus, receive my spirit' ... And Saul approved of his execution ... Devout men buried Stephen and made great lamentation over him. But Saul was ravaging the church, and entering house after house, he dragged off men and women and committed them to prison ... But Saul, still breathing threats and murder against the disciples of the Lord, went to the high priest and asked him

> for letters to the synagogues at Damascus, so that if he found any belonging to the Way, men or women, he might bring them bound to Jerusalem. Now as he went on his way, he approached Damascus, and suddenly a light from heaven shone around him. And falling to the ground he heard a voice saying to him, 'Saul, Saul, why are you persecuting me?' (Acts 7:58–8:3; 9:1-4).

Did the witnesses lay their garments 'at the feet of ... Saul' (Acts 7:58) because he was the ringleader of the opposition to Stephen? He certainly approved of his stoning.

Why then did Saul of Tarsus become so furious—by his own testimony, *the most furious* (Phil. 3:6)? It was not, as is sometimes assumed, because he was a Pharisee (Phil. 3:5). Nicodemus, and presumably his friend Joseph of Arimathea, were Pharisees and had not persecuted the Lord Jesus. Even more significantly, Saul's own theology professor, the learned Gamaliel (Acts 22:3), had urged the Sanhedrin not to persecute the church (Acts 5:33-39). Some other force was at work in Saul's heart.

When we join up these various dots on the pages of the New Testament a picture begins to emerge of a young man, fiercely driven and confident in his religious superiority. He had, presumably, never been in a position in which he 'could not withstand the wisdom and the Spirit' with which any of his contemporaries spoke. He knew no contemporary whose gifts, religious advance, and zeal surpassed his. But he now encountered a contemporary marked by a different, higher, better order of religion—in quality of life, in ability in the Scriptures, in the possession of the graces, in a life lived in the Spirit promised in God's new covenant. Stephen was a living embodiment of the Sermon on the Mount—his righteousness exceeded that of the scribes and Pharisees (Matt. 5:20). He possessed everything Saul lacked but wanted—and, yes, we might say '*coveted*.' And even in the hour in which Saul was approving of his destruction he heard Stephen pray, Jesus-like, 'Lord, do not hold this sin against them' (Acts 7:60—was Paul remembering that prayer when he wrote 2 Cor. 5:19?). This man had everything Saul of Tarsus aspired to; everything he wasn't; everything he might covet. When such a believer is encountered the non-believer has only two options—ask, seek, knock, and join; or seek to destroy (even if by slow and sophisticated means).

This, then, may well be the best way to understand when, how, and why the commandment against coveting is the one to which Paul draws attention: He thought he was 'alive' but now 'the law came'; now sin 'came alive' and Paul died (verse 9). But men like Saul do not go gently into the night; they rage. Many a sweet-spirited Christian since has experienced the same viciousness of opposition that Saul directed towards the early Christians—an antagonism out of all proportion to the simplicity and grace in which they (like Stephen) have borne witness to their Saviour.

There is, therefore, no necessary tension between Paul's reflections on his past in Philippians 3:3-6 and the words of Romans 7:7-13 being a reflection of his experience. In fact the Saul of the former passage needed to become the Saul of the latter.

The picture that is now being built up from these verses is that the revelation of Christ on the Damascus Road took place in a larger context of a divine work of conviction that was already underway in Saul of Tarsus—he was finding it hard 'to kick against the goads' (Acts 26:14). But that simply inflamed his rage.

If, in the light of a gracious Christian's life and testimony, the law revealed its power to unmask him in this way, Paul now maintains it has the same power still. When, in the power of the Spirit, God's law comes to a Christian believer, his or her sin is exposed. It cannot be any other way. And when that takes place, what Paul writes in the rest of Romans 7 becomes a reality.

What we have therefore in Romans 7:14-25 follows the pattern we have already seen established. In Adam we were in bondage to sin. In Christ we are set free from its guilt and reign, but we are not yet free from its presence. That inevitably leads to an inner tension. We are, in Christ, free from the law's condemnation of our sin. But since we are not yet delivered from the presence of sin, whenever we view our lives in the light of the law, the tension Paul describes here is surely the inevitable result.

To this tension we must turn in the next study.

21

The Good Reveals the Bad

Did that which is good, then, bring death to me? By no means!
It was sin, producing death in me through what is good, in order
that sin might be shown to be sin, and through the commandment
might become sinful beyond measure. [14] *For we know that the*
law is spiritual, but I am of the flesh, sold under sin. [15] *For I do*
not understand my own actions. For I do not do what I want,
but I do the very thing I hate. [16] *Now if I do what I do not*
want, I agree with the law, that it is good. [17] *So now it is no*
longer I who do it, but sin that dwells within me. [18] *For I know*
that nothing good dwells in me, that is, in my flesh. For I have
the desire to do what is right, but not the ability to carry it out.
[19] *For I do not do the good I want, but the evil I do not want is*
what I keep on doing. [20] *Now if I do what I do not want, it is*
no longer I who do it, but sin that dwells within me.

[21] *So I find it to be a law that when I want to do right, evil*
lies close at hand. [22] *For I delight in the law of God, in my*
inner being, [23] *but I see in my members another law waging war*
against the law of my mind and making me captive to the law of
sin that dwells in my members. [24] *Wretched man that I am! Who*
will deliver me from this body of death? [25] *Thanks be to God*
through Jesus Christ our Lord! So then, I myself serve the law
of God with my mind, but with my flesh I serve the law of sin.
(Rom. 7:13-25)

Paul has answered the question—perhaps criticism—'If we needed to die to the law, to be released from it, then this suggests there is something sinister about the law. Your view virtually suggests that the law itself is sin, doesn't it?' In reply he has established that the law is 'good' and not 'sin' (verse 12). But it reveals sin.

But that answer simply raised another question: 'Did that which is good, then, bring death to me?' (verse 13). Once again he recoils instinctively: 'By no means!' (cf. 6:1, 15; 7:7). He has demonstrated that the law is both holy and good. It is sin—the breach of the law—that is perverse and heinous. *That* is what the law exposes—sin in its utter sinfulness. Just as there is matter that festers in the heat of the sun, so it is with our sin under the searching rays of the holy and righteous and good commandment of God.

Paul now goes on to explain the function of the law in verses 14-25. What he says is not in itself difficult to follow, but it is especially at this point that discussions about the 'problem' of the identity of the 'I' in this chapter have reached a critical point.

THE ELUSIVE 'I'

If you were to ask a group of theological students 'What is the key issue and problem in Romans 7?' they would almost certainly respond 'the identity of the "I".' It is a major feature in commentaries, scholarly articles and doctoral dissertations. But we must not lose sight of the fact that *this was not Paul's problem*! We need to be careful that we do not allow this (understandable) question to divert us from what was central in his thinking at this point in the letter, namely the role and function of the law.

Paul's main point is that in Christ we have died to the law—but the law is not sin, and the law has not died; it remains good, holy, righteous, and spiritual (verse 12). And that has implications for us.

When we grasp this—that throughout the chapter Paul is speaking about the ongoing character and function of the law—then his teaching becomes clearer to us.

In verses 7-13 Paul had spoken of himself (as we have maintained) in the *past* tense. Now there is a shift to the *present* tense which is consistently maintained throughout the rest of the passage.

There are several good reasons for thinking that this use of the present tense is not merely a rhetorical device but indicates Paul is describing his own experience.

(i) *Positively*: this is the most natural way to read the shift from the past tense (verses 7-13) to the present tense as the long history of interpretation tends to demonstrate, even if the exact nature of that experience is debated.

(ii) *Negatively*: the dominant modern interpretations have, by and large, taken two millennia to develop and suggest that for a period of two thousand years the church has failed to see what modern scholars seem to regard as now clearly demonstrated. This seems unlikely.

(iii) *Negatively*: the dominant modern interpretations demand a degree of literary and even academic sophistication greater than what Paul could expect from readers in churches he had never visited.

(iv) *Positively*: a nuanced expression of the classical interpretation takes account of what Paul is doing in this and the surrounding chapters. It is consistent with the fact that this chapter focusses on the nature and function of the law, and aptly describes the experience of the believer in the light of its spirituality and righteous perfection.

PARALLELS

In the previous chapter we saw that there are parallels in the theological structures of chapters 6, 7, and 8. In chapter 6 we learned that in Christ we have died to the reign of sin. But since we are not yet sinless, we must continue to resist its influence. Later, in chapter 8 we will learn that we are free from condemnation, and yet we continue to live in a world that is under that condemnation. Here, then, in chapter 7, Paul is teaching that in Christ we have also died to the law. Nevertheless, neither he nor we are perfect according to the standards of the law. Thus, when we view ourselves in its light the presence and power of indwelling sin is revealed. It cannot be otherwise. Hence the sense of tension in what Paul says about himself in the second half of Romans 7.

So Romans 7:14-25 is a *real description* of the Christian life. But it is a *partial picture*. It is not the whole truth. For the 'whole truth' involves not only these verses but the entire section 3:21–8:39. This is Paul's self-analysis of his life in the light of the law; it is not everything that can be said about the Christian life (*that* at minimum requires both Romans 6 and Romans 8).

Whenever Christians view themselves exclusively from the perspective of the law it is inevitable that internal contradictions will be exposed. Thus there are statements here that *taken on their own, abstracted from the whole passage*, give the impression that the speaker is not a Christian. These include: 'I am of the flesh, sold under sin ... I do not do what I want, but I do the very thing I hate ... nothing good dwells in me ... I have the desire to do what is right, but not the ability to carry it out ... the evil I do not want is what I keep on doing ... Wretched man that I am ... with my flesh I serve the law of sin' (verses 14, 15, 18, 19, 24, 25).

Such statements do not seem to sit comfortably alongside 'having been set free from sin [we] have become slaves of righteousness' (6:18), and 'the law of the Spirit of life has set you free in Christ Jesus from the law of sin and death' (8:2) and 'the righteous requirements of the law' are 'fulfilled in us who walk ... according to the Spirit' (8:4).

But there are other statements in this passage which do sound like the words of a Christian believer. Paul recognizes not only the spirituality of the law (verse 14) but distinguishes between himself and the presence of indwelling sin (verses 17, 20). He says 'I delight in the law of God' (verse 22). In addition, he not only recognizes his personal sinfulness (verse 18—something that does not seem to have overly troubled Saul of Tarsus, Phil. 3:6), and at the same time expresses his desire to fulfil the law (verse 19, 22). In addition he specifically confesses Jesus Christ (verse 25a) as the one who will 'deliver me from this body of death' (verse 24).

These are apparently contradictory words. But that is precisely the point. It is not that Scripture is contradicting itself, but that there is a deep contradiction in Paul the apostle. The strands that have led readers to conclude either 'This is not Paul the believer,' or, alternatively, '*Only* a believer could say this,' are both present. But rather than allow one strand to overwhelm the other, the key to understanding these verses is to recognize that both are present when Paul sees himself through the lenses of the law. There is a contradiction in him, and it will remain all the days of his life.

This, however, should not be misunderstood. Romans 7:14-25 may describe Paul the believer (and ourselves); but it is only a *partial* description. He is not here describing an uninterrupted state of mind. He has other perspectives on his new life in Christ. This one does not negate them. Nor do they negate this one. But so long as he experiences these radically contradictory realities—*Christ dwells in Paul* and *Sin continues to dwell in Paul*—so long will this experience be part and parcel of his Christian experience.

UNDERSTANDING PAUL'S SOLILOQUY

We can express what Paul is saying then in a series of propositions that lead to a final conclusion.

In Christ, believers 'died to the law through the body of Christ' (7:4).

(i) But the law itself has not died; it continues its holy function.

(ii) The law's function is to forbid and reveal sin.

(iii) Although we have died to the law, it continues to reveal our sin.

(iv) The law therefore has a double effect:

(a) It reveals—even to an excruciating degree—that while I have died to the dominion of sin in Christ I am far from being free from the presence of sin in myself, and,

(b) This inevitably means that if I see myself in the mirror of God's holy, righteous, good, and spiritual law I will inevitably lament my sin and long more for Christ and the final deliverance from sin that he will bring.

It is surely not too difficult to imagine someone describing such an experience:

> I know the law is spiritual—and when I see myself in its light, and especially when I remember Jesus' teaching in the Sermon on the Mount (Matt. 5:17-48), God's law seems to reveal how unspiritual and unholy, and unrighteous I am in myself.
>
> As a result the law of God makes me feel I am still carnal, as though I were still paying a mortgage to sin. I am doing things I don't want to do, and I hate myself for doing them.
>
> I know that God's law is meant to promote what is good and righteous in my life, and I want that for myself; but it is not what I always do. Is it any wonder then that there are times when I see myself in the mirror of the law and feel wretched?
>
> I draw what may seem to be a strange conclusion from this. It may sound like an excuse, but it is not. In Christ I have been delivered from the *reign* of sin. But I have not yet been delivered from the *presence* of sin. Sin is still present and operative in me. I

can maybe put it this way: it is as though sin is doing in me what I myself don't want to do!

God help me! When I see myself in the light of the perfect law of God I feel there is nothing good in me by nature. I want to do what is right, but I do what is wrong instead. It feels as though the sin in me is making me do what I don't want to do! Why, just when I want to do the right thing, does evil always seem to be waiting at the door to get me?

And yet, the truth is, I love God's law and I know it is right and good. I understand that it is spiritual. That is it. That is why it makes me feel there is an unholy war going on inside me. Sin feels like a kind of Trojan horse within that wants to take over the whole city of my life. I confess that there are times when I feel my life as a whole doesn't seem to be in the same place as my mind! Sometimes I find myself almost overwhelmed with my sense of sinfulness and crying out to God, 'God, can somebody set me free from this "body of death"?'—because honestly that's what it feels like.

But it is just then that—by God's grace—I remember that I am in Christ. It is true that I am still sinful. *But that is not the whole truth about me!* Sometimes I almost forget who I really am. But when I do remember I find myself shouting out, 'Thank you, Lord! Thank you for Jesus Christ! I know that he will set me free!'

So, when I think about all this, here is where I am:

I really do love the Lord with my heart and soul and mind, and I want to serve him with all my strength. I know that's who I am in Christ.

But I also know that sin continues to indwell me. I am not yet fully or finally delivered from this 'body of death.'

And so long as that is the case, I know that this will be true of me: 'with my flesh I serve the law of sin; but with my mind I serve the law of God' (verse 25).

TWO OBSERVATIONS

Two comments are worth making here:

1. An important key to understanding this whole section is remembering that we are living constantly in the outworking of Romans 5 and 6 and 7 and 8—not just one of those chapters. We have to read them in sequence, but what they describe is a single reality rather than a series of sequential experiences. We do not move in a straight line through these chapters as though we experience chapter 5 and then chapter 6 and then, sometime afterwards, chapter

7, and perhaps finally we manage to 'get into Romans 8.' Rather they are all true of us, all of the time, even if we experience particular elements of them at various times.

What is being expressed here in this distinctive way is that whenever we see ourselves from the perspective of the law *alone* we are bound to sense the 'not yet' dimension to the salvation we have 'already' experienced. We are, as Luther insisted, *simul justus et peccator*—'at one and the same time justified and yet a sinner.' We experience the continuing down-drag of sin, and the frustration with self this produces even while we are new men and women in Christ. To follow up on Paul's marriage metaphor at the beginning of the chapter, we still bear the marks of our former abusive marriage. We are loved by our second husband, the Lord Jesus; his Holy Spirit bathes us in his love (5:5). And yet at the same time we have not fully or finally escaped the effects of our abusive marriage to our first husband.

No wonder then if there are times when Paul—and we too—long for the deliverance only Christ can give (verses 24-25). But it has not yet arrived. And until it does, the tensions of the self-assessment in verse 25b, and this apparent contradiction, will remain true until we are finally delivered from the body of death—which, thank God, we will be one day (7:25; cf. 8:21-25). Until then there will be moments, even seasons, in life when we will be more conscious of Romans 7 than we are of Romans 5, 6, and 8 (just as at other times we may be more conscious of the reality expressed in chapter 5 or chapter 6 or chapter 8).

It is precisely then that we need to remember that all four of these chapters, not just one of them, describe our present experience in Christ.

Thus while we rejoice in the knowledge that we have 'died to the law through the body of Christ,' until sin dies in us that same law will expose the fact that while we are free from sin's dominion over us we are not yet free from its presence in us.

2. The effort to harmonize everything Paul says in these verses may be a misstep. Almost inevitably it will lead to downplaying some statements. Because we are committed to a high view of Scripture's inspiration and inerrancy we may feel a certain discomfort in thinking that the Bible contains such 'contradictions.' But that

ceases to be a problem when we understand that in fact Scripture is not contradicting itself. The contradictions are in us:

- *Jesus Christ dwells in me the Christian* (Gal. 2:20; Col. 1:27).
- *Sin also dwells in me the Christian* (Rom. 7:17, 20).

This being the case it should not surprise us if there are times when the Christian believer feels, with Augustine, 'In your eyes I have become a problem to myself, and that is my sickness.'[1]

THE RESOLUTION

So long as we view ourselves through the microscope of the law we will see, sense, and feel this contradiction between what we are in Christ and what we are in ourselves. But this will have the blessed effect on us that it did on Paul—making us long to be free from indwelling sin, and leading us to thank God that one day Christ will finally deliver us from 'this body of death.'

But for the moment, the reign of grace (5:12-21) is being worked out in the Adamic domain that has been under the reign of sin. So long as this remains true, from time to time this sense of inner contradiction will flare up and we will say with Paul 'I do not understand my own actions' (verse 15). For who can take in all the ramifications of Christ indwelling us while sin simultaneously continues to indwell us? That double reality is surely a massive 'ought not to be'! But it is. And that is precisely the point, and the best explanation of Paul's teaching: we are in Christ, and yet 'what ought not to be'—indeed, what we ourselves do not want to be—remains.

In Romans 6 Paul had viewed Christian experience from the perspective of 'already' being delivered from the dominion of sin but 'not yet' being free from its presence, and therefore having to battle against its presence in his life.

Now in Romans 7 Paul is looking at his Christian experience from the perspective of 'already' having died to the law, but 'not yet' being finally delivered from the indwelling sin that the law continues to expose and condemn. There are moments of high emotion when all he can say is that he longs to be free from the 'body of death.'

[1] *Saint Augustine: Confessions*, translated with an introduction and notes by Henry Chadwick (Oxford: Oxford University Press, 1991), 208.

Only then, when Jesus Christ finally delivers him to glory, will his whole being harmonize with his renewed mind. Only then will a life of sinless perfection be 'easy.'

Thank God, Jesus Christ will deliver him—and us too! But until that day dawns, let us share Paul's resolution: *So then, I myself serve the law of God with my mind, but with my flesh I serve the law of sin.*

But one day, by God's grace, *in Christ and through the power of his Spirit, I will indeed 'be saved to sin no more.'*[1]

[1] From the hymn 'There is a fountain filled with blood' by William Cowper. (1731–1800).

22

The Un-condemned Life

There is therefore now no condemnation for those who are in
Christ Jesus. [2] *For the law of the Spirit of life has set you free in*
Christ Jesus from the law of sin and death. [3] *For God has done*
what the law, weakened by the flesh, could not do. By sending his
own Son in the likeness of sinful flesh and for sin, he condemned
sin in the flesh, [4] *in order that the righteous requirement of the*
law might be fulfilled in us, who walk not according to the flesh
but according to the Spirit. [5] *For those who live according to*
the flesh set their minds on the things of the flesh, but those who
live according to the Spirit set their minds on the things of the
Spirit. [6] *For to set the mind on the flesh is death, but to set the*
mind on the Spirit is life and peace. [7] *For the mind that is set on*
the flesh is hostile to God, for it does not submit to God's law;
indeed, it cannot. [8] *Those who are in the flesh cannot please*
God. [9] *You, however, are not in the flesh but in the Spirit, if in*
fact the Spirit of God dwells in you. Anyone who does not have
the Spirit of Christ does not belong to him. [10] *But if Christ is*
in you, although the body is dead because of sin, the Spirit is
life because of righteousness. [11] *If the Spirit of him who raised*
Jesus from the dead dwells in you, he who raised Christ Jesus
from the dead will also give life to your mortal bodies through
his Spirit who dwells in you.

(Rom. 8:1-11)

The famous Scottish preacher Alexander Whyte (1836–1921) warned his congregation against the mantra of the 'Higher Life' movement, that struggling Christians 'need to get out of Romans 7 and into Romans 8: 'You will not "get out of Romans 7 into Romans 8" as long as I am your minister!' he affirmed.

It was shrewd advice. But, as we have seen, it might have been even better to have said, 'You'll not get out of Romans 5, 6, 7, or 8 as long as I am your minister!' These chapters need to be taken together. Their repeated refrain suggests that they are unfolding various dimensions of our union with Christ: 'through our Lord Jesus Christ' (5:11); 'through Jesus Christ our Lord' (5:21); 'in Christ Jesus' (6:11); 'in Christ Jesus our Lord' (6:23); 'through Jesus Christ our Lord' (7:25); 'in Christ Jesus' (8:1); 'in Christ Jesus our Lord' (8:39). We are no longer in Adam, under wrath, in bondage to sin, and condemned by the law. In Christ we are *already* free, and we will ultimately be delivered from all opposition and even death itself. But until Christ returns there remains a *not yet* dimension to the Christian life.

The New Testament scholar Oscar Cullmann famously illustrated this by means of the events that brought to a conclusion World War II (1939–45). Between 'D-Day' (marked by the Normandy Landings on 6 June 1944, the decisive moment in the war) and 'V-Day' (the day when the war actually ceased), war and casualties continued—even although the outcome was certain. So it is in the Christian life. We live between God's D-Day (the death, burial, resurrection, ascension of Christ, and the Day of Pentecost) and his V-Day (Christ's final return when all things will be made new).[1]

As he continues to expound the significance of no longer being in Adam but living in Christ, Paul now turns his attention to further dimensions of the Christian life.

ALREADY, BUT NOT YET

Although we are *not yet* fully or finally delivered from the entail of Adam's sin, we are *already* fully justified. Nothing can reverse this, since we are justified in the risen Christ and his status is irreversible (4:25; he 'will never die again,' 6:9). Because of this it is certain that we will be 'glorified' (8:30). As Paul will argue, nothing can destroy our justified status because nothing can separate us from God's love in Christ (8:39).

Paul now continues to explore the theme of our union with Christ. 'There is therefore now no condemnation for those who are

[1] O. Cullmann, *Christ and Time*, 3rd ed., tr. Floyd V. Filson (London: SCM Press, 1951), xix, 84, 87, 141-42.

in Christ Jesus. For the law of the Spirit of life *in Christ Jesus* has set you free from the law of sin and death' (verses 1-2).

Here we might have expected Paul to say that there is no condemnation for us because of the work of Christ on the cross *for us*. But he gives a different reason. There is 'no condemnation' for us because of the work of the Holy Spirit *within us*.

But it is not the work of the Spirit *within us*, but the work of Christ *outside of us* that constitutes the basis for our justification. So what is Paul's logic here?

When he says that there is 'no *condemnation*' he is not referring to the *verdict* God pronounces on us in Christ ('not guilty,' 'justified'), but to the *prison sentence* that would follow a guilty verdict. Justification frees us from the guilt of sin; but in addition the Spirit enables us progressively to experience the implications of our new status—we are not condemned to a life in prison, in bondage to sin, self, and Satan. We are now 'free.'

Paul is not reneging on what he said in 7:14-25. The 'contradiction' we continue to experience is real; but it is neither the whole story nor the final story. We will be delivered from 'this body of death' (7:24). But even now in Christ there are additional dimensions to our experience. Romans 7 is not the only chapter in our lives. It sits alongside chapters 5, 6, and 8.

The Christian life is marked by freedom in the Spirit. It is not a life of bondage. True, the 'law of sin' (7:25) continues to operate in our flesh. But it is not the only 'law' at work. Some commentators understand 'law' here as a reference to the law of Moses. But it is more natural to understand it as 'a principle,' as in 7:21 ('I find it to be a law'). The law of the Spirit of life in Christ sets us free from the law of sin and death.

Think of a giant plane rumbling along the runway with hundreds of people on board, weighed down by the fuel it is carrying (not to mention the hundreds of 23-kg bags on board). Does it reach its cruising altitude of 33,000 feet because mysteriously the 'law of gravity' ceases to function? No. It does so because the laws of aerodynamics are called into service. These do not abolish the law of gravity; but they 'overcome' it; they 'set free' the plane to fly.

So it is with the Christian: 'For the law of the Spirit of life has set you free in Christ Jesus from the law of sin and death' (verse 2).

The law of Moses could not accomplish this (verse 3). Paul is not denigrating the law. While it was given to direct obedience it could not empower it. And in addition, because of our sinfulness, the law is 'weakened.' It cannot effect obedience; and furthermore it cannot give life to those who are dead in trespasses and sins (Eph. 2:1). But now, in Christ, God has not only 'condemned sin in the flesh' (verse 3); he has also given us the Spirit of Christ the perfect law-keeper, to accomplish in us what the law commanded but could never effect (verse 4).

Commentators who adopt the view that in the previous chapter Paul is *not* describing his experience as a Christian point to these words as confirmation. They are said to stand in stark contrast to 'with my flesh I serve the law of sin' (7:25). But we have suggested that believers do in fact experience this very real contradiction. The resolution of the issue lies in this formula:

- The Christian is no longer 'in the flesh' but 'in the Spirit' (8:9).
- But the flesh remains in the Christian.
- The forceful language of the implied imperative in 8:13 that those who are 'in the Spirit' and not 'in the flesh' should 'put to death the deeds of the body' confirms that this contradiction does in fact continue and that left to itself the flesh in its own nature serves the law of sin (7:25).

How could it be otherwise for anyone in whom the Lord of glory *and* remaining sin dwell simultaneously? But what Paul is underlining now is that while the two sides of this contradiction are *opposite*, they are not *equal*. The flesh remains in us, but we are no longer 'in the flesh but in the Spirit' (verse 9).

This is so because, in order to 'condemn sin in the flesh,' God sent his Son 'in the likeness of sinful flesh and for sin' (8:3). 'Likeness' here (*homoiōma*—used earlier in 1:23; 5:14; 6:5) suggests *similarity*, but not *identity*. It is used here in order to carefully delineate the nature of the incarnation. Paul does not say that the Son assumed *sinful* flesh. 'Likeness' here is not 'identity.' But had Paul said that he came 'in the likeness of flesh' we would be left wondering if the incarnation was real. Thus his careful choice of language. In Jesus the last Adam, God did not begin again with a *creatio ex nihilo* (creation out of nothing), for then Christ would not really have been one of us (see Heb. 2:10-18). He began with the seed (*sperma*) of David. He was 'descended from David according to the flesh' (1:3). Nor could he have begun again with someone with a sinful human nature, since such a person would die because of their own sins. He would not be able to offer himself as a substitute for others.

God's Son took genuine human nature, our human nature (sin apart) in the womb of the virgin Mary (Luke 1:35). He was therefore liable to temptation (as was Adam). He experienced this fallen world in our frail flesh. One with us he was qualified to act for us.

These words confirm what is known as the Definition of Chalcedon (written in AD 451). The incarnation did not involve mixing together deity and humanity. Rather, two natures, divine and human, were united in the one divine person of the Son of God 'without confusion, without change, without division, without separation; the distinction of natures being in no way annulled by the union.'

But although Jesus was like Adam (in the sense that he was created without sin), in sharp contrast to the first man, Jesus the second man was not placed in a garden of great beauty and fruitfulness, surrounded by an animal kingdom subject to him. The last Adam, God's Son, faced the direct onslaught of the devil in the wilderness where wild beasts surrounded him (Mark 1:12-13). His initial victory there was later completed in his death and resurrection, in which God condemned sin in his flesh. For us God 'made him to be sin who knew no sin' (2 Cor. 5:21). In Christ's atonement sin's penalty was paid, and our guilt dealt with; sin was judged and condemned, and Satan was disarmed of his weapon of guilt. In his resurrection Christ drew the sting of death. Consequently there is no condemnation remaining for those who are in Christ. True, we battle against indwelling sin in our flesh, as well as the world and the devil. But we do so as freed men and women, not as prisoners. And now that the risen Christ has given us his own Spirit, just as he enabled him to fulfil the law's demands, he will help us progressively to do so.

Thus the point Paul had made earlier in passing is fully vindicated. The gospel sets us free from the condemnation of the law.

But it does not eliminate the law. In fact it establishes it (3:31). In Christ we are set free from the condemnation of the law in order to live a law-fulfilling life of new obedience through the ministry of the Spirit. Already justified, we also experience 'no condemnation' as we 'walk not according to the flesh but according to the Spirit' (verse 4).

TWO MINDSETS

This contrast (even contradiction), between the old pattern of life and the new, between the flesh and the Spirit, between death and life, is now worked out in detail, in terms of two settled attitudes or mindsets—two tendencies in the way we think, and in the instincts that are developed in us (verses 5-8).

These mindsets function like magnets. The mind of the flesh is naturally drawn to the influence of the flesh and the Adamic world. In sharp contrast, those who 'walk … according to the Spirit' (verse 4) and have the mind of the Spirit have instincts that are drawn to what pleases Christ. The mind of the flesh wears the marks of death because it is riddled with our enmity with God. It is 'hostile to God' and unsubmissive to his law; indeed it is incapable of submitting to it (verse 7). The flesh can never please God (verse 8); it serves the law of sin (7:25). The 'mind of the Spirit,' however, breathes spiritual air, and leads to life and peace (verse 6b). Paul had earlier described it thus: 'I myself serve the law of God with my mind' (7:25).

Paul—like every believer—is no longer 'in the flesh' (verse 9). But the flesh is still in Paul. Regeneration is not yet glorification. Sin remains in us. And so long as that is true there will be what the *Westminster Confession* describes as 'a continual and irreconcilable war; the flesh lusting against the Spirit, and the Spirit against the flesh.'[1] But the battalions are not equal. The law of the Spirit of life sets the believer free from the down-drag of the law of sin and death. But notice that Paul does *not* say that it sets us free *here and now* from the *presence* of sin and death.

The Spirit of Christ indwelling the believer thus overcomes sin's gravitational pull. We are no longer 'in the flesh but in the Spirit' (verse 9). Paul unpacks what this means in stages:

[1] *The Confession of Faith*, XIII.ii.

1. This is true 'if the Spirit of God dwells in you' (verse 9). Here is a further dimension to the new identity which is ours in Christ. To be 'in the flesh' is to be 'in Adam,' to be an enemy of God, to be outside of his family, to be under the tyranny of sin and Satan and condemned by the law. But to be in the Spirit is to be 'in Christ,' to live in superabundant grace in his kingdom (5:12-21), and to be set free from the dominion of sin (6:1-23) and the condemnation of the law (7:1-6; 8:1-4). Believers belong to a new order of reality, a 'new creation' (2 Cor. 5:17).

2. This is *always* true, and true of *every* Christian. For 'anyone who does not have the Spirit of Christ does not belong to him' (verse 9).

Here Paul identifies the Spirit as the 'Spirit of God' and as 'the Spirit of Christ.' The Holy Spirit is 'of' the Son just as truly and fully as he is 'of God' (in this context, the Father). Although we cannot penetrate into the fullness of what this means, it indicates the wonder of the inner-trinitarian relationships: the Father and the Son are intimately and similarly related to the Spirit, and on his part the Spirit is intimately related to both the Father and the Son. This is the impenetrable light of the being of God the Trinity. But it is the light in which we see light (Psa. 36:9).

3. Paul is also implying here that the way Christ indwells believers is through the presence of the Spirit in their lives. This is what Jesus had first taught his disciples in the Upper Room (see John 14:15-21; 15:26-27; 16:7, 14; 17:20-23). The Spirit of God indwelling the Christian is the Spirit of Christ. His indwelling means that 'Christ is in you' (verse 10). How are we to understand this breathtaking statement?

THE GIFT OF THE INDWELLING SPIRIT

Undergirding Paul's thinking here lies the incarnation. Our Lord's conception was effected by the Holy Spirit and his life was lived in his power (Luke 1:35; 4:1, 14, 18; Matt. 12:28). The Spirit was present in him from Mary's womb through to the Garden tomb and beyond to the throne of heaven. Jesus described him as 'another Helper'—that is, 'another [*allos*] of the same kind' as Jesus himself. And he is so because he was our Lord's constant and intimate companion throughout the whole course of his life. The ascended

Christ then asked his Father for the same Spirit to be sent to the church. This is what happened on the Day of Pentecost (John 14:16; Acts 2:33).

To be indwelt by the Spirit is to 'have the Spirit of Christ,' one and the same Spirit as our Lord himself. Thus Paul can say, 'Christ is in you.' And the result? 'Although the body is dead because of sin, the Spirit is life because of righteousness' (verse 10).

The ESV rightly interprets spirit (*pneuma*) here as a reference to the Holy Spirit, as elsewhere in Romans 8 (verses 13-14, 16, 23, 26-27). Paul's point is that while we still live in 'this body of *death*' (7:24), the Spirit of Christ who indwells us is '*life* because of righteousness' (verse 10).

This unique and somewhat enigmatic statement is explained in what follows. The Spirit who indwells us as the Spirit of Christ is the Spirit of God who 'raised Christ Jesus from the dead.' That event was simultaneously a resurrection to life and a declaring and confirming of Christ's righteousness. And since we have now believed 'into' Christ, are united to him, and are indwelt by his Spirit, both righteousness (in Christ) and life (through the Spirit) are ours too (cf. 4:24-25). For God has given us the self-same Spirit by whom he raised Christ from the dead. And since we are united to Christ, what God the Father did by the Spirit to Christ he will also accomplish in us: he 'will also give life to your mortal bodies through his Spirit who dwells in you' (verse 11). Eternal life is ours now and resurrection life will be ours in the future.

Thus not only (i) There is no condemnation now because the Spirit sets us free from the down-drag of sin; but (ii) There will be no ultimate death for us because the Spirit will also set our bodies free from the down-drag of death in the final resurrection. God means to save us in a holistic way, body and spirit!

We should not leave these verses without noting the remarkable trinitarian character of our salvation. If the Trinity—the Father, Son, and Holy Spirit—works on our behalf, we have good reason to believe we will be helped to set our minds on what is spiritual, will be enabled to put sin to death, and will be strengthened to live a Spirit-filled, Christ-honouring, God-centred life.

23

Adopted

So then, brothers, we are debtors, not to the flesh, to live according to the flesh. [13] *For if you live according to the flesh you will die, but if by the Spirit you put to death the deeds of the body, you will live.* [14] *For all who are led by the Spirit of God are sons of God.* [15] *For you did not receive the spirit of slavery to fall back into fear, but you have received the Spirit of adoption as sons, by whom we cry, 'Abba! Father!'* [16] *The Spirit himself bears witness with our spirit that we are children of God,* [17] *and if children, then heirs—heirs of God and fellow heirs with Christ, provided we suffer with him in order that we may also be glorified with him.*

(Rom. 8:12-17)

Paul's exposition thus far in 8:1-11 has described the Spirit–flesh tension which the believer experiences. Two realities mark our lives in Christ. We are not 'in the flesh' but 'in the Spirit.' But the flesh is still in us even while the Spirit is also indwelling us. We are under the Lordship of the Spirit, but not yet delivered from the presence or influence of the flesh. Conflict is inevitable.

Now the apostle develops a point he had noted earlier. While the conflict (Adam-sin-law-flesh *versus* Christ-righteousness-grace-Spirit) is between two opposites; it is not between two equals. In Christ we not only live *because of* the Spirit but we live *to* the Spirit and, as Paul later says, we will be 'more than conquerors' (verse 37).

Illustrations have limitations. But imagine you have moved from the United Kingdom to the United States of America and have become a citizen. You are no longer 'in' the United Kingdom. But in addition, you are 'free' from it since you are now an American citizen. The United Kingdom no longer commands your loyalty (you no longer do jury duty, serve in the armed forces, vote in the elections). Not only so, but neither the King nor his parliament has authority over you. But this in itself does not immediately change your accent, your instincts, your habits, and a multitude of other things. These may indeed change—some by a single decision, others slowly over time. But your past will never disappear completely. There is a saying, 'You can take the boy out of Glasgow (or Belfast), but you cannot take Glasgow (or Belfast) out of the boy'—certainly not immediately; not for a long time; and probably never in this life! So it is in our new life in Christ. We are no longer 'in the flesh,' citizens in Adam's kingdom. And yet the flesh remains in us. Like Israel brought out of Egyptian bondage, we are constantly faced with the choice between the way of life and the way of death (cf. Deut. 30:19-20). The craving of the exodus-generation for 'the melons, the leeks, the onions, and the garlic' did not disappear overnight (Num. 11:5)!

It is true that in some believers past addictions seem to be broken immediately and dramatically. For others being set free in Christ is the beginning of a lifelong battle against them. As we begin to appreciate our new identity in Christ, and our new citizenship (Phil. 3:20), we have an obligation to 'put to death the deeds of the body' and thus live (8:13). For we are 'debtors not to the flesh, to live according to the flesh' (8:12). We are no longer 'in the flesh,' and no longer belong to the kingdom of the flesh, under the dominion of sin. Now our former obligation to serve sin and the flesh has been rescinded. We belong to the new creation in Christ; we have a new citizenship under a new monarch—King Jesus. The claims of the old world on us have come to an end. No matter what remnants of our old feelings and instincts remain, we are to remind ourselves that our former king has no right to enlist us in his service. Getting this clear gives strength to our resistance.

We are to 'put to death the deeds of the body.' 'Deeds' here (verse 13) has a negative connotation (as in Acts 19:18), hence the translation 'misdeeds' in the NIV. The body is not evil in and of itself. But it has become the vehicle of sin in the present evil age (Gal. 1:4). Sin comes to expression through our bodily activities for the simple reason that while our bodies are not all there is to us, nevertheless we are our bodies. Our sinful tendencies and their physical and bodily expressions must be put to death and superseded by new expressions of holiness (cf. 6:12-13). Sanctification is bodily, or it is non-existent (cf. 12:1-2).

BRICKS WITHOUT STRAW?

The apostle Paul sometimes seems to provide us with exhortations, or imply them, without pausing to provide us with the counsel we need to effect them. Here is an obvious example. He implies that we should 'mortify' indwelling sin, but he apparently does not answer our 'How to …?' questions. Is he asking us to make spiritual bricks without straw (cf. Exod. 5:6-8)?

Our tendency is perhaps to turn to other resources for help—books, seminars, social media, and the like. These certainly can be helpful. But they should never be our first port of call. *First*, we should linger on the words of Scripture. We may well find that the answers to our 'How to …?' questions are already embedded in the passage we are studying. If not we will surely find directives to help elsewhere in Scripture.

Here, for example, Paul refers to the importance of mortifying sin. If we ask 'how?' his answers seem to be embedded in the context. For the apostle builds into his teaching here both (i) the motivation we require; (ii) the assurance that we will be able to put to death the misdeeds of the body; and (iii) the support we need to accomplish the task.

The *motivation* is simple: we are under obligation to live this way (verse 12) because of who we now are in Christ. Know who you are in Christ, and you will want to live for Christ!

And the *assurance* that helps us? If we feel we are still in bondage to sin our hope of success in dealing with sin will be minimal. But when we recognize our new identity in Christ involves deliverance from the reign of sin, and therefore from all obligation to live to the flesh, we are also set free from the curse of the inevitability of sin. The paralysis it produces is lifted.

Furthermore, the *support* we need is found in the ministry of the Spirit ('… if *by the Spirit* you put to death the deeds of the body …'). Remember, Paul indicates, that we have not received a spirit of slavery that produces the spiritual paralysis that marked us before we came to faith in Christ. Instead we enjoy a new status as adopted sons. We have received 'the Spirit of adoption as sons' (verse 15). He helps us realize what it means to belong to a loving Father; he reassures us of our filial relationship to him. And the more that is true the greater will be our motivation never to bring shame on the family name, and to grow in expressing in our lifestyle the family likeness of our Elder Brother Jesus.

Furthermore we now see the *destination* to which sin was leading us, namely 'death,' and the glorious destiny at which holiness finally arrives, namely eternal life (verse 13). So both positively and negatively we have powerful incentives and encouragements to put sin to death.

Here then is very practical, attitude- and desire-transforming teaching that helps us answer the 'How to …?' question when it comes to dealing with indwelling sin. It is in order to put it to death that we are 'led by the Spirit' (verse 14).

THE 'LEADING' OF THE SPIRIT

When some Christians speak about being 'led by the Spirit' they do not always mean the same as Paul does here.

We should notice the context of these words. Paul is not talking here about special, individual guidance ('the Spirit led me … to become an architect, to marry Mary, to live in Nairobi …'). Nor does this 'leading' refer to inner promptings that may come to us. Rather Paul is referring to holiness of life—to biblically informed behaviour patterns that conform to the gospel. His leading is not occasional, intermittent, or unusual; it is permanent and constant.

The Spirit of God is the 'Spirit of adoption' (verse 15). He therefore leads us to behave like children of our Heavenly Father. He develops within us family instincts, so that we turn away from everything that grieves the Spirit (Eph. 4:30), or dishonours our Elder Brother Jesus, or causes a frown to appear on our heavenly Father's face, or brings shame on the family name. 'For all who are led by the Spirit of God [to put away sin, as in the previous words of verse 13] are sons of God.'

There have been only three references to the Spirit in Romans prior to chapter 8—in 1:4; 2:29; 7:6. But Paul now develops his exposition of his ministry and builds up his portrait of the Spirit's person and work. He is 'the Spirit of God' (verses 9, 14), 'the Spirit of Christ' (verse 9), 'life' (verse 10), 'the Spirit of him who raised Jesus from the dead' (verse 11), 'the Spirit of adoption as sons' (verse 15), the one 'by whom we cry "Abba! Father"' (verse 15), and 'the Spirit who bears witness with our spirit that we are children of God' (verse 16). Verses 12-17 thus provide us with the most concentrated New Testament teaching on the Holy Spirit outside of John chapters 14–16.

- When Christians live according to the Spirit he leads them to mortify sin (verses 13-14).
- He reassures us of our new relationship to God as our Father (verse 15).
- Through him we express this consciousness when 'we cry "Abba! Father!"' (verse 15).
- Thus 'the Spirit himself bears witness with our spirit that we are children of God' (verse 16).

Paul then draws out the implications: if we are children, then we are heirs, not of course in and of ourselves but in and with Jesus Christ. But then he adds, in words that link this section to the next: if we are 'in Christ' we will not only share in his inheritance in glory, 'there and then' as it were; we will also share with him in his sufferings 'here and now' (verse 17).

THE ADOPTED LIFE

There is rich and thrilling instruction here about our new life in Christ.

1. 'We cry, "Abba! Father!"' (verse 15). Jesus addressed his Father in the Garden of Gethsemane in this way (Mark 14:36). The Aramaic noun '*abba*' is a term of intimacy. But we should not bypass the force of Paul's verb—'cry' (*krazō*). It is an onomatopoeic word (one whose sound echoes its sense). It sounds like a sharp cry, or a cry of pain. The picture here is not of an infant resting quietly in its mother's arms, but of a child in need or in danger crying out for his or her father to help.

Notice the implication of this, because it is an expression of the tender grace of our Father in heaven. Our crying out to him in our time of need is itself an instinctive confirmation that we know that we have a loving and caring heavenly Father. Nor is this assurance reserved only for those who have attained great spiritual maturity. It is the birthright of every child of God, however young, however immature. And it is given especially in times of need. Only if, but also because we are God's children, in times of need and trial we instinctively call out to him, 'Abba!'

2. Paul indicates that in this cry of 'Abba, Father' the Holy Spirit 'bears witness with our spirit that we are children of God' (verse 16).

The translation here is debated. Did Paul mean 'bears witness *with* our spirit …' or 'bears witness *to* our spirit …'? Commentators disagree. But since the fruit of this joint witness is the single cry that issues from the believer, the first alternative is better and is expressed in the compound verb Paul uses (*summartureō*)—to bear witness along with. There are two testimonies here: the believer's and the Spirit's. But they are joined together in the single cry of the believer, 'Abba.' Just as Paul had earlier written to the Corinthians that 'no one can say "Jesus is Lord" except in the Holy Spirit' (1 Cor. 12:3; or 'by' the Holy Spirit), so no one can say 'Abba, Father' except by the same Spirit.

Here we have one of the distinguishing marks of a Christian. A formally religious person can say 'the *Pater Noster*' (the Lord's Prayer, beginning 'Our Father in heaven,' Matt. 6:9). But, in moments of crisis and need, formal religion rises no higher than 'O God …' By contrast, those who have been born again and adopted into the family of God have this deep instinct—as Jesus himself had—to call him 'Abba, Father!' And in that cry, issuing from our lips because of the Spirit's ministry within us, he 'bears witness with our spirit that we are children of God.'

This is more than a matter of logical deduction (what is sometimes called 'the practical syllogism': 'because of the evidence of my transformed life, I conclude I am a child of God'). It is a new, Spirit-given, intuition in us—one of which we knew nothing before we were in Christ. It is not surprising that John Calvin wrote that 'Spirit of adoption' should be placed first in any list of 'titles … applied to the Holy Spirit in Scripture, when the beginning and whole renewal of our salvation are under discussion.'[1]

[1] Calvin, *Institutes*, III.ii.3.

3. Paul also draws out the logic implicit in all this: if we are children it follows that we are heirs, 'fellow heirs with Christ' (verse 17). The implications of this are manifold. Paul focusses on one in particular. If we are united to the incarnate Christ and are fellow heirs with him, we will share not only in his glory but also in his sufferings. We will 'suffer with him [now] in order that we may also be glorified with him [then]' (verse 17).

A humble reading of these words would surely cause the so-called 'prosperity gospel' of 'health, wealth, and happiness' to disintegrate. The Spirit does not lead us to such a false interpretation of the gospel but to a Christ-centred one. He produces in us what has sometimes been called *Christiformity*—the forming of our lives in the shape and pattern of Jesus' life. And since that pattern led him through suffering to glory it will lead us similarly. Thus coming to trust Christ means we 'know him and the power of his resurrection, *and may share his sufferings, becoming like him in his death* …' (Phil. 3:10). In this way our lives are progressively reshaped into the likeness of the life experience of our Lord.

4: We should not neglect the closing words of verse 17: 'we suffer with him *in order that* we may also be glorified with him.' It is true that glory *follows* suffering. But the relationship stated here between the two is not only *chronological*; it is *causal*. Through our union with Christ, our suffering becomes the raw materials out of which God creates glory. By it he both weans us from this world and polishes our graces. This perspective is typical of Paul's teaching. Here is an echo of the martyr Stephen in whose life and death Saul of Tarsus probably first saw what *Christiformitas* looked like and meant (Acts 6:15; 7:59-60; cf. 2 Cor 4:10-12, 17-18; Phil. 3:10-12; Col. 1:24-29).

Thus the inheritance that comes to us in Christ involves sharing in his sufferings as well as in his glory (cf. 2 Cor.1:5). In this way, God's children inherit what has been lost through sin (3:23); they rejoice already in the hope that is theirs (5:2; cf. 1 Pet.1:8). And ultimately, as we shall see, this will lead to full and final conformity to Christ (8:29; cf. 1 Cor.15:48-49; Phil 3:20-21).

24

Future Glory

For I consider that the sufferings of this present time are not
worth comparing with the glory that is to be revealed to us.
19 *For the creation waits with eager longing for the revealing of*
the sons of God. 20 *For the creation was subjected to futility, not*
willingly, but because of him who subjected it, in hope 21 *that the*
creation itself will be set free from its bondage to corruption and
obtain the freedom of the glory of the children of God. 22 *For*
we know that the whole creation has been groaning together in
the pains of childbirth until now. 23 *And not only the creation,*
but we ourselves, who have the firstfruits of the Spirit, groan
inwardly as we wait eagerly for adoption as sons, the redemption
of our bodies. 24 *For in this hope we were saved. Now hope that*
is seen is not hope. For who hopes for what he sees? 25 *But if we*
hope for what we do not see, we wait for it with patience.

26 *Likewise the Spirit helps us in our weakness. For we do*
not know what to pray for as we ought, but the Spirit himself
intercedes for us with groanings too deep for words. 27 *And*
he who searches hearts knows what is the mind of the Spirit,
because the Spirit intercedes for the saints according to the will
of God. 28 *And we know that for those who love God all things*
work together for good, for those who are called according to
his purpose. 29 *For those whom he foreknew he also predestined*
to be conformed to the image of his Son, in order that he might
be the firstborn among many brothers. 30 *And those whom he*
predestined he also called, and those whom he called he also
justified, and those whom he justified he also glorified.

(Rom. 8:18-30)

'Sufferings'—the word touches a raw nerve in us. But in Romans 8:17 Paul has indicated that suffering is integral to the Christian life in this present age. To one degree or another, we all experience it. But Scripture teaches us a distinctive world-view that frames our understanding and experience of suffering within the context of God's multi-layered and multi-dimensional purpose.

Paul later alludes to this in verse 28, at the end of this section. But he begins it with a summary: our sufferings are 'not worth comparing with the glory that is to be revealed to us' (verse 18). This is also the teaching of our Lord Jesus. He has prayed we will be protected and preserved until we see him in his glory (John 17:24). Part of his motive in asking this was surely because he wants us to see that everything we may have been through has been worthwhile.

This is an article of faith, not of sight. Paul uses a favourite verb here (*logizomai*—to reckon, calculate, evaluate, ponder). It is not our natural response to think about suffering in this way. It therefore calls for us to 'act faith' (as our spiritual forefathers said)—that is, deliberately to hold on to the promises of God and to trust him to fulfil them.

GLORY

What is to be revealed to us is 'glory'—the harmonious manifestation of God's attributes. As his image and likeness we were made both to love him for his glory and to reflect it. It is this that we have fallen short of because of our sin (3:23). But now we anticipate its recovery and its full manifestation to us because in Christ we have been justified (5:1) and because God is at work in us (5:3-5). So the hope is not rooted in our personal resolve or wishful thinking, but in our re-creation in Christ.

This glory will be revealed '*to* us.' True, we will be spectators of God's glory. But perhaps Paul's preposition here (*eis*—in, towards, into) hints at more. Ultimately in God's presence we will be encompassed by his glory; it will draw us into its orbit and atmosphere so that we reflect it. Just as on the Mount of Transfiguration our Lord's humanity was metamorphosed (Luke 9:29) and seemed to absorb and express God's glory, so it will be for the believer. We shall be like him because we will see him as he is (1 John 3:2). In fact we are already being changed ('metamorphosed') 'from one degree of glory to another' (2 Cor. 3:18, literally 'from glory into glory'). Our union with Christ in his resurrection is glory begun; our glorification is regeneration consummated. At present we live in between these two realities. Life in the present age therefore is marked by an inevitable 'groaning.' But it is the groaning of longing and expectation ('we groan inwardly *as we wait eagerly*'), not the groaning of despair.

Paul points to three aspects of this groaning: the groaning of *creation*, the groaning of *the believer*, and then (perhaps most remarkable of all) the groaning of *the Spirit*.

CREATION'S GROANING

First of all, Paul speaks about the condition of the created order (verses 19-22). He introduces his comments with the connective 'For' (verse 19) which suggests that what follows helps ground the affirmation of verse 18.

The very creation is groaning—like a mother in childbirth—longing for the Day of Glory (verse 22). And the 'birth' for which creation groans is 'the revealing of the sons of God' (verse 19). At present who they really are is 'hidden with Christ in God' (Col. 3:3). But when Christ appears in glory they will be both with him and like him (Col. 3:4; 1 John 3:2). In anticipation of that Day, it feels as if (as J. B. Phillips vividly renders verse 19) 'The whole creation is on tiptoe to see the wonderful sight of the sons of God coming into their own.'[1]

What explains this phenomenon? It is that Adam's sin led to the disordering of the entire creation of which he was both head and caretaker (see Gen. 1:26-28; 2:15; 3:17-19). Its original design was fractured, its purpose frustrated, and its life disordered. The Second Law of Thermodynamics, the principle of entropy, is now part and parcel of the life of the cosmos; both the times and the fabric of things are somehow 'out of joint.'[2] It is as though the purpose and goal of the whole cosmos have been thwarted.

But there is hope. A day will come, Paul affirms, when the One who thus subjected it to its present inbuilt corruption will set it

[1] J. B. Phillips, *New Testament in Modern English*, 324.

[2] The expression is Hamlet's in William Shakespeare, *Hamlet*, Act 1, scene 5.188.

free. Then creation itself will 'obtain the freedom of the glory of the children of God' (verse 21).

Paul does not pause to provide his readers with a full biblical-theological explanation. But we can piece it together from his writings as a whole. If the goal of the cosmos was frustrated by the disobedience of the first man, the first Adam, this will be reversed by the obedience of the second man, the last Adam, Jesus Christ (1 Cor. 15:47-49). This reversal has in fact already begun in Christ's resurrection. It was the harbinger of the day when he will subdue all things to himself, renew the face of the earth and bring it, perfected, to his Father. In this way, as the last Adam he will fulfil and complete the work he inaugurated with his resurrection (1 Cor. 15:20-28). He will thus consummate the submission to the Father that Adam was originally called to express (Gen. 1:28). Then at last creation will cry 'Freedom!' Until this magnificent vision is fulfilled, however, creation must continue to experience what Paul calls 'the pains of childbirth' (verse 22).

Creation is 'groaning' for 'the glory that is to be revealed to us' (verse 18). That glory will not appear only on a distant horizon; it will surround us; it will invade us and transform us. Then it will be clear why Paul did not 'consider the sufferings of this present time ... worth comparing with' it. They will pale into insignificance by comparison.

But creation is not alone in its groaning. In verses 23-25, Paul points to a second sphere in which groans can be heard. For the condition of the created order is related to ours.

BELIEVERS ALSO GROAN

Christians have 'the firstfruits of the Spirit' (verse 23). Paul does not mean that we receive only part of the Holy Spirit. He is a person; he cannot be received in bits and pieces. Rather, the Spirit's presence in our lives is the firstfruits of the harvest of our full and final salvation. Contrary to what is sometimes taught, when we receive the Holy Spirit his presence results in us groaning! But, as with creation, this groaning is not an expression of despair but of longing. We 'groan inwardly *as we wait eagerly* for adoption as sons, the redemption of our bodies' (verse 23). The groaning is real, but its nature is not complaining so much as longing and expecting.

Having 'the firstfruits' makes us long for the final harvest: 'adoption as sons, the redemption of our bodies' (verse 23).

But are we not already adopted into God's family? Yes, we are already his children (1 John 3:2). Here, therefore, Paul is referring to something more than the legal act of adoption, namely its full manifestation in us of the final resurrection-redemption. Then the reality of our sonship will pervade our whole being. Then God's ultimate goal will be expressed in us fully reflecting the image of God's Son (verse 29).

We have been saved into the hope of glory, as Paul had already said (5:2-3). But, as he explains here in verses 24-25, hope is different from sight. If we can already see something we do not need to hope for it. But since it does not yet appear what we shall be, we wait for it eagerly with patience and in holiness of life (verse 11; cf. 1 John 3:3).

We 'have the firstfruits of the Spirit' (verse 23). Genitives ('of') can be slippery little words. Here the genitive clearly refers to the Spirit himself as the firstfruits of our full and final salvation. He is a person, and therefore we do not receive him only in part. But his work in us and ministry to us have only begun. It awaits completion—and his indwelling presence is the guarantee of the final harvest of his work.

What Paul is saying here aligns with his earlier two-dimensional analysis of Christian experience—the 'already' and the 'not-yet.' As he has indicated, our having died in Christ to the dominion of sin does not mean that sin has died in us (chapter 6); nor does our having died to the law in Christ mean we are already perfect according to its standards (chapter 7).

So here, the fact that we have the Spirit does not mean we are raised above the struggles and discouragements of life. Far from being silenced by the Spirit's presence in our lives, groaning is actually caused by it! How could it be otherwise? The indwelling presence of the Spirit of the Lord Jesus is bound to make us groan as we long for the day when we will see him face to face and be like him, when salvation will be completed in 'the redemption of our bodies.' We groan inwardly as we wait eagerly *because* we have the firstfruits of the Spirit, not *despite* having those firstfruits.

How beautifully balanced Paul's words are. Because our hope is sure, 'we wait eagerly' (verse 23) for the Great Day that is still to come. Our anticipation is enthusiastic; our enthusiasm is patient! For what a day that will be!

THE SPIRIT ALSO GROANS

'Likewise' (verse 26) introduces a third groaning (verses 26-27). It looks back to verses 18-25. But to what in these verses?

Paul is now giving a further reason for 'hope' (verses 24-25). Suffering is a prelude to the glory for which creation 'waits with eager longing' (verse 19), and for which we hope. Earlier he had reassured the Romans that this hope 'does not put us to shame, because God's love has been poured into our hearts through the Holy Spirit who has been given to us' (5:5). Now he further develops this indwelling ministry of the Spirit. The Spirit through whose ministry we taste the love of God for us also 'helps us in our weakness.'

The use of the noun in the singular ('weakness' not 'weaknesses') is perhaps significant. This is our permanent condition as well as something we may be especially conscious of at particular times.

The verb Paul uses in verse 26 is even more evocative. It is a triple compound composed of two prepositions: 'along with' (*sun*) and 'over against' (*anti*) and a verbal root, to take, take up, hold, or even lift (*lambanō*). It conjures up the picture of, for example, a piece of furniture too heavy for someone to lift and move on their own. But if a friend takes the opposite end to ours (*anti*), we are able to lift it (*lambanō*) together with (*sun*) them.

There is a dual encouragement here.

The first is that in our weakness the Spirit comes to help us. He is a true Helper (*paraklētos*—one called alongside; John 14:16-17). We are not left to our own resources.

But a further encouragement is that we are not marginalized by the sovereign Spirit. He is, after all, the Spirit of Christ (verse 9). He does not despise us in our frailty and say, 'Out of my way, you pathetic weakling. I'll do it!' No. In his mercy the Spirit works *with* us and thus *enables us to do* what we cannot in ourselves accomplish. He works *in us*, and *with us*, not *instead of us*. He enables us to cope with our infirmity. In doing so he shares the disposition of the Lord Jesus whose Spirit he is (Isa. 42:1-4, cited in Matt. 12:18-21).

What follows (verse 26b) appears to be a specific illustration of this—perhaps the supreme illustration.

Intercessory prayer is itself an expression of our weakness—we ask God to act because we know we are too weak to accomplish what we desire or need. But there are times when the weakness we confess in prayer is heightened. We bow to pray—but we do not really know what we need and therefore we do not know what to pray! We bow to pray—expressing our weakness to act—but we are so weak that words do not come, or if they come they are halting and even confused. A friend has an incurable disease, or a situation arises for which we can see no good resolution. Under these circumstances, says Paul, 'the Spirit himself intercedes for us with groanings too deep for words. And he who searches hearts [*i.e.* God the Father] knows what is the mind of the Spirit, because the Spirit intercedes for the saints according to the will of God' (verses 26c-27).

This is now the third of the three parallel statements in 8:18-30. Creation groans physically (verse 22); believers groan inwardly (verse 23); now Paul adds that the Spirit groans inexpressibly—'with groanings too deep for words' (verse 26). But the Father is able to interpret these wordless groans. He understands their language; and he knows the Spirit's mind because his mind is always one with the Father's.

This is, surely, one of the most remarkable and intimate trinitarian statements to be found anywhere in Scripture. Here we are given a momentary glimpse into 'the depths of God' (1 Cor. 2:10—an expression also used in the context of the relationship between the Spirit and the Father). Perhaps our best access to its meaning is in the way a mother understands the wordless communications of her child; or in the way a loving carer understands the sounds of a parent, child, friend, or patient who through physical incapacity is able to communicate only by inarticulate sounds—groanings that lack words—and yet love develops the ability to interpret the groans and knows how to respond to every need.

Paul is telling us here that when our weakness is at its most extreme, and situations are beyond our wisdom not only to solve but even to know what to pray for, God does not abandon us. 'Child, I will do it for you,' says the Spirit; 'in your utter weakness I will intercede in perfect accord with the will of your Father! He understands my groans.' This, surely, is the wonder of effectual prayer being made when we are too weak even to know how to pray.

HIS PURPOSES ARE SURE

Paul points to a further encouragement that strengthens hope. It lies in the sovereign providence of God. Those who love God are reassured that 'all things work together for good, for those who are called according to his purpose' (verse 28).

Paul is not here mouthing the platitude 'It will all turn out all right in the end.' In one sense that is true. God will right all wrongs. But Paul is not promising that everything will turn out 'well' for everyone. We have already read his sobering words of judgment in 1:18–3:20. This promise of ultimate good is given to 'those who love God ... who are called according to his purpose.' Our God rules the universe for the good of his own people. All believers are able to confess:

> I am not my own,
> but belong with body and soul, both in life and in death,
> to my faithful Saviour Jesus Christ ...
> He also preserves me in such a way that
> without the will of my heavenly Father
> not a hair can fall from my head;
> indeed, all things must work together for my salvation.[1]

But *how* do we know this, and *what* is this 'purpose'?

Paul answers these questions in verses 29-30. His explanation of why *all things* work for our good lies in the nature of the 'good' that God has in view, namely the destiny he has planned for us. He has 'predestined us to be conformed to the image of his Son, in order that he might be the firstborn among many brothers' (verse 29). Every providence in our lives, rough and smooth, sad or glad, painful or pain-free, is subservient to this goal. Our Father is determined to transform us progressively into the likeness of the Lord Jesus. *That* will be glory revealed in us! We should not be surprised therefore if the 'all things' through which he works turn out to be a sovereignly mixed compound that at times may feel abrasive on our skin. But it is designed to polish our graces. God's goal, after all, is not only the restoration of the original divine image of Genesis 1:26-28 but its consummation in glory in Christlikeness!

This goal, however, is not reached by *sovereign providence* alone; it requires *saving grace*. God's providences in the believer's

[1] Answer to Question 1 in the *Heidelberg Catechism*.

life are predicated on God's provision in Christ for the believer's redemption. Paul analyzes this by describing the way God provides for the complex nature of our fallen condition. Those God foreknew he predestined; those he predestined he called; those he called he justified; those he justified he glorified (8:29-30). There is here a steady drumbeat of grace marching us from lostness in sin to a final transformation in glory.

There are several noteworthy features in what Paul says here.

For one thing he moves from eternity ('foreknew') to eternity ('glorified'). The whole of our life is encompassed here.

For another, his verbs are all in the past tense—'foreknew,' 'predestined,' 'called,' 'justified'—even 'glorified.' This doubtless reflects the absolute certainty that God will accomplish his work. There is, of course, a sense in which the believer already tastes glory (Rom. 5:5; 2 Cor. 3:18). But what Paul has in mind here is the irresistibility of God's sovereign grace.

It is also noteworthy that Paul does not include every aspect of the application of redemption. For example, he makes no reference to either adoption or sanctification, both of which are key elements in what is often called the *ordo salutis* (order of salvation).

For this reason it may be wise to avoid the common description of these words as 'the chain of salvation.' It is understandable why this metaphor is so often used, but it can be somewhat misleading. For Paul gives no indication here that he is thinking of the application of redemption as a series of links in a chain. To that extent the metaphor has been superimposed on the text rather than derived from it.

There is another reason for avoiding the chain metaphor here: links in a chain close round each other. The metaphor conveys the idea that calling, justification, and glorification connect directly to each other. But it is not so clear how each one is connected to the Lord Jesus Christ himself. It is therefore better to think of calling, justification and glorification as complementary aspects of our union with Christ which together lead to the fulfilment of God's plan to transform us into 'the image of his Son in order that he might be the firstborn of many brothers' (verse 29). This is the heart of the matter—the transformation and adoption that are involved in our union with the risen Christ.

God's foreknowledge here refers to his prior love for us and engagement with us. The foreknowledge in view is of persons, not merely an advance knowledge of facts or events about those persons. God made us the object of his intimate love long before we were conscious of it. 'Know' in such contexts in Scripture stresses the idea of personal relationship with, not merely 'informational knowledge about' someone (cf. Gen. 4:1; Amos 3:2; Matt.1:25).

Thus, in his foreknowledge of us, God views us in his grace in Christ rather than under his wrath in ourselves. In his predestination of us, he has in his mind's eye the ultimate goal of our salvation. In his calling of us, he effectually summons us into union and communion with his Son (1 Cor. 1:9). In his justifying of us he counts us righteous with the righteousness of the Christ whom we receive by faith. And since, through our faith union with him, we are justified in the resurrected Christ (4:24-25), our status is irreversible. And the unexpected tense of his final verb ('glorified') suggests that the final outcome is certain. The divine goal will be reached. We shall be transformed into the image of Christ; he will be the firstborn of many brothers. This is 'full salvation.'

No wonder the closing section of Romans 8 begins as it does: 'What then shall we say to these things? If God is for us, who can be against us?' (verse 31). For when these great truths illuminate our understanding and flood our hearts, courage and confidence are born.

25

Everlasting Love

What then shall we say to these things? If God is for us, who can
be against us? [32] *He who did not spare his own Son but gave him*
up for us all, how will he not also with him graciously give us
all things? [33] *Who shall bring any charge against God's elect?*
It is God who justifies. [34] *Who is to condemn? Christ Jesus is*
the one who died—more than that, who was raised—who is at
the right hand of God, who indeed is interceding for us. [35] *Who*
shall separate us from the love of Christ? Shall tribulation, or
distress, or persecution, or famine, or nakedness, or danger, or
sword? [36] *As it is written,*

'For your sake we are being killed all the day long;
we are regarded as sheep to be slaughtered.'

[37] *No, in all these things we are more than conquerors through*
him who loved us. [38] *For I am sure that neither death nor life,*
nor angels nor rulers, nor things present nor things to come,
nor powers, [39] *nor height nor depth, nor anything else in all*
creation, will be able to separate us from the love of God in
Christ Jesus our Lord.

(Rom. 8:31-39)

At several points Paul's exposition of salvation in chapters 5 to 8 has pointed to its consummation in glory (5:2-3, 10-11; 6:23b; 7:24-25a; 8:30). He now draws the entire section to a triumphant conclusion in a series of challenges to every power or influence that could thwart God's purposes or our assurance of that final glory. His words echo the spirit of the Servant of the Lord expressed in Isaiah 50:8-9:

… He who vindicates me is near.
Who will contend with me?
 Let us stand up together.
Who is my adversary?
 Let him come near to me.
Behold, the Lord God helps me;
 who will declare me guilty?
Behold, all of them will wear out like a garment;
 the moth will eat them up.

The question 'What then shall we say *to these things*?' may have verses 28-30 specifically in view. But they should also be read in the context of this whole chapter, and perhaps even 5:1–8:27, or indeed Paul's entire argument thus far (from 1:18 to 8:27). If God is for us, and has worked for us in Christ, and is working inexorably for our salvation by his Spirit, what opposition can stand against us?

Paul does not mean—indeed cannot mean—that he or we will never face opposition. The reverse was clear in his own life (*e.g.* 2 Cor. 11:23-28) and will be in ours too. Opposition abounded for him and continues to abound for us. His point is that no opposition can be victorious 'if God is for us.'

The words '*if* God is for us' form what is called a 'first class conditional' where 'if' is the equivalent of 'since it is true that …' It introduces a logical syllogism or argument of the form: 'If "A" is true then "B" follows inevitably.' Clearly if God is for us—and he is indeed, as Anselm of Canterbury said, 'the One than whom no greater can be conceived'—then not even the sum total of all the dark and sinister powers at work in the cosmos can ultimately overwhelm or destroy us.

But this prompts a fundamental question: *How do we know that God is for us?* Paul answers in one of his greatest statements of the gospel: because 'He … did not spare his own Son but gave him up for us all' (verse 32). On that basis we can say with confidence, 'how will he not also with him graciously give us all things?'

THE GREATEST ARGUMENT EVER

This is what logicians call an *a fortiori* argument, a form of reasoning that argues from a stronger, more difficult, demanding, or costly consideration or situation to a lesser one. A man who spends £5,000 to buy a watch for his wife will surely be willing to pay an extra £10 to purchase an attractive box in which to present it to her (even if he complains that the box should have been included in the price!). So here: If God the Father has been willing to sacrifice his Son for our salvation (the greatest possible sacrifice he could make for us), then certainly he will let nothing stand in the way of that sacrifice achieving the purpose for which it was made. He will providentially govern 'all things' for our good. The gift of Christ to us in the incarnation and then for us on the cross is the ultimate, irreversible, incontrovertible and invincible guarantee of God's commitment to fulfil his covenant purposes for us, in us, and through us.

The Christians in Rome would have recognized that the words 'spare not his own Son' were an echo of one of the most familiar father-and-son stories in the Old Testament—that of Abraham's willingness to sacrifice his son Isaac—the son of the promise. God commended Abraham because he had 'not withheld your son, your only son' (Gen. 22:16). What Abraham was willing to do (not spare his son), God prevented him from doing by providing a substitute. In the event, God himself—not Abraham—was the one who would not spare his own and only Son! For our sake, the Father did not spare him, but 'delivered him up' to the cross. As we have seen before, this is the verb that is used of the judicial condemnation of our Lord Jesus Christ (cf. Matt. 20:19; 26:15-16; 27:2, 18, 26. Cf. Isa. 53:6, 10).

What is so staggering about God not sparing the Lord Jesus is that in the Garden of Gethsemane *he asked that he might be spared* ('Father ... Remove this cup from me ...,' Mark 14:36). The measure of the sacrifice Paul contemplates here is that the Father did not spare his own Son, and that his Son was willing not to be spared even though that would mean the God-forsakenness of the cross. For us the Father and the Son were willing to bear the unbearable. For it was not possible that both we and the Son could be spared.

Paul's logic is simple, irrefutable, and profoundly moving: If the Father has gone to such lengths, will he let anything subvert his purpose to save us? It is inconceivable. There can be no greater reassurance of God's love. Nothing that is against us can ultimately withstand his commitment to us.

QUESTIONS AND PRONOUNS

The questions Paul asks in verses 31, 33, 34, and 35 share a common but perhaps surprising feature: they all use the *personal interrogative pronoun* (Who ...? Who ...? Who ...? Who ...?). Each of them is framed in personal rather than impersonal terms This personal quality suggests that Paul has a supernatural opponent in view.

Satan is not mentioned by name in Romans until 16:20, but his activity can be detected in various places in the letter. He lurks in the shadows of 1:18-32. He lies behind the fall of Adam in 5:12-21. And here, in 8:31-36, his dark shadow appears again. He is against us (verse 31). And he also seeks to accuse and condemn us (verses 33-34). Since he cannot ultimately destroy us or our faith he seeks to separate us from our sense of the love of God in Christ (verse 35). He surely knows that he cannot destroy God himself, so he therefore seeks to destroy his people's fellowship with him and thus thwart his grace.

Thus (verse 33) Satan attempts to bring a 'charge' against us ('There you go, failing again, sinning again. You are as guilty as ever!'). But the charge cannot stick. That knowledge provides both relief and assurance.

But why can this charge not stick? Because it is presented before the Judge who is not only 'for us' but is in fact the One who 'justifies' us (verse 33). There is an inbuilt folly in Satan's activity—a frenzied desperation in bringing charges against us in the very courtroom in which God justifies us! For all charges against us have already been met and dealt with in the death and resurrection of Christ (cf. 4:24-25).

Here, then, is a valuable lesson. When Christians are struggling with a sense of guilt and lack assurance as a result, the resolution is to be found not by looking within (at our sanctification-levels as it were), but by a fresh and deeper appreciation of the justification God has granted to us in Jesus Christ.

Paul now asks, 'Who is to condemn?' (verse 34).

As we have seen (in relation to 8:1), the nuance of the verb 'condemn' takes us beyond the verdict on our lives to the 'jail sentence' that follows a 'guilty' verdict. Although a verdict of justification has been pronounced over us, Satan seeks to persuade us otherwise. Justified we may be, but he attempts to obscure from us the fact that we have received 'the Spirit of adoption as sons' and seeks to recreate in us 'the spirit of slavery [or *bondage*]' (verse 15; cf. Heb. 2:15). He seeks to deceive us into thinking of ourselves as prisoners, not as sons.

Is there no remedy? Yes, there is. Paul provides it here: we are to remember that the only one who has the authority to condemn us has in fact died for us to save us from condemnation! Realize that and the prison door will open, and we will escape the evil one's clutches.

Paul now adds a statement that further strengthens his reasoning. Far from condemning us, Christ died *for us*. It is unthinkable that he would then condemn us. In fact he has also been raised *for us* and is seated at the right hand of God *for us.* He 'is interceding *for us.*' He is *for* us, not *against* us. The one who is for us will not condemn. Thus the knowledge of Christ's love for us, in all its aspects, has the power to silence the insinuations of Satan. If then we know what the Lord Jesus has done for us, and how his Father's love is revealed in his work, the lurking fear of condemnation will be dissolved.

So, no opposition can stand, no accusation stick, and no condemnation can prove lasting. But Satan is not finished yet. He will surely employ 'tribulation, or distress, or persecution, or famine, or nakedness, or danger, or sword' (verse 35), to seek to separate us from the love of Christ, will he not?

But in fact, Paul hints that such experiences are to be expected. They are in keeping with biblical patterns and promises, as Psalm 44:22 makes clear: 'For your sake we are being killed all the day long; we are regarded as sheep to be slaughtered' (verse 36). The operative words are 'for your sake.' Even such dark experiences prove to be instruments in our Father's hands to transform us; in every context God is working together for the good of those who love him. We have been called according to his purpose. And that purpose means that everything that might separate us from him he will use to draw us closer to him and to conform us to the image of his Son, Jesus Christ (8:29). No wonder Paul speaks about believers being 'more than conquerors through him who loved us' (verse 37). For all things do indeed 'work together for the good of those who love God' (verse 28).

As he brings his teaching in this chapter, and indeed in the whole first half of the letter, to a climax Paul now traverses the cosmos in his imagination, spotting all the destructive forces that might be ranged against the Christian—death, life, angels, rulers, present things, future things, powers, the dimensions of height and depth, anything we can name (verses 38-39). But none of these things can withstand the purposes of God. Therefore he concludes—and we can conclude with him—that in Christ 'we are more than conquerors' (verse 37). Nothing 'can separate us from the love of God in Christ Jesus our Lord' (verse 39).

What more is there for Paul to say? From one point of view, perhaps, very little. But from another, enough to fill a further eight chapters of this great letter! There is yet more for us to discover in what Paul calls 'my gospel.'

26

Anguished Apostle

I am speaking the truth in Christ—I am not lying; my conscience bears me witness in the Holy Spirit— [2] that I have great sorrow and unceasing anguish in my heart. [3] For I could wish that I myself were accursed and cut off from Christ for the sake of my brothers, my kinsmen according to the flesh. [4] They are Israelites, and to them belong the adoption, the glory, the covenants, the giving of the law, the worship, and the promises. [5] To them belong the patriarchs, and from their race, according to the flesh, is the Christ, who is God over all, blessed forever. Amen.

(Rom. 9:1-5)

Was there a pause for breath and for Tertius to refresh his writing materials following the climactic eloquence of the closing verses of Romans 8? If so, it was by no means the final breath. For what follows immediately in chapters 9–11 is integral to Paul's concerns in writing to the Roman church and indeed to the exposition of what he calls 'my gospel.'

This becomes immediately clear. In 1:16-17 Paul had announced as his theme that 'the gospel is the power of God for salvation to everyone who believes, *to the Jew first* and also to the Greek.' He had expounded the first part of this statement in chapters 1–8. But the second part required explanation too, not least for himself, a Jew. And in addition he knew there had been tensions in the house churches in Rome between Jewish and Gentile believers. Following their permitted return to Rome, after their expulsion under Claudius, Jewish believers, like Priscilla and Aquila (16:3), may have discovered that in their absence '*our* (Jew and Gentile) church' had become '*their* (Gentile) church.'

In addition, Paul's theme text had said that 'the righteous shall live by faith.' How, then, were they to live? Rome was the place where 'Caesar is Lord.' Working out how to live in a mixed Jewish-Gentile community as spiritual 'aliens' in a pagan world, where the adjective '*divus*' ('divine') was bestowed on emperors but not on Jesus, presented multiple challenges. So here, just as much as in the first half of his letter, Paul wanted to 'impart' his 'spiritual gift' by showing how his gospel answered both the deep questions of history and the practical questions of daily Christian living.

So chapters 9–16 are not a mere appendix to chapters 1–8. And in particular chapters 9–11 are germane to Paul's concerns. Nor should they be bypassed because their teaching on both the sovereignty of God and the place of Israel in his purposes are often seen as 'controversial' topics and treated as a battleground.

Paul has thus far emphasized *both* that the gospel is for all, and that in terms of redemptive history it is 'for the Jew first and also for the Greek.' Furthermore, he has argued that in his gospel justification by faith does not depend on our obedience to the law, or on circumcision, but nevertheless it is consistent with the teaching of the Old Testament and in fact fulfils it.

WHY THE SUDDEN CHANGE?

But why the apparently sudden change of theme at 9:1? The transition seems all the more abrupt because of the lofty and joyful heights that had been scaled in the closing words of chapter 8.

But the glory of the gospel that creates such rhetoric, and the fact that it is for all—both Jew and Gentile (and indeed for 'the Jew first')—is the explanation. For Paul, the apostle to the Gentiles, was brought up as the quintessential Jew (Phil. 3:5). Jews were his people, his 'kinsmen according to the flesh' (verse 3). He has both natural and spiritual reasons for having 'great sorrow and unceasing anguish' in his heart because of their unwillingness to receive Jesus as the Messiah (verse 2). On his missionary journeys, his first port of call wherever there was a Jewish enclave was the local synagogue. There he would proclaim that the Messiah was Jesus (Acts 13:5, 14; 14:1). But time and again his message encountered opposition and he experienced rejection and worse (Acts 13:45; 14:4, 19).

Paul, as much as John, was 'the apostle of love.' In the face of all that he had experienced he was heartbroken that God's covenant people, the people he also loved, were refusing their Messiah. Although designated an apostle *to the Gentiles* (Acts 9:15; Gal. 2:8-9), he cared no less for his own people.

So there is deep emotion in his words. He is 'speaking the truth in Christ'; he is 'not lying'; his 'conscience bears … witness in the Holy Spirit' to the 'great sorrow and unceasing anguish' in his 'heart' (verses 1-2). More than that, he 'could wish' himself 'accursed and cut off' from Christ if this would serve the salvation of his 'kinsmen according to the flesh' (verse 3). These words echo Moses' response to Israel's idolatry in the incident of the golden calf (Exod. 32:30-32).

The ESV translates Paul's verb, which is in the imperfect tense, not as 'I was wishing' but as 'I could wish …'—there is a similar use in Galatians 4:20. He seems to mean something like 'Just for a moment I found myself wishing …,' or 'the thought crossed my mind …' He knows he cannot make atonement for the unbelief of his people. But he would do anything for them. Clearly he loves them more than his own life. He was 'willing to endure everything for the sake of the elect' (2 Tim. 2:10).

PRIVILEGES

Paul's anguish over his kinsmen is directly proportional to the privileges he and they had received. He gives a brief catalogue of them. Since they are Israelites, to them belong:

- the adoption,
- the glory,
- the covenants,
- the giving of the law,
- the worship,
- the promises,
- the patriarchs,

and (the climactic privilege):

- from their race, according to the flesh, is Christ who is God over all, blessed forever.

These are the fundamental blessings progressively and cumulatively offered to Abraham and his seed. They tumble from Paul's lips, perhaps in no particular order except for the last mentioned which climaxes the whole.

Most of these privileges are self-explanatory. God had made his covenants with the patriarchs Abraham, Isaac, and Jacob in pursuit of his original saving promise enshrined in Genesis 3:15 (see Gen. 15:8; 17:21; Exod. 2:24). In his covenant with Moses at Sinai he had given the law to guide his people, and its liturgy to point them to the way of forgiveness and of access into his presence in worship.

But there is something arresting about the way he mentions 'the adoption' (*huiothesia,* being placed as a son) as the first privilege in the list. He had already used the term in 8:15.

In Paul's world, adoption was a practice regulated by Roman law but apparently absent from the law of Moses—in Israel family needs were met within the family. We are accustomed to Paul using old covenant concepts to explain new covenant privileges. Here he does the reverse. He uses new covenant terminology ('adoption') to describe a privilege experienced by the old covenant people as a whole. This is simply one more hint that the people of God are one throughout the whole of redemptive history. They participate in the grace of the same covenant Lord and taste the same salvation, albeit first by means of shadows, types, and ceremonies, and only later in its fullness in Christ. 'The adoption' belonged to old covenant believers even though their experience of God's fatherhood was limited. A survey of the Old Testament suggests that 'Abba, Father' (8:15-16) was not the instinctive cry of the old covenant believer. Nevertheless they knew that 'as a father shows compassion on his children, so the Lord shows compassion to those who fear him' (Psa. 103:13).

To Israel also belonged 'the glory' (verse 4). They had seen it in the pillar of cloud and fire that guided and guarded them in the wilderness (Exod. 13:21-22), in its appearance on Sinai when Moses ascended the mountain of God (Exod. 24:15-18), when Moses entered the tent of meeting (Exod. 33:9-11), and as it filled the temple when the ark of the covenant was brought into it (1 Kings

8:10-11). Ultimately, of course, this glory would be seen in Jesus Christ (John 1:14; 2 Cor. 3:18).

All of these privileges were pointers to the climax of God's saving revelation in the incarnation: 'from their race, according to the flesh, is the Christ, who is God over all, blessed forever. Amen' (verse 5).

THE DEITY OF CHRIST

In many translations (including the ESV) these words constitute a classic 'proof text' for the deity of Christ. To describe him as 'God over all, blessed forever' unambiguously affirms his divine person.

Some scholars have contested this translation. It should be said that their number includes some who believe the New Testament does in fact teach the deity of the Lord Jesus in other passages (unlike, for example, Jehovah's Witnesses who deny that the New Testament anywhere teaches the full deity of Christ).

Why the dispute? A literal translation of Paul's words might be as follows: '… and from whom is the Christ the one being over all God blessed for ever amen.' A difference in translation arises—in part because ancient manuscripts used punctuation marks sparsely. How then are these words to be punctuated? Should there be a period or a comma after the word 'Christ'?

(i) If a period ('from their race, according to the flesh, is the Christ. God, who is over all, be blessed forever') then this is a statement about Christ's descent from the Jewish people followed by a separate doxology addressed to God.

(ii) If a comma ('from their race, according to the flesh, is the Christ, the one who is God over all, forever blessed') then the words clearly ascribe deity to the Lord Jesus.

The debate here can become very technical. But faced with questions like this we are wise to ask not only about the grammar of a statement but also about the context in which it appears. There are technical reasons for the ESV translation. For example, Paul's independent doxologies are typically in the form 'Blessed be God …' (2 Cor. 1:3; Eph. 1:3), rather than 'God be blessed for ever.'

But there is a simple, non-grammatical reason for believing Paul is referring here to Jesus as 'God over all.' He has just listed the privileges his people have rejected. The rejection of the Lord Jesus is the most heinous of all rejections. It is not likely that he would break out in praise to God as a response to listing them. A cry for mercy would be far more appropriate from a theological point of view, and much more likely from a psychological one.

It will take a further three chapters of exposition to bring Paul (and with him his friends in Rome) to the place where he bows in wonder and praise for God's sovereign purposes (11:33-36). But the journey begins in 9:6.

Paul's expression of 'unceasing sorrow and anguish' leads him to ask a question about God's faithfulness, and this in turn develops into a discussion of the ways of God. He has acted righteously in justifying Gentile sinners and making provision for any and for all who will turn to Christ.

But what, then, is the explanation for the tragic condition of his kinsmen? Is God unjust in their case? Has his word 'failed' (verse 6)?

THE BROKEN HEART

Before we turn to Paul's extended discussion and answer, we should pause to reflect on the fact that his heart is breaking over the lost condition of his own people. There is something profoundly Jesus-like in this. He too wept over his kinsmen according to the flesh: 'O Jerusalem, Jerusalem, the city that kills the prophets and stones those who are sent to it! How often would I have gathered your children together as a hen gathers her brood under her wings, and you were not willing! See, your house is left to you desolate' (Matt. 23:37-38).

True, if we are Gentiles then our kinsmen have not enjoyed the privileges of Paul's kinsfolk (listed in verses 4-5). But many of our kinsmen according to the flesh have had access to the (even greater) message of 'the Christ, who is God over all, blessed forever,' and yet are not saved. Should not our hearts, like Paul's, be broken and filled with compassion?

Paul feels this deeply. Questions arise in his mind. And so in the chapters that immediately follow (9–11) he faces up to three major ones:

1. Has God's word failed in connection with the Jews? (ch. 9).

2. Is there no salvation for the Jews? (ch. 10).

3. Has God rejected the Jews? (ch. 11).

In the chapters that follow we will turn our attention to Paul's resolution of each of these questions. But before we do, should we not pause to pray for Paul's ' kinsmen according to the flesh'—and also for our own?

27

Questions Answered

But it is not as though the word of God has failed. For not all
who are descended from Israel belong to Israel, [7] and not all
are children of Abraham because they are his offspring, but
'Through Isaac shall your offspring be named.' [8] This means
that it is not the children of the flesh who are the children of
God, but the children of the promise are counted as offspring.
[9] For this is what the promise said: 'About this time next year
I will return, and Sarah shall have a son.' [10] And not only
so, but also when Rebekah had conceived children by one man,
our forefather Isaac, [11] though they were not yet born and had
done nothing either good or bad—in order that God's purpose of
election might continue, not because of works but because of him
who calls— [12] she was told, 'The older will serve the younger.'
[13] As it is written, 'Jacob I loved, but Esau I hated.'
[14] What shall we say then? Is there injustice on God's part?
By no means! [15] For he says to Moses, 'I will have mercy on
whom I have mercy, and I will have compassion on whom I
have compassion.' [16] So then it depends not on human will
or exertion, but on God, who has mercy. [17] For the Scripture
says to Pharaoh, 'For this very purpose I have raised you up,
that I might show my power in you, and that my name might
be proclaimed in all the earth.' [18] So then he has mercy on
whomever he wills, and he hardens whomever he wills.

(Rom. 9:6-18)

Paul's anguish leads him to a question. Unusually, we have access to it first of all in the answer he gives: 'But it is not as though the word of God has failed' (9:6). He had already affirmed this in principle. Man's faithlessness does not nullify God's faithfulness. Yes, God is true even if every man turns out to be a liar (3:3-4)! The issue here is specific: What of God's covenant promise to be the God of Paul's kinsmen the Jews? Already his earlier words point us towards the answer: *It is not God who has been faithless, but his people.*

There is a basic principle enshrined in all of God's covenants: the making of the covenant is entirely his sovereign act, but the implications of its outworking in history are related to the response of those with whom he has made it. Thus faith leads to the ongoing blessing of the covenant, but faithlessness leads to alienation from God and being exposed to the curse (illustrated, for example, in Deuteronomy 27–28 and 29–30).

The fault here lies not in God but in his people. Yet Paul does not have a calloused heart. This does not alleviate his personal pain. The two belong together. Here he helps his readers to think this through in detail.

His argument is punctuated by three questions:

QUESTION ONE: A GOD WHOSE WORD HAS FAILED?

Paul's first question is whether God's word (*i.e.* his covenant promise and purpose) has failed (verse 6). The answer, already given in the way he asked the question (a feature of Greek grammar), is elaborated in the verses that follow (verses 6-13). It is, clearly, 'No!'

How can this be true when Paul experiences such personal grief at Israel's unbelief? What can give him a sense of stability when God's promises seem to have been contradicted by events? He answers by pointing to the fact that God's covenant promises have always involved a distinguishing election: 'not all who are [naturally] descended from Israel [whether immediately or long-term] belong to [God's] Israel' (verse 6). Natural descent does not in and of itself guarantee the response of faith that leads to the enjoyment of the blessings of the covenant.

This was already evident in the immediate families of the 'patriarchs' (verse 5), and two examples prove the point.

Example 1 (verses 7-9) comes from the story of Abraham. He received the covenant promise of God. But in God's sovereign purposes it was his son Isaac, not Ishmael, who received the covenant blessings. The line of God's purpose descended from Abraham, but it did so according to God's word of promise, not merely according to genetic descent. It was Sarah's son (not Hagar's) who was the promised heir (verse 9). God chose the line of Isaac (verse 7), not Ishmael. In this his word did not fail (See Gen. 18:1-15; 21:1-7).

Example 2 (verses 10-13) takes the argument a stage further. In the case of Isaac and Ishmael it might be thought that the reason for God's election was that Isaac was the son of both Abraham and Sarah and therefore the legitimate heir, whereas Ishmael had been fathered with Hagar, Sarah's servant. Perhaps the distinction was grounded in these human differences and in Isaac's 'qualifications'? After all, well into the twentieth century illegitimacy was still regarded as a social stigma.

Paul had already made the point that Isaac was specifically the son of the promise (verses 8-9). To prevent any possibility of a misunderstanding, Paul's second biblical illustration is drawn from Isaac's own sons Jacob and Esau. The distinction made between them was not rooted in any difference in them or in their circumstances, but entirely in the purpose of God—as Paul indicates:

- Jacob and Esau had the *same father*. This was also true of Isaac and Ishmael.
- But Jacob and Esau had the *same mother* as well as the same father.
- Not only so, but Jacob and Esau were *twins*, and were therefore *conceived simultaneously* and were present in *the same womb* at *the same time*.
- Moreover of the two *it was Esau who was the elder* and therefore the *natural heir*. But in fact *the inheritance* (the blessing) went to *the younger twin Jacob*.
- That this would happen was declared *before the twins were born* (Gen 21:12), when '*they had done nothing good or bad*' (verse 11).

Thus the fact that the line of promise came down through Jacob and not through Esau was not dependent on anything in them but entirely on the purpose of God. Not only so, but Jacob, through whose line the covenant promise would be fulfilled, gained his position by deceit and fraud! The electing purpose of God was clearly not rooted in any moral qualification. In fact, the heir of the promise was by nature a cheat, a liar, and a deceiver!

In a word, the grace of God expressed in his 'purpose of election' is 'not because of works but because of him who calls' (verse 11). Paul can therefore appeal to the words of the prophet Malachi to confirm his teaching: 'Jacob I loved; Esau I hated' (Mal. 1:2-3).

This is strong language and calls for comment.

STRONG LANGUAGE

It is regularly claimed that 'hate' here (and elsewhere in Scripture) is hyperbole—exaggeration for the sake of effect—and amounts to an emphatic way of saying 'love less.' Jesus' affirmation that if we do not 'hate' mother and father and even our own lives we cannot be his disciples (Luke 14:26) is often called in as a witness to this understanding. But whatever the connotation of 'hate' may be elsewhere in Scripture, in this context it cannot be reduced to hyperbole for 'love less.' For in its context Malachi's language indicates rejection: 'Esau I have hated, and I have turned his mountains into a wasteland and left his inheritance to the desert jackals.' This is not merely a lesser love.

Does God hate? This question is all the more acute because Paul seems to be suggesting that God's 'hate' is prior to anything Esau has done. There is no way round this.

Here again we should bear in mind the larger context in which Paul is speaking. Paul has already set the whole of human history within the context of the sin of Adam (5:12-21). Implicitly, therefore, both Jacob and Esau are viewed by God as 'in Adam.' In him all are sinners, 'brought forth in iniquity and conceived in sin' (Psa. 51:5). We should not interpret Paul's words outside of that context. We are all by nature children of wrath (Eph. 2:1-3)—including both Jacob and Esau. The apostle is thinking and speaking of God's purposes for Esau and Jacob only within that context of viewing them, like ourselves, as members of a fallen race.

We must constantly affirm our recognition of the biblical teaching that there remain mysteries to God's ways (Deut. 29:29). We must never reject what God has plainly revealed; but we ought not to stray beyond the boundaries of biblical revelation. And in this context—the Letter to the Romans—Paul is speaking against the background of 1:18–3:20 and 5:12-21. He believes that there was a sovereign election at work in the distinction between Jacob and Esau. God's electing purposes precede creation and the fall; but throughout the letter Paul's teaching is set within the context of the divine perspective on our sinful condition. It would therefore be unwise to speculate outside of that context.[1]

There is a third issue— one that is usually seen to ameliorate the shock of Paul's words. It is again often argued that the election and rejection in view here are restricted to the roles of Jacob and Esau in God's overall purposes in biblical history, not to their individual salvation. The implication drawn is that his discussion of Jews and Gentiles in these chapters is related not to salvation but to roles in redemptive history.

But Paul's concern in these chapters *is* salvation, not merely roles in redemptive history. He has hinted at this already in 9:1-5; if anything he makes it even clearer later when he says: 'brothers, my heart's desire and prayer to God for the Israelites *is that they may be saved*' (10:1). The exposition which follows in 9:14-16 also implies this concern, as do his comments about wrath and mercy, destruction and glory in 9:22-23.

To return then to Paul's discussion. His response to this first question, 'Has God's word failed?' is therefore, 'No.' In fact there is a consistent pattern of distinguishing election running through all of his covenant purposes. Far from God's word failing, he has been resolutely faithful to it throughout the ages.

That this is the right way to understand Paul is confirmed by the second question he addresses: Is God unjust?

[1] Paul clearly teaches here that in God's decree his purposes were in place before Esau and Jacob were born or had done either good or evil. A minority of theologians have gone beyond the view stated above and argued that in the logical order within that decree the decision to 'elect' or to 'pass by' preceded that related to the fall (a position known technically as 'supralapsarian'). The view adopted here is that this takes us beyond Paul's teaching set within the framework of its exposition in Romans. A fine discussion of this point can be found in Herman Bavinck, *Reformed Dogmatics: volume 2, God and Creation*, Ed. John Bolt, tr. John Vriend (Grand Rapids: Baker Academic, 2004), 361-70, 382-99.

QUESTION 2: A GOD WHO IS UNJUST?

Paul's instinctive response, his 'gut reaction' ('By no means!') is all of a piece with his earlier reactions in 6:2, 15; 7:7, 13. And as before he follows this up with biblical-theological exposition, citing God's response to Moses' request to see his glory: 'And he [God] said, "I will make all my goodness pass before you and will proclaim before you my name 'The Lord.' And I will be gracious to whom I will be gracious and will show mercy on whom I will show mercy"' (Exod. 33:19).

How does this ground Paul's instinctive reaction? It indicates that God is righteous in his distinguishing election, because men and women have neither grounds in themselves nor rights to salvation; they cannot qualify for it or gain it by their own efforts or merit; it is entirely a matter of God's grace and mercy (verse 16).

Paul's teaching humbles us. God's election is not rooted in any qualities in us, or in anything that distinguishes us from others. God is free to exercise his grace and mercy as he pleases precisely because it is grace. Moreover, where it is a matter of grace that he chooses someone (*e.g.* Jacob and not Esau), no question of divine injustice can arise, since no appeal to 'what we deserve' is relevant. What we deserve is condemnation. Grace and mercy are, by definition, not a matter of our deserts.

It is worth noting once again that Paul's language of mercy here implies that he is thinking of God viewing humanity in its fallen and sinful condition in Adam. His teaching is memorably echoed in the words of Portia in Shakespeare's *Merchant of Venice*:

> … consider this—
> That in the course of justice none of us
> Should see salvation. We do pray for mercy.[1]

The absoluteness of God's sovereignty in election is well illustrated by the event that had preceded Moses' request to see God's glory, face-to-face—namely his encounter with Pharaoh and the subsequent hardening of Pharaoh's heart.

This divine hardening had been announced even before Moses returned to Egypt to confront him (Exod. 4:21; 'I will harden his

[1] William Shakespeare, *The Merchant of Venice*, Act IV, Scene i, 206-208.

heart, so that he will not let the people go'). The Exodus narrative that follows is punctuated by the interplay between divine and human activity. 'Pharaoh's heart was hardened' (Exod. 8:19; 9:7, 35). In that hardening, God hardened (Exod. 7:3; 9:12; 10:20, 27; 11:10; 14:4, 8), while Pharaoh himself persistently hardened his heart against God (Exod. 7:3, 13; 8:15, 32; 9:34; 14:4). God's hardening, announced before the event, does not take place in a vacuum. It is an act of just judgment.

The Exodus narrative makes clear that God acts in righteousness. The vehicle by which God hardens Pharaoh's heart and against which Pharaoh hardens his own heart is the divine word of command that implicitly offered mercy to Pharaoh if he would allow God's people to go into the wilderness to worship. It is worth noting here that the issue is *worship* (reminding us of the way Paul had handled that theme in 1:21-25).

Pharaoh's response reveals a heart of ungodliness and unrighteousness that suppresses the truth (1:18): 'Who is the Lord that I should obey his voice … I do not know the Lord, and moreover, I will not let Israel go' (Exod. 5:2). Not only is he disobedient to the Lord's word; he is arrogantly so, and even dismissive of God himself. In the process he reveals the truth about himself in a way that underlines God's justice in hardening his heart.

Once again Paul cites Scripture but introduces the words of Exodus 9:15 in an arrestingly different way from his appeal to Scripture in verse 15. Here the wording is: 'For the Scripture says to Pharaoh' (verse 17). In the original context these are God's words spoken through Moses. Here we have an indication of the way Paul viewed the words of Scripture as the word of God.

Paul's main point, of course, is to indicate that, already in the Pentateuch, Scripture had stressed the sovereign will and activity of the Lord. He had 'raised … up' Pharaoh 'to show his power' and to make known his name (verse 17). Already in the Pentateuch then, God's people had been taught that God '… has mercy on whomever he wills, and he hardens whom he wills' (verse 18). His distinguishing election implies both saving and hardening, according to his own will.

However challenging we find this, Paul's further question, 'You will say to me then, "Why does he still find fault? For who can resist his will?"' indicates that we are tracking accurately with his argument. Isn't this distinguishing election unjust?

No doubt Paul had heard this complaint often enough. But now he answers it in writing. And in the following chapter we will examine his answer in detail.

Before we do so, it is helpful to remember again the wise words of Anselm of Canterbury to his struggling pupil Boso a millennium ago. Objections to Paul's teaching are often rooted in the notion that we have 'inalienable rights' and in particular that we all have some entitlement to salvation. It is often that mistake that lies at the root of our complaints about, or rejection of the biblical teaching on God's electing grace. If we are tempted to question why we need it, Anselm reminds us that 'You have not yet considered the greatness of the weight of sin.'[1]

[1] Anselm, *Cur Deus Homo*, Book 1, chapter 21.

28

Who Do You Think You Are?

You will say to me then, 'Why does he still find fault? For who
can resist his will?' 20 But who are you, O man, to answer back
to God? Will what is moulded say to its moulder, 'Why have
you made me like this?' 21 Has the potter no right over the clay,
to make out of the same lump one vessel for honourable use and
another for dishonourable use? 22 What if God, desiring to show
his wrath and to make known his power, has endured with much
patience vessels of wrath prepared for destruction, 23 in order to
make known the riches of his glory for vessels of mercy, which
he has prepared beforehand for glory— 24 even us whom he has
called, not from the Jews only but also from the Gentiles? 25 As
indeed he says in Hosea,

> 'Those who were not my people I will call "my people,"
> and her who was not beloved I will call "beloved."'
> 26 'And in the very place where it was said to them, "You
> are not my people,"
> there they will be called "sons of the living God."'

27 And Isaiah cries out concerning Israel: 'Though the number of
the sons of Israel be as the sand of the sea, only a remnant of them
will be saved, 28 for the Lord will carry out his sentence upon
the earth fully and without delay.' 29 And as Isaiah predicted,

> 'If the Lord of hosts had not left us offspring,
> we would have been like Sodom
> and become like Gomorrah.'

30 What shall we say then? That Gentiles who did not pursue
righteousness have attained it, that is, a righteousness that is
by faith; 31 but that Israel who pursued a law that would lead

to righteousness did not succeed in reaching that law. [32] *Why? Because they did not pursue it by faith, but as if it were based on works. They have stumbled over the stumbling stone,* [33] *as it is written,*

> *'Behold, I am laying in Zion a stone of stumbling, and a rock of offence;*
> *and whoever believes in him will not be put to shame.'*

(Rom. 9:19-33)

Paul has carefully explained that God's covenant promises have not failed. The Jews' own Scriptures revealed a pattern of God's distinguishing election. He has also shown why God cannot be accused of injustice. But now he faces another question, one that had perhaps exploded in public whenever he had preached or taught on the themes he is handling in Romans 9. This—Question 3—is as much a complaint and a protest, as it is a question.

QUESTION THREE: HOW CAN GOD BLAME US?

If God has always fulfilled his purposes by means of a distinguishing election—choosing Isaac and not Ishmael, Jacob and not Esau (as Paul has argued), showing mercy as he pleases, hardening as he wills—in the face of such divine sovereignty, how can we be held responsible and, more especially, how can we be liable to blame?

The implication of the question and questioner here seems to be: 'So, Paul, if what you are saying is true, how can God blame us for doing what he has decided we will do? You are implying that we really have no choice. "For who can resist his will?" (verse 19b). If that is the case, then clearly there is "injustice on God's part" (verse 14)—isn't there?'

Paul's response here seems to belong to a different register from his earlier patient explanations. In essence he says: 'You are forgetting yourself' ('Who are you, O man, to answer back to God?' verse 20). But once again his thinking is rooted in Scripture. He alludes to a biblical illustration (Isa. 29:16 and 45:9). A potter can make whatever he wants out of his clay (vessels for either 'honourable' or 'dishonourable' use, verse 21). God is the potter here; we are the clay. Who then do we think we are (mere clay) 'to answer back to God' (verse 20)?

What, exactly, is Paul affirming here? Some commentators complain that he is being unreasonable—human beings are not lumps of clay. But again we need to remember the background of Romans 1:18-32; 3:1-20; 5:11-21. We are sinners, rebels, God-rejectors. We have no claim on God. Left to ourselves we choose to reject God. The 'clay' is impure and corrupt.

There are mysteries about God's distinguishing election because the reasons for it lie in God. And there may be questions that occur to inquisitive minds that will remain unanswered. We can all benefit from John Calvin's advice: 'The best limit of sobriety for us will be not only to follow God's lead in learning, but when he sets an end to teaching, to stop trying to be wise.'[1] We are sinners, and our mouths are shut because we are guilty before the judgment seat of God (3:19). We have no mitigating features in ourselves to avert the righteous wrath of God. It will never be possible therefore for anyone to say, 'I do not deserve this,' unless they are talking about God's gracious salvation. Paul's point is that the salvation of any—even of only one—is entirely a matter of grace and mercy—'in the way of *justice*—with respect to what we "deserve"—none of us would see salvation.'

God, then, has the right to work out his purposes to show both his wrath and his power (verse 22). But he has also shown his patience with the 'vessels of wrath prepared for destruction' (verse 22) because of his purpose to 'make known the riches of his glory for vessels of mercy, which he has prepared beforehand for glory' (verse 23).

Once again here, Paul is simply expounding Scripture by spelling out the general implications of the Lord's words through Moses to Pharaoh before the seventh plague (hail) on Egypt: 'By now I could have put out my hand and struck you and your people with pestilence, and you would have been cut off from the earth. But for this purpose I have raised you up, to show you my power, so that my name may be proclaimed in all the earth' (Exod. 9:15-16). His emphasis on God's purpose to display his glory in his triumph over Pharaoh is but a further exposition of the text of the book of Exodus (in this case 14:4, 17-18).

[1] Calvin, *Institutes*, III.xxi.3. The whole chapter is introduced with wise counsel.

Some interpreters have suggested that Paul's language in verses 22-23 is deliberately precise here. He says that the vessels of wrath have been 'prepared' (*katērtismena*), whereas the vessels of mercy are said to have been 'prepared *beforehand*' (*proētoimasen*). This is seen as a similar distinction to one Jesus makes: the kingdom is prepared 'from the foundation of the world' for 'the sheep,' whereas the eternal fire 'those on the left' experience was 'prepared for the devil and his angels' (Matt. 25:34, 41). Implied here is that election and reprobation are not in every respect mirror images of each other. There is nothing in the vessels of mercy to ground their salvation; it is grounded exclusively in God's gracious will towards them. But while reprobation is no less rooted in God's will, it also involves a righteous judgment. Since they are sinners, God is sovereign in 'passing by' (technically known as 'preterition'); his reprobation of them is a just action.

It often comes as a surprise to Christians familiar with Calvin's reputation, but not with his writings, to discover his wise words of counsel again in this context. He issues a strong warning to us not to go beyond what is clearly stated in Scripture or we will find ourselves in a labyrinth in which prying minds may get lost and from which they may never be able to extract themselves.[1] So we need to remember that Paul's concern here is not to answer the questions of prying minds but to vindicate God's covenant faithfulness to his word.

In summary, then, God has remained faithful to his word. His covenant promises were never automatic guarantees of salvation to Abraham's natural seed. For 'Not all who are descended from Israel belong to Israel.' That is the foundational principle he had laid in verse 6.

THE DISTINCTION

This distinguishing feature in the outworking and reception of God's promise was not Paul's novel idea. Hosea had prophesied that those who were 'not my people' would become 'my people' (Hos. 2:23 and 1:10). Hosea had God's ancient people in view—rejected but restored. Paul sees that principle coming to fulfilment in the present inclusion of Gentiles who have come to faith in Christ—once

[1] Calvin, *Institutes*, III.xxi.1.

'alienated from the commonwealth of Israel and strangers to the covenants of promise,' they are 'now in Christ Jesus ... brought near' (Eph. 2:12-13).

Isaiah in turn had indicated that 'not all who are descended from Israel belong to Israel.' Paul points out (quoting from the Greek translation of the Old Testament) how Isaiah 10:21-23 had prophesied that only 'the remnant of Jacob' would return to the Lord. Once again, then, the Old Testament bore witness to the principle Paul has enunciated. God's distinguishing election had already been clearly expressed in prophecy and illustrated in biblical history.

Paul's second quotation, from Isaiah 1:9, further emphasizes that if there were any survivors ('offspring') of God's judgment it was entirely a matter of his mercy. It would have been entirely within God's righteous prerogative not to save any of his ancient people if they rejected his covenant. That he saved a 'remnant' is proof of his sovereign mercy. In addition it shows that God's purposes have always worked in a distinguishing way. And it is also proof positive of Paul's earlier contention that 'it is not as though the word of God has failed' (verse 6).

This section of the argument now draws to a conclusion in verses 30-33.

Paul began the chapter reflecting on the privileges Israel had received and expressing his grief at their rejection of them. Now he has shown that this present situation is entirely in keeping with (i) the character of God and (ii) the teaching of the Old Testament Scriptures. Gentiles, who were 'not my [God's] people,' who 'did not pursue righteousness,' have found true and saving righteousness in Christ as they have turned to him in faith (verse 30).

Israel, on the other hand, who 'pursued a law that would lead to righteousness did not succeed in reaching that law' (verse 31). By the mistaken and self-justifying way in which they sought the end in view ('righteousness' before God) they failed to find or gain it. They chose the way of righteousness 'based on works,' not the divinely revealed way of faith. But, as Paul had demonstrated, 'by works of the law no human being will be justified [*i.e.* counted righteous] in his sight' (3:20). That effort was doomed to failure from the start. God's ancient people failed to pursue righteousness 'by faith, but as if it were based on works' (verse

32). Their path to righteousness therefore clashed with the path God provided—ultimately in Jesus Christ—the grace-way, the faith-way Paul had earlier expounded.

Lest there be any further word of complaint about this teaching being a Pauline novelty, Paul again quotes from Isaiah. He welds together Isaiah 28:16, 'Behold, I am the one who has laid as a foundation in Zion, a stone, a tested stone, a precious cornerstone, of a sure foundation: "Whoever believes will not be in haste,"' and Isaiah 8:14, 'a stone of offence and a rock of stumbling.' God's word (now fulfilled in Christ) is both cornerstone and stumbling block. God's covenant ways have always involved these two dimensions. Rather than the covenant word of God failing, in fact it has come true.

As Paul concludes this extended section with its majestic emphasis on God's sovereignty, he indicates that Israel is responsible for her own position. The God of Abraham, Isaac, and Jacob had laid down the 'stone' who would be the foundation and means of saving righteousness for all who believe in him. But in their determination to gain by their own works the righteousness God provides by grace alone (and through faith in Jesus Christ), that stone had instead become 'a stone of stumbling and a rock of offence.' As Peter had told the Jewish Sanhedrin, 'This Jesus is the stone that was rejected by you, the builders, which has become the cornerstone' (Acts 4:11).

By contrast, 'whoever believes in him will not be put to shame' (verse 33). The way of salvation is the way of faith. It always was; it always will be. And it is open to all who will believe.

This leads us into chapter 10 and Paul's further exploration of his theme.

29

The Message of Salvation

Brothers, my heart's desire and prayer to God for them is that
they may be saved. 2 *For I bear them witness that they have a*
zeal for God, but not according to knowledge. 3 *For, being ig-*
norant of the righteousness of God, and seeking to establish their
own, they did not submit to God's righteousness. 4 *For Christ*
is the end of the law for righteousness to everyone who believes.
5 *For Moses writes about the righteousness that is based on the*
law, that the person who does the commandments shall live by
them. 6 *But the righteousness based on faith says, 'Do not say in*
your heart, "Who will ascend into heaven?"' (that is, to bring
Christ down) 7 *'or "Who will descend into the abyss?"' (that*
is, to bring Christ up from the dead). 8 *But what does it say?*
'The word is near you, in your mouth and in your heart' (that
is, the word of faith that we proclaim); 9 *because, if you confess*
with your mouth that Jesus is Lord and believe in your heart
that God raised him from the dead, you will be saved. 10 *For*
with the heart one believes and is justified, and with the mouth
one confesses and is saved. 11 *For the Scripture says, 'Everyone*
who believes in him will not be put to shame.' 12 *For there is no*
distinction between Jew and Greek; for the same Lord is Lord of
all, bestowing his riches on all who call on him. 13 *For 'everyone*
who calls on the name of the Lord will be saved.'
14 *How then will they call on him in whom they have not*
believed? And how are they to believe in him of whom they
have never heard? And how are they to hear without someone
preaching? 15 *And how are they to preach unless they are sent?*
As it is written, 'How beautiful are the feet of those who preach
the good news!' 16 *But they have not all obeyed the gospel. For*
Isaiah says, 'Lord, who has believed what he has heard from

us?' [17] *So faith comes from hearing, and hearing through the word of Christ.*

[18] *But I ask, have they not heard? Indeed they have, for*

> *'Their voice has gone out to all the earth,*
> *and their words to the ends of the world.'*

[19] *But I ask, did Israel not understand? First Moses says,*

> *'I will make you jealous of those who are not a nation;*
> *with a foolish nation I will make you angry.'*

[20] *Then Isaiah is so bold as to say,*

> *'I have been found by those who did not seek me;*
> *I have shown myself to those who did not ask for me.'*

[21] *But of Israel he says, 'All day long I have held out my hands to a disobedient and contrary people.'*

(Rom. 10:1-21)

Romans 10 is a shorter chapter than the ones that precede and follow it (twenty-one verses rather than the thirty-three of chapter 9, and the thirty-six of chapter 11). But it is no less instructive (and parts of it are no less challenging to interpret).

Before Paul continues he pauses briefly at a base camp in his discussion. God's purpose in his dealings with Israel is not an academic matter for him, something that can be kept within the bounds of detached intellectual inquiry. At the beginning of chapter 9 he made it clear that it was an issue that had deep existential implications for him (and also for his Jewish-Christian brothers and sisters in Rome). He had 'great sorrow and unceasing anguish' in his heart because his 'kinsmen according to the flesh'—who had known so many spiritual privileges—had not recognized Jesus as their promised Messiah (9:1-5).

Now in 10:1-4 he gives further expression to his personal investment in the spiritual condition of his own people. His doing so was a further hint of the special empathy he felt for the Jewish Christians in Rome (as is clear later in chapters 14 and 15). They belonged to a despised minority among their own Jewish family and friends, who may well have disowned and disinherited them because of their Christian faith. In addition, as we will see, at least some if not most of them were regarded as 'weak' and perhaps felt demeaned by their Gentile brothers and sisters. Paul's deep personal and pastoral sensitivity towards them runs throughout the whole letter. But it comes very near to the surface here in the way he provides pastoral care for them, by helping them to understand as far as possible the ways of God with both Jew and Gentile.

And so he returns to his burden announced earlier. His concern for his kinsfolk, his 'heart's desire and prayer to God is that they may be saved' (verse 1). This language, as we have seen, confirms that Paul's concern here is not merely Israel's role in redemptive history, but their salvation. His people are not lacking in 'zeal'; but it is misplaced (cf. 9:31-32). It is 'not according to knowledge' (verse 2). They have been 'ignorant of the righteousness of God' (verse 3)—that is, the way of justification God has provided in Christ. The terrible implication is that they have insisted on doing it 'my way.' Implicitly they have demanded that God submit to their plan of salvation rather than his own (verse 3). And this is all the more heinous because they had the revelation of God but rejected it.

THE END

What had Paul discovered in submitting 'to God's righteousness' rather than seeking to establish his own (verse 3)? He answers: 'Christ is the end of the law for righteousness to everyone who believes' (verse 4).

Paul's word 'end' (Greek: *telos*) has a range of meanings, just as it does in English. It can mean 'finish' (like the words 'The End' at one time printed on the last page of a book). It can also mean 'goal,' 'the end in view.' Commentators are by no means in agreement about its meaning here. Does Paul mean that Christ 'brings to an end' the law as a way of righteousness when we come to believe in him? Or does he mean that Christ is the 'goal' in view in the law and that those who believe see this? Or some variation of these two interpretations?

Arguments can be made for each interpretation (and for variations on them). And, since we often use words without reflecting on which precise dictionary definition we are intending, it is possible that both senses may be in view. Both are in fact true—the law did point to Christ —he is its *telos*. And Paul knew from personal experience that when he came to believe in Christ any notion he had that obedience to the law could justify him came to an end (cf. Phil. 3:4-9).

The connective word 'for' (*gar*) at the beginning of verse 5 may suggest that the second view was uppermost in Paul's mind. His kinsmen were seeking to establish their own righteousness 'based on the law.' In this they were 'ignorant of the righteousness of God' (verse 3). But this ignorance and effort both come to an end when someone discovers that 'the gospel (*i.e.* Christ) is the power of God for salvation to everyone who believes ... For *in it* the righteousness of God is revealed from faith for faith' (1:16). If God-provided righteousness is to be found only in Christ, then that discovery ends all the efforts of those who 'pursued a law that would lead to righteousness ... as if it [righteousness] were based on works' (9:31-32). Because Paul himself had come to realize this, it pained him deeply that so many of his kinsmen remained 'ignorant of the righteousness of God' (verse 3) and continued to seek to establish their own. Would that their pursuit were brought to an end through faith in the Lord Jesus, the Christ of God!

Paul's connecting words are usually significant. Another 'for' appears at the beginning of verse 5 and links what he has just said to the argument that follows. On the one hand Christ ends the law for righteousness for those who believe, and on the other hand he also provides righteousness for them.

Once more we see both the apostle's deep instinct to refer to Scripture and also to think from the first principles it provides. This is also a pastoral master-stroke. Earlier, in discussing justification by faith he had appealed to Abraham, the father of the faithful—if something was true for Abraham, then, to the Jew, it was, quite simply, true (4:1-5). Now, discussing whether righteousness comes by the law or by faith, he appeals to Moses through whom God had originally given the law.

This is, of course, an appeal to authority (the Scriptures that were given through Moses). But there is also an element of sanctified psychology here. If Paul can prove his point about obtaining righteousness by faith *by appealing to Moses the law-giver*, his case will not only be established intellectually, it will also be persuasive emotionally. For how could what was true for Moses not also be true for his kinsmen?

In the words of Moses recorded in Scripture Paul finds two principles stated:

(i) Concerning the view that 'righteousness is based on the law,' Moses writes 'that the person who does the commandments shall live by them' (verse 5).

By way of contrast (signalled by 'But' in verse 6):

(ii) 'But the righteousness *based on faith* [which, ultimately means faith in Christ] says … 'The word is near you … (that is *the word of faith* that we proclaim) … if you confess with your mouth that Jesus is Lord and *believe in your heart* that God raised him from the dead, you will be saved … For the Scripture says "Everyone *who believes* in him will not be put to shame" … there is no distinction between Jew and Greek; for the same Lord is Lord of all … For everyone who *calls on the name of the Lord* will be saved' (verses 6-13; the italicized phrases indicate Paul's emphasis on believing in distinction from 'doing').

Paul here runs together several Old Testament passages:

- He paraphrases Leviticus 18:5 (which he had cited earlier in Gal. 3:12): 'If a person does them [*i.e.* God's statutes and rules], he shall live by them.'
- *By contrast* in verses 6-11 (signalled by the introductory word 'But') he refers to Deuteronomy 9:4 ('Do not say in your heart …')—a passage that warns the people not to assume that the possession of the land would come as a result of their own righteousness; it was a gift of grace.

He links this with Deuteronomy 30:12-14. Here the covenant commandment God is giving is not 'too hard for you' or 'far off,' as though considerable exertion was needed to bring it down from heaven, or a long journey required to bring it from beyond the sea. Instead it is 'very near you. It is in your mouth and in your heart so that you can do it.'

These apparently contrasting passages are drawn from the law and are about the law as God's word. Yet Paul understands these last words to refer to faith. This is 'the word of faith that we proclaim' (verse 8).

At first glance this may seem to be a sleight of hand. If both passages refer to God's law, it seems arbitrary for Paul to use one of them as a description of faith. On reflection, however, we can see Paul the pastor here. He is demonstrating *from the law* that stated the principle, 'Do the commandments and you will live by the commandments,' that this could only become a reality *by faith*—not by exertions to obey the law, but by receiving the word by faith; as Jeremiah would later put it, by having the law graciously written into the believing heart (Jer. 31:33).

This Old Testament principle embedded in Deuteronomy is now filled out in the gospel. Paul's explanation follows the order of the text in Deuteronomy: 'confess with your mouth ... believe in your heart' and then reverses it, now following the order of his own (and our) experience: 'with the heart one believes and is justified, and with the mouth one confesses and is saved' (verse 10).

What, exactly, is Paul doing here through these references to Scripture?

ONLY ONE WAY

Paul uses the words of Scripture to present two ways to righteousness: on the surface, one is the way of law-keeping ('Do this and live') while the other is the way of faith ('based on faith'). However, we should not draw the conclusion that he thought the Old Testament taught that these two ways equally lead to righteousness—as though it were a matter of 'take your choice.'

Nor should we draw the conclusion that 'Do this—keep the law—and you will live' is false. For the principle itself is true. Be perfectly obedient to God's law and life will be yours. When the Rich Young Ruler asked what he needed to do to inherit eternal life, the Lord Jesus replied: 'If you would enter into life, keep the commandments' (Matt. 19:17). Jesus knew that no one has ever attained life this way, but that did not invalidate the principle itself. The Young Ruler thought he had kept the commandments from the day he became responsible to do so (Matt. 19:20). Saul of Tarsus similarly had believed he was 'as to righteousness under the law, blameless' (Phil. 3:6). But both men discovered (and it seems by means of the same tenth commandment—Matt. 19:21-22; Rom. 7:7-10) that the pathway of 'Do this and live' was not attainable by them. Already within the context of the law itself it was clear that the way of establishing one's own righteousness by law works was never effectual. But it was also clear already in the writings of Moses (the law-giver) that righteousness is provided only by grace and received only by faith. This is the point of his contrasting second biblical reference.

The way Paul cites the words of Deuteronomy 30:12-14 here in verses 6-8 may seem a little unusual:

> But the righteousness based on faith says, 'Do not say in your heart, "Who will ascend into heaven?"' (that is, to bring Christ down) 'or "Who will descend into the abyss?"' (that is, to bring Christ up from the dead). But what does it say? 'The word is near you, in your mouth and in your heart' (that is, the word of faith that we proclaim).

Paul is doing here what preachers sometimes do—taking a passage of Scripture and transposing its teaching into the form of a soliloquy or a dialogue. He personifies the message of righteousness by faith. It speaks for itself in telling us that, in sharp contrast to the most strenuous efforts on our part to obtain righteousness before God (ascending to heaven or descending into the abyss), true right standing with God is a gift—we do not 'go' to it; instead 'it' comes to us!

Thus Paul is saying again what he has said before: it is only in the gospel of Christ, the gospel of sovereign grace, that righteousness is found. And whether it was found in the shadowy form of the days of the Mosaic administration, or in the full light of Christ's incarnation, it has always been 'from faith for faith' (1:17).

In passing, here we should remember that when old covenant saints appealed to their own righteousness (*e.g.* Psa. 7:8; 18:20, 24) this was not an appeal for justification on the basis of their obedience, but an appeal to their faithfulness as those established in a covenant relationship with God by grace and faith.

Paul also indicates here that this faith-way of righteousness was always implicitly available *to all* by referring once again to Isaiah 28:16 (as he had done in 9:33): '*Everyone* who believes in him will not be put to shame.' True, that was read restrictively by the Jewish people as 'Every one *of us*,' and doubtless Paul himself read the text that way in his pre-Christian life. But there had been a veil over his eyes (2 Cor. 3:14-15). But now, in Christ, that veil had been removed. The core message of the way of salvation revealed in the Old Testament itself had become clear to him. If 'everyone *who believes*' means '*everyone* who believes' then 'there is no distinction between Jew and Greek ... For everyone who calls on the name of the Lord will be saved' (verse 13; cf. Joel 2:32). Simon Peter had cited the same words in explaining the events of the Day of Pentecost, even though it would be some time before he and the other apostles recognized their full significance (Acts 9:10–10:48).

And so once more Paul returns to the point he made repeatedly: there is only one way of salvation. It is the only way for everyone; it is open to anyone. It is the way of faith in Christ, of calling on the name of the Lord, of believing on him in the heart and confessing him with the mouth. And this was the way that had been taught by Moses.

In verses 14-21 Paul now explores a series of questions. Some commentators read them as objections, formulated as a kind of reactionary self-defence on the part of Jews who had heard Paul's teaching. That may be true. But what follows may simply be Paul's explanation of (i) how someone is enabled to call on the name of the Lord (verses 13-17), and (ii) how this applies to Israel (verses 18-21).

PREACHERS NEEDED

There are always links in the chain of circumstances and events that together bring any individual to faith. Paul expresses the sheer generosity in God. He bestows 'his riches on all who call on him' (verse 12). But people cannot call on Christ unless they believe in him (verse 14a). And they cannot believe 'in him of whom they have never heard' (verse 14b). And, in turn, they cannot hear unless someone preaches Christ to them (verse 14c). And preachers will not preach unless they are sent (verse 15).

The import of Paul's quotation from Isaiah 52:7 ('How beautiful are the feet of those who preach the good news!' verse 15) is, therefore, 'Thank God, preachers have been sent—and how beautiful their feet are to us!' As Christians we love those who first brought the message of the gospel to us.

Some modern translations (including ESV reference versions) include an important footnote to verse 14b, indicating an alternative translation: 'And how are they to believe *him whom they have never heard*?' The issue here is one of translation, not (as it was in 5:1, 3) of different manuscript traditions. It arises because of what (at least to English speakers) is an unusual feature of the Greek verb 'to hear' (*akouō*). It takes the genitive case of the object. The result is that two translations are possible:

(i) ESV text: 'And how are they to believe in him *of whom* they have never heard?'

(ii) ESV margin: 'And how are they to believe in him *whom* they have never heard?'

These lines may seem like an optical illusion. The difference between them is the absence of the word 'of' in the marginal translation.

> Translation (i) suggests Paul is referring to *hearing someone preaching about Christ*.
>
> Translation (ii) suggests Paul is speaking about *hearing Christ himself preaching*.

Both translations are possible. Here context is of little help. But asking broader questions about Paul's understanding of preaching (and indeed about our own experience of hearing preaching) may help. For we come to faith not only by hearing *about Christ*, but by *hearing Christ himself*.

Other passages also point us in this direction. It is only when Christ's sheep hear and recognize his voice that they follow him (John 10:1-6, 16). After explaining to the Ephesians that Christ made peace by shedding his blood on the cross (his *finished* work, Eph. 2:13-16), Paul tells them that 'Christ came and preached peace to you' (his *ongoing* work, Eph. 2:17). But Christ did not visit Ephesus during his earthly ministry; nor is Paul suggesting he paid a personal visit there after his crucifixion! The Ephesians heard Christ preaching peace to them when they heard Paul preaching! His accent was heard through Paul's voice. That reality has been repeated again and again throughout the centuries:

> I heard the voice of Jesus say,
> *'Come unto Me and rest;*

Lay down, thou weary one, lay down
Thy head upon My breast.'
I came to Jesus as I was,
Weary, and worn, and sad;
I found in Him a resting place,
And He has made me glad.

I heard the voice of Jesus say,
'Behold I freely give
The living water—thirsty one,
Stoop down, and drink, and live.'
I came to Jesus, and I drank
Of that life-giving stream;
My thirst was quenched, my soul revived,
And now I live in Him.

I heard the voice of Jesus say,
'I am this dark world's Light;
Look unto Me, thy morn shall rise,
And all thy day be bright.'
I looked to Jesus, and I found
In Him my Star, my Sun;
And in that light of life I'll walk
Till travelling days are done.[1]

In this little phrase, then, Paul gives expression to an important element in his understanding of preaching. As God's word is proclaimed in the grace and power of the Spirit, the accent of the preacher becomes secondary. The voice of Christ becomes primary. As we listen we hear not only God's words being spoken, but his Living Word, the Lord Jesus himself. Then our experience of preaching is that his word 'is living and active, sharper than any two-edged sword, piercing to the division of soul and of spirit, of joints and of marrow, and discerning the thoughts and intentions of the heart. And no creature is hidden from his sight, but all are naked and exposed to the eyes of him to whom we must give account' (Heb. 4:12-15).

DEAF ISRAEL

In verses 14-15 Paul had explained how we are brought to call on the name of the Lord. But not all do: 'they have not all obeyed the gospel'

[1] Horatius Bonar (1808–89).

(verse 16; notice again Paul's understanding of 'the obedience of faith,' 1:5). This expectation was already enshrined in Isaiah's prophecy about the coming Suffering Servant (Isa. 52:13–53:12). He laments, 'Who has believed what he has heard from us?' (Isa. 53:1). Faith comes by hearing, and hearing comes through the word of Christ (verse 17).

What, then, of those who do not believe? Did they not hear (verse 18)? Paul again answers with an appeal to Scripture, this time from Psalm 19, the first half of which expounds the reality of the 'surround sound' of divine revelation. God has revealed himself in everything he has made; there is no escape from that revelation.

This perspective undergirded what Paul had said already in 1:18-32. But why does Paul cite a passage on general revelation in this context? He is indicating that through this revelation *all have heard*—'to all the earth… to the ends of the world' (verse 18). But how does this apply to Israel?

Usually the employment of a biblical citation assumes some knowledge of its context. Psalm 19 traces two dimensions of God's revelation in succession: first, *general* revelation (verses 1-6); but then the *special* revelation of God's word, 'the law of the Lord' (verses 7-14). So perhaps the link in Paul's mind is that if all who have had the wordless general revelation have heard (Psa. 19:1-6) then there can be no doubt that the children of Israel in particular have heard since they have, in addition, received the special revelation of the word of the law of the Lord (Psa. 19:7-14).

Then, 'Did Israel not understand?' (verse 19). That may be the case, but if so more than a lack of intellectual comprehension was involved. Paul highlights this with a further series of quotations from the Old Testament.

The first is from the Song of Moses. Here, in the light of the wilderness wanderings and the people's disobedience, Moses calls them to account. He speaks as the mouthpiece of God: 'I will hide my face from them … They have made me jealous with what is no god … So I will make them jealous with those who are no people …' (Deut. 32:20-21).

The second quotation is from the penultimate chapter of Isaiah where God speaks about being ready to be found by those who did not seek him because he revealed himself to them (Isa. 65:1-2).

Paul believed these words were being fulfilled in his own day. God's word has certainly not failed—and God's word proves it! The Gentiles who did not seek the God of Israel have been found by him in Jesus Christ. He is the Lord on whose name all may call. By contrast, 'Of Israel he [God] says, "All day long I have held out my hands to a disobedient and contrary people"' (Isa. 65:2).

According to Scripture, Israel has indeed heard (verse 18). The responsibility for their present spiritual condition lies at their own door—as Isaiah prophesied, they have been 'a disobedient and contrary people.' And as Jesus had later made plain, what happened at the time of his coming was consistent with his people's entire history: 'O Jerusalem, Jerusalem, the city that kills the prophets and stones those who are sent to it! How often would I have gathered your children together as a hen gathers her brood under her wings, and you were not willing ...' (Matt. 23:37).

The apostle Paul was profoundly moved and concerned about the response of his own people to the Lord Jesus Christ (9:1-2; 10:1). The opening section of each of these three chapters, 9, 10, and 11, provides us with all the evidence we need that Paul was a devoted son of Abraham. He had an intense love for, and loyalty to, his own people, so real and deep that it caused his heart to break because only a remnant of them recognized Jesus as the Messiah for whom they professed to be waiting.

Paul was a Jew. Those of us who are Gentiles might sympathize with his need to wrestle with 'the Jewish question.' But in Romans 9–11 he is not only helping his fellow Jewish believers. He is helping Gentile believers to understand and appreciate the purposes of God.

We continue to need that help. There was a time when Christians prayed regularly for the Jewish people to discover and trust Messiah Jesus. Perhaps political tensions and theological controversies have diminished that concern. Or perhaps it is that we have glossed over these chapters in Romans. Or could it be that our indifference here is an expression of a general indifference to the need of the world as a whole?

The words Paul quotes from Isaiah in the closing verses of this chapter looked forward to the day when God would be found by those who did not seek him and would show himself to those who did not ask for him (verse 20, quoting Isa. 65:1). Those of us who are Gentile Christians are the fulfilment of that prophecy. But is there no hope for Israel? Has God wiped his hands of his ancient people? And should we? Isaiah's next words give us a clue: 'All day long I have held out my hands to a disobedient and contrary people' (verse 21, citing Isa. 65:2). In centuries past God had extended overtures of grace to Israel.

But are God's hands still held out? To that question Paul now turns in chapter 11.

30

Conclusions Reached, Warnings Given

I ask, then, has God rejected his people? By no means! For I
myself am an Israelite, a descendant of Abraham, a member of
the tribe of Benjamin. 2 God has not rejected his people whom
he foreknew. Do you not know what the Scripture says of Elijah,
how he appeals to God against Israel? 3 'Lord, they have killed
your prophets, they have demolished your altars, and I alone
am left, and they seek my life.' 4 But what is God's reply to
him? 'I have kept for myself seven thousand men who have not
bowed the knee to Baal.' 5 So too at the present time there is a
remnant, chosen by grace. 6 But if it is by grace, it is no longer
on the basis of works; otherwise grace would no longer be grace.
7 What then? Israel failed to obtain what it was seeking. The
elect obtained it, but the rest were hardened, 8 as it is written,

> 'God gave them a spirit of stupor,
> eyes that would not see
> and ears that would not hear,
> down to this very day.'

9 And David says,

> 'Let their table become a snare and a trap,
> a stumbling block and a retribution for them;
> 10 let their eyes be darkened so that they cannot see,
> and bend their backs forever.'

11 So I ask, did they stumble in order that they might fall? By
no means! Rather, through their trespass salvation has come to
the Gentiles, so as to make Israel jealous. 12 Now if their trespass
means riches for the world, and if their failure means riches for
the Gentiles, how much more will their full inclusion mean!

13 Now I am speaking to you Gentiles. Inasmuch then as I am an apostle to the Gentiles, I magnify my ministry 14 in order somehow to make my fellow Jews jealous, and thus save some of them. 15 For if their rejection means the reconciliation of the world, what will their acceptance mean but life from the dead? 16 If the dough offered as firstfruits is holy, so is the whole lump, and if the root is holy, so are the branches.

17 But if some of the branches were broken off, and you, although a wild olive shoot, were grafted in among the others and now share in the nourishing root of the olive tree, 18 do not be arrogant toward the branches. If you are, remember it is not you who support the root, but the root that supports you. 19 Then you will say, 'Branches were broken off so that I might be grafted in.' 20 That is true. They were broken off because of their unbelief, but you stand fast through faith. So do not become proud, but fear. 21 For if God did not spare the natural branches, neither will he spare you. 22 Note then the kindness and the severity of God: severity toward those who have fallen, but God's kindness to you, provided you continue in his kindness. Otherwise you too will be cut off. 23 And even they, if they do not continue in their unbelief, will be grafted in, for God has the power to graft them in again. 24 For if you were cut from what is by nature a wild olive tree, and grafted, contrary to nature, into a cultivated olive tree, how much more will these, the natural branches, be grafted back into their own olive tree.

(Rom. 11:1-24)

Paul now begins to bring his extended discussion of the spiritual condition of his kinsmen to a series of conclusions, a resolution, and a response. He asks and answers two questions (in verses 1 and 11), and then works through their implications. In the process he comments on his own sense of apostolic calling (verses 13-16), gives an important admonition to the Romans as a (probably) predominantly Gentile church (verses 17-21), and makes a significant observation about the ways of God (verses 22-24). He then comes to a final resolution of his burden (verses 25-32) before closing the entire section with an ascription of praise to God (verses 33-36).

And so, as we shall see, this long section that began in 9:1 with deep sorrow ends in an exalted doxology.

HAS GOD REJECTED HIS PEOPLE?

Paul now comes to his bottom line issue: 'I ask, then …' (verse 1). His language summons us to pay close attention to both his question and his answer.

Question: 'Has God rejected his people?' The only other time in the New Testament this verb is used is Acts 7:27. It conveys a sense of finality, of thrusting something away, repudiating, or (as here in the ESV), rejecting it.

Answer: Once again Paul's initial response is indicative of a conviction so profound it emerges intuitively: 'By no means!' 'Never!' (cf. 3:4, 6, 31; 6:2, 15; 7:7, 13; 9:14). He has developed biblical instincts. Here is a further indication that exposure to the word of God increasingly sanctifies our instincts, theologically as well as morally, even if imperfectly.

Although not obvious in our English translations, the form in which Paul asks the question (in Greek) already indicates that he expects a negative answer. Nevertheless he spells it out: *'By no means!'* While this response—that God has not abandoned Israel—will require an extended explanation, we must not lose sight of the basic answer. While the situation and condition of his own people is heartbreaking for Paul, it is not one of total rejection. He now goes on to explain this in several stages: verses 1-10; 11-12; 13-16; 17-24; 25-32, climaxing in his magnificent doxology in verses 33-36.

EXHIBIT 1

Paul himself is exhibit number one in demonstrating that God has not completely abandoned the Jews. In essence he says, 'I am as Jewish as they come,' and points to his own lineage and pedigree (verse 1; as he does, for a different reason, in Phil. 3:4-5). He himself is an Israelite, a descendant of Abraham, and indeed a Benjaminite. So if *he* has come to faith , then God has not completely thrust his people away.

But beyond the *personal* illustration, there is a *theological* explanation: 'God has not rejected his people *whom he foreknew*' (verse 2). God loved his people—that is why they were his people in the first place. And Paul is convinced that God never revises his electing purposes—although, as he has indicated, those purposes have never been a blanket guarantee that every natural-born Israelite is a faith-filled Israelite (cf. 9:6).

Once again the apostle views things through biblically-crafted lenses. In verses 2-4 he appeals to the account of Elijah and specifically to his complaint to God in 1 Kings 19:10ff. He saw himself as in a minority of one: 'I alone am left' (verse 3; cf. 1 Kings 19:9-18). In fact there were seven thousand who had not 'bowed the knee to Baal' (verse 4). And just as there was then, so there is also in Paul's day, 'a remnant, chosen by grace' (verse 5).

But the fact that there is a 'remnant' (an idea we met before in the quotation of Isaiah 10:22 in 9:27) should not be seen as an indication that those who constituted it somehow merited their election. The remnant is 'chosen by grace' (verse 5). Thus Paul safeguards us from misreading his illustration. It was not their refusing to bow the knee to Baal that rendered the seven thousand acceptable to God. That was the fruit, not the root. Not even heroism of that order grounds God's distinguishing election. It is the other way round.

The word 'grace' appears four times in verses 5-6, and three times in verse 6 alone. Paul's logic is simple. It is also honouring to God and devastating to our pride. Salvation is all of grace, only by grace, and always by grace. The moment we begin to imagine that God's election might be rooted in something—anything—in us, including courage bordering on heroism, or radical commitment to the Lord himself, or for that matter our suffering—'grace would no longer be grace' (verse 6).

'What then?' (verse 7)—that is, 'What has happened to Israel? And what is the current situation?'

Paul's answer is multi-layered:

(i) Israel, viewed as a whole, has 'failed to obtain what it was seeking' (verse 7). As he had explained in 10:3, they sought but did not come into possession of righteousness because they sought to establish their own righteousness rather than submit to God's way of righteousness by grace alone in Christ alone.

(ii) The 'elect' in Israel have obtained that righteousness by God's grace and by means of salvation in Jesus Christ.

(iii) 'The rest were hardened.' These last words come from

Paul's broken heart and must have fallen on Jewish-Christian ears like a hammer blow. The verb form is passive, and the quotation that follows makes clear that it is a 'divine passive.' God hardened the hearts of those whose hard hearts refused his Christ.

Once again Paul appeals to Scripture. He is saying only what the Hebrew Bible had already said. His teaching is not novel. He demonstrates this by weaving language from Isaiah 29:10 into Deuteronomy 29:4 (the way a preacher might bring together two texts that shed light on each other) and then citing Psa. 69:22-23.

In one of his prayers, the Scottish reformer John Knox spoke about God 'judging sin with sin.' Paul had enunciated that principle earlier in this letter (in 1:22, 24, 26). God gives people over to the consequences of their rejection of him. The result (verse 8) is that they develop a spirit that is indifferent to him ('a spirit of stupor'), eyes that are not fixed on his will (they 'would not see'), and ears that will not listen to his voice (they 'would not hear'). What they seek enslaves them, the way in which they walk causes them to stumble; ultimately they are given over to their diseased vision and cannot see; and what they have created for themselves proves to be spiritually back-breaking (verse 10).

This is a sobering description of Israel. But it is a description Paul found in the Hebrew Bible with which he and his kinsmen were so familiar. Scripture's words, he says, are not only a description of Israel's past history; they were being fulfilled 'down to this very day' (verse 8). Given that this is what we find in Scripture, 'it is not as though the word of God has failed' (9:6).

This sombre conclusion leads Paul to a second question, introduced with the same formality that characterized the first one ('I ask ...'): Did Israel 'stumble in order that they might fall?' (verse 11).

STUMBLING AND FALLING?

Having stressed God's righteous judgment in the preceding verses it is noteworthy that the apostle frames this new question in terms of Israel's own activity and responsibility ('did *they* stumble that *they* might fall?' verse 11).

Once again the form in which he asks the question anticipates a negative answer. We could almost predict that his response would be—as in fact it is—'By no means!'

Paul's answer is relatively brief (verses 11-12). But it leads to the extended exposition and application that dominates the rest of the chapter until he breaks out in doxology in verses 33-36. Israel's rejection is not *total*; now Paul raises a further question: Did Israel 'stumble *in order that* they might fall?'

Interpretations and therefore translations of these words differ. The ESV translates them as a *purpose* clause ('in order that'); others interpret them as a *result* clause ('with the result that').

At this stage in the chapter the ESV seems to be correct. Paul goes on to spell out various aspects of what that purpose is. Thus, in verses 11-12 he gives a short-form answer to his question; in verses 13-24 he applies its significance for the (probably dominant) Gentile group in the church; this then leads him in verses 25-32 to unveil the mystery of God's long-term purposes for Jew *and* Gentile.

Here, in passing, it may be worth mentioning that *Romans was written in order to be read aloud*. And in fact that is still the best way to read it—not least the sections in which he is reasoning things out. No doubt members of the churches in Rome would have made copies of his letter and read it in private. But first they must have gathered to hear it read to them. In fact, in antiquity even reading in private was done 'out loud.'[1] There is no doubt that the power of both the logic and the deep emotion of Romans 9–11 come alive when read aloud. It is an experiment worth trying.

Later, Paul will describe what he now begins to discuss as a 'mystery' (11:25).

THE MYSTERY

A 'mystery' is something we could not understand apart from divine revelation, something hidden within the providential purposes of God that requires divine illumination to enable us to grasp. Here Paul begins to unravel the mystery enshrined in God's providential governing of history with respect to the relationship of Jews and Gentiles (i) to the gospel and also (ii) to each other.

The basics are as follows:

In the divine economy, Israel's rejection of Christ has led to

[1] Our practice of 'reading into ourselves' was apparently so unusual that as late as the end of the fourth century AD Augustine expressed surprise that he would come across Ambrose the bishop of Milan reading a book silently to himself.

the gospel being brought to the Gentiles. Through the trespass (stumbling) of the Jews, salvation has come to Gentiles (verse 11). This reflected Paul's own experience. It is a pattern that punctuates the record of his ministry in the Acts of the Apostles (*e.g.*, 13:44-47; 18:1-7; 19:8-10; 28:13-28).

But Paul saw a deeper process at work here—a providential process governed by the sovereign Lord. Deeply inscribed within the story of this Jewish rejection of the gospel was not only the Gentile reception of it, but—since that did not happen apart from God's sovereign purposes—the salvation of the Gentiles would 'make Israel jealous' (verse 11).

On this basis Paul now creates a logical argument or syllogism:

If it is true that
The *trespass* of the Jews leads to *riches* for the world, and their *failure* means *riches* for the Gentiles

Then it will also be true that
Their *full inclusion* will mean *much more*.

The argument seems clear enough. If Jewish trespass (their rejection of Jesus) has brought blessing to the Gentiles (their salvation through faith in Jesus), then, surely Jewish inclusion will lead to even greater blessing.

The ESV's 'full inclusion' translates the word 'fullness' (*plērōma*). But what does Paul mean by *plērōma?* Since it stands in antithesis to the *stumbling* or *trespass* of the Jewish people, it would seem to refer to their coming to faith and the new obedience that results from it.

Since this statement cries out for further exposition, Paul will return to explain it in verses 25-32. But in the meantime he immediately applies its significance to the Gentile section of the church (who were, perhaps, already in danger of becoming a faction): 'Now I am speaking to you Gentiles' (verse 13).

What will he say to them?

A WORD FOR GENTILES

God had commissioned Paul as 'an apostle to the Gentiles' (cf. Acts 9:15). But he understands that an element in the divine purpose in the conversion of Gentiles is that it would cause Jews to be envious. This in turn adds a fresh layer of significance to his own ministry to the Gentiles. He magnifies it with a view to promoting such envy (verse 13). Although he has been sent to the Gentiles he continues to have a burden for his own people. In fact, even in going to the Gentiles he has the salvation of his own people on his heart. Deep within his passion to serve Christ as an apostle to the Gentiles is his love for his own people, the Jews! In his jealousy-inciting preaching of Christ and his kingdom, some Jews were saved (verse 14).

We are now taken a stage further as Paul returns to his logical argument and elaborates it from the Jewish Scriptures. The parallel with his syllogism in verse 12 is obvious:

> If the *trespass of the Jews* has led to *riches for the Gentiles*,
> the *fullness of the Jews* will mean *much greater riches.*

Similarly:

> If the *rejection of the Jews* has led to the *reconciliation of the world* (as in 5:10-11),
> the *acceptance of the Jews* will mean nothing less than *'life from the dead'* (verse 15).

WHAT OF THE JEWS?

Paul's teaching here has given rise to major differences in interpretations. The road divides into two (albeit there are side roads, further junctions, and individual nuances in the interpretations). Much simplified, the most frequently adopted views are as follows:

(i) Paul teaches that throughout the Christian ages there will be conversions to Christ among the Jewish people until all the elect of God are gathered. Thus 'all Israel will be saved' (verse 26). In different forms of this view 'all Israel' is interpreted as 'the church, the true "spiritual" Israel' (the view of Augustine and Calvin), or more literally and simply as 'all the elect of ethnic Israel in every age' (verse 26).

(ii) Paul teaches that at some time in the future the Jews *as a people* (*i.e.* in substantial numbers, but not necessarily without exception) will turn to Jesus Christ, recognize him as their Messiah, trust him as their Saviour, and bow to him as their Lord. Thus in a very visible way the Jewish people as a whole will be seen to turn to Christ, and this will have significant repercussions. This view too comes in variant forms and there are some significant differences in interpreting the timing of this event.

It is not possible here to expound these various views at length or in detail. What follows adopts interpretation (ii) as generally more faithful to Paul's meaning.[1] The basic reasons for taking such a view at this stage in the chapter are:

(i) When Paul refers to 'Israel' in these chapters he is referring to ethnic Israel. Even when he draws a distinction in Israel in 9:6 his language in that context is restricted to the seed of Abraham (*i.e.* ethnic Israelites). When therefore he says (in 11:26) that 'all Israel will be saved,' it would be illegitimate to understand him in any other way unless he made that different meaning crystal clear.

(ii) Paul has been speaking thus far about the Jewish people *as a people*. True, there are Jewish knees that have bowed to Christ, but they have been a minority and the apostle distinguishes them as such ('a remnant,' verse 5). They are by no means 'Israel' as a whole. But when he speaks about 'full inclusion' and 'all Israel' he does seem to be referring to the people as a whole and not merely to an ongoing succession of remnants.

(iii) The form of argument used ('much more,' verse 12, and implied in verse 15), set within the context of the 'acceptance' and 'fullness' of the Jewish people, anticipates something on a much larger scale than Paul's present experience. In his day only a relatively small number of Jews were coming to faith in Christ. It is true that if that present pattern continued there would be a much larger total number of individuals saved. But it would be strange to describe the total as 'life from the dead' (verse 15). That expression seems to look beyond a simple accumulation of numbers and points to a climactic and quantum difference—not so much a slow 'accumulation' but a remarkable 'event' in which multitudes of Jews come to faith in Jesus as the Messiah. Here, perhaps, we should underline that Paul envisages their salvation in no other way than by faith in Christ.

Of course Paul says that in Christ there is no longer 'Greek [*i.e.* Gentile] or Jew … barbarian, Scythian, slave, free' (Col. 3:11). God's people are no longer one distinct people-group. But there is

[1] A form of view (i) will be found in: William Hendriksen, *Romans*, listed later among commentaries suggested for further study.

no inherent theological problem in believing that God has ongoing purposes of grace for the Jewish people any more than there is in recognizing that, in his providence, he has at times worked powerfully in specific Gentile nations in ways he has not done in others. This may be a mystery to us, but it is certainly not a theological contradiction of the universal nature of the Christian church.

Paul has now expanded on the 'how much more' of the 'full inclusion' (fullness) of the Jewish people. Jewish failure has led to Gentile riches. Jewish 'full inclusion' will surely lead to even greater riches: 'their acceptance' can mean nothing less than 'life from the dead' (verse 15).

In verse 16, Paul confirms his argument by means of a biblical allusion: 'If the dough offered as firstfruits is holy, so is the whole lump, and if the root is holy, so are the branches.'

The background to this statement lies in the liturgical regulations given to Moses (Num. 15:17-21). The first loaf baked from a lump of dough was 'holy to the Lord' and was devoted to him as a token of the whole lump of dough being sanctified to him. Again, if the root is holy, the branches will be too. As Paul says later, Israel remains beloved by God 'for the sake of their forefathers' (verse 28).

The patriarchs were 'the firstfruits of the dough'; they were the 'root' from which the branches grew. The implication is that the principle that was true in the liturgy of God's ancient people holds good historically: God's ancient people still have a place in his economy.

But all this is 'not yet' for Paul. The present situation, by and large, is one of Jewish rejection leading to Gentile acceptance. Salvation has come to those who were 'not my people' (9:25).

Paul was well aware of the temptation this situation presented and to which some Gentile believers yielded. They stumbled into a spiritual trap that was the mirror image of the one into which he and his own kinsmen had fallen—thinking of themselves as superior. The gospel had come to the Gentiles having been by and large rejected by Jews throughout the empire. Gentile Christians might therefore be tempted not only to demean Jewish people in general, but also their Jewish-Christian brothers and sisters. Later in chapters 14 and 15 Paul tackles the side effects of that attitude.

GENTILES

Verses 17-24 are dominated by the picture of an olive tree. The imagery was familiar, and Old Testament prophets had already used it as an image of God's covenant people (Jer. 11:16; Hos. 14:5-6).

Here then is the situation: 'natural' branches (Israelites) have been broken off from the olive tree God planted. Wild shoots (Gentiles) have been grafted in. But the grafts (Gentiles) need to understand their situation: they 'now share in the nourishing root of the olive tree' (verse 17). The implication is this: Gentiles *share* the life-giving root; they are not the root itself! It supports them, not the other way round. There is therefore no room for Gentile grafts to display arrogance towards the natural branches (Israel) that the root of God's electing grace had long ago produced.

Paul had probably already encountered such arrogance. Here he anticipates it in a Gentile believer's potential words: 'Branches were broken off that I might be grafted in' (verse 19; cf. verse 17). He responds: 'True; but they were not broken off because you are superior to them; it was the result of their own unbelief.' So the ingrafting of the Gentiles is not a matter of superiority, or merit, but only of the grace that effects the faith that rests on Christ alone. No believer should ever forget that the faith-way is the grace-way, and the grace-way is the faith-way. It leaves no room for boasting in ourselves—Paul had made that clear (3:19-20, 27).

Thus, knowing that natural branches were broken off because of their unfaithfulness should cause Gentile 'grafts' (verse 19) to have godly fear, and a spirit of humility towards the Jewish people. For if God dealt thus with the natural branches (Israel) it would be folly to assume he would spare unfaithful Gentiles (verses 20-21).

IMPLICATIONS

The 'takeaway' from this is clear: in his ongoing providence God displays both his mercy and his justice, his severity and his kindness (verse 22). He has taken Jewish rejection of his Son seriously (severity); he has called Gentiles into his kingdom (kindness).

How then are Gentile believers to respond? By recognizing God's kindness to them and continuing to receive it, appreciate it, and enjoy it—by embracing Christ in faith, repentance, and obedience (cf. 2:4). Go the way of disobedient Israel, and Gentiles will share

Israel's rejection. But the reverse is also the case: if Israelites turn to Christ in faith, yielding him obedience as Lord, they will be 'grafted in again.' God is well able to do that (verse 23)!

Paul concludes this section with a final 'much more' argument: If in God's grace a cutting from a wild olive tree can be grafted in—unnaturally as it were—into a cultivated olive tree, how much more will God regraft a broken-off natural branch into the tree that first gave it life (verse 24)?

How mysterious, how marvellous, and how kind, are the ways of God! And yet Paul is undeviating in the way he has shown that he is also always just.

Later Paul will address the tension between Jewish and Gentile believers in the church at Rome. Underneath all he will say there lies this substratum that runs through the letter from the announcing of its theme text in 1:16-17 ('to the Jew first and also to the Greek'), through his exposure of Gentile and Jewish sin in 1:18–3:20, in his appeal to Abraham and Moses, and now in these verses. He is displaying tremendous pastoral wisdom as well as great theological acumen. Here, in the context of chapters 9–11, before we (contemporary readers) even know there is a problem in the Roman church, he has been shaping the way Gentile believers think about their Jewish brethren, and vice-versa.

Paul urges humility on both Jew and Gentile. For where humility reigns, fellowship will be both preserved and strengthened (cf. Phil. 2:1-11).

31

Mystery Revealed, God Glorified

Lest you be wise in your own sight, I do not want you to be
unaware of this mystery, brothers: a partial hardening has
come upon Israel, until the fullness of the Gentiles has come
in. 26 *And in this way all Israel will be saved, as it is written,*

> *'The Deliverer will come from Zion,*
> *he will banish ungodliness from Jacob';*
> 27 *'and this will be my covenant with them*
> *when I take away their sins.'*

28 *As regards the gospel, they are enemies for your sake. But as*
regards election, they are beloved for the sake of their forefathers.
29 *For the gifts and the calling of God are irrevocable.* 30 *For*
just as you were at one time disobedient to God but now have
received mercy because of their disobedience, 31 *so they too have*
now been disobedient in order that by the mercy shown to you
they also may now receive mercy. 32 *For God has consigned all*
to disobedience, that he may have mercy on all.
33 *Oh, the depth of the riches and wisdom and knowledge of*
God! How unsearchable are his judgments and how inscrutable
his ways!

> 34 *'For who has known the mind of the Lord,*
> *or who has been his counsellor?'*
> 35 *'Or who has given a gift to him*
> *that he might be repaid?'*

36 *For from him and through him and to him are all things.*
To him be glory forever. Amen.

(Rom. 11:25-36)

We all have characteristic speech patterns. You might, for example, have met a Christian with the (sometimes irritating) habit of constantly addressing you as 'brother' or 'sister.' By contrast Paul seems to use the address 'brothers' only in moments of heightened emotion or concern. He had appealed to the Roman believers in this way (essentially as 'family') only a handful of times (1:13; 7:1, 4; 8:12; 10:1). When he does so once again here (verse 25), it is a signal he is coming to the climax of the discussion that began in chapter 9.

Paul now points both Gentile and Jewish Christians to an important spiritual safeguard (they are not to 'be wise in your own sight,' verse 25). It is a call for humility. John Calvin and Augustine (from whom he derived the illustration) refer in their writings to a famous comment made by the great Greek orator Demosthenes. When asked about the key to eloquence he replied, 'Delivery, delivery, delivery.' In a comparable way, these two major theologians commented that if they were asked to identify the key to Christian living their answer would be, 'Humility, humility, humility.'[1]

To curb pride Paul says, 'I do not want you to be unaware of this mystery ...' (verse 25). Once again he emphasizes a positive by stating it in a negative way: 'I do not want you to be unaware ...' But unaware of what? A 'mystery' (*mustērion*). The word appears (in the singular and plural) some twenty-seven times in the New Testament. Twenty of those occurrences are in Paul's letters. It refers to something known exclusively to God to which we have access only when he reveals its meaning to us.

In verses 25-32, Paul (1.) states the mystery (verse 25), (2.) explains its consequence (verses 26-27), and (3.) stresses its significance (verses 28-32) before breaking out in the magnificent doxology with which the chapter concludes (verses 33-36).

MYSTERY UNVEILED

The mystery itself is that 'a partial hardening has come upon Israel until the fullness of the Gentiles has come in' (verse 25) so that 'in this way all Israel will be saved' (verse 26)—according to the prophetic words of Isaiah (59:20-21, nuanced with some further wording from Isaiah 27:9).

[1] Calvin, *Institutes*, II.ii.11.

The significance of this is that we are to view Israel from two perspectives: both as enemies of God—which status, paradoxically, has benefited Gentiles—and also as the elect of God—beloved by him for the sake of the forefathers because God does not renege on his word—'the gifts and calling of God are irrevocable' (verses 28-29).

We are also to view the historical outworking of the Lord's dealings with them from two perspectives:

(i) Israel's disobedience has, in God's providence, led to Gentiles receiving mercy.

(ii) The mercy shown to Gentiles is to result in that same mercy being received by Jews. Both Jews and Gentiles—as Paul had already demonstrated in 1:18–3:20—are 'consigned … to disobedience.' Nevertheless, the underlying purpose of our gracious God is 'that he may have mercy on all,' both Jew and Gentile (verses 30-32).

Here we come to another passage in Romans whose meaning has been much debated. But Paul believed his readers would be able to understand it. After all he said that he did not want them to 'be *unaware* of this mystery' (verse 25).

Paul had already explained in the previous verses what he meant by saying 'a partial hardening has come upon Israel.' But three questions remain, all related to verses 25-26. The answers to them should enable us to get to the heart of the 'mystery.'

QUESTIONS

(i) What does 'the fullness of the Gentiles' mean (verse 25)?

(ii) What does the phrase 'in this way' mean (verse 26, Greek *kai houtōs*)?

(iii) What does 'all Israel will be saved' mean (verse 26)?

Given the fact that the apostle refers to a 'mystery' here, we need to remember his counsel to beware of being 'wise in your own sight' (verse 25). We must approach these verses patiently with humility of heart and mind.

Paul sees what he says in verse 25 as a fulfilment of the prophecy of Isaiah 59:20-21, clarified by the words added from Isaiah 27:9 ('when I take away their sins').

Some questions about these words remain difficult to resolve dogmatically. Why, for example, does Paul change Isaiah's original 'a Redeemer will *come to Zion*' into 'The Deliverer will *come from Zion*'?

Different answers have been given to this question, and they are often related to the interpreter's broader understanding of the Bible.

Many understand the change in preposition to indicate that Paul is thinking about the return of Christ from heaven (cf. the reference to the 'heavenly Zion' in Heb. 12:22), and therefore connect the ingathering of Israel to Christ's return.

However, the reason for the subtle change of preposition may simply be to stress again the debt Gentiles owe to God's ways with the Jews. Christ the Deliverer who came *to* Zion (*i.e.* to the Jewish people, cf. Matt. 15:24; Mark 7:27; Luke 13:33) now comes to the world '*from* Zion' (cf. Jesus' words to the Samaritan woman, 'salvation is from the Jews,' John 4:22). Paul would thus be driving home his earlier words to Gentile Christians, 'do not be arrogant toward the branches ... it is not you who support the root, but the root that supports you ... as regards election they are beloved for the sake of their forefathers' (verses 18-19). If so this was a further admonition to Gentile believers to curb their pride, as well as an encouragement to Jewish believers that they were not second-class citizens in Christ's kingdom.

Expressed negatively, the 'mystery' that is revealed *cannot* be merely that the kingdom of Christ would consist of both Jews and Gentiles. That would not have been a 'mystery' to Paul. It had been revealed virtually from the beginning, enshrined in the Abrahamic covenant (cf. Gen. 12:1ff.), and clearly expressed in many different ways in the Old Testament. Rather, the 'mystery' lies at least in part in the way in which this takes place, through the divine dialectic in history: the salvation of Gentiles results from the rejection of Jews; the salvation of Jews follows that of Gentiles!

But what does Paul mean by '*until the fullness* of the Gentiles has come in' (verse 25)? There are two possible interpretations here:

'Until' means that this partial hardness will persist right up to the point of this 'fullness.' But the preposition *by itself* does not determine whether Paul means this hardness will persist:

(i) 'up to that point' without suggesting any implications for what follows; or

(ii) 'up to that point and then cease.'

In favour of view (ii) that when 'the fullness of the Gentiles has come in' the hardness will cease are the following considerations:

(a) If all Paul meant (as some interpretations hold) was that the *status quo* of Gentiles coming to faith and becoming the means of the conversion of a Jewish remnant would continue throughout history there would have been an easier and clearer way of saying it than this.

(b) If that was what he meant, it seems unusual to think of this as a 'mystery.' In this case he would be saying no more than 'the *status quo* will continue to the end.'

(c) In stating that when 'the fullness of the Gentiles has come in' 'all Israel will be saved,' Paul cites words from Isaiah that describe something more climactic and remarkable than that the *status quo* would simply continue.

(d) If 'all Israel will be saved' means no more than 'the *status quo* of a remnant of Jewish converts will continue' it is more difficult to see the logical and psychological connection to verses 33-36 which constitute the supreme doxological passage in the letter, if not in the whole Bible.

Paul began dictating this argument in 9:1 in 'great sorrow and unceasing anguish' (9:2). His 'heart's desire and prayer to God' was for all of his Israelite brethren to 'be saved' (10:1). To point to the continuation of the *status quo* seems inadequate to alleviate Paul's own spiritual anguish and to lead to the heart-bursting praise of God that follows.

The whole thrust of this chapter suggests that Paul expects something bigger, something grander than the continuation of the present situation. The divine dialectic in history will reach its 'omega-point.' Jewish rejection leading to Gentile acceptance, and Gentile acceptance increasing throughout history to the point of 'fullness,' will be climaxed when the veil is taken from the eyes of the Jewish people as a whole (even if not without exception).

The fact is that an ongoing *status quo* could hardly create the excitement Paul clearly feels in the conclusion he draws for *both* Jew and Gentile: 'God has consigned all to disobedience that he may have mercy on all.' The 'all' here surely refers to a climactic reality: for thus 'all Israel will be saved.'

In summary, then: We have already seen that in Romans 9–11, Paul refers to 'Israel' twelve times (9:6 twice; 9:27 twice; 9:31; 10:19; 10:21; 11:2; 11:7; 11:11; 11:25; 11:26). Leaving the reference here aside, in all but one instance he is clearly referring to the Jewish people as a whole. The one exception is his carefully nuanced words in 9:6, 'not all who are descended from Israel belong to Israel,' where he distinguishes between 'ethnic Israel' and 'believing Israel.' But even here, in both instances he was referring to *Jewish* people. Whatever may be true elsewhere (Gal. 6:16), in no instance in these chapters does 'Israel' include 'Jew *and* Gentile.' It would surely be redundant and anticlimactic to have said 'all Israel will be saved' if what was meant was simply that 'all believers will be saved.' That would be no 'mystery' at all.

'All Israel will be saved' does not necessarily imply that each and every individual Jewish person will come to faith in Christ. The expression 'all Israel' is used regularly in the Old Testament in a general sense (*e.g.* 1 Kings 1:20; 2:15; 3:28). It denotes the people as a whole rather than each and every individual without exception. Paul anticipates 'Israel as a whole' will be 'saved.' The context of Romans 9–11 makes it clear that this salvation will come in the same way Jews in his own day were experiencing it, namely by faith in the Lord Jesus Christ.

Paul is looking forward to the conclusion of the providential pattern he has been unfolding. It will reach a climax which he describes as nothing less than 'life from the dead' (verse 15). Again this indicates something far greater than the present *status quo* or its continuation. The apostle to the Gentiles anticipates a day dawning when the Jewish response to Messiah Jesus will be transformed. What a day that will be!

The phrase 'life from the dead' (verse 15) is used only here. Some understand it to mean that the salvation of Israel will be a *forerunner* of the return of Christ and the general resurrection. Others have held more specifically that it will take place *as a result of* Christ's return. But Paul refers to the event that will result from the return of Christ as 'resurrection.' So it may be better to take 'life from the dead' here as implying a glorious resuscitation of Israel to covenant faithfulness and fulfilment.

Paul's language here echoes his earlier comment on God's faithfulness to his covenant promise that Abraham would have a son when his own body was 'as good as dead' (4:19). He is 'the God … who gives life to the dead …' (4:17). As with the birth of Isaac, so with the conversion of Paul's kinsmen: the observable situation provided no grounds for hope except in God's promise. It is, therefore, easy to imagine the transformative impact on the world the widespread conversion of God's ancient people would have. The olive tree (verse 17) would be seen to bear superabundant fruit from both the grafted-contrary-to-nature-branches and the re-grafted-natural-branches.

The mystery that is now revealed through Paul is then a divinely-planned wonder. Not only are Gentiles being brought to Christ as a result of Israel's rejection of him, but in turn the 'fullness' of the Gentiles will lead to the salvation of Israel—'life from the dead' among God's ancient people, and life for the world as a result.

THE VIEW FROM THE SUMMIT

Thus Romans 11:28-32 brings us almost to the summit of the theological mountain whose base camp was pitched at Romans 9:1. The climb has been arduous; but the view is spectacular. From this high vantage point we can better see the panorama of God's purposes. From the perspective of history, and of Paul's day, in terms of their response to the gospel, Israel (remnant apart) 'are enemies' (verse 28). Yet, paradoxically, in the economy of God, this proves to be for the benefit of the Gentiles.

But also, from this summit we are given a view that stretches into the distance—both behind us and in front of us. As we look back we see that Israel was and remains 'beloved for the sake of their forefathers' (verse 28). God chose the patriarchs in love and gave them covenant promises. He does not change his mind ('the gifts and calling of God are irrevocable,' verse 29).

God's word of promise has not failed. Nor has the God of promise changed. The God of grace is never defeated, nor has he 'rejected his people' (verse 1). 'God is working his purpose out as year succeeds to year.'[1] The wonder is that Israel's disobedience has resulted in disobedient Gentiles receiving mercy from God—a display of mercy that will lead in turn to Israel receiving mercy. The words of 11:33-36 are the only proper response.

THE DOXOLOGICAL CLIMAX

The eloquence of the closing verses brings us not only to the conclusion of Romans 9:1–11:32 but to the climax of the entire letter thus far.

In 1:18–3:20 Paul had explained at length how and why it is that 'God consigned all to disobedience' (verse 32) before explaining (in 3:21–8:39) how he has had 'mercy on all' (verse 32).

Truly, all have sinned, Jew and Gentile alike, and have fallen short of the glory of God. His wrath is therefore righteously revealed from heaven against all ungodliness and unrighteousness, whether in Jew or in Gentile. But there is good news: the gospel is 'the power of God for salvation *to everyone who believes, to the Jew first and also to the Greek*. For in it the righteousness of God is revealed from faith for faith' (1:16-17).

Truly, where sin has abounded, God's grace has abounded all the more. With Augustine we can say, 'I see the depth; I cannot reach the bottom.' He was singing from the same songbook as Paul does here in the words with which these chapters now climax. Embedded in them are quotes from two Old Testament passages of soaring rhetoric—Isaiah 40:13 and Job 41:11.

The power of these words rivals, indeed may even surpass (if possible) the closing section of chapter 8 in their recognition of the incomprehensibility (but *not unknowability*), the absoluteness of the sovereignty, and the perfection of the knowledge and wisdom of the One who is the Creator, Sustainer, and the Ultimate End of all things—the One to whom all glory is to be ascribed, world without end.

> Oh, the depth of the riches and wisdom and knowledge of God! How unsearchable are his judgments and how inscrutable his ways! 'For who has known the mind of the Lord, or who has been his counsellor?' 'Or who has given a gift to him that he might be

[1] The opening line of the hymn by Arthur Campbell Ainger (1841–1919).

> repaid?' For from him and through him and to him are all things. To him be glory forever. Amen (verses 33-36).

The words are both self-explanatory and at the same time carry implications that are beyond our ability fully to grasp. It would seem almost an impertinence to comment further on such exalted praise. Perhaps the only appropriate response is to repeat them and to say: 'Amen, and Amen.'

32

Living Sacrifices

I appeal to you therefore, brothers, by the mercies of God, to present your bodies as a living sacrifice, holy and acceptable to God, which is your spiritual worship. [2] Do not be conformed to this world, but be transformed by the renewal of your mind, that by testing you may discern what is the will of God, what is good and acceptable and perfect.

(Rom. 12:1-2)

We come now to a major transition point in Romans, but one that has a deep connection to everything that precedes it. The conclusion of the previous section was signalled by the climactic doxology in 11:33-36. But Paul now connects chapters 1–11 to chapters 12–16 by the conjunction 'therefore' (verse 1). Truth has consequences.

Paul's gospel includes consequences for Christian living. Everything Paul has said thus far—about our need for but lack of righteousness (1:18–3:20), God's provision and our reception of that righteousness (3:1–4:25), how this transforms our lives personally (5:1–8:39) and then how God's righteousness is worked out in history in relation to Jews and Gentiles (9:1–11:32)—all to his praise (11:33-36)—now leads to the ways in which righteousness comes to expression in daily Christian living in the church and in the world (12:1–15:21).

Paul then bookends the letter with personalized comments, sharing his plans for future mission, and sending greetings to the brothers and sisters he knows in the churches in Rome (15:22–16:27).

Metaphorically we might say that Paul has taken us on a ski-lift up the theological mountain of the mercies of the saving righteousness of God so that we can now keep our spiritual balance as we negotiate our way down the slopes of life.

He begins with a summons to unreserved consecration to the Lord.

GOSPEL GRAMMAR

The high emotion of 11:33-36 is still echoing in Paul's mind and ours. Once again he addresses the Romans as 'brothers' (cf. 1:13; 7:1, 4; 8:12; 10:1; 11:25) in a way that is not only powerful and personal ('I appeal to you') but illustrative of how Paul understands the way the word of God works (cf. 1 Thess. 2:13).

In these two verses, we have one of the clearest illustrations in the apostle's letters of the inner logic and grammar of the gospel. Noticing it writ large here provides us with a basic grounding in how the gospel works to transform our lives. Once grasped, this apostolic logic and grammar become ingredients in the way we think and live as Christian believers.

Here, then, is a summary of the gospel grammar Paul employs in these verses:

> *The indicatives of God's grace in the gospel*
> *give rise to*
> *imperatives which direct us in righteous Christian living.*
> *Consecration is therefore both energized by,*
> *and the logical implication of,*
> *God's grace*
> *and leads to*
> *both negative and positive practical responses and effects in our lives.*

Here in 12:1-2, the *indicative* of 'the mercies of God' forms the *logical* ground ('therefore') for the *imperative* summons to *consecration* ('present your bodies as a living sacrifice'). And this imperative carries *implications* that are both *negative* ('Do not be conformed to ...') and *positive* ('but be transformed by ...') that in turn have *practical effects* ('that ... you may ...').

MERCY

Paul had specifically spoken of 'the mercies of God' in the previous three chapters (9:15-16, 18, 23; 11:30-32). But that same mercy had been demonstrated earlier in his exposition of the work of Christ (3:21-24). He is the ultimate Good Samaritan—'the one who showed mercy' (Matt. 10:37), rescuing us from sin and destruction. God is indeed 'the God who is rich in mercy' (Eph. 2:4).

In this mercy, as we embrace Christ we are united to him by faith and have been justified. But in that union we have also died to the dominion of sin and been set free from its bondage—in order to do battle with it (ch. 6); we have also died to the law—although we are not yet perfect according to its standards (ch. 7); and in addition we have been set free from a life of condemnation and have become 'more than conquerors'—called to live according to the Spirit and not according to the flesh in a world in which we also continue to experience tribulation but are never defeated (ch. 8).

This same merciful God is working out his purposes in, through, and for, both Jews and Gentiles (chs. 9–11). He means to have mercy on both (11:32). Paul's gospel thus far has bathed us in mercy. How should we respond?

LIVING SACRIFICE

We now possess a new status and identity in Christ while we continue to live in a world dominated by sin. We have the same bodies that were once sin's servants. So while our sanctification is real and radical, it is also progressive and arduous (as 6:11-14 had made clear). We are therefore called to present our whole selves sacrificially to God in bodily form ('present your bodies as a living sacrifice,' verse 1). We are not disembodied spirits. Consecration that is not physical is not spiritual!

Paul describes this consecration as a 'living sacrifice.' It is not the atoning sacrifice of a substitutionary death. Christ alone had made that for us once and for all. Rather it is a 'living' thank offering. But it is nonetheless a sacrifice. It will prove costly. Taking up the cross and following Christ always is (Luke 14:25-33). It cannot be otherwise when we are united to a risen Saviour who was once crucified.

Some translations render the Greek word here (*sōmata*) more generally as 'yourselves,' but as the ESV suggests, its basic meaning is 'bodies.' The exhortation has a special relevance to our age. In societies where God is not honoured, the creature is worshipped rather than the Creator (Rom. 1:25) and a kind of body-narcissism develops. Thus the message we find in advertisements in virtually every glossy magazine (and many that have no gloss) is: 'Offer your body to yourself and satisfy the desires of your heart. Decorate and admire yourself. You are worth it and deserve it.' How different the Christ-recovered life where we are summoned to present our bodies to the Lord in worship (thus reversing the trend of 1:25). For true beauty comes through holiness (the principles Peter applies to women in 1 Pet. 3:3-4 surely have a parallel form that is applicable to men). The goal is likeness to Christ, the restoration of the image of God.

NEW LIFE PATTERNS

This work of restoration, Paul tells us, inevitably involves two basic elements that should never be separated. One without the other will lead to spiritual malformation.

(i) Being living sacrifices involves non-conformity to the world. In J. B. Phillips's memorable paraphrase, 'Don't let the world around you squeeze you into its own mould.'[1]

(ii) But non-conformity alone is not holiness. A positive conformity is essential since true sanctification involves being 'conformed' to the likeness of Christ (Rom. 8:29). And so the old influencers of the world must give way to the only worthy Influencer, our Lord Jesus Christ. This is why we are exhorted to keep our eyes fixed on him (Col. 3:1; Heb. 12:1-2). The new life of righteousness is Jesus-shaped.

If, at this stage, Tertius the scribe had interjected and said, 'But Paul, *how does this take place?*,' verse 2 suggests his reply would be, 'I am glad you asked!' His answer points us to a central aspect in spiritual growth. Transformation takes place 'by the renewal of your mind.'

The dynamic here is as follows. Through the ministry of the Holy Spirit, the truth of the gospel is addressed to our minds and absorbed by us as rational, *thinking* beings. But as it percolates our thinking it impacts us as *affectionate* beings. Our dispositions are cleansed and recalibrated, and our desires transformed and redirected. This also influences us as *volitional* beings: we desire what is attractive to us. We come to love (affections) and want (will) what we

[1] J. B. Phillips, *New Testament in Modern English*, 332.

know to be good and spiritually healthy (mind); we understand what conforms to God's will (mind); we admire and desire it (affections) and determine to follow through its implications for our lives (will).

These are not three separate 'parts' of our human nature, as though one 'part' was impacted and then, perhaps some time later, another 'part.' They are, rather, three dimensions of the complex unity of our human nature.

The result is that 'by testing [*i.e.* in experience] you may discern what is the will of God, what is good and acceptable and perfect' (verse 2). Here mind ('discern'), affections (recognizing and loving the 'good and ... perfect') and will (finding 'acceptable' and responding to 'the will of God') unite in leading to a life of glad, unreserved, fulfilling consecration to the Lord.

But if this transformation-producing renewal is to take place our minds need to be instructed and informed by the gospel. This is exactly what Paul has been aiming at in the previous eleven chapters of his letter. This is the 'spiritual gift' he has been imparting to the Romans to strengthen them (1:11). Hence his reasoned exposition. And hence his occasional asking, 'Do you not know ...?' (6:3; 6:16; 7:1), and such statements as 'I do not want you to be unaware ...' (11:25). This too is why we engage in Bible study.

GRAMMAR: PRESENT, PASSIVE, IMPERATIVE

These two verses are especially helpful because they illustrate the way the dynamic of the gospel is enshrined in its grammar. Here we move on to a further lesson. At first sight there appears to be something paradoxical about Paul's exhortation, 'be transformed.'

Verbs come in different shapes and sizes. They have *moods* (indicative and imperative), *tenses* (past, present, future) and *voices* (active and passive). Here Paul's verb 'be transformed'—

- is in the *imperative mood:* it is a command addressed to us;
- is also in *the continuous present tense*: it is to be an ongoing reality, not a once-for-all-time event;
- but paradoxically (since it is a command directed to us), the verb is in the *passive voice*: the exhortation is not 'transform yourself' but '*be* transformed'!

What does Paul mean? How does this take place? Of course there is vigorous activity called for in the Christian life, as the many all-demanding imperatives that follow in Romans make clear (12:3-21). But at the heart of everything, energizing our response, is this principle: *spiritual transformation is initiated by the renewing of our minds*. And this is not self-generated. It takes place as we yield our minds to the word of God so that its truth and grace shape our thinking, our affections, our desires, and our wills. Then the word of God is at work in us (1 Thess. 2:13). The exhortation in Romans 12:2 is a subset of the broader exhortation in Philippians 2:12-13: 'Work out [*not* 'work for'!] your own salvation in fear and trembling, for it is God who works in you [by his word and Spirit], both to will and to work for his good pleasure.'

Now that these fundamental structures are in place, Paul can move on to explain their concentric spheres of application. This he will do in terms of:

(i) Christian commitment in church and society (12:3–13:14);

(ii) Christian fellowship with one another, especially in the light of conscientious differences (14:1–15:13);

(iii) Christian mission to the world (15:14–16:24).

Unsurprisingly, this leads Paul, once again, to break out in doxology (16:25-27).

'Practice makes perfect' is an old adage. Sportsmen and women speak about 'putting in the "reps" (repetitions).' Growth in any area of life involves getting the right principles and practices in place and repeating them with sufficient frequency for them to become instinctive. Something similar is true in the Christian life. The lessons, principles, and practices of *gospel logic and grammar* need to be regularly reviewed. As we notice how deeply embedded they are in the New Testament they will begin to take deep root in our minds and affections, transforming our desires, and energizing our wills.

So as we move on in our studies to the rest of Romans, we must never leave these two verses behind.

33

Life Together

For by the grace given to me I say to everyone among you not to think of himself more highly than he ought to think, but to think with sober judgment, each according to the measure of faith that God has assigned. [4] *For as in one body we have many members, and the members do not all have the same function,* [5] *so we, though many, are one body in Christ, and individually members one of another.* [6] *Having gifts that differ according to the grace given to us, let us use them: if prophecy, in proportion to our faith;* [7] *if service, in our serving; the one who teaches, in his teaching;* [8] *the one who exhorts, in his exhortation; the one who contributes, in generosity; the one who leads, with zeal; the one who does acts of mercy, with cheerfulness.*

(Rom. 12:3-8)

What does consecration to the Lord look like in practical terms? Paul now turns to consider this question in relationship to the concentric spheres in which we live out the life God has implanted in us in Christ. He begins 'at home.'

SERVING IN THE BODY.

'Charity begins at home.' Being a living sacrifice to the Lord means becoming a servant of others in our church family. That transformed way of living is rooted in a new way of thinking about them that in turn is effected by the renewing of our minds through God's word. Thus a basic key to living well within the church family is: 'I say to everyone ... *not to think of himself more highly than he ought to think ...*' (verse 3).

Paul issues this exhortation 'by the grace given to me.' This is not an exhortation to develop a grovelling spirit that is always proclaiming its own sense of inferiority. In fact it is characterized by the self-forgetfulness that arises from loving Christ and therefore wanting to love and serve those who belong to him.

The apostle's own life modelled the balance created by the gospel: an awareness of his gifts and calling ('the grace given to me') with a consciousness that all he was and all that he accomplished was by that grace. He sheds light on this balance elsewhere: 'I am ... unworthy to be called an apostle ... But by the grace of God I am what I am, and his grace toward me was not in vain. On the contrary I worked harder than any of them, though it was not I but the grace of God that is with me' (1 Cor. 15:10). He ascribes the transformation of his life to the Lord without demeaning his own hard work; and he stresses his hard work without detracting from the grace of God. It is by the grace of God that we are what we are. But that does not diminish our responsibility to work hard (and even to work harder than others!). But the stress here is on grace.

Paul knows that our native tendency is towards pride, not humility. In the Western world (but by no means only there), in sharp contrast to the past, our own era has transformed 'pride' in more than one way. What was once regarded as a vice is now heralded as a virtue. But pride has always had very subtle ways of injecting poison into how we view ourselves.

So how do we learn to think rightly? Not by denying what God in his grace has made us, or accomplished through us, but by developing what Paul calls 'sober [not sombre!] judgment' (verse 3). We learn in Christ to assess our lives and gifts by seeing through biblically-crafted lenses, all the while understanding that our perception is limited (there is a telling illustration of this in 1 Cor. 4:1-5). This leads to us seeing our lives in two dimensions. As Martin Luther famously noted, we are justified yet still sinners (*simul justus et peccator*). We are unworthy, but we have been engraced and gifted. The real issue is, have we been faithful? Do we serve 'each according to the measure of faith that God has assigned' (verse 3)?

Here Paul gives us a principle that helps us develop the sober judgment he has just mentioned, and at the same time encourages humility without grovelling. Each of us has different gifts, and spheres of service; but it is God who gives them to us. As he writes elsewhere, 'What do you have that you did not receive? If then you received it, why do you boast as if you did not receive it?' (1 Cor. 4:7).

We are to be transformed by the renewal of our minds. The use of the mind involves thinking (*phronein*). Verse 3 is packed with the importance of using our minds. Paul uses the compound verb 'think *more highly*' (*huperphronein*) as well as the simple form 'ought to think' (*phronein*); and 'but to think' (*phronein*), and in addition another compound verb, to 'think with a sober judgment,' *i.e.* with sound judgment (*sōphronein*). Think! Think! Think! Think! The root word must have sounded like a drumbeat in the ears of the first hearers—and we need to continue to hear it. The key to living a sanctified life and using our gifts spiritually begins with what goes on in our minds (a similar pattern appears later in verse 16). Paul knew long before modern psychologists discussed the topic that how we think, and especially how we think about ourselves and others, influences the way we live.

THE BODY

Paul now supplies an illustration to help us to think clearly (verses 4-5). The church is fundamentally a family since we are children of God. But the church also functions like a human body and its members. There has been much discussion about the source of Paul's use of this picture for the church (no other biblical writer employs it). But the implications he draws from it are far more important than the source from which he may have derived the idea. Each member has a different, unique, and essential role to play if the whole body is to function properly; all the members belong together in an interdependent, not independent, way. So it is in the church: we are 'one body in Christ.' We all belong to each other and therefore serve one another in that body.

The implication Paul draws from this metaphor is a simple one: our personal task is to use the gifts Christ has given to us for the sake of the whole body. When we think about ourselves 'with sober judgment' we see the simple wisdom of this. How foolish to be jealous of another's gifts when God has given us our own. How short-sighted if, having our distinctive gifts—each one needed by the church in order to function well—we fail to 'use them' (verse 6). How self-depriving if we do not realize how much we also need to be the recipient of others using their gifts to serve and help us.

Seeing the body as a picture of how a community should function was a commonplace in antiquity. The Roman author Livy famously recorded the story of how Menenius Agrippa (Consul in 503 BC) tried to smooth the rebellion of the plebians against the senate by arguing that each part of the body has its own function in enabling the body to work well. But in essence his point was that the plebs should stay in their servile place![1] How different Paul's view is! Service in the body of Christ is mutual, interdependent, harmonious—all are one in Christ Jesus. The members of the church in Corinth who were with him (16:23) would surely have remembered how he had written in similar terms to them and even emphasized that 'the parts of the body that seem to be weaker are indispensable, and on those parts of the body that we think less honourable we bestow the greater honour' (1 Cor. 12:22-23).

Essential to this harmony is that we each come to recognize that the gift or gifts the Lord has given us are only marginally *for ourselves.* While they enable us to do something to serve our Lord, they are maximally *for others.* Our Lord wants us to be able to show by our service that we love them because he loves both them and us. We are, after all, in Paul's arresting expression, 'individually members of one another' (verse 5).

Verses 6b to 8 provide seven illustrations of the kind of gifts we are given. The list is not comprehensive (cf. 1 Cor. 12:27-31; 1 Pet. 4:1-11). Here Paul mentions 'prophecy ... service ... teaching ... exhortation ... contributing ... leading ... doing acts of mercy ...' Several of these gifts involve the reception of our fellow Christians if they are to be fully exercised. Interestingly Paul gives the Romans no specific directives for how these gifts were to be exercised. What he does emphasize is the spirit and disposition required—wholeheartedness in using them for others.

USE YOUR GIFTS

The first gift Paul mentions here is 'prophecy.' In the Bible 'to prophesy' has a variety of connotations ranging from *fore*-telling the

[1] The story is told in Livy (c. 59 BC–AD 17) , *History of Rome*, 2.32.9.

future and *forth*-telling (expounding and applying to the present) the word of God to more general ideas like giving verbal expression to God's praise. Like the gifts of 'teaching' and 'exhorting' and 'leading' it was a gift employed in the public sphere for the church family as a whole.

Other gifts—serving (since Paul uses the word *diakonia*, some commentators take this to be a reference to the specific ministry of deacons) and contributing (presumably, but perhaps not exclusively, financially) are gifts that are often best exercised discretely, in private and hidden contexts. The public nature of the exercise of the gift is not what matters; using it for the benefit of others does. We are rightly suspicious of individuals who treat the church family as a platform, satisfying themselves by using people rather than serving them. If 'the Son of Man came not to be served but to serve' (Matt. 20:28), Christlikeness means that we do the same.

So Paul's chief concern here is not with specific details of these gifts; it is that we use whatever gifts God has given us for the sake of others. And perhaps the nature of his directives (if this is your gift, *use it*!) is intended to encourage each believer that their specific gift is vital for the health of the church (even if—as the friends with him in Corinth well knew some believers give the impression others' gifts are incidental while theirs are vital). We should never fall into the trap of allowing the gifts we have received to become inactive because we would prefer to have someone else's gifts.

Again we are mistaken if we think that our gifts make us superior to any of our fellow Christians. For one thing the gifts are not 'ours' but Christ's. And they are 'for' his people, not 'for' us. They enable us to say, in concrete ways, 'I count you as someone more significant than myself' (Phil. 2:3, which is Rom. 12:3 expressed positively with respect to others). In addition we should never forget that gifts are not graces, although they require grace if they are to be used well.

This not only explains the apostle's pattern of speech in verses 6-8 (if you have a gift then use it!); it also indicates his concern that each of us should employ our gifts in a way that is in accordance with their character. With respect to some gifts his exhortation is simply 'So, use them!' But in others he is more specific, and his comments are enlightening.

Prophecy: If someone has the gift of 'prophecy' it should be exercised 'in proportion to our faith' (verse 6). These words have been interpreted in different ways, to mean:

(a) 'in proportion to the faith we have—small or great'; or

(b) 'in proportion to the content of our shared faith,' *i.e.* 'according to the *analogy of faith*' (he uses the word *analogia*), that is, regulated by the objective content of the revelation God has already given.

The former view is the more likely here since in mentioning the other gifts, Paul refers to the attitude of the individual while exercising them. It should go without saying that the exercise of any gift should be consistent with divine revelation in Scripture. That is obviously the case today with preaching—which earlier interpreters often took to be the significance of 'prophecy' here.

Contributing. The person who contributes should do so with a generous spirit. Unnecessary counsel? Hardly. No doubt Paul was familiar with the story of Ananias and Sapphira (Acts 5:1-11). They contributed substantially but not with genuine generosity. Instead they used their 'gift' for self-serving ends. They 'sold a piece of property' and ostensibly donated the proceeds to the church. But under the guise of giving the whole they gave only part. Perhaps their goal was to purchase the kind of reputation Barnabas had (Acts 4:36-37) and of which they were jealous. They did not give 'in generosity' (verse 8). The word itself can mean 'simplicity' or 'sincerity'—that is having no other motive than to do good to others, knowing that it is more blessed to give than to receive (Acts 20:35). After all we can donate everything we have, but if we do it without love we do it without generosity (1 Cor. 13:3).

Leading. The verb translated 'lead' here is *proïstēmi.* Training young people to be leaders has become a minor industry in the church. But there is a distinctive element in Paul's vocabulary that is not always emphasized. 'Lead' is a compound of the preposition 'in front of' and the verb 'to stand.' But the concept is not so much that the 'leader' holds the prime position, as that he takes responsibility for others and, like Paul, is willing to 'endure everything for the sake of the elect' (2 Tim. 2:10). The leader is willing to put his body in front of those he leads in order to protect them, as well as model before them the Christian lifestyle. He is *for them* before he is anything else. Leading is primarily a 'responsibility role' rather than a 'promoted position'! And those who exercise it are required to be 'all in' for the sake of others. For this gift, like the others, is not for me and about me, but for Christ and for others.

Showing mercy. Like giving, it is possible in a formal way to show mercy simply because we have, for example, the financial capacity to do so. But our model here is the Christlike figure of the Good Samaritan ('the one who showed … mercy,' Luke 10:37). He exhibited genuine 'compassion.' He demonstrated loving care for the Jewish man who had been 'mugged' ('He went to him and bound up his wounds'). His 'contributing' was a sacrificial self-giving. He used his own oil and wine for the wounds. He presumably walked as his donkey carried the injured man to the inn. He took care of him himself, and a day later—now, presumably delayed on his journey—he not only paid for the injured man's care, and committed himself to meeting any further debts, but also promised to return. That is what it means to do 'acts of mercy, with cheerfulness' (verse 8).

Like his Master before him, Paul is saying, 'You go, and do likewise' (Luke 10:37). It is not surprising that his next words are about love (12:9). For it was as true in Rome as it was in Ephesus that 'the whole body, joined and held together by every joint with which it is equipped, when each part is working properly, makes the body grow so that it builds itself up in love' (Eph. 4:16).

Exactly the same is true for our church family. So, in using your gifts, 'go, and do likewise'!

34

An Imperative Life

Let love be genuine. Abhor what is evil; hold fast to what is
good. 10 *Love one another with brotherly affection. Outdo one*
another in showing honour. 11 *Do not be slothful in zeal, be*
fervent in spirit, serve the Lord. 12 *Rejoice in hope, be patient*
in tribulation, be constant in prayer. 13 *Contribute to the needs*
of the saints and seek to show hospitality.
14 *Bless those who persecute you; bless and do not curse them.*
15 *Rejoice with those who rejoice, weep with those who weep.*
16 *Live in harmony with one another. Do not be haughty, but*
associate with the lowly. Never be wise in your own sight.
17 *Repay no one evil for evil, but give thought to do what is*
honourable in the sight of all. 18 *If possible, so far as it depends on*
you, live peaceably with all. 19 *Beloved, never avenge yourselves,*
but leave it to the wrath of God, for it is written, 'Vengeance is
mine, I will repay, says the Lord.' 20 *To the contrary, 'if your*
enemy is hungry, feed him; if he is thirsty, give him something to
drink; for by so doing you will heap burning coals on his head.'
21 *Do not be overcome by evil, but overcome evil with good.*

(Rom. 12:9-21)

In the previous section Paul's focus was on the employment of the specific gifts Christ gives to individuals. Now he turns to the lifestyle of grace that should mark every Christian.

When we find ourselves caught up in the flow of Paul's reasoning in Romans it is surprisingly easy to miss one of its significant features: its first eleven chapters contain only a handful of imperatives (*e.g.* 6:13; 11:18). True, a lifestyle that corresponds to the gospel was implied in these earlier chapters; but Paul's overwhelming focus was on expounding our need for salvation and God's provision of it in Christ. Now, it becomes clear in chapter 12 that this massive concentration on God's grace has been necessary in order to provide a strong enough foundation to sustain the all-demanding character of the exhortations that follow. Now we are caught up in a flood of imperatives. These constitute a detailed exposition of 'the obedience of faith' which Paul's ministry aimed at producing (1:5). Here, in verses 9-21 alone, there are some thirty imperatives. The good news is this: the gospel is able to sustain us in obedience to all of them.

At first sight these exhortations could drown us in their sheer number and variety. How can we cope? But in fact they are many different applications of the one basic principle 'Let love be genuine' (verse 9a). Intriguingly there is no verb in this statement. A literal translation would read simply: 'Genuine Love.' What follows is in some respects a variation on the apostle's more famous exposition of love in 1 Corinthians 13. Although we are not justified by love but by faith, the justified are not without love. Indeed faith 'works by love' (Gal. 5:6). As Martin Luther put it, 'Oh, it is a living, busy, active, mighty thing, this faith.'[1]

It has become a commonplace that 'love is all you need.' From one point of view Paul agrees. But for him 'love' is not an amorphous concept. Specifically it fulfils the law (13:8; cf. Gal. 5:14). And here he is teaching us that it requires more than two dozen imperatives to explain what love is, how it acts, and what it looks like in daily life.

Christian love should be 'genuine'—behind which translation lies a readily recognizable Greek word—*anupokritos*. A *hupokritēs* was an actor. He addressed the audience through the mask he wore. Unlike modern theatre and film, actors in antiquity went into 'mask-up' rather than 'make-up.' Hence the use of the word in the New Testament to denote a 'hypocrite'—someone who appears to be one thing in public but is a different thing in private—a person who plays a part and wears a mask.

The Lord Jesus taught that knowing that God is our loving and all-providing heavenly Father means that we no longer need to pretend to him. And if that is true then we do not need to pretend at all (Matt. 6:1-18). This is why love will 'abhor what is evil' and 'hold fast to what is good' (verse 9). There is no room here for pretence.

[1] Martin Luther, *Commentary on Romans*, tr. J. Theodore Mueller (Grand Rapids: Zondervan, 1954), xvii.

The fruit of love is meekness; but it also produces moral strength rather than weakness. It has a backbone of a godly intolerance of evil, and also a gritty stickability in its commitment 'to what is good'—that is, to what is pleasing to God and conforms to his will (cf. 12:1-2).

This is in fact simply the outworking of the two great commandments (Matt. 22:36-40). And so in what follows Paul explains what love for God with heart, mind, soul, and strength, and love for our neighbour will look like in practice and in detail. He does so not to condemn us but to encourage and direct us in Christian living. For love needs eyes to see and paths on which to walk. At the end of the day, as Paul later says, 'love is the fulfilling of the law' (13:10).

Paul's style of speech here—a series of imperatives directing behaviour patterns—was a well-recognized form of moral teaching in antiquity (its technical name is *paraenesis*—advice or counsel). But the distinctive thing in Paul's *paraenesis* is that he has expounded the saving power of God that enables us to sustain ongoing obedience to his imperatives.

There is no minute logical pattern of development in Paul's imperatives. But they do divide roughly into two categories, expressing (i) our attitude to others *within* the church (verses 10-13) and (ii) our reaction to others, especially *outside* the church (verses 14-21).

ATTITUDES

Tertullian of Carthage (AD 160–225), the early Christian theologian to whom we owe some important words in our Christian vocabulary like 'Trinity,' was able to say in his *Apology*:

> It is mainly the deeds of a love so noble that lead many to put a brand upon us. *See*, they say, *how they love one another*, for themselves are animated by mutual hatred; how they are ready even to die for one another, for they themselves will sooner put to death [*i.e.* kill each other].[1]

Paul begins therefore with a command for Christians not only to show genuine love but '*brotherly* affection' (*philadelphia*, verse 10).

[1] Tertullian, *Apology*, tr. S. Thelwall, in *Ante-Nicene Fathers*, eds. Alexander Roberts and James Donaldson; revised by A. Cleveland Coxe, vol. 3 (New York: Christian Literature Publishing Co., 1885), 46 (Chapter 39).

Perhaps it would be even better to translate this as 'family love.'[1] In Christ God is our Father. We are his 'family' and thus enjoy the closest of relationships with one another. 'Body,' 'flock,' 'temple' are metaphors for the church—we are not arms or sheep or stones! But 'family' is not a metaphor; it is what we *are*—born into a new family, adopted by the heavenly Father, brothers and sisters of Jesus Christ and of each other. This is why Paul elsewhere urges us to treat older men as fathers, older women as mothers, and younger men as brothers, and younger women as sisters (1 Tim. 5:1-2). It is a beautiful portrayal of affectionate relationships.

In a world of family dysfunction and disintegration this is an important and powerful element in the church's witness. In the church a restoration of what family life was meant to be is taking place. Even those who despise the Christian gospel may be awakened by the realization that its truth and power are evidenced in its fellowship of family love.

God's grace is thus evidenced in an attractive self-forgetfulness, in 'a heart at leisure from itself, to soothe and sympathize.'[2] Love delivers us from our bondage to self and enables us therefore to 'outdo one another in showing honour' (verse 10). But this beautiful grace needs to be deliberately cultivated. It is not the dominant disposition in a society in which people clamber over others in order to gain position, or are jealous of the privileges or gifts that others possess. Love is never slovenly in displaying this other-directedness. It sees that the world does not revolve around 'me.' It knows that by honouring others it honours Christ. The Christian therefore has nothing to lose and everything to gain by outdoing others in showing honour!

Nor is love exercised reluctantly. There is no sloth in love (verse 11). Instead there is 'zeal,' even fervency 'in spirit.' Commentators debate whether 'spirit' here refers to our own spirits or to the Holy Spirit. In either case such zeal and fervency are disciplined (cf. 2 Tim. 1:7). They are directed by the Lord whom we serve and

[1] As the ESV frequently indicates in footnotes, 'brothers' implies 'brothers and sisters.' The Greek word *adelphos* has a broader range of meaning than the masculine 'brother.'

[2] From the hymn by Anna Laetitia Waring (1823–1910), 'Father, I know that all my life.'

therefore by his word. There is no room here for a zeal that is 'not according to knowledge' (cf. 10:2).

There may seem to be little or no connection between verses 11 and 12 or, for that matter, between each of the exhortations in verse 12 itself. If so this should not trouble us; we often make statements in a relatively random way. Nevertheless, it may well be the three-fold encouragement in verse 12 recognizes that while we are new men and women in Christ we remain sinful people in a fallen world. Living an 'other-focussed life' is by no means plain sailing.

So how can we maintain a spirit of cheerfulness? First by remembering the hope of the gospel; then by patience under pressure, committing ourselves to bearing it because of the hope the gospel gives us; and in addition by remembering that we always have recourse to our heavenly Father in prayer. It is surely true—

O what peace we often forfeit,
O what needless pain we bear,
All because we do not carry
Everything to God in prayer.[1]

With these characteristics in place, genuine love will play its role when other believers have needs, including providing for them in practical ways by learning to 'show hospitality' (verse 13). In Paul's context that had special relevance to those Christians who were 'home-owners' (like Gaius, his Corinthian host, 16:23). But even those who had no home of their own (some of them were almost certainly slaves in someone else's house) could be welcoming to their brothers and sisters in Christ. A warm heart is always the best hospitality (Prov. 15:17).

At verse 14 there is a change of atmosphere as Paul now turns largely to challenging situations, including how we respond to those who do not love Christ (and may not love Christians either).

REACTIONS

How we react in situations over which we have no control is often a clearer indication of the presence (or absence) of love than how we act in situations we can control. It is often more revealing of what is in our hearts.

[1] From the hymn 'What a Friend we have in Jesus!' by Joseph Scriven (1819–86).

Perhaps we can best absorb and apply Paul's quick-fire *imperatives* by reformatting them as *questions*. How do we react to:

- Persecution (verse 14). *Do we bless in response?* (The root meaning of the verb 'bless' [*eulogeō*] is 'to speak well of.')
- The success of others (verse 15). *Do we rejoice in it?*
- The sorrow of others (verse 15). *Do we also shed tears?*
- Those who are difficult (verse 16). *Do we seek to live in harmonious and affectionate fellowship with them?*
- Those on society's bottom rungs (verse 16). *Do we see ourselves as above them and wise in our own eyes? Or do we sit alongside them and count them as our friends?*
- People who do us harm or evil (verse 17). *Do we behave honourably towards them, remembering the dignity that we find in Christ?*

But how can we engage a fallen world so that we are not 'overcome by evil, but overcome evil with good' (verse 21)? Paul gives both positive and negative directives:

If we are to respond well in any situation we need to develop a settled disposition *before* it arises and be committed to 'live peaceably with all' (verse 18). It should become a fixed principle with us that we are called in Christ to be peacemakers (Matt. 5:9; Prov. 20:3). There will be times when the Christian should not bend, adjust, or wrongly compromise. But Proverbs 15:1 is a word of wisdom for us: 'A soft answer turns away wrath, but a harsh word stirs up anger.' (The Hebrew word translated 'soft' here does not mean 'weak,' but 'gentle, tender.') The Christian is at peace with God; the gospel is a message of peace; peacemakers are blessed because they exhibit the family likeness seen in Christ. We ourselves are by nature 'children of wrath,' and yet the Lord has spoken his 'soft' and 'tender' word to us in Christ. Knowing that enables us to imitate him.

In addition, although others may express their anger against us, Christians may safely leave to God the issue of wrath being directed against them (verse 19; here Paul alludes to Deut. 32:35). The knowledge that their wrath against us is a symptom of their alienation from God stimulates in us the compassion that enables us to absorb their enmity rather than retaliate against them. More than that, the knowledge that Christ has borne the wrath of God on our behalf will enable us to fulfil the wise counsel of Proverbs 25:21-22 (quoted here in verse 20).

The meaning of the expression 'heap burning coals on his head' (a proverbial saying now as it was then) has been much discussed. It may mean that the Christian's response of grace simply highlights the fact that those who do evil are only increasing the judgment of God against themselves. Alternatively, since the expression originates in the wisdom literature of the Old Testament, it has been suggested that this may be a proverbial allusion to a practice in Egypt in which wrongdoers were compelled to carry a plate or tray of burning coals over their head as a sign of penitence. If this is the background then the force of the proverb is that a gracious response to opposition may lead our persecutors to repentance and faith, just as God's kindness converted us (2:4).

In either case we are able to leave things with the Lord.

In this way, then, the Christian whose life is characterized by genuine love will not be overcome by evil but will overcome evil with good (verse 21). We are called not only to a counter-cultural life, but a culture-overcoming life too!

Here, then, are more ways in which Christians are 'more than conquerors through him who loved us' (8:37)!

35

The Christian and the State

Let every person be subject to the governing authorities. For there is no authority except from God, and those that exist have been instituted by God. [2] *Therefore whoever resists the authorities resists what God has appointed, and those who resist will incur judgment.* [3] *For rulers are not a terror to good conduct, but to bad. Would you have no fear of the one who is in authority? Then do what is good, and you will receive his approval,* [4] *for he is God's servant for your good. But if you do wrong, be afraid, for he does not bear the sword in vain. For he is the servant of God, an avenger who carries out God's wrath on the wrongdoer.* [5] *Therefore one must be in subjection, not only to avoid God's wrath but also for the sake of conscience.* [6] *For because of this you also pay taxes, for the authorities are ministers of God, attending to this very thing.* [7] *Pay to all what is owed to them: taxes to whom taxes are owed, revenue to whom revenue is owed, respect to whom respect is owed, honour to whom honour is owed.*
(Rom. 13:1-7)

The outworking of the righteousness of God by which we are counted righteous is expressed in different spheres of life. It follows the order of the great commandments to love God with heart, soul, mind, and strength, and then also to love our neighbour as ourselves.

Paul's application of this neighbour-love is expressed in the concentric circles in which our fundamental devotion to God (12:1-2) comes to expression: in our personal relationships within the church (12:3-13) and then in our actions and reactions in a world that is often antagonistic to our Christian testimony (12:14-21).

Now, in 13:1-7, Paul extends his exposition of the Christian's righteous living into the context of life in the state.

No doubt the house churches in Rome were composed of members of several social classes. Some may have been immigrants; others would have been Roman citizens from birth; yet others, freedmen and women. And others were almost certainly slaves, even if in daily life they held significant positions in the running of the empire.[1] But now, in this section, Paul's focus is not on how church members in different social strata should relate to one another (as in Eph. 5:5-9 and Col. 3:22), but on their shared responsibilities to the state. The rubric for the entire section is 'Let *every person* be subject to the governing authorities' (13:1). That principle was the same for both masters and slaves.

In addition to belonging to a variety of social classes, the members of the church in Rome would undoubtedly have come from different backgrounds, had different temperaments, and been at different stages of spiritual understanding and maturity. It is easy to forget that in all likelihood none of them owned a copy of the Old Testament, or a Gospel, and perhaps only Priscilla and Aquila had read any of Paul's other letters. They had no Christian literature. Any creeds they had were a few sentences long; they did not own hymn-books whose contents expressed centuries of reflection on Christian doctrine and lifestyle. And perhaps against that background, some of them had actually unwisely contributed to the trouble that had taken place a number of years earlier 'at the instigation of Chrestus' (probably 'Christ'). They needed therefore to be reminded that they had responsibilities for 'the good of the city' to live as the best and most helpful of its citizens, as salt and light.

So it is possibly against that background that, now, Paul calls all the believers, free or bound, Jew or Gentile (and perhaps even more conservative and more radical in temperament) to see everything as under Christ's sovereign Lordship, to submit in all things to him, and within that context to 'be subject to the governing authorities' (verse 1).

[1] As noted earlier (p. 170), estimates of the number of slaves in the city of Rome vary considerably, some as high as 300,000, amounting to approximately one third of the population. Scholars have believed that some of the individuals mentioned in Romans 16 probably have 'slave names.'

BEING SUBJECT

The key to the Christian's disposition and action here is the principle 'For there is no authority except from God, and those that exist have been instituted by God' (verse 1). Ultimate authority resides in the throne room of heaven; earthly thrones have only derived authority. This is in fact a liberating principle whose implication is as clear as it is simple: God himself—not the state, nor any individual 'Caesar'—is the Christian's Lord. Our eyes are ultimately fixed on him; our civic life (as well as our life in church fellowship) is lived in tribute to him; he is the one we obey and serve.

Because of this, our being 'subject to the governing authorities' is not ultimately rooted in their authority and our earthly citizenship, but on God's authority and our glad submission to him 'whose service is perfect freedom.'[1] Since 'our citizenship is in heaven' (Phil. 3:20), our being 'subject to the governing authorities' is not a mindless obedience but a form of service to our Lord. An awareness that there is a higher throne in heaven than any throne on earth is what distinguishes the Christian's unique disposition towards secular authority. It makes believers the best servants of the state without being subservient to it.

As Christians, therefore, we are 'subject to the governing authorities' as Christ's free men and women. Martin Luther enunciated this principle in the thesis statement of his great Reformation treatise *The Freedom of a Christian* (1520):

- A Christian is a perfectly free lord of all, subject to none.
- A Christian is a perfectly dutiful servant of all, subject to all.[2]

Our service of and obedience to others, including the state, is not ultimately derived from their authority. 'All authority ... on earth' is not given to them but to Jesus Christ (Matt. 28:18). We serve them as a way of expressing our submission to him.

The first implication Paul draws from this is a negative one: to resist the authorities is to resist God's providential appointments. It can only lead to judgment.

[1] The expression comes from the Collect for Peace in Thomas Cranmer's *Book of Common Prayer*.

[2] Martin Luther, *The Freedom of a Christian*, tr. W. A. Lambert, rev. J. J. Grimm, in Martin Luther, *Three Treatises* (Philadelphia: Fortress Press, 1970), 277.

Paul does not specify the source or the nature of this judgment—God's or man's—the two may well be intertwined: rebellion against lawfully constituted authority in the state inevitably leads to coming under the judgment of the civil law; in turn, if such rejection of the state's authority is contrary to the commandment of God, to breach it also places us under God's judgment.

THE STATE'S GOD-GIVEN CALLING

Lest we misunderstand our new-found Christian freedom at this point ('It's OK to break the speed limit because I'm under the Lordship of God, not man—not under law but grace'), the apostle spells out the principle: God has appointed the state for the good of society. Its divinely-ordained *raison d'être* is not to create fear in those who seek to do good but to restrain the bad that destroys the stability and well-being of a society (verse 3).

In fact Paul emphasizes that the magistrate is a minister of God (*diakonos* twice in verse 4 and *leitourgos* in verse 6). In the economy of God he serves for the good of the community. And that is true as much when he punishes as when he expresses approval (verses 3-4). The immediate implication is spelled out: 'being subject to the governing authorities' is the pathway to a comfortable conscience that is not paralyzed by fear of the state. It exists to serve God by encouraging and approving conduct that is good, not what is bad (verses 3-4a).

On the other hand, it is appropriate that we should be afraid of the consequences if we disobey the state, for the civil magistrate (in whatever form) 'does not bear the sword in vain' (verse 4). While positively he has been called to encourage and establish good behaviour in the community, negatively he also has authority to give this-worldly expression to the opposition of God against social disintegration and its causes (stealing, murder, etc).

This being the case, as believers we are helped by the double motive Paul gives us for being 'subject to the governing authorities' (verse 1): (i) *negatively*, to avoid the wrath of God (verse 5); (ii) *positively*, to maintain a clear conscience before God so that we walk in fellowship with him in his righteousness (verse 5).

'The authorities are ministers of God' (verse 6). Earlier, in verse 4, Paul had used the word *diakonos* (a generic word for servant);

now he uses the word *leitourgos*. In classical literature it refers to a public servant who acts for the good of the people, often at his own expense. It has a distinctive theological sense in Hebrews 8:2 where it refers to Christ as our *leitourgos*, our ministering priest in the heavenly sanctuary, our 'liturgist'—the one who leads in worship. Paul himself later uses the term of his own ministry and also that of his friend Epaphroditus (15:16; Phil. 2:25).

Thus the apostle uses the same terminology to describe the role of the civil ruler that he uses elsewhere to describe Christ's ministry. He is both *diakonos* (Rom. 15:8) and *leitourgos* (Heb. 8:2). Within the realm of the state, in temporal affairs, the civil magistrate also has a divinely appointed diaconal and servant role.

In its own sphere, therefore, the state is a servant of God. So as Christians we pay (personal) 'taxes' and (business) 'revenue' where these are owed (verses 6-7). We are called to integrity as tax-owing citizens, and to faithfulness if we are business-owning employers. Significantly Paul adds that we are also to 'Pay … honour to whom honour is owed' (verse 7). This exhortation carries implications for state officials as well as for citizens. The former are to serve in a way that is worthy of honour; the latter are to pay honour where it is due; bad-mouthing state officials is not a Christian virtue.

LIVING AT PEACE

All this is a further expression of the fact that we are called 'so far as it depends on you, [to] live peaceably with all' (12:18). The Christian is not a loud-mouthed complainer. After all we are those whose mouths have been 'stopped' (3:19). We have bowed before the God who has had mercy on us; submission to the state as God's minister is simply one application of our reverence for God himself.

All three of the Synoptic Gospels record a watchword of Jesus that directs us here. Challenged about the sensitive issue of paying taxes to Caesar, he borrowed a denarius and asked, 'Whose likeness and inscription is this?' (Matt. 22:19-20). It was, of course, Caesar's image that was on the coin. 'Therefore,' our Lord said, 'render to Caesar the things that are Caesar's.' But he did not stop there. He added: 'Render … to God the things that are God's' (Matt. 22:19-21). The implication of his words must have been obvious—if the coin belonged to the one whose image it bore, then in turn we belong to the One whose image we bear. So we render to Caesar what is his—tax payments; and we render to God what is his—our everything! Our lives are his currency in the world. Our submission to 'Caesar' is always set within the context of our primary submission to God.

Paul's words here have prompted lengthy discussion throughout the centuries and have given rise to a variety of social and political theories. It is worth noting that, while written in the context of the Roman Empire, Paul does not indicate that his teaching requires or is applicable only to one form of government (monarchy, democracy, oligarchy, or dictatorship). We should therefore be careful about the 'yes, but ...' approach that wants to rewrite his principial statements in the light of potentially difficult exceptions. The implication of Paul's words are that the Roman Christians—and we following them—are called to be models of what true citizenship means. They—and we—should be able to say (as some courageous believers have been bold to say to governments that have persecuted them): 'Your Christians are your best citizens.' The gospel works in every political context.

Paul's teaching is finely summarized in *The Confession of Faith* composed by the Westminster Assembly in London in the 1640s—which was, significantly, a period of civil unrest and even civil war in Great Britain (the document was written only a few years before King Charles I was executed):

> God the supreme Lord and King of all the world, hath ordained civil magistrates to be under Him, over the people, for His own glory, and the public good; and, to this end, hath armed them with the power of the sword, for the defence and encouragement of them that are good, and for the punishment of evil doers.
>
> It is lawful for Christians to accept and execute the office of a magistrate, when called thereunto: in the managing whereof, as they ought especially to maintain piety, justice, and peace, according to the wholesome laws of each commonwealth ...
>
> It is the duty of people to pray for magistrates, to honour their persons, to pay them tribute and other dues, to obey their lawful commands, and to be subject to their authority, for conscience' sake. Infidelity or difference in religion doth not make void the magistrate's just and legal authority, nor free the people from their due obedience to him.[1]

[1] *The Confession of Faith*, XXIII.1, 2, 4.

Paul's teaching is straightforward enough. But what about the problem questions?

PROBLEM QUESTIONS

Questions about the application of these words in societies where governments are hostile to the gospel inevitably arise. What are Christians to do when the state becomes a threat to the church, or requires conformity to laws and regulations that are contrary to God's law? And why does Paul say nothing about such circumstances?

Whole treatises have been written on such questions and it would take us beyond the scope of these pages to discuss them in detail. But we can draw some guidelines on the basis of what Paul says here.

1. In thinking about our relationship to civil authorities we must never lose sight of 'first principles' and become obsessed with exceptions. No particular situation creates the general principle. We have two New Testament anchors to hold us steady:

(i) Romans 13:1: we are to be subject to the governing authorities—the general principle is that the state is to be obeyed.

(ii) Acts 4:19: we must obey God (in his word) rather than man.

This is quite different from the assumption that because the state is not the church it has no authority over us. We have seen that it has a God-given diaconal ministry (verse 4). But by the same token, as a servant of God, the state also has responsibilities to him as it exercises its responsibilities towards its citizens.

2. There are reasons why Paul does not give us a list of 'exception clauses' here. He does not say: 'Be subject to the governing authorities ... *but NOT in the following instances* ...' Clearly there is wisdom in this—it would be impossible to provide permanent universal legislation for exceptions. And in any event, the principles governing exceptions are either clearly taught in Scripture or can be deduced from Scripture 'by good and necessary consequence.'[1]

[1] *The Confession of Faith*, I. vi. The combination 'good and necessary' is again important. If a doctrine or practice is to be required of us, it must not only be consistent with Scripture ('good' consequence), it must in addition be necessitated by Scripture, *i.e.* no other application would be consistent with the principle. These

3. So the Christian's basic attitude to the state is to respect it as a divinely ordained societal good. It was never ordained to save society; but it does have a God-given responsibility to regulate it for the general well-being. Any form of civil government exists in a world that is both fallen and sinful (as 13:3-4 indicates). It cannot provide perfect justice or right all society's wrongs. Governments may make laws we think could be better made, as well as at times make laws we feel sure will never solve the problem they are devised to resolve. In addition, sin complicates as well as mars our life together; there will therefore always be disagreements about whether governments are operating well. Christians themselves may not be in complete agreement about the best form of government or about their own government's performance—none of us is omni-wise, omniscient, or omni-competent. Since there are no perfect churches it is unlikely there will be any perfect secular governments!

The upshot of this is that we need to distinguish between occasions when a government performs imperfectly in its ministry to society, and when it acts in blatant opposition to the commandments of God and dictates disobedience to them. When that happens we are surely called to stand with Shadrach, Meshach and Abednego (Dan. 3:13-18), and with Daniel himself in the days of Darius (Dan. 6). But at the same time it is instructive to notice that while these young friends declined the royal menu (Dan. 1:8-16), and themselves continued to use their given Hebrew names, they do not seem to have made even a mild fuss over the fact that in Babylonian society they were known by pagan names (Dan. 1:6-7).

Wisdom enables us to negotiate the difference between active participation in breaking God's laws and the recognition that we live in a fallen world. We are not yet living in the new heavens and the new earth. Most Christians recognize this without much reflection.

---

two concepts are often confused. A 'good consequence' (*i.e.* something that is consistent with the teaching of Scripture) may not be the only 'good consequence' that is consistent with it. To give a trivial illustration: a 'good consequence' of Scripture historically in a rural community was that worship should begin say at 11 a.m. to allow people time to (a) care for their animals if necessary and (b) walk several miles to church. But while the practice of an 11 a.m. time for worship has been remarkably enduring in some places, so much so that to change it might seem 'wrong,' it is not a 'necessary consequence' binding a village church in the twenty-first century where no one owns cows, or walks miles to the service.

Few if any Christians lobby their governments to re-title the days of the week from their present gospel-offending pagan-rooted names, or regard using them as a breach of God's commandments.[1]

Paul's letter to the Romans was written around the mid-50s. The teenage Nero had been emperor for a few years at most. The horrors of his persecution of Christians still lay in the future. Some of those who were present at the first reading of these words may well have been among those who suffered at the emperor's hands—as indeed, according to tradition, Paul himself would later do, and Simon Peter too.

Would Paul have written differently were he corresponding with the church in Rome a decade later? Perhaps—in the sense that his letters always address specific situations. Later on he might well have echoed Peter's counsel for persecuted believers. But we can be sure he would not have written anything that would *contradict* what he says here about the nature of government and the Christian's responsibility in relation to it. And we should remember that some time later he urged Titus to remind believers 'to be submissive to rulers and authorities, to be obedient, to be ready for every good work' (Titus 3:1).

It is tempting when we are Bible readers sitting in comfortable chairs to raise hypothetical 'But what about …?' questions. But it is significant that believers who have suffered opposition and antagonism from the state do not accuse the apostle of misspeaking. Rather they have reflected, often at great cost, on how they are to apply in *their* context what Paul wrote to *this* context. But that question is not confined to our relationship to civil government. It is simply another form of the broader responsibility we always have—to apply all Scripture to all of life.

Writing to believers facing 'trials of various kinds,' James counsels them to ask God for wisdom which is 'pure, then peaceable, gentle, open to reason, full of mercy and good fruits, impartial

[1] It is a curious fact that even in times of ascendancy and political influence the church failed to reform this phenomenon. So much so that we rarely think twice about the fact that we describe the days of the week as though they were dedicated to various pagan gods: Moon day (Monday); the Norse god Tyr (Tuesday), the chief of the Anglo-Saxon gods Woden (Wednesday), the hammer-wielding god Thor (Thursday), another Norse god, Fryer (Friday), the planet Saturn (Saturday), and the Sun (Sunday)—even if we resolutely refer to the last as 'the Lord's Day.'

and sincere' (James 1:5; 3:17). Thankfully, God always provides it according to our need as the Spirit helps us apply Scripture to our own contexts and situations. But at the end of the day, our permanent calling as Christians is to be the best citizens our own country could ever have.

The question for us to answer is therefore: Could that be said of us?

36

Love and Law

Owe no one anything, except to love each other, for the one who loves another has fulfilled the law. [9] For the commandments, 'You shall not commit adultery, You shall not murder, You shall not steal, You shall not covet,' and any other commandment, are summed up in this word: 'You shall love your neighbour as yourself.' [10] Love does no wrong to a neighbour; therefore love is the fulfilling of the law.

[11] Besides this you know the time, that the hour has come for you to wake from sleep. For salvation is nearer to us now than when we first believed. [12] The night is far gone; the day is at hand. So then let us cast off the works of darkness and put on the armour of light. [13] Let us walk properly as in the daytime, not in orgies and drunkenness, not in sexual immorality and sensuality, not in quarrelling and jealousy. [14] But put on the Lord Jesus Christ, and make no provision for the flesh, to gratify its desires.

(Rom. 13:8-14)

Paul now moves on from his focus on the obligation Christians have to live righteous lives in the context of the state to fulfilling the same obligation more broadly in society in general. Here he beautifully enunciates the relationship between law and love. We have one basic obligation to the state—*to serve it well* as it fulfils its God-given calling to serve us (verses 1, 7). We have a different basic obligation to our neighbours: *to love them*. For when we love them we fulfil the law (verse 8).

This is a simple statement with massive implications. How are we to love? For Paul, the answer is: the law of God gives us eyes to see what to do, the word of God as a whole shows us how to apply that law, and the Spirit of God enables us to do so with wisdom. For the apostle, as for his Saviour, love and law are in harmony with one another, not in tension (cf. Matt. 5:17-48; John 14:23; 15:10).

The commandment to love our neighbour is both the focus and summary of what is sometimes called the 'second table of the law' (Commandments 5 to 10).[1] Paul lists four of the six, but presumably implies the others (honouring parents and not bearing false witness) by his equivalent of our 'etc.'—'and any other commandment' (verse 9).

NEGATIVES ARE POSITIVE

The commandments Paul lists here are all expressed in negative terms ('You shall not ...'), hence his own negative summary: 'Love does no wrong to a neighbour' (verse 10a). They were delivered to Moses in this limiting form because God's people were sinners, and in terms of redemptive revelation they were still in a state of spiritual infancy.

When children are small the simplest and most effective way to protect them from their tendency to waywardness is to tell them what *not* to do. We do not give them lectures on how electricity works; we simply tell them 'Don't ...' We build a protective fence around them by telling them *what not to do.* But enshrined in each negative command is a positive goal—their security.

So it was with the Ten Commandments given to Moses. Implicit in each of its negative commands (and explicit in the one command without negatives, the honouring of parents) is a positive exhortation to reflect life as the restored image of God. We learn the full scope

[1] The language of 'second table' is derived from the fact that the Ten Commandments were written on two tablets of stone (Exod. 31:18). It was traditionally assumed that the commandments governing our relationship to God were inscribed on one tablet and the laws governing human relationships on another (hence the language of 'the first table' and 'the second table' of the law). More recently scholars have suggested that in fact the tablets were duplicates—representing the fact that there were two parties to the covenant of which the laws were an expression—so that all of the commandments were written on both of them. A modern analogy is found in the way each party to a business 'covenant' (or contract) receives a copy of the deed detailing the implications of the relationship that has been established between the parties. An indication of how foundational the Decalogue was to the covenant bond is underlined by the fact that it was the only element in the Mosaic law code that was placed within the ark of the covenant (Deut. 10:5; Heb. 9:4).

of each commandment when we detect the *positive* grace that is hidden within its negative expression.[1]

Paul had indicated in 8:3-4 that the law is 'weak' because of our sinfulness. It can tell us what we are not to do and imply what we are to do; but it is powerless to create the loving heart of obedience that fulfils its commands. Only the Spirit can effect this in us. His first 'fruit' is love. And this in turn produces in us 'joy, peace, patience, kindness, goodness, faithfulness, gentleness, self-control.' Paul adds, tellingly, 'against such things there is no law.' The reason? Because these qualities are in themselves the fulfilment of the ultimate goal of the law (verse 10; Gal. 5:22-23).

It is in this way that in the new covenant God's promise is fulfilled in Christ and by the Spirit: 'I will put my law within them, and I will write it on their hearts' (Jer. 31:33). It is therefore a form of double-think when someone appeals to the gift of the Spirit as justification for indifference to the law. For Jeremiah's prophecy of the Spirit's coming (cited in Hebrews 8:10; 10:16) affirms that what he writes on our hearts is ... the law! In this way the image of God is being redrawn in our lives. For Paul there is no contradiction, antipathy or even tension between law and love. The Spirit-filled life is a law-loving and commandment-fulfilling life.

NEW AGE LIFE

Having given us directives for our life in Christ, Paul now sets our obedience within the new context in which Christians live—the inauguration of the last days signalled on the Day of Pentecost by the coming of the Holy Spirit (Acts 2:16-17). Daytime has arrived: 'the hour has come ... to wake from sleep' (verse 11); 'The night is far gone; the day is at hand' (verse 12).

The outpouring of the Spirit at Pentecost was the visible evidence of an otherwise invisible heavenly transaction that took place on the ascension of Jesus. As he had promised, he asked the Father for the gift of the Spirit to be sent to the church (John 14:16; cf. Acts 2:17, 32-33). Thus took place the fulfilment of the promise of Psalm 2:8 (among other Old Testament prophecies): 'Ask of me,

[1] This is a principle taught by Jesus (Matt. 5:17-48) and the approach adopted, for example, in the exposition of the Ten Commandments in the *Shorter Catechism* questions 39–81 and the *Larger Catechism* questions 93–151.

and I will make the nations your heritage, and the ends of the earth your possession.'

Now the new age has begun. We belong to it. Our lives are hidden with Christ in God (Col. 3:3). In Christ we belong to the new creation; the old has gone and the new has come (2 Cor. 5:17). But as we have seen, while in the kingdom of Christ we have died to sin and been raised to new life, sin has not yet died in us and needs to be mortified (8:13). While our citizenship is in heaven (Phil. 3:20) we are not yet fully conformed to Christ (Phil. 3:21). So we have a calling that is both urgent and challenging: to learn to live in this present evil age as citizens of the new age, and conduct ourselves as citizens of earth as those who are already citizens of heaven. Furthermore, every day that passes means that our 'salvation [*i.e.* the final redemption referred to in 8:23] is nearer to us now than when we first believed' (verse 11).

Paul expresses the urgency of his exhortation to live for Christ by means of metaphors. In verses 11-12 he tells us we need to wake up from our slumber. Since the night is almost over, and the full light of the new day is dawning, believers' lives should not be marked by 'the works of darkness' (verse 12).

We might expect Paul's antithesis to be (i) 'cast off *the works* of darkness' (verse 12) and (ii) put on *the graces* of light.' But he makes his point by means of a more vivid expression: we are to put on '*the armour* of light.' We have been spiritually awakened in a war zone, to spend the day fighting, not playing! The 'heavenly places' in which we are 'blessed ... in Christ with every spiritual blessing' (Eph. 1:3) are also the realms in which we encounter 'the spiritual forces of evil in the heavenly places' (Eph. 6:12).

Paul is reminding us that the new life in Christ is a battle; we need to wear the appropriate spiritual armour (cf. Eph. 6:10-18). It is time to remember his earlier exhortation: 'Do not present your members to sin as instruments [*hopla*—weapons] for unrighteousness, but present yourselves to God as those who have been brought from death to life, and your members as instruments [*hopla*—weapons] for righteousness' (6:13). And the armour we wear is that provided by our General, Jesus Christ. He is the Light of the world (John 8:12). He has field-tested the armour we need to wear and the weapons we need to wield. He has called us out of the moral darkness of the night into the light of the new day. And we need to 'dress' appropriately for daytime.

Here again, Paul expresses the effect of the gospel both negatively and positively. The 'no-no's' are: orgies and drunkenness; sexual immorality and sensuality; quarrelling and jealousy (verse 13). The combination is instructive. The first two pairs refer to what traditionally are thought of as 'high level sins.' The apostle's exhortation to avoid them was by no means theoretical. As is clear from the literature of antiquity, the city of Rome had its considerable share of moral degradation. But the sins in the final pairing in Paul's list ('quarrelling and jealousy') should not be regarded as little more than irritating personality defects. They too are destructive and wrath-deserving like the others.

All that is sinful must be put off. We do not pick and choose, as though God might be satisfied with semi-sanctification; or as if putting away some of 'the works of darkness' compensated for clinging on to others. Quarrels may do as much damage as orgies both by their effect on others and by the distorted soul-shape they create in ourselves. For the quarrelsome spirit is simply an orgy of the heart and of the tongue. And the 'green-eyed monster' of jealousy can kill. Perhaps Paul was conscious that in his own life it was in part *this* that had led to his approval of the death of Stephen.

Paul concludes this section by once again illustrating an important principle: mortification is essential to sanctification, but it is not the whole of it. At the end of the day holiness is conformity to Christ (8:29). For that to be effected in us there needs to be transformation. And for transformation there needs to be a 'putting on' as well as a 'casting off.' Hence the double-sided exhortation to '*put on* the Lord Jesus Christ, and *make no provision* for the flesh, to gratify its desires' (verse 14).

Here, again, is the apostolic pattern for growth in Christlikeness. We are to:

(i) deliberately, consciously, even painfully if necessary, deconstruct the lifestyle to which we have become addicted, and 'make no provision' for it. Here is a simple but powerful principle with which to face temptation adequately equipped with the armour of light.

(ii) fix our gaze on Christ, growing in appreciation of our union with him. As we learn to 'put on the Lord Jesus' (verse 14), to clothe ourselves in Christ, we will become increasingly like him. And—it is worth remembering—nothing that is un-Christlike will have any place in the final kingdom of God.

HOW TO?

But how do we do this? By meditating on Christ as he reveals himself in his word; by loving to read about him in the Gospels and observing him there. By remembering that 'Jesus … is the same yesterday, today and forever' (Heb. 13:8)—that is, he is the same 'today,' in our lifetime, as he was in the days of the Gospels (the 'yesterday' of 'the days of his flesh,' Heb. 5:7). And he will be like that forever!

We are not Nicodemus, or Jairus, or Zacchaeus, or Peter, or James, or John, or Andrew. But Jesus is exactly the same person today for us as he was 'yesterday' for them. And as we gaze on him in the Gospels we, 'beholding the glory of the Lord, are being transformed into the same image from one degree of glory to another. For this comes from the Lord who is the Spirit' (2 Cor. 3:18).

So, the last days have already come. The new age has dawned in the midst of the present evil age. We live 'between the times' of Christ's decisive triumph over sin, death and Satan. So we no longer sleep spiritually (verse 11). We neither clothe ourselves in the inappropriate garments of the night (verse 12), nor live under cover of darkness (verse 13). Rather we walk in the light of the dawn of a new day; we put on the Lord Jesus Christ; we wear his armour. And as we do so, we make no provision for feeding the flesh (verse 14).

It was these last words in Romans 13 that led to what, from a human point of view, was almost certainly the most significant conversion in the four centuries that followed, namely that of Augustine of Hippo.

Aurelius Augustinus was born in AD 354 in Thagaste (in modern Algeria), of a pagan father and a Christian mother. Having long pursued rest for his restless soul, when he was in his mid-thirties he was drawn into a circle of Christian believers in Milan. He had gone there seeking rhetorical fame and financial fortune. But it was there, a lost soul, that Jesus Christ found him. He recorded the story in his own words:

> I felt my past to have a grip on me. It uttered wretched cries: 'How long, how long is it to be?' 'Tomorrow, tomorrow.' 'Why not now? Why not an end to my impure life this very hour?'
>
> As I was saying this and weeping in the bitter agony of my heart, suddenly I heard a voice from the nearby house chanting as if it might be a boy or a girl (I do not know which), saying and repeating over and over again, 'Pick up and read, pick up and read.' At once my countenance changed, and I began to think intently whether there might be some sort of children's game in which such a chant is used. But I could not remember having heard of one. I checked the flood of tears and stood up. I interpreted it solely as a divine command to me to open the book and read the first chapter I could find … So I hurried back to the place where Alypius was sitting. There I had put down the book of the apostle when I got up. I seized it, opened it and in silence read the first passage on which my eyes lit: 'Not in riots and drunken parties, not in eroticism and indecencies, not in strife and rivalry, but put on the Lord Jesus Christ and make no provision for the flesh in its lusts' (Rom. 13:13-14).
>
> I neither wished nor needed to read further. At once, with the last words of this sentence, it was as if a light of relief from all anxiety flooded into my heart. All the shadows of doubt were dispelled.[1]

Romans 13:13-14 thus became the life text of the man who would later say to God, 'You have made us for yourself, and our heart is restless until it rests in you.'[2] At last he found peace and rest in Jesus Christ, and the beginnings of a new life of holiness.

Paul bids us share the same life text.

[1] *Saint Augustine: Confessions*, translated with an introduction and notes by Henry Chadwick (Oxford: Oxford University Press, 1991), 152-53.

[2] Ibid., 3.

37

You Are Very Welcome!

*As for the one who is weak in faith, welcome him, but not to
quarrel over opinions. 2 One person believes he may eat any-
thing, while the weak person eats only vegetables. 3 Let not the
one who eats despise the one who abstains, and let not the one
who abstains pass judgment on the one who eats, for God has
welcomed him. 4 Who are you to pass judgment on the servant
of another? It is before his own master that he stands or falls.
And he will be upheld, for the Lord is able to make him stand.*

*5 One person esteems one day as better than another, while
another esteems all days alike. Each one should be fully convinced
in his own mind. 6 The one who observes the day, observes it
in honour of the Lord. The one who eats, eats in honour of the
Lord, since he gives thanks to God, while the one who abstains,
abstains in honour of the Lord and gives thanks to God. 7 For
none of us lives to himself, and none of us dies to himself. 8 For
if we live, we live to the Lord, and if we die, we die to the Lord.
So then, whether we live or whether we die, we are the Lord's.
9 For to this end Christ died and lived again, that he might be
Lord both of the dead and of the living.*

*10 Why do you pass judgment on your brother? Or you, why
do you despise your brother? For we will all stand before the
judgment seat of God; 11 for it is written,*

> *'As I live, says the Lord, every knee shall bow to me,*
> *and every tongue shall confess to God.'*

12 So then each of us will give an account of himself to God.
(Rom. 14:1-12)

In Romans we witness the way the Holy Spirit superintended the mind of the apostle Paul to enable him to apply the truth of the gospel to the life of the church. His summons to unreserved consecration (12:1-2) was more than a call to inner spiritual commitment. Holiness is always visible, relational, and physical (because we are visible, relational, and physical). It always needs to be worked out in the church family (because we belong to that family); it carries implications for our relationship to the organized life of the state (because we are citizens of it); it is a life in which love is expressed in our conformity to the law of the Lord, as we do battle for Christ and wear his armour of light and the graces he gives.

Now Paul turns to a problem in the house churches in Rome. Chapter 14 transports us into the middle of a disagreement, even controversy, about diets and days, cuisine and calendars. But if this were merely a one-of-a-kind parochial issue it is difficult to understand why he would devote thirty-six verses (14:1–15:13) to resolving the issue. Evidently although the presenting symptoms were particularly evident in Rome, the apostle saw that the undergirding issues were of wider significance.

DIETS AND DAYS

As we read Romans from beginning to end, and not merely our favourite verses in the letter, it becomes clear that what we might have thought of as isolated passages are in fact integrally related to the whole letter. Having read it through from the beginning we can see almost immediately how this section is connected to one of the themes that runs through the letter.

As Paul prepares to visit Jerusalem with a gift to the Jewish church from the Gentile churches, the relationship of Jew and Gentile, and with it the relationship of the old covenant to the new, is on his heart and mind. Although he has been accused of demeaning the law, he stresses that far from being a novelty, the gospel he preaches was announced in the Law and the Prophets and is perfectly consistent with their teaching (1:2, 16-17; 3:21; 4:21 etc.). Both Jews and Gentiles need it (3:9b) and, thankfully, its message of redemption in Christ is for both—'the Jew first and also ... the Greek' (1:16).

But from the earliest days of the church's existence believers had been wrestling with the question 'How does the new relate to the old? Is there continuity, or discontinuity, or elements of both?' That was a particularly pressing issue for Jewish believers who had come to faith in Jesus as the Messiah. What was to remain from their past and what was to go—if anything? What do Gentile converts have to do, or not do, to be fully-fledged people of God? What specific Old Testament practices, if any, continue and what (if any) have become obsolete and are no longer mandatory? The issue was of course complicated because God had brought Gentiles to faith and into the church; the Mosaic ordinances had played no part in their past life. It is not surprising that challenges and tensions arose in the light of these different backgrounds and the almost inevitably different answers being given to these questions (cf. Acts 10:1–11:18; 14:24–15:35; Gal. 2:1-21).

From the outset Paul had emphasized that the gospel was for both Jew and Gentile (1:16-17). And although he had been called to be an apostle to the Gentiles, he has made it clear, especially in chapters 9–11, that he was burdened for his own people, the Jews. Indeed he believed that his own ministry to the Gentiles was integrated with God's purposes for the Jews. That was the reason he was in the process of pursuing his plan to give practical expression to the unity in Christ to which both Gentile and Jewish believers were called (cf. 15:25-27).

Spiritual regeneration does not immediately perfect our understanding of the gospel. Nor does it lead to infallible wisdom in applying it. And since our doctrine affects our behaviour, differences in understanding the gospel can easily lead to different behaviour patterns emerging—and sometimes clashing—within the church family. Disagreements and, sadly, divisions can easily arise because of tension between 'tradition' and 'relevance.' And tension is likely to be sharpest when *both* sides believe that their view or practice is solidly built on biblical teaching and authority.

That was the kind of situation Paul was now turning to address.

THEN AND NOW

Believers with a Jewish background had Old Testament instincts when it came to their diet (cf. Lev. 11:1-47) and to the way they viewed the days of the year (the weekly sabbath, the annual festivals, and other 'days of rest' or sabbaths). The regulations that governed them had *biblical authority* as far as they were concerned. That was embedded in the Jewish conscience from childhood. But Gentile converts had no such instincts—they had never lived by the Jewish religious calendar, and their diet was certainly not determined by Levitical food laws. If, as is possible, these two groups gathered in different house churches, their physical separation in worship, instruction, and fellowship would only highlight their differences—and doubtless increase the possibility of alienation.

This is the situation with which Paul is seeking to deal both theologically and pastorally in Romans 14:1–15:7. Believers from a Gentile background (and perhaps some Jews like Priscilla and Aquila who had a better understanding of the gospel) believed they were free to eat all kinds of food without any pangs of conscience. In sharp contrast, others from a Jewish background naturally felt it would be a breach of God's law, and therefore of their own consciences, to eat what God had said was 'unclean.'

Although debated, it is possible that believers with a Jewish background who had been forced to leave Rome under Claudius may have now returned to find less sensitivity to 'the old ways' (Jewish religious practices). We can imagine that feelings would run high. The rapid changes in the culture, lifestyle, and forms of worship that have characterized evangelical churches in the past few decades have similarly given birth to tensions between those who loved the 'old' and those who have pushed for the 'new.' The question is relatively commonplace today, 'Is your church "traditional" or "contemporary"?' People have left churches they once loved over such issues. In Rome, the stakes were even higher because the opposing views *both* claimed specific biblical authority.

Notice first how pastoral Paul's approach is. From a theological point of view he recognizes that some believers are 'weak' (14:1) while others are 'strong' in faith (15:1). And in addition he has the discernment to recognize the paradox that the 'weak' in faith would be the ones who would view themselves as having a 'strong' conscience with regard to certain foods and specific days—and therefore also imagine that they therefore have 'strong' faith—when the reality was the reverse. Clearly, this was not an easy situation to deal with pastorally.

Paul's own position is clear. The kosher food laws and the Jewish calendar were designed to govern Israel between the first Exodus (from Egypt) and the new Exodus in Christ (Luke 9:31 uses the word *exodus* of his death and resurrection). In God's purposes these laws had a specific function. But it was an interim one: to keep Israel separate from other nations and distinct in their lifestyle.

There were hints already in the Old Testament itself that while the Decalogue was intended to be permanent, the ceremonial and civil laws were always interim in nature. Only the Decalogue was spoken by the voice of God (Deut. 4:12), written by the finger of God (Deut. 4:13), and placed in the ark of God (Deut. 10:5). The ceremonial and civil implications and outworkings of it were intended to be observed 'in the land' (Deut. 4:5, 14) when the people of God were constituted ethnically (as one nation) rather than internationally (from all nations) as they were following Pentecost (Matt. 28:18-20; Luke 24:46-49; Acts 2:17). And so now, in the new internationalism Christ had inaugurated, these calendrical and dietary regulations were abrogated; they had fulfilled their purpose. Paul therefore clarifies the principle of the gospel with respect to the Mosaic food laws: 'I know and am persuaded in the Lord Jesus that nothing is unclean in itself' (14:14; cf. Mark. 7:19; Acts 10:14-15). But he also adds an important qualification: 'but it is unclean for anyone who thinks it is unclean.'

How then are these Christians to think and act in the context of these differences of conviction and practice?

WELCOME

Paul's first priority is devastatingly simple, but also profoundly challenging. It is summed up in the word 'welcome': 'As for the one who is weak in faith, welcome him' (verse 1).

This is not Paul's *only* word on the issue. But it is his *first* one, and it is an expression of loving pastoral wisdom. Many difficult situations and potential divisions would be diffused, and problems eased, if the 'strong' welcomed the 'weak' (and for that matter vice versa). For to 'welcome' is an action of love, an expression of fellowship instead of alienation, a coming together rather than a pushing away. It is a recognition that believers have far more in common than what divides them. It is also a recognition that when division takes place the reason for the division almost immediately becomes more important than it was in the past because it now becomes what defines us *over against* each other.

Paul is not telling the Romans to close their eyes to their different convictions. *Ignoring* theology can never lead to a permanent solution![1] But while he does make his theological position clear it is noteworthy that he returns to the 'welcome principle' at the end of his discussion, with even greater emphasis and motivation: Christ welcomed us when we were weak (15:7). It was 'while we were still weak … Christ died for us' (5:6). It is therefore a sign of un-Christlikeness, indeed a symptom of spiritual sickness, if our first reaction to fellow believers is to focus on differences in practices, rather than welcoming them because Christ himself has welcomed them. We need to remember that if they are Christ's they are ours too (1 Cor. 3:21).

Clearly Paul's principle has a much wider application than the specific issue he is addressing here. How easily (and sadly how often) when a fellow believer's name is mentioned in conversation the first thing said about them is negative and expresses this un-Christlike, unwelcoming spirit. That is, alas, to 'make provision for the flesh, to gratify its desires' rather than to 'put on the Lord Jesus Christ' (13:14). For of him it was written: 'a bruised reed he will not break, and a faintly burning wick he will not quench' (Isa. 42:2-3; cf. Matt. 12:19-20).

In the light of the principle of verse 1, verses 2-4 deal with different convictions about food while verses 5-9 take up the question of the observance of certain days as sacred.

[1] It is important to remember here that Paul is speaking within the context of debates about how patterns of life established in the Mosaic covenant apply to believers' lives in the light of the gospel of the new covenant in Christ. Specifically his focus is on the foods Christians may eat and whether they should regard certain days in the calendar as 'sacred.' He is not speaking about, for example, the deity of Christ, the Trinity, the atonement, justification by faith in Christ alone, or similar cardinal Christian doctrines the rejection of which causes the gospel to disintegrate. In such matters his response is quite different. See, for example, Galatians 1:8-9.

YOU ARE WHAT YOU EAT!

Perhaps this issue of diets came to its sharpest point at the church's *agapē* meals—the suppers Christians seem to have shared together as part of their church family fellowship (cf. 1 Cor. 11:20-22). We can imagine the scene—Gentile believers cheerfully 'tucking in' to pork chops while their fellow believers from a Jewish background retreated into a corner to eat their 'kosher' meals.

These two groups faced subtly different temptations. The 'strong' (*i.e.* 'the one who eats') is likely to 'despise' the person who abstains ('the weak'); while 'the one who abstains' is likely to 'pass judgment on the one who eats' (verse 3). The 'strong' insist on their freedom to eat anything, and look down on 'the weak.' Paradoxically 'the weak' has 'a strong conscience' about eating meat and condemns 'the strong' for his or her 'weakness'!

But whether it is 'the strong' who 'looks down his nose' at 'the weak,' or 'the weak' sitting on the judge's bench with an accusatory stare at 'the strong'—both have lost sight of what is fundamental and essential. They have failed the apostolic test of Christlikeness: 'in humility count others more significant than yourselves. Let each of you look not only to his own interests, but also to the interests of others' (Phil. 2:3b-4).

So Paul's summons is to mutual acceptance (verse 3a). And that is rooted in a call to recognize God's acceptance. What is needed is what Thomas Chalmers famously called 'the expulsive power of a new affection'[1]—a love for God as our Father that responds to his welcome of us and is reflected in our 'welcome' of each other (verse 1)—'For God has welcomed him' (verse 3b). The gospel directs, empowers, and equips us to respond in love to one another. To fail to welcome our brother or sister, weak or strong, reveals and expresses a misshapen view of God. It is at root the expression of a distorted theology. Every action we take and every reaction we have with respect to a fellow Christian turns out to be a revelation of how we think about God.

Paul takes this one step further. To fail to welcome each other and instead 'to pass judgment' on a fellow believer is to forget our position. It is not our place to pass judgment on someone else's

[1] Thomas Chalmers, *Sermons and Discourses* (New York: Robert Carter and Brothers, 1856), II. 271-78. The text of the sermon was 1 John 2:15.

servant—servants stand or fall before their own masters (verse 4a). To pass judgment on a fellow Christian (verse 3) is to arrogate to ourselves what belongs only to the Lord Jesus. And, Paul adds, the Lord is well able to make his own servants 'stand' in the judgment (verse 4b). Therefore how dare I demean or condemn a brother or sister whom God has justified? There is a faint echo here of Paul's earlier question, 'Who is to condemn?' (8:34). If Christ died, rose, and is at the right hand of God interceding for this brother or sister, who do I think I am to judge them?

Remember, therefore, your welcoming God. And remember, too, you are not the lord of your fellow believers; Jesus Christ is.

THE JEWISH CALENDAR

At verse 5 Paul turns to the second issue: Should Christians continue to observe the sacred days in the Old Testament calendar? He states the two different views:

(i) Some days are 'better' than others, 'sacred' according to the teaching of the Old Testament; therefore we should still treat them as such;

(ii) On the contrary, in Christ all days are 'alike,' just as all food is 'clean' (verse 5).

Here Paul adds a further principle: each of us should be 'fully convinced in his own mind' as to lifestyle pattern (verse 5), but we should also recognize that underneath our differences lies a common heartbeat: a desire to honour the Lord and give thanks to him (verse 6). As Christians we neither live nor die to ourselves but to the Lord who died for us. We are not our own, but his, and we are called to honour him just as we will eventually have to give an account to him (verse 12; cf. verses 7-9; cf. 1 Cor. 6:20).

If this is to be true, then it should be mutually recognized. We must not fall into the trap of confusing differences in practice of the order Paul is discussing with lesser devotion to the Lord than our own, and sometimes also with a lower view of Scripture (the issue here was not biblical authority but biblical interpretation). If we recognize we have in common a heartfelt devotion to the Lord, that will go a long way to enabling us to live in harmony with each other until a unity of mind joins our unity of heart-devotion to our common Saviour and Lord. At present we must not deny conscience; but nor should we fail to have respect for each other's love for Christ. That, alas, is all too easily and frequently done. It seems it was being done in Rome.

Passing condemnatory judgment on or despising our fellow believer is thus brought into question (verse 10a). We misunderstand ourselves; for we are the judged, not the judge. All of us—Jew and Gentile alike—stand or fall not in one another's court of opinion but 'before the judgment seat of God' (verse 10; cf. 2 Cor 5:10). There—as Isaiah had prophesied (Isa. 45:23)—we will all agree. For there, 'every knee shall bow.' There only one Lord will be confessed by 'every tongue.' There we will give account for our own lives, not the lives of our fellow believers (verse 12). So, Christians who live in the light of God's assessment of their lives will not view themselves as standing above their brothers or sisters, whether 'weak' or 'strong,' but kneeling alongside them.

This is Paul's prescription to help the believers in Rome to dissolve and dispel the false attitudes of either judging or despising their brethren (verse 10-12). Although these seem to be opposite sicknesses, they evidence a common disorder and require the same prescription. Seeing ourselves before the judgment seat of God and knowing that there 'each of us will "give an account"' (verse 12) makes us think about our brothers—whether 'weak' or 'strong'—in an entirely different light and with a humbler disposition.

So we need to keep taking the medicine.

38

A Major Decision

Therefore let us not pass judgment on one another any longer,
but rather decide never to put a stumbling block or hindrance in
the way of a brother. 14 *I know and am persuaded in the Lord*
Jesus that nothing is unclean in itself, but it is unclean for anyone
who thinks it unclean. 15 *For if your brother is grieved by what*
you eat, you are no longer walking in love. By what you eat, do
not destroy the one for whom Christ died. 16 *So do not let what*
you regard as good be spoken of as evil. 17 *For the kingdom of*
God is not a matter of eating and drinking but of righteousness
and peace and joy in the Holy Spirit. 18 *Whoever thus serves*
Christ is acceptable to God and approved by men. 19 *So then*
let us pursue what makes for peace and for mutual upbuilding.
20 *Do not, for the sake of food, destroy the work of God.*
Everything is indeed clean, but it is wrong for anyone to make
another stumble by what he eats. 21 *It is good not to eat meat or*
drink wine or do anything that causes your brother to stumble.
22 *The faith that you have, keep between yourself and God.*
Blessed is the one who has no reason to pass judgment on himself
for what he approves. 23 *But whoever has doubts is condemned*
if he eats, because the eating is not from faith. For whatever
does not proceed from faith is sin.

(Rom. 14:13-23)

Law and love—there is a tendency to divorce them, and they are often presented as opposites. But Paul sees them as happily married, partners intimately related, since 'love is the fulfilling of the law' (13:10). The same may be said of freedom and discipline. For if we fail to exercise discipline we will lose the liberty we claimed we had.

RESOLUTIONS

Paul has already urged us not to 'pass judgment on one another' (verse 3). Judgmentalism is asphyxiated by the principle of 'welcome.' Now he spells out what this means in practice.

The disposition of 'welcome' does not 'just happen' although it should increasingly become the Christian's default reaction to his or her fellow believers.

Paul's verb in verse 13 is significant. He had used it in verse 4 ('Who are you *to pass judgment* ...?'). But now he uses it both negatively and positively: we are *not* called to 'decide' (pass judgment) on one another; but we are called to 'decide never to put a stumbling block or hindrance' in their way.

Thus welcoming others is not merely a matter of emotion; it involves a deliberate act of the will, a decision on our part. In contexts where there may be differences of viewpoint and practice, it involves the resolution '*never* to put a stumbling block or hindrance in the way of a brother.' Not 'in general,' or 'not usually,' but 'never,' that is, 'not even one more time from now on.'

As Christians we are called to the following unchanging 'Jonathan Edwards-type' resolution:[1]

> *Resolved*: I will never put a stumbling block or hindrance in the way of a brother or sister.

Paul gives us two pictures that express the potential results of failure to do this:

(i) a fellow believer being tripped up (by a 'stumbling block') to their spiritual harm because of what I am doing;

(ii) a fellow believer being caught in a snare ('hindrance'), trapped in a situation where they feel pressurized to imitate my actions but in doing so act in a way that runs contrary to their own conscience. This weakens conscience rather than informs it; ignoring it a second time becomes easier because its strength has been, possibly irrevocably, broken.

[1] Jonathan Edwards famously penned some seventy personal resolutions between December 1722 and August 1723 and committed himself to reading them on a weekly basis to aid his consecration to the Lord. They are listed in Sereno Dwight's Memoir of Edwards in *The Works of Jonathan Edwards* (1834, repr. Edinburgh: Banner of Truth Trust, 1974). I. xx-xxii.

Even though we are believers, we can still be reluctant, even averse, to making concrete commitments like this. To some it seems to smack of 'legalism,' rather than love. But if making such a decision is a biblical exhortation (which it is, verse 13), we dare not think of it as 'legalism.' It is in fact an expression of genuine love and of the humility that considers others more important than ourselves (Phil. 2:3). To be unwilling to make such decisions is an expression of un-Christlike self-love.

Our spiritual ancestors strengthened their resolve in matters like this by the practice of making personal covenants, or (like Jonathan Edwards) 'resolutions'—specific, concrete, written expressions of their commitment to live in a way that would please Christ. Whether we follow their writing practices or not, these verses make clear that the voice of love says, 'I commit myself to never causing a brother or sister to stumble.' The principle of 'welcome' requires a rejection of self-love and its spouse, self-pleasing.

The resolution (verse 13) is now followed by an explanation of why we need to put it into practice.

EXPLANATION

Paul himself was persuaded 'that nothing is unclean in itself' (verse 14; cf. Mark 7:19). But he was wise enough to know that to the person who regards a particular meat as 'unclean' it is indeed *unclean to him*—and therefore 'off limits' (verse 14). Eating it would not only be emotionally repulsive, but it would also sully that person's conscience. It is both natural and almost inevitable therefore for such individuals to be grieved when they see someone doing what their own conscience forbids (verse 15); it offends their conscience as if they had done it themselves. Their conviction is that they should no more eat meat that has been forbidden by Old Testament law than steal or break the Sabbath. Conscience tells them it would be sinning against God. And it is natural for them to ask and even assume that if that is true for them, surely it should be true for everyone?

It is all too easy for the 'strong' to adopt a dismissive attitude, and with a shrug of the shoulders think or even say, 'Well, that's your problem.' If so, however, these words cut us down to size: 'you are no longer walking in love.' By such an attitude we may be in danger of destroying a brother or sister for whom Christ died (verse 15). To 'despise the one who abstains' (verse 3) is not a trivial matter.

Paul had spoken about the role of 'conscience' earlier in Romans (2:15; 13:5), and although he does not use the word in this context the idea is clearly present. 'Conscience' is the aspect of our self-awareness that exercises moral judgment as to right and wrong, wise and foolish actions. Paul's understanding is that conscience should be heeded, while at the same time he recognizes that it is fallible. For the Christian it will reflect his or her understanding of the teaching of God's word and its implications. But that does *not* mean he or she rightly understands the Scriptures or their application to life. So, with Martin Luther, we need to learn to have a conscience that is 'captive to the word of God'—that is, submits to its authority and is informed by its teaching.

This whole section then is dealing with the sensitive issue of two groups of believers whose consciences dictate different responses to the same situations (in this case diets and days). But—as in every context where he is addressing issues in the church—the principles Paul enunciates derive not from the problem but from the gospel. They therefore prove to be broadly applicable to many situations in church life.

Paul's response here is to put the onus on himself and others who consider themselves to be 'strong'—that is, whose consciences, informed and shaped by the gospel of Christ, allow them behaviour patterns that the consciences of others forbid.

This is a challenging approach, for two reasons. *First,* because those who are sure they are 'right' also tend to assume others should fall into line with them. And *second*, because it means that although the question of 'What is right?' is important, it is not the only important question. There is also the question, 'In this situation, how can I best love my brother and sister as myself?' Fail to ask it, and it is almost certain that our first reaction will be to judge (and then to demean and perhaps even to condemn) rather than to 'welcome.'

'WEAK' AND 'STRONG'

Paul hopes that the 'weak in faith' will come to be more fully instructed by the gospel and enjoy the liberty of conscience it brings.

But meanwhile he has made a personal commitment not to demean, or to put an obstacle in the way of, or do anything that would cause the stumbling of a believer whose conscience is still bound by the regulations of the Mosaic law code (verse 13).

We have already noted the paradox in this situation. But it bears repetition. The person who has a 'strong' conscience—and therefore refuses to eat non-kosher meat—is the one who is 'weak in faith' (verse 1). As we have seen, the pastoral problem here is twofold:

- those who regard themselves as having a 'strong' conscience usually assume they are also 'strong' in faith and do not need instruction. But strong convictions of conscience can be mistaken and may need correction.

On the other hand,

- those who actually are 'strong in faith' sometimes react to the weak by insisting on and even flaunting their liberty of conscience. But that is to sin against members of our family. It is not the way of welcoming love nor is it the way of humility. What is required is patience coupled with a loving commitment to self-discipline and self-sacrifice.

If we fail here the result may be spiritual damage. How so? In three ways. It may (i) grieve fellow Christians, (ii) indicate that I am no longer walking in love, and (iii) risk the destruction of someone for whom the Lord Jesus Christ shed his precious blood (verse 15). Hence Paul's sober exhortation: *Don't do it*. If we do, we are risking what we regard as our 'good' being spoken of as 'evil' (verse 16). The result will, alas, be increased alienation and exacerbated antagonism, and then, possibly, painful division that could have been avoided by the self-denying exercise of love.

DESTROYING?

When Paul urges us not to '*destroy* the one for whom Christ died' (verse 15), he is not implying that one believer's actions can lead to another believer's apostasy. That would contradict his earlier statement that those God predestined, called, and justified he also glorified (8:30), as well as negate his reassurance that *nothing* can separate us from the love of Christ (8:39). Rather he is indicating that confusion of conscience, a disintegration of stability, and a loss of assurance may result. Satan then has a field day; joy diminishes; faith is paralyzed.

But while 'destroy' does not mean 'cause apostasy,' the strength of Paul's language underlines that we ignore his exhortation at great cost—first to our brother, but then also to ourselves, since we will surely be judged (we will be not 'acceptable to God,' as he later says, verse 18). For we have shown a deliberate lack of love to a member of our family—God's family!

WHAT REALLY MATTERS TO YOU?

The verses that follow (verses 17-23) further elucidate the rationale for, and the implications of, this teaching. Paul clearly empathized with all Jewish believers who now felt themselves being treated as a marginalized minority even in the church, and perhaps found themselves becoming resentful and judgmental, or on the other hand, tempted to act against conscience by conforming.

At the same time, Paul (whose own conscience has been set free by the gospel), expresses a principle that, once grasped, should motivate Gentile believers to share his self-denying, other-loving resolution. It puts the divisive issue in perspective for everyone in the church. And it is applicable far beyond the specific issues he highlights here. 'For the kingdom of God is not a matter of eating and drinking but of righteousness and peace and joy in the Holy Spirit' (14:17). Were we all to grasp this principle our church would become a 'safe place' for all believers, whether 'weak' or 'strong.'

The principle here, although challenging, is simple. Issues of the kind that were here causing tensions between Jewish and Gentile believers need to be seen in the much larger context of the whole gospel and of the rich blessing *all believers share.* What is eating and drinking compared to *justification* ('righteousness') before God? How can we be so foolish as to profess to have *peace* with him but to care little for the peace of conscience of other members of his family? How can we have *joy* through the Spirit when we are giving grief to our fellow believers?

Paul's words here are reminiscent of the triumphant exultation he had earlier expressed in 5:1-2—*righteousness* (justification) brings both *peace* and *joy*. In essence he is reminding the church in Rome, and teaching us, that if we keep the gospel central and together focus on Christ and the blessings we have in him, other matters will surely (even if slowly) fit into place. Keep our eyes fixed on Jesus and we will develop the loving patience required for that to happen.

A small object brought close to the eye can obscure the entire world. Similarly when our vision is dominated by one issue on which we differ, we will lose sight of what unites us. We will end up majoring on the minors and minoring on the majors. Clearly this was happening if Gentile believers were despising Jewish ones and Jewish believers were condemning their Gentile brothers and sisters. They were blinding themselves to the gospel and its fruits—which united them. Imagine the folly of thinking that your views of meat and drink were more important than 'righteousness and peace and joy in the Holy Spirit'!

Sadly, we can imagine it because we have too often made similar mistakes.

But grasp the principle of verse 17 and we will fulfil our responsibility to serve Christ. For this is the lifestyle that is 'acceptable to God.' Plus it also leads to being recipients of our fellow believers' favour—our self-disciplined love will be 'approved by men' (verse 18). There is a dual effect: peace—the well-being of the church family—on the one hand, and its mutual upbuilding on the other (verse 19). Then, 'when each part is working properly,' the body to which we belong 'builds itself up in love' (Eph. 4:16).

What Paul calls for here is not an added extra in the Christian life. Rather it is the specific application and outworking of the response to God's mercy he had spelled out in 12:1-2. Consecration to the Lord as living sacrifices works itself out in the church family when we 'pursue what makes for peace and for mutual upbuilding' (verse 19).

Here, again, Christian love, neighbour-love, 'does not insist on its own way' (1 Cor. 13:5). The poison that threatened to destroy fellowship in Rome was the spirit of 'self first and others afterwards.' That turns the church from being a maternity hospital, a school of learning, a gymnasium where fitness is developed, into a demolition company. And sadly the company may end up bankrupting itself! By contrast, in the church family everything is to be done with a view to upbuilding (15:2; cf. 1 Cor. 14:26).

SUMMING UP

In verses 20-23 Paul sums up his argument thus far:

He underscores *the seriousness of the issue*: some of the Christians in Rome are in danger of destroying 'the work of God' among them 'for the sake of food' (verse 20). The stakes are indeed high. The 'strong' may be 'right' theologically but misguided and even foolish spiritually, for the sake of food destroying both 'the one for whom Christ died' (verse 15) and also being willing to 'destroy the work of God.' True, sometimes churches necessarily divide over the foundational elements of the gospel—but what folly has taken hold of us if, over the issue of food, we are prepared to destroy rather than build up? That is not caused by love of orthodoxy. That is caused by love of self.

Several principles arise from Paul's teaching thus far:

(i) Self-control and self-discipline are a 'good': 'It is good not to eat meat or drink wine or do anything that causes your brother to stumble' (verse 21). Had some of the Roman Christians begun to think 'It would be bad for me *not* to exercise my liberty'?

(ii) There is a simple axiom we should practise: 'The faith that you have, keep between yourself and God' (verse 22). Paul is not speaking here about not sharing our faith with unbelievers. Rather the thought is: you do not need to exercise your freedom in order to enjoy it.

(iii) If we *insist* on exercising our liberty (here, eating meat) we are in danger of forfeiting the liberty we claim to have. That inner necessity is the seed of a new bondage. True freedom in the matter of eating meat means I can *either eat it or abstain from eating it*. It is not a new binding of my conscience so that I *must* eat it!

(iv) The blessedness of a conscience informed by Scripture lies in being free both to exercise and not to exercise the liberties the gospel brings (verse 22b). I step into spiritual danger if, insisting on my right to exercise my liberty, I *flaunt* that liberty and demean those whose consciences differ from mine. Then my insistence on exercising my freedom has silenced God's command to love my neighbour as myself. The spiritual sickness and ultimate bondage of self-love has infected me.

In Galatians 2:11-14 Paul describes a situation in which similar forces were at work, although in the reverse direction. Simon Peter had come to Antioch and (presumably in the light of his experiences described in Acts 10–11) was happily eating and drinking with the Gentile Christians there. But then a group of Jewish Christians arrived from Jerusalem. Peter withdrew from table fellowship with his Gentile brothers. Others—even the reliable Barnabas—were 'led astray.' In this instance, the consciences of these Christians—a Jewish one in Peter's case—had been set free from observing the Levitical food laws. But they acted against conscience *because of the intimidating judgmentalism of their Jewish Christian brethren.* It could so easily have wrought havoc and destruction in the church at Antioch. That explains why the tense moment Paul describes in Galatians 2:11-14 was necessary. For the sake of the gospel and the church, he courageously rebuked Peter to his face (which makes Peter's later description of Paul as 'our beloved brother' very impressive indeed, 2 Pet. 3:15).

Paul realized there was a similar, if reversed, danger in Rome to the one he had witnessed in Antioch. In Rome, Jewish believers might feel so intimidated by their Gentile brethren that they would act against their consciences. They might then eat non-kosher food, but from fear not from faith. And doing that, says Paul, leads to self-condemnation and subsequent spiritual distress. 'For whatever does not proceed from faith is sin' (verse 23). What they needed was patient instruction, not Gentile demeaning! Only then would they be able to approve of eating all meats (verse 22).

Our Christian freedom rests in our conscience being informed by the truth of the gospel, and our appreciation of what it means to belong to the kingdom of God. Our 'meat and drink' is no longer 'meat' or 'drink'—but delighting in righteousness, peace, and joy in the Spirit. Possessing these, we can enjoy our liberties without expressing them, and at the same time be patient with those whose consciences differ from ours in such matters of practice. And so, in the light of this, each of us is called to a simple act of consecration:

> *Resolved*: Never to use any freedom I have if by doing so I would demean or destroy a brother or sister for whom Christ died.

Are *you* thus resolved?

39

Christ Our Example

We who are strong have an obligation to bear with the failings of the weak, and not to please ourselves. [2] *Let each of us please his neighbour for his good, to build him up.* [3] *For Christ did not please himself, but as it is written, 'The reproaches of those who reproached you fell on me.'* [4] *For whatever was written in former days was written for our instruction, that through endurance and through the encouragement of the Scriptures we might have hope.* [5] *May the God of endurance and encouragement grant you to live in such harmony with one another, in accord with Christ Jesus,* [6] *that together you may with one voice glorify the God and Father of our Lord Jesus Christ.* [7] *Therefore welcome one another as Christ has welcomed you, for the glory of God.*
(Rom. 15:1-7)

Paul now concludes his extended discussion of a potentially divisive pastoral issue in the church in Rome. Set as it was in the capital city of the empire it may have been the most multi-ethnic church in the world. But it was also probably the church with the largest *mixture* of Jewish and Gentile Christians. And the complexion of the church had possibly changed around AD 50 when the Emperor Claudius had expelled Jews, including Jewish Christians (at first Rome had probably viewed Christianity simply as a sect of Judaism). Now Jewish believers had returned—like Priscilla and her husband Aquila whom Paul had first met in Corinth (Acts 18:1-3; Rom. 16:3).

Whether this was a contributing cause, it is not difficult to imagine the heightening of tension in the church if at the *agapē* meals Jewish believers saw Gentile believers eating meat proscribed by the Levitical laws. How dare they? The danger then was that in reaction the Gentile believers might insist on exercising their freedom from the ceremonial law code, and in the process demean their Jewish Christian brothers. In turn the latter would either be scandalized by such behaviour or, intimidated by it, conform to it contrary to their consciences.

The situation was by no means easy to negotiate wisely. What principles could Paul derive from the gospel that would help? Here were people who thought of themselves as having 'strong' consciences but who had 'weak' faith. The situation was further complicated when those who knew that in Christ the Levitical food laws had been abrogated were regarded as having 'weak' consciences when in fact they were 'strong' in faith. In such situations it is all too easy to adopt entrenched views and practices. What was needed was the exercise of the love and patience of the Lord Jesus and making 'welcome' the watchword.

Paul, although a Jewish believer, places himself among 'the strong' ('We who are strong,' 15:1). He had earlier indicated this with an appeal to the teaching of the Lord Jesus: 'I know and am persuaded in the Lord Jesus that nothing is unclean of itself' (14:14a). At the same time, he displays a marvellous pastoral intelligence. He was sensitive to what this issue felt like to his fellow Jewish believers. While 'nothing is unclean of itself ... it is unclean for anyone who thinks it unclean' (14:14b). What is to be done in such a complex and sensitive situation?

From the outset of his discussion Paul had laid down his 'welcome principle': *fellowship must be maintained even while divisive issues like this remain unresolved*. What the Roman Christians had in common in the kingdom of God was far greater than what divided them (14:17). Therefore both 'weak' and 'strong' had responsibilities to each other: 'Let not the one who eats despise the one who abstains, and let not the one who abstains pass judgment on the one who eats, for God has welcomed him' (14:3).

BEARING UP

But now, in the context of this principle of *mutual* responsibility and forbearance, Paul places a special responsibility on the 'strong'—including therefore himself. Characteristically he states it both positively and negatively. But now he increases his typical two beats to the bar to a rhythm of three beats—*positive*, *negative*, *positive*.

Positive: 'bear with the failings of the weak' (verse 1). He does not deny that there are 'failings' and that those who have them are 'weak.' But he urges forbearance. He must have known that this response might itself be accused of weakness (and, alas, even compromise); but it actually requires great strength. The verb *to bear* means 'to carry.' The 'strong' must be willing to take the weight and the strain required in exercising patience. The 'strong' must carry the weak! The attitude of 'not suffering fools gladly' is anathema to the apostle.

Negative: let us '*not* ... please ourselves.' Here again is the key issue: are we willing to deny self because of the priority of neighbour-love?

Positive: 'Let each of us please his neighbour for his good, to build him up' (verse 2). Once again we hear the same note: neighbour love always seeks to please and do good, with the goal of upbuilding, edifying, and maturing. This is a radically different disposition from demeaning, despising, and destroying.

But now in addition Paul adds a motivation of overwhelming power: Jesus Christ himself is our example: 'For Christ did not please himself' (verse 3). That is a word that demolishes self-love and promotes the disposition he is inculcating.

Earlier in Romans Paul had majored on the way our union with Christ energizes a new lifestyle of holiness (6:1-14). The knowledge that Christ is our life is transformative. United to him in his death and resurrection, we died to the dominion of sin and now live to God. But Christ is our example as well as our life. The mind of Christ is our mind too (Phil. 2:5).

The application of this to our fellowship life is not complex rocket science. It involves only a simple syllogism:

> *My Master, Jesus Christ, did not please himself,*
>
> Therefore:
>
> *As his servant I will not please myself.*

Clearly the temptation of 'the strong' with respect to 'the weak' is to say, or at least imply, 'Whatever you think, I have a right to express my liberty.' But that is tantamount to saying, 'I intend to please myself.' And that for Paul is a contradiction of the Christlikeness that is God's goal for our lives (cf. 8:29).

ON NOT PLEASING SELF

In verses 3 and 4 we are given a further explanation of the importance of this principle by way of an example: *the example of Jesus.*

Christ not only did not please himself; in addition, he was willing to bear reproach. Paul hears the Saviour applying Psalm 69:9 to himself: 'The reproaches of those who reproached you have fallen on me.'

No psalm is more frequently quoted or alluded to in connection with the passion of the Lord Jesus than Psalm 69. In it we are given a moving pre-description of the forbearance of Christ. More than endure 'weak' believers, for the sake of sinners he was willing to endure reproach he had not deserved, and the suffering of the cross, and not insist on his own 'rights.' If this is the way the Master went, is it not a small thing by comparison for 'the strong' to follow his example and 'bear with the failings of the weak'?

This text—Psalm 69:9—like other Old Testament Scripture 'was written in former days … for our instruction' (verse 4). It was 'breathed out by God and profitable for teaching …' (2 Tim. 3:16). Paul uses the same word in both passages. The 'teaching' or 'instruction' (*didaskalia*) in Scripture is 'profitable for … reproof, for correction, and for training in righteousness, that the man of God may be complete, equipped for every good work.' So Paul is not only admiring Jesus here; he is also implicitly using the Scriptures for the 'reproof, correction, and training in righteousness' of the Roman believers.

In our union with Christ, he becomes both our life and our example. For the 'strong' to bear, to endure, to put up with the 'weak' is a small thing by comparison with our Lord's willingness to endure the hostility of sinners (Heb. 12:3). We are being asked only to endure and to patiently put up with the weakness of some fellow believers! This is trivial by comparison with,

Bearing shame and scoffing rude,
In my place condemned He stood.[1]

[1] From the hymn 'Man of sorrows' by Philip P. Bliss (1838–76).

The Scriptures thus give us 'encouragement and hope' (verse 4). While Paul does not specify what he means, the 'hope' in view here may be that when the 'endurance' of 'the strong,' and their willingness to take the weight of 'the weak,' are coupled with the teaching of the Scriptures, 'the weak' will gradually become 'strong' too and begin to enjoy the freedom they have been given in Christ.

A COLLECT FOR PEACE

In verses 5-7, Paul rounds off his emphasis on Christ himself as the motivation and model for harmony in the church family. He expresses a prayer-wish that God would enable the believers in Rome to be conformed to Christ ('in accord with Christ Jesus') in whom their unity and harmony are rooted and grounded. For when that harmony is present and evident then 'together ... with one voice' they will 'glorify the God and Father of our Lord Jesus Christ' (verses 5-6).

These words refer to our worship. But they also echo the prayer of Christ for the whole life and lifestyle of the future church (recorded in John 17:20-26). He prayed that through our union with him we might also be united to each other in a way that reflects the loving and attractive harmony that he has with his Father. It is not difficult to understand why Jesus added 'so that the world may know that you sent me and loved them even as you loved me' (John 17:23). When Jewish and Gentile believers live in the loving harmony Paul has in mind, unbelievers are bound to ask for the explanation. And, of course, there is only one—Christ! But when that loving harmony is absent in the church—when this evidence of salvation is lacking among us—why would the world believe that the Father sent his Son to be the Saviour, or that in Christ we have been reconciled?

Could there be stronger motivation for the Roman Christians, Jewish and Gentile, to 'welcome one another as Christ has welcomed you, for the glory of God' (verse 7)? What began as an exhortation to the 'strong' (14:1) has now extended to them all. Here, then, was the question they all needed to ask: *What attitude to our fellow Christians will most tend to bring glory to God?*

That is a question *we* should ask too. And we should ask it about everything.

40

Christ—for the Jew and Gentile

For I tell you that Christ became a servant to the circumcised to
show God's truthfulness, in order to confirm the promises given
to the patriarchs, [9] and in order that the Gentiles might glorify
God for his mercy. As it is written,

> *'Therefore I will praise you among the Gentiles,*
> *and sing to your name.'*

[10] And again it is said,

> *'Rejoice, O Gentiles, with his people.'*

[11] And again,

> *'Praise the Lord, all you Gentiles,*
> *and let all the peoples extol him.'*

[12] And again Isaiah says,

> *'The root of Jesse will come,*
> *even he who arises to rule the Gentiles;*
> *in him will the Gentiles hope.'*

[13] May the God of hope fill you with all joy and peace in
believing, so that by the power of the Holy Spirit you may
abound in hope.

(Rom. 15:8-13)

The Letter to the Romans is punctuated by the little connective word 'for' (*gar*). It occurs almost constantly as the link between one part of Paul's argument and the next. In this way it leads us into the undergirding logic of his gospel. Following his reasoning is a theological education in itself.

The word appears again here in 15:8 in what serves as both a *final word* on the tensions between Jewish and Gentile believers in the churches in Rome and an *introductory word* to the closing section of Paul's exposition of his gospel. The unity of Jewish and Gentile believers is an integral part of that gospel and indeed of the entire history of redemption (as Gen. 12:3; Psa. 2:8; Isa. 52:15, and many other Old Testament passages had indicated). The consummation of that history is found in Christ.

Here Paul gives us one of several New Testament statements that help us to answer Anselm of Canterbury's famous question *Cur Deus Homo—Why the God-Man?* Why did Christ come, and what did he intend to accomplish? The New Testament authors focus on various aspects of the work of Christ (*e.g.* 1 John 3:8: 'The reason the Son of God appeared was *to destroy the works of the devil*'). Here, in this passage, Paul provides us with a gospel triptych—three dimensions of our Saviour's work.

A GOSPEL TRIPTYCH

(i) Jesus Christ came 'as a servant (*diakonos*) to the circumcised.' He came *to the* Jews; and he came 'to serve and not to be served' (Mark 10:45). The gospel is 'for the Jew first' (1:16-17), a principle that, as we have seen, Paul's invariable practice mirrored.

The link to his previous discussion is clear: Gentile believers need to remember that they are branches grafted into what God had been doing down through the centuries in the fulfilment of the Abrahamic promise that the nations would be blessed in his seed (and Eve's—Gen. 12:1-2; 3:15; Rom. 11:17-24). They should rejoice in conversions among the Jews, not despise those who struggle with, and are slow to appreciate, the new liberty and lifestyle the gospel brings. Did they not know that the apostles themselves had been slow to understand this fully?

If Gentile believers would only remember that the Son of God became a *diakonos* to the Jews (verse 8) surely any attitude of superiority would be dissolved. The lessons remain the same for Gentile believers today. And, in passing, Paul's words remind us that the Christian faith is not 'western' in origin and 'white' in colour-tone. It never was (and statistically is not today either).

(ii) The coming of Christ demonstrates the veracity of God ('to show God's truthfulness') expressed in 'the promises given to the patriarchs' (verse 8). God had promised Abraham that it was in his seed that the families of the earth would be blessed. That blessing was not a blanket guarantee to all of Abraham's natural seed irrespective of faith (cf. 9:7), nor was it confined to them. But it did come through them and was intended to be sustained among them.

This divine truthfulness in turn expresses the divine reliability. God has kept his longest-standing promise (for Gen. 3:15 lies behind Gen. 12:1-3) and his most-difficult-to-keep promise (since it would cost the death of his only Son—Rom. 8:32; Gal. 3:13).

(iii) The original plan of God always had Gentiles in view as well as Jews. Christ came 'in order that the Gentiles might glorify God for his mercy' (verse 9). Both Jewish and Gentile believers in the church in Rome needed to realize that this world-surprising unity was not an afterthought in the divine plan and economy. It was already in view in the Abrahamic covenant promise. Even before that, the promise enshrined in Genesis 3:15 was available to Adam and Eve who were 'pre-Israelites'! God's redemptive purposes have always been universally orientated. And now they have begun to come to a glorious new stage of fruition. The Gentiles have received mercy.

Once again Paul echoes themes he has already explored: mercy coming to the Gentiles through God's sovereign superintending of history (chs. 9–11) and our consecration to the Lord seen as a response to 'the mercies of God' (12:1). As he moves towards the conclusion of the letter it becomes increasingly clear that his gospel is woven from the single cloth of grace. Could anything make it clearer to these Roman Christians that Jew-Gentile fellowship, mutual love, and church family harmony are built into the covenant purposes of God? It is *that important.* They therefore should be nurtured, not deconstructed.

BIBLICAL CONFIRMATION

All this is substantiated in the verses that follow (verses 9b-12) by a series of quotations from the Old Testament. Each one indicates that already in the old covenant the conversion of Gentiles was in view in the divine purposes (notice the words in italics):

- verse 9 is a quotation from Psalm 18:49 (cf. 2 Sam. 22:22): 'Therefore I will praise you *among the Gentiles*, and sing to your name.'
- verse 10 is quoted from Deuteronomy 32:43: 'Rejoice, *O Gentiles*, with his people.'
- verse 11 comes from Psalm 117:1: 'Praise the Lord, *all you Gentiles*, and let *all the peoples* extol him.'
- verse 12 is from Isaiah 11:10: 'The root of Jesse will come, even he who arises to rule *the Gentiles*.'

Paul seems to have selected these quotations deliberately from the three divisions of the Hebrew Bible: the Law, the Prophets, and the Writings. In this way he again emphasizes that his gospel is in perfect continuity with the Old Testament Scriptures as a whole and fulfils them.

The cumulative effect of the quotations highlights the word 'Gentiles' in each. The quotations in verses 9 and 11 stress the way in which the Lord will be worshipped by the Gentiles ('I will praise you among the Gentiles,' verse 9; 'let all the peoples praise you,' verse 11). In the other two citations the unity of Jewish and Gentile believers is established ('Rejoice, O Gentiles, *with his people*' verse 10; 'The *root of Jesse* will come, even he who arises to rule *the Gentiles*. In him will *the Gentiles* hope,' verse 12).

No doubt Paul had often linked these verses together before. Perhaps his first glimpse of this Christ-centred-prophecy-fulfilling way of reading the details of the Old Testament had been when he heard Stephen preach. Now, in turn, hearing the way he interpreted Scripture must have been a similar eye-opening experience for both Jews and Gentiles in Rome. Only a few Christians in Rome would have owned parts or all of the Scriptures (the invention of the printing press, economical 'publishing,' was almost a millennium and a half distant; indeed in the Roman Empire perhaps only ten per cent of the population were literate). Yet these growing young Christians had undoubtedly memorized as much Scripture as they could. So we can imagine them going home after the first reading of this letter saying to each other, 'I never put those verses together that way—did you? Now I see it!'

The last words in verse 12, 'in him will the Gentiles hope,' link up with Paul's earlier comment that the Old Testament Scriptures were written that 'we might have hope' (15:4) and also with the concluding prayer-wish for 'the God of hope' to act (verse 13).

We have seen that 'hope' in Scripture is not wishful thinking but an assured conviction that what is promised will come to pass. The coming of the gospel through the Jews to the Gentiles has fulfilled the 'hope' enshrined in the promises given by God and recorded in Scripture. He has kept the covenant promise he gave to Abraham who 'in hope … believed against hope' (4:18). Such 'hope' was never wishful thinking when it was hope in God!

That is why the children of Abraham in the days of the old covenant were able to say, 'I wait for the Lord, my soul waits, and in his word I hope' (Psa. 130:5).

Thus, in the fulfilment of his greatest, longest-lasting, and most-difficult-to-keep promise God has proved himself to be 'the God of hope' (verse 13). So Paul prays that this God will fill the believers in Rome, both Jew and Gentile, with joy and peace—the keynotes of life in the kingdom of God as he had earlier indicated (14:17)—and that through the ministry of the Spirit in their lives they will 'abound in hope.'

Since the ancient promises had been fulfilled in Jesus Christ, the Roman Christians had every reason to have a well-grounded and assured hope. Paul is calling them to learn 'to act faith' (as our forebears put it). God's promises do not give rise to hope in us simply by 'being there.' We are responsible to take hold of them in faith, consciously meditating on them, deliberately committing ourselves to believing them, holding on to them, and never letting go of them until they come to pass. Our faith is receptive with respect to justification. But throughout our growth in grace it is active in taking hold of the word of promise—we contribute nothing to God and his word; but we are called to take everything from it that it contains!

Martin Luther was indeed right: 'Oh, it is a living, busy, active, mighty thing, this faith.'[1]

[1] Luther, *Commentary on Romans*, xvii.

41

Reflections on a Ministry

I myself am satisfied about you, my brothers, that you yourselves
are full of goodness, filled with all knowledge and able to instruct
one another. [15] *But on some points I have written to you very*
boldly by way of reminder, because of the grace given me by God
[16] *to be a minister of Christ Jesus to the Gentiles in the priestly*
service of the gospel of God, so that the offering of the Gentiles
may be acceptable, sanctified by the Holy Spirit. [17] *In Christ*
Jesus, then, I have reason to be proud of my work for God.
[18] *For I will not venture to speak of anything except what Christ*
has accomplished through me to bring the Gentiles to obedi-
ence—by word and deed, [19] *by the power of signs and wonders,*
by the power of the Spirit of God—so that from Jerusalem and
all the way around to Illyricum I have fulfilled the ministry
of the gospel of Christ; [20] *and thus I make it my ambition to*
preach the gospel, not where Christ has already been named,
lest I build on someone else's foundation, [21] *but as it is written,*

> *'Those who have never been told of him will see,*
> *and those who have never heard will understand.'*

[22] *This is the reason why I have so often been hindered from*
coming to you. [23] *But now, since I no longer have any room for*
work in these regions, and since I have longed for many years to
come to you, [24] *I hope to see you in passing as I go to Spain, and*
to be helped on my journey there by you, once I have enjoyed
your company for a while. [25] *At present, however, I am going*
to Jerusalem bringing aid to the saints.

(Rom. 15:14-25)

Paul is now coming towards the conclusion of his letter. It is bookended both at the beginning and end with personal reflections, aspirations, and plans. Although hundreds of miles away from the church in Rome, he has been fulfilling his desire to 'impart to you some spiritual gift to strengthen you' (1:11; his teaching in 1:18–15:13 constituting at least some part of that gift). Now, in the lengthiest conclusion to any of his letters, he reflects on his present situation and his hopes for the future (15:14-33). He then concludes with his customary greetings to a remarkably numerous list of his friends in Rome.

The opening words of this section may come as a surprise after fourteen and a half chapters of careful instruction. He is in fact 'satisfied' with (*i.e.* 'persuaded of') the spiritual maturity of the Christians in Rome. They are 'full of goodness, filled with all knowledge and able to instruct one another' (verse 14). He had urged Gentile Christians in the churches not to demean their Jewish brethren. Here he makes it clear to all of them that his extended and detailed exposition of what he has called 'my gospel' should not be read as though he were demeaning them, or their understanding of the faith, or the quality of their Christian lives.

This is very instructive in an age when evangelical Christians are sometimes quick to write off brothers and sisters in Christ. Too frequently there is a carping note heard on social media platforms, criticizing other believers or ministries but without any apostolic note of thanksgiving (contrast Paul's attitude in Phil. 1:15-18). Paul may have occasionally asked his Roman readers penetrating questions like 'Do you not know ...?' (6:3, 16; 7:1). But he is not suggesting the church in Rome is immature—far from it. His underlying motive has been to explain what he preaches, expound it, where necessary defend it from misunderstanding, and to commend it to them—in the expectation that they will recognize its authenticity. If there has been a boldness in anything he has said (verse 15) it has been simply to remind them of the importance of the gospel they share in common. As an apostle to the Gentiles he sees it as is part of his responsibility to fulfil his ministry in the capital of the Gentile world as he has done elsewhere (verses 14-16).

MINISTRY

Paul describes himself here in a unique way. He is 'a minister [*leitourgos*] of Christ Jesus to the Gentiles in the priestly service of the gospel of God [literally, 'ministering as a priest,' *hierourgeō*]. This is a self-description he uses only here. His goal is that 'the offering of the Gentiles may be acceptable, sanctified by the Holy Spirit' (verse 16).

The Levitical 'ring' to the vocabulary here (liturgical minister, priestly service, acceptable offering, sanctified) should not be misinterpreted. It is in line with his similar use of liturgical language in 12:1-2. All Christians are to present themselves as a 'sacrifice' that involves 'service' or 'worship' (*latreia*) and is 'well-pleasing to God' (cf. Eph. 5:2; Phil. 4:18). As he often does, Paul is using the language of old covenant liturgy to describe the way it is fulfilled in the new covenant in Christ, and in this case in his own ministry.

But as Peter had indicated on the Day of Pentecost, quoting Joel 2:28-32, new covenant believers enjoy greater privileges. Under the old covenant only the high priest could enter the holy of holies—and he only once a year (Heb. 9:7). Now all who are united to Christ have 'access' to the Father (Rom. 5:2; Eph. 2:18) and bring their sacrifice to him. But now their sacrifice is not of the atoning blood drained from the dead body of an animal substitute. It is the thanksgiving and praise they bring as they consecrate their own bodies in response to Christ's once-for-all sacrifice (12:1-2).

Paul further applies this old covenant liturgical pattern to his own ministry as an apostle. He pictures himself as a new covenant liturgist who is bringing the Gentiles to God as a thank-offering. The liturgy Paul conducts is evangelistic. His ministry applies the fruits of the unique priesthood of Christ who by his 'death upon the cross for our redemption … made there (by his one oblation once offered) a full, perfect, and sufficient sacrifice, oblation, and satisfaction' for our sins.[1] Now the sanctification of the offering is effected not by following Levitical regulations but by the power of the Holy Spirit (verse 16).

Paul is also conscious that he has come to a new stage in his ministry. Ministers sometimes do—whether that is to be within

[1] From 'The Order for Holy Communion' in the *Book of Common Prayer* (1549).

their current sphere of service or in their calling to serve in new ones. The apostle is conscious that 'From Jerusalem to Illyricum [the Roman province north of Macedonia on the opposite side of the Adriatic from Italy] I have fulfilled the ministry of the gospel of Christ' (verse 19).

From the time Paul's ministry commenced with his commissioning by the church at Antioch (Acts 13:1-3) he has traversed a vast area by land and sea, preaching the gospel. He is not claiming to have preached in every town and hamlet. Nor is he claiming that the gospel has reached everyone. Nor does he credit himself with its fruitfulness (even though he has worked harder than anyone else); any fruitfulness has been the effect of the grace of God, not his personal merit (1 Cor. 15:10): 'I will not venture to speak of anything except what Christ has accomplished through me to bring the Gentiles to obedience' (verse 18).

This is a changed man from the one God had humbled on the road to Damascus. *That man* had cherished the ambition to belong to the front rank of Jews, not only in terms of pedigree and commitment but in personal performance (Gal. 1:13-14; Phil. 3:4-6). *This man* attributes all to the grace of God. He would not dare ('venture,' verse 18) to speak otherwise.

And the goal? It has been to fulfil his divinely given apostolic commission 'to preach to the Gentiles the unsearchable riches of Christ' (Eph. 3:8) in order 'to bring about the obedience of faith for the sake of his name among all the nations' (Rom. 1:5). That calling had been embedded in him from the days surrounding his Damascus Road experience. By God's grace it had never left him despite 'many dangers, toils, and snares' (Acts 9:15-16; 2 Cor. 4:7-12; 11:23-29).

This glorious calling had been fulfilled 'by word and deed, by the power of signs and wonders, by the power of the Spirit of God' (verses 18-19). These constitute what Paul had earlier significantly described as 'the signs of an apostle' (2 Cor. 12:12).

These words should inform our general thinking about 'signs and wonders.' From time to time in the history of the church the view has emerged that 'the Bible is full of them, and we should be full of them too.' It became especially influential again during the twentieth century. But this view has almost always failed to observe that such 'signs and wonders' (miraculous healings and similar phenomena effected by or through individuals) are not presented in Scripture as normative in either the history of redemption or the life of the church.

Paul specifically related these phenomena to the significance of the ministry of the apostles. They are 'the signs of a true apostle' (2 Cor. 12:12). They were confirmations of their calling, of the divine origin of their message, and of their direct commissioning by Christ (1 Cor. 9:1). Such 'signs and wonders' done through the mediation of individuals appear spasmodically in Scripture rather than constantly. They are infrequent rather than frequent. They were not constant features of God's superintendence of his people, and in that sense the Bible is not in fact 'full' of them. Thus Scripture tells a quite different story from contemporary claims that 'the Bible is full of signs and wonders, and the church today should be too.' It records only a few periods, usually lasting around a generation, during which 'signs and wonders' were effected through God's servants. These were typically seasons when the kingdom of God faced a crisis in which its very existence was threatened, or in which God was giving new revelation and wanted to confirm his messengers and their message—and sometimes both.

Thus 'signs and wonders' were absent during vast tracts of biblical history. And it is striking how little attention Paul gives to them in his letters. Particularly noteworthy is that in preparing Timothy to minister in the future he gives no indication that he expected 'signs and wonders' to be permanent features in the life of the church. His focus is on the ministry of the word and the ministries to which this will give birth. After all, the word of God, the New Testament, is the great gift of the Spirit (John 14:26; 15:26-27; 16:13-15). And it is by the Spirit's supernatural ministry that we interpret, proclaim, apply, and obey it.

THE NEW WORK

A sense of completion had developed in Paul's heart and mind: 'I no longer have room for work in these regions' (verse 23). His role had been to establish living congregations in the cities he has visited with a view to their reproducing themselves in the areas that surround them (and perhaps beyond). His calling has been to plant first-generation churches that would act as catalysts for further expansion, and thus 'to preach the gospel, not where Christ has already been named' (verse 20). He is a foundation-layer. Hence his motto text is Isaiah 52:15, which he cites (in verse 21): 'Those who have never been told of him will see, and those who have never heard will understand.'

We are probably more familiar with the passage that follows the verse Paul quotes:

> Behold, my servant shall act wisely;
> he shall be high and lifted up,
> and shall be exalted.
> As many were astonished at you—
> his appearance was so marred, beyond human semblance,
> and his form beyond that of the children of mankind—
> so shall he sprinkle many nations;
> kings shall shut their mouths because of him;
> *for that which has not been told them they see,*
> *and that which they have not heard they understand.*
> Who has believed what he has heard from us?
> And to whom has the arm of the Lord been revealed? …
> He was despised and rejected by men,
> A man of sorrows and acquainted with grief.
> (Isa. 52:13–53:3)

Isaiah's words point forward to the atoning death and triumphant resurrection of the Lord Jesus. Why then does Paul cite them in relation to his own ministry? Because he realized that the fulfilment of this prophecy of Christ's ministry extended through his ministry. Through his preaching of the gospel, and the 'signs and wonders' that accompany it, the words 'Kings shall shut their mouths …' were being fulfilled. Indeed, Paul had been commissioned as an instrument of God to bring this to pass. Had not Ananias been told that this once-persecutor 'is a chosen instrument of mine to carry my name before the Gentiles and kings …' (Acts 9:15)?

This call of God on his life explains why Paul has not yet been able to visit Rome, despite his aspirations (verse 22). But that major stage in his ministry was now coming to a close. He is not planning to 'retire,' but to head west, to Spain. And he means to visit Rome *en route*, to spend some time with the believers there, and hopefully 'to be helped on' (*i.e.* given personal, spiritual, and, if possible, material assistance) to continue to fulfil his calling in these new regions (verse 23). The apostle's vision encompassed the fulfilment of Isaiah's words about the Suffering Servant.

But Paul was also familiar with the fulfilment-vision Isaiah recorded in the closing chapter of his prophecy:

> The time is coming to gather all nations and tongues. And they shall come and shall see my glory, and I will set a sign among them. And from them I will send survivors to the nations, to Tarshish, Pul, and Lud, who draw the bow, to Tubal and Javan, to the coastlands far away, that have not heard my fame or seen my glory. And they shall declare my glory among the nations (Isa. 66:18-19).

How significant is it that Isaiah mentions 'Tarshish'—the very region to which Jonah sought to flee from God's commission? Perhaps because it is the next staging post in Paul's calling. 'Tarshish' is probably Spain. But before the apostle goes there *via* Rome there is one more task to be completed.

THE DELAY

Paul's hopes—and those of the Romans—were now raised. The apostle was coming to visit them! Little did they imagine that he would arrive much later than he hoped and in a different way from what the Christians in Rome would have desired. But in the meantime, he had a burden to discharge—a burden that would cause a considerable delay in his plans.

Reading these words in Romans in the light of the Acts of the Apostles reminds us that 'The heart of a man plans his way, but the Lord establishes his steps' (Prov. 16:9), or as Thomas à Kempis wrote, 'man proposes, but God disposes.'[1] That was as true of the apostle Paul as it is for us. His next step—an apparently brief delay in the plan to visit Rome—would in fact lead to that visit being postponed for several years. And when he did eventually reach the capital it was not as a free man but as a prisoner coming for trial before the Imperial Court. Perhaps when he said 'I *hope* to

[1] Thomas à Kempis (c. 1380–1471) *The Imitation of Christ*, Book 1.19.

see you in passing on my way to Spain' he was using the word in a 'non-theological' sense. It was certainly what he wanted to do—but his life was not his own.

God is sovereign over our lives. He 'disposes.' Nevertheless it is also appropriate for us to 'propose,' always subject to God's will (cf. James 4:15). And so, before heading west to Rome, Paul is heading east to Jerusalem, on a mission that dovetails with the concern he has expressed in this letter to see Gentile and Jewish believers living in mutual harmony and caring for each other as family. The reason for the delay was ... *the collection.*

The details of this emerge in the verses that follow.

42

The Collection

This is the reason why I have so often been hindered from coming
to you. [23] But now, since I no longer have any room for work in
these regions, and since I have longed for many years to come
to you, [24] I hope to see you in passing as I go to Spain, and
to be helped on my journey there by you, once I have enjoyed
your company for a while. [25] At present, however, I am going
to Jerusalem bringing aid to the saints. [26] For Macedonia and
Achaia have been pleased to make some contribution for the poor
among the saints at Jerusalem. [27] For they were pleased to do it,
and indeed they owe it to them. For if the Gentiles have come to
share in their spiritual blessings, they ought also to be of service to
them in material blessings. [28] When therefore I have completed
this and have delivered to them what has been collected, I will
leave for Spain by way of you. [29] I know that when I come to
you I will come in the fullness of the blessing of Christ.
[30] I appeal to you, brothers, by our Lord Jesus Christ and
by the love of the Spirit, to strive together with me in your
prayers to God on my behalf, [31] that I may be delivered from
the unbelievers in Judea, and that my service for Jerusalem may
be acceptable to the saints, [32] so that by God's will I may come
to you with joy and be refreshed in your company. [33] May the
God of peace be with you all. Amen.

(Rom. 15:22-33)

Paul is 'book-ending' his letter. He began (in 1:1-15) with indications of his plans and some personal news; he ends (in 15:23–16:27) with more detailed personal news and individual greetings. As he had indicated (1:11-13) he had often hoped to visit Rome. Now he had explained in some detail why that wish had never been fulfilled. His primary 'obligation' (1:14), and therefore his 'ambition,' had been to preach the gospel where Christ had not 'already been named' (15:20). A major stage of his calling had now been fulfilled in the area 'from Jerusalem all the way round to Illyricum' (15:19).

Why, then, if the plan was to go to Spain, was Paul not already on a ship heading for Rome to be helped on further west so that 'Those who have never been told of him will see, and those who have never heard will understand' (verse 21)? Was this another example of Paul being guilty of saying 'yes' when he did not really mean it—a fault of which he had been accused before (2 Cor. 1:15-24)?

WHY DELAY?

In fact the reason for the apostle's delay was related to his understanding of the 'mystery of Christ'—that in him 'the Gentiles are fellow heirs' with Jewish believers (Eph. 3:4-6). If then Gentile Christians belong to the same family as their Jewish-Christian brothers and sisters, family unity and mutual love should result and be expressed in practical ways. That was his desire for the churches in Rome (14:1–15:7). But Paul's vision stretched far beyond believers who lived in the same city. For some time now he had been sharing a burden with the churches he had planted in the Gentile world: they should together demonstrate their love for, and unity with, their needy Jewish brothers and sisters in Jerusalem. What a demonstration of the gospel that would be—Gentiles loving and sacrificing for Jews! Was this a world first?

There are indications in the New Testament that relationships between the church in Jerusalem and the congregations planted through Paul's ministry were not always easy. What was happening in Rome was a microcosm of it. As we have seen, there was a major debate about the continuing role of the Mosaic law code for followers of 'the Way' (Acts 9:2; 22:4; 24:14).

It was in Jerusalem, understandably, that continued adherence to the Levitical laws was most likely to linger. And it did—as is clear from the conversation James would soon have with Paul when he arrived in Jerusalem with the collection.[1] In response,

[1] This gift was a 'one-off' special offering, not what churches refer to today as 'the offering' (or sometimes 'the collection'). Paul had urged the Corinthians to

far from despising the Jerusalem believers, Paul practised what he had preached earlier in this letter. He wanted to see the theology he had taught turned into practice; he wanted to see Gentiles who had received mercy display mercy. Unity in love was his goal, and therefore he was very willing to act in accordance with the counsel of James to be sensitive to Jewish-Christian consciences (Acts 21:17-26).

Although relatively little is said about it in the New Testament, it is clear that to be a Christian in Jerusalem involved both social and material privation. Paul himself hints at this when he says that he 'suffered the loss of all things' (Phil. 3:8). Perhaps other believers were disowned and disinherited. The author of Hebrews refers to such experiences among his readers (Heb. 10:32-36). In addition there had been seasons of famine. So Jewish believers in Jerusalem were suffering on several fronts. Now was the time for the Gentile churches to act. And despite his fellow believers' concern that he would pay dearly if he followed through on his plan (Acts 20:22-23; 21:10-14), Paul was committed to 'bringing aid to the saints' (verse 25).

Paul was not slow to hold up the example of other believers. He does so in naming individuals (*e.g.* Phil. 2:19-30; Col. 4:12-13) and churches (1 Cor. 16:1; 2 Cor. 8:1). So here: 'Macedonia and Achaia have been pleased to make some contribution for the poor among the saints in Jerusalem.' He repeats the point: 'For they were pleased to do it' (verses 26-27). In fact Paul presses the point home even more forcefully: 'indeed *they owe it* to them' (verse 27).

There is an important general principle to be learned here. It has already appeared in various forms in Romans: *God's gift of grace always creates obligations for the recipients.* These obligations are built on God's provision, as here: 'For if the Gentiles have come to share in their spiritual blessings, they ought also to be of service to them in material blessings' (verse 27).

But why? Because Gentile and Jewish believers in Christ are not only members of the same body (cf. 12:4), they have also become one family. They share the same heavenly Father who has adopted

develop a regular and disciplined pattern of contributing to it on a weekly basis (1 Cor. 16:2). Its significance is underlined by the way he discusses it at length in 2 Corinthians 8–9.

them, the same Elder Brother whose sacrifice has redeemed them, the same Spirit who indwells them and creates in them the family likeness. In such a family the question should never arise, 'Am I my brother's keeper?' (Gen. 4:9). We are, simply because we are brothers and sisters in Christ. Nor should our question about neighbour-love ever be 'Who is my neighbour?' (Luke 10:29). Our calling is not to ask *who our neighbour is* but to *be a neighbour* like the Samaritan who 'proved to be a neighbour' by showing mercy (Luke 10:37). That was how it had been in the fellowship of the first churches in Jerusalem (Acts 2:44-45; 4:32). That is how Paul saw it should be in the fellowship between the Gentile and Jewish churches. Indeed, that is how it should always be. He wanted to give practical expression to his doctrine of 'all one in Christ Jesus' (Gal. 3:28). So should we.

The plan, then, is: 'When therefore I have completed this and have delivered to them what has been collected, I will leave for Spain by way of you. I know that when I come to you I will come in the fullness of the blessing of Christ' (verses 28-29).

Fast forward to Acts 21:1–28:31 and Paul's words are fulfilled. But his 'when I come to you' lay several years off in the future. And the manner in which he would come was quite different from the way he had planned—not as a missionary to Spain but as a prisoner of Rome.

THE MYSTERY OF PROVIDENCE

The events recorded in Acts 21–28 are remarkable for many reasons, some more important than others. What at first sight might seem trivial in an extended narrative can, however, prove to be very illuminating. And one such feature in these chapters is the unusual frequency of time-markers. They punctuate the extended story in a manner that is unparalleled in the New Testament (Acts 21:1, 4, 7-8, 10, 15, 18, 26-27; 22:30; 23:11-12, 23, 32; 24:1, 24, 27; 25:1, 6, 13, 23; 27:1-3, 7, 9, 12, 18-20, 23, 27, 33, 39; 28:7, 11, 13-14, 17, 23, 30). So, when we turn from Romans 15:28-29 to discover how Paul's plans were fulfilled, it almost seems as if his friend Luke is telling the story in slow motion, frame by frame.

Acts 24:27 is an especially significant time-marker because it is given not in days or even months, but in years. Yes, *years* would pass before Paul reached Rome. Providence seems to frown on his plans. It was not the first time Paul had discovered that

God moves in a mysterious way
His wonders to perform,
He plants his footsteps in the sea,
And rides upon the storm.[1]

The challenge to his faith was, as it is to ours, that footprints in the sea are invisible (Psa. 77:19).

Did the providence of God—being brought to Rome as a prisoner—mean that Paul did not arrive there 'in the fullness of the blessing of Christ' (verse 29)?

Part of the answer is already found in the narrative of Acts 21–28. Wherever Paul went, on sea or on land, his life and ministry were attended with blessing. And when he at last arrived in Italy he found a welcome (Acts 28:14b-16). That must have been a major encouragement to him when at the time he was sending this letter he found it necessary to explain and defend his apostolic ministry and teaching.

Unanticipated blessings emerge from that still-to-come ministry in Rome. While there he was able to share 'some spiritual gift' (1:11) not only with the Romans, but also with others. For it is probably from there that he wrote his letters to the Ephesians, the Philippians, the Colossians, and to his friend Philemon. And these particular letters certainly express 'the fullness of the blessing of Christ' (verse 29).

He gives us a glimpse of this in writing to the Philippians. Prisoner he may be, but he has not ceased to be a fruitful witness or failed to be an encouragement to his fellow believers (Phil 1:12-14). The lesson is clear enough: nothing can 'separate us from the love of God in Christ Jesus our Lord' (8:39), and nothing can ultimately prevent our living and serving 'in the fullness of the blessing of Christ' (verse 29). As he would write to Timothy during a later imprisonment in Rome, 'The word of God is not bound' (2 Tim. 2:9).

In the light of what is yet to come—unknown for Paul but known to us—his powerful, appeal for support in prayer (verses 30-33) takes

[1] The first verse of the hymn by William Cowper (1731–1800) entitled 'Light shining out of darkness.'

on a significance beyond the words themselves. For we know from elsewhere in the New Testament how those prayers were answered.

PRAYER FOCUS

Paul's request for prayer is full of feeling: it is an 'appeal' from his heart, and it is addressed to 'brothers'—a form of address we have noticed occurs only in moments of high emotion or affection. But this is more than a simple request. Paul virtually puts the Romans under oath: he appeals to the church in Rome 'by our Lord Jesus Christ and by the love of the Spirit' to 'strive together with me in your prayers to God on my behalf' (verse 30).

This appeal is wonderfully trinitarian and alerts us again to the fact that Paul's trinitarianism is not isolated to a single chapter in which he expounds the doctrine but is woven into the warp and woof of his letters. Glancing through them, noting occasions when he mentions two or all three persons of the Godhead in a single breath, is an exercise that can be as thrilling as it is instructive. The bonds he shares with others who have been adopted by the Father through the Son and in the Spirit form the foundation of his appeal to them to be energetic and persistent in prayer. They are not just praying for him but also with him.

In verse 31, Paul requests that prayer be specifically focussed in a threefold way:

First, that he might be 'delivered from the unbelievers in Judea.' He had already shared with the Ephesians elders his awareness that there were dangers attached to his visit to Jerusalem (Acts 20:22-24). This helps to explain why he resisted the urging of the believers in Caesarea to pay heed to the words and action of the prophet Agabus who had given dramatic expression to what lay ahead if Paul persisted in delivering the collection in person (Acts 21:7-14). Apparently even Luke begged him not to go, since he includes himself ('we') in the protest (Acts 21:14).

Paul's determination was a measure of the high importance he attached to the collection, and to his role as an apostle (the money could easily have been delivered by someone else). It is also an indication of his courage. He knew that he was suspect among some of the Jerusalem believers as well as openly opposed by others. And he was not immune to pain. But his response to the prophecy of

Agabus is very instructive. The fact that a prophecy might come true (as Agabus's prediction had previously done—Acts 11:27, 28—and as this prophecy also would), was not in itself a decisive indication of what he should do. He knew he needed to take it into account in drawing conclusions about how he himself should act. But in this case he believed he should be guided not by *outcomes*, nor by a *prophecy* of what would happen, but by his *commitment to the ministry to which he had been called.*

Second, Paul also urged the Romans to pray that his service would be 'acceptable'—that is, to the Jerusalem church. It was not a foregone conclusion that a gift from the Gentile churches would be welcomed by the Jewish believers in Jerusalem—especially when it was being brought by a man some of them suspected of demeaning God's law. In the event both James and Paul were wisely sensitive to the situation (Acts 21:17-26).

Paul was well aware that responses in Jerusalem might fluctuate between the hoped-for 'Praise God for the Gentile churches' fellowship with us and their love for us,' and the discouraging 'Who do these Gentiles think they are? And who do they think we are? We'd rather suffer with little than have plenty presented to us by this man and coming to us from hands that have fed unclean food to their mouths.'

There is a lesson for us all here, perhaps especially for pastors: Paul did not make the mistake of assuming that because he meant to do good the intended recipients would regard what he did as 'good.' He teaches us that love needs to be accompanied by wisdom. As Calvin somewhere comments, it is possible to lose what we seek to gain by the manner in which we seek to gain it.

Third, Paul asks his brothers and sisters to pray that what he had intimated at the beginning of his letter might come to pass: 'that by God's will I may come to you and be refreshed in your company' (verse 32). Three elements stand out here.

- Paul did 'come' to them—but not until several years had passed.
- Paul was 'refreshed' in their company—as Luke records in Acts 28:15-17, 30-31, and Paul himself indicates in Philippians 1:12-14.

• Paul did reach Rome 'by the will of God.'

YOUR WILL BE DONE ON EARTH

Paul was eventually brought to the refreshing fellowship for which he longed by a path he had not planned, and according to a timetable that was out of his control. Nevertheless it was all under the sovereign and wise superintendence of his heavenly Father. He need have no fear. In retrospect he could have sung,

Praise to the Lord, who o'er all
things so wondrously reigneth,
Shieldeth thee gently from harm,
or when fainting sustaineth:
Hast thou not seen
How thy heart's wishes have been
Granted in what He ordaineth?[1]

Paul had truly been shielded *en route*; but at times the shelter must have seemed very flimsy (*e.g.* during the two weeks recorded in Acts 27:13-44). Yet all through it he had sought the glory of God, lived for the honour of Christ, and depended on the help of the Spirit. He was willing to fill up what was 'lacking in Christ's afflictions for the sake of his body, that is, the church' of which he was a minister (Col. 1:24-25). His will was to do God's will (12:1-2). And whatever forebodings he may have had about the path by which he would reach Rome, his prayer request was that it might be God's way and not his, and that God's will and not just his own plans might be brought to fruition. He was determined; but he was not foolishly stubborn.

Perhaps Paul's sense of his own needs, and any concerns he had about what he would find when he did eventually reach Rome (potential division within, opposition and persecution from the Roman Empire without), naturally leads to his prayer-wish: 'May the God of peace be with you' (verse 33).

[1] From the hymn 'Praise to the Lord the Almighty' by Joachim Neander (1650–80). The translation cited here, by Catherine Winkworth (1827–78), has sometimes been 'softened' to, *e.g.* 'Have you not seen *all that is needful has been* [not: *how thy heart's wishes have been*] met by his gracious ordaining?' This may be an understandable attempt to guard the hymn from misunderstanding, but Catherine Winkworth better captures Neander's wording, which underlines that if our heart's wish is 'Your will be done,' then it will indeed be granted.

Earlier he had expounded at length the way in which peace flows from our justification in Christ (5:1). He had also explained how, from that peace with God, peace with others develops—in general in the church family, particularly between Jews and Gentiles in Christ, and also in believers' relations with outsiders (12:18). Now it becomes clear that this peace is rooted in God himself. Like love, peace characterizes him. He is 'the God of peace' (cf. 1 Thess. 5:23). His very being as Father, Son, and Holy Spirit is *shalom*—an inner relational peace so intense that it is part of the very definition of his being. Peace characterizes him. And the wonder of the gospel is that the God of peace promises to be with us. Not only so, but in order to bring us to taste his *shalom* his Son was 'pierced … crushed … [and] upon him was the chastisement that brought us peace' (Isa. 53:5).

Later Paul would write from Rome:

> He himself is our peace, who has made us both one and has broken down in his flesh the dividing wall of hostility … that he might create in himself one new man in place of the two, so making peace, and might reconcile us both to God in one body through the cross, thereby killing the hostility. And he came and preached peace to you who were far off [*i.e.* Gentiles] and peace to those who were near [*i.e.* Jews]. For through him we both have access in one Spirit to the Father. So then you are no longer strangers and aliens, but you are fellow citizens with the saints and members of the household of God … (Eph. 2:14-19).

In what follows in Romans 16 Paul gives beautiful expression to this reality.

43

Friends

I commend to you our sister Phoebe, a servant of the church at
Cenchreae, 2 *that you may welcome her in the Lord in a way*
worthy of the saints, and help her in whatever she may need from
you, for she has been a patron of many and of myself as well.
3 *Greet Prisca and Aquila, my fellow workers in Christ*
Jesus, 4 *who risked their necks for my life, to whom not only I*
give thanks but all the churches of the Gentiles give thanks as
well. 5 *Greet also the church in their house. Greet my beloved*
Epaenetus, who was the first convert to Christ in Asia. 6 *Greet*
Mary, who has worked hard for you. 7 *Greet Andronicus*
and Junia, my kinsmen and my fellow prisoners. They are
well known to the apostles, and they were in Christ before me.
8 *Greet Ampliatus, my beloved in the Lord.* 9 *Greet Urbanus,*
our fellow worker in Christ, and my beloved Stachys. 10 *Greet*
Apelles, who is approved in Christ. Greet those who belong
to the family of Aristobulus. 11 *Greet my kinsman Herodion.*
Greet those in the Lord who belong to the family of Narcissus.
12 *Greet those workers in the Lord, Tryphaena and Tryphosa.*
Greet the beloved Persis, who has worked hard in the Lord.
13 *Greet Rufus, chosen in the Lord; also his mother, who has been*
a mother to me as well. 14 *Greet Asyncritus, Phlegon, Hermes,*
Patrobas, Hermas, and the brothers who are with them. 15 *Greet*
Philologus, Julia, Nereus and his sister, and Olympas, and all
the saints who are with them. 16 *Greet one another with a holy*
kiss. All the churches of Christ greet you.

(Rom. 16:1-16)

Paul's letters typically begin and end with greetings. Sometimes he mentions those who are with him or individuals in the church to which he is writing. But no other letter contains such an extensive catalogue of individuals and groups as listed here.

NAMES

Lists of names can be off-putting. If an author fills the first chapter of a biography with a detailed genealogy of his subject our eyes probably glaze over. But we would be making a mistake if the sight of the names in Romans 16 made us turn the page to 1 Corinthians!

We may perhaps recognize a few names because of their close relationship to Paul (Prisca and Aquila, and Timothy, for example); but the complete list is a touching one because it introduces us to the otherwise hidden heroes of the Christian church. These are the first men and women who lived for Christ at the heart of one of the most powerful empires the world has seen—and one that would soon prove to be viciously hostile to the gospel. Even as Paul was dictating his letter to Tertius (verse 22), Lucius Domitius Ahenobarbus had recently become emperor and would reign for another decade and more. We know him better as Nero. Perhaps a cruel 'fate' awaited some of the men and women who are so warmly greeted here. We do not know. But what we do know is that it awaited the sender of the letter.

These believers were 'ordinary' Christians— like ourselves. They belonged to at least three different house churches: one met in the home of Priscilla and Aquila (verse 5—they earlier hosted a church in Corinth, 1 Cor. 16:19); another met with Asyncretus and others (verse 14); yet another met with Philologus and other saints (verse 15). Other groupings of names probably represent additional house churches (commentators are not agreed on the number). While this may shed light on some of Paul's earlier comments (were there Jewish and Gentile house churches?) it is significant that only now, at the end of the letter, the multi-congregational character of the Roman church actually comes into view. Paul's central concern has been its unity.

A further fascinating feature of the chapter is the sheer number of names Paul seems able to rhyme off as though they were no further away than the other side of town. Twenty-six individuals' names are listed. Paul may have known the names of others he greets without mentioning them individually. Not many Christians can provide a list of more than two dozen fellow-believers who belong to a church they have never visited located hundreds of miles away! This perhaps speaks to the extent to which Paul himself and some of the Christians in Rome may have travelled (and thus encountered one another). But it is also indicative of the apostle's life of prayer (cf. 1:9-10). We tend to remember the names of people who have been on our prayer lists or for whom others have prayed in our church prayer gatherings.

Paul varies his descriptions. He knew Priscilla and Aquila (verse 3), Mary (verse 6), Urbanus (verse 9). Tryphaena and Tryphosa (presumably sisters and perhaps twins) and Persis had all 'worked hard' in serving Christ (the first mentioned with Paul himself; verse 12). His married friends Prisca (or Priscilla) and Aquila had at some point 'risked their necks' for him (verse 4). Did he mean that literally? Epaenetus had the distinction of being 'the first convert to Christ in Asia' (verse 5—perhaps he had come from Ephesus with Prisca and Aquila). Andronicus and Junia (verse 7) were fellow Jews. They had become Christians (were 'in Christ') before Paul himself was, and at some point had been imprisoned, perhaps with him. They were 'well known' in the wider church. Others like Epaenetus (verse 5), Ampliatus (verse 8) and Stachys (verse 9) are 'beloved.' Apelles is 'approved in Christ'—a well-tested and faithful believer (verse 10).

Some names merit special comment for quite different reasons.

PHOEBE

In verses 1 and 2 Paul prefaces his greetings by introducing and commending an otherwise unknown 'sister' by the name of Phoebe. He provides no explicit reason for doing so beyond asking the Romans to 'help her in whatever she may need from you' (verse 2), although it has generally been assumed that she is travelling to Rome at the same time as the letter. The assumption is also usually made that Phoebe was carrying the letter and had been charged with the responsibility of delivering it to the church.

Paul does not explicitly say this, however. Travel in the first century AD could be difficult and dangerous. So it quite certainly over-reads Paul's comments if we imagine Phoebe setting off on her own with Romans in her carry-on bag. It is probably wiser to think of her setting out with her household staff (she was a woman of means, verse 2) or accompanied by a small group of people (perhaps also believers) heading for Rome. The fact that Paul indicates she may need help when she arrives (verse 2) perhaps suggests that a business enterprise or possibly some family matter was the reason for her journey.

Paul describes her in two ways that have undoubtedly made Phoebe a more controversial figure in church history than either she herself or the apostle would ever have chosen! She is (i) 'a servant [*diakonos*] of the church at Cenchreae [the port of Corinth]' (verse 1), and (ii) has been 'a patron [*prostatis*] of many' including Paul himself (verse 2).

Two debated questions have arisen in the light of these descriptions. (i) Since Paul calls her a *diakonos*, was Phoebe a *deaconess* in the church at Cenchreae? And (ii) since he also describes her as a *prostatis* was she a 'leader,' perhaps even serving (the suggestion has been made) as a 'president' in the congregation?

The answer to the second question is relatively straightforward. The word *prostatis* means 'patron.' Phoebe was a woman who was prepared to take responsibility for the welfare of others. Paul does not describe her by a term that refers to a specially recognized 'position' in the church. But she had been a help to many, including Paul himself. The suggestion that as a 'patron' (*prostatsis*) she had served as 'president' or 'leader' in the church at Cenchreae is absurd. Paul mentions she had served in this capacity *for him*. Apostles did not have a non-apostolic 'president'! Rather this highly-valued believer was widely known as a well-to-do, generous-spirited helper in Christ's kingdom.

The more widely contested question is whether Paul is here describing Phoebe as a deacon. If so then presumably other women served in that capacity in the New Testament church and therefore may do so in our churches. This has proved to be a more difficult exegetical issue. Individual interpreters (and whole denominations) of unquestioned commitment to Scripture have taken differing views. The two most common approaches to the question can be simply stated:

Reasons for believing Phoebe was a deacon(ess) include:

(i) Paul describes her as a *diakonos*, the term used for deacons in the church (Phil. 1:1; 1 Tim. 3:8, 12). The verb (*diakoneō*) is also used of deacons in 1 Tim. 3:10, 13.

(ii) He specifically connects Phoebe with a particular church. She is not only a 'servant of Jesus Christ' but of a specific church—the one at Cenchreae. This suggests she had a specific role in that church.

(iii) The Greek text of Romans 16:1 reads more literally (if woodenly), 'I commend now to you Phoebe the sister of us *being also* a servant of the church in Cenchreae.' Paul appears to be describing a permanent state of being, a role, not merely a servant spirit.

(iv) In the context of discussing the qualifications for deacons in 1 Timothy 3:11, Paul interjects an apparently parallel statement ('likewise ...') about 'the women.' If this is taken as an indication that there were women deacons, the case for regarding Phoebe as an 'office holder' in the church at Cenchreae is as good as certain.

(v) The noun *diakonos* is regularly translated 'minister' and in these cases, while not referring to the 'office' of the deacon, nevertheless it does seem to refer to individuals who had a recognized role in the life of the church (Paul in Eph. 3:7, Col. 1:23, 25; Tychicus in Eph. 6:21, Col. 4:7; Epaphras in Col. 1:7).

(vi) There were women deacons in the post-apostolic church.[1] This suggests the early church understood Paul to have provided guidelines for deacons like Phoebe, and therefore she is (probably?) described here as holding a specific 'office' in the church, even if 'church office' was not as formal a role in the house churches of the New Testament as it is in our larger churches today.

[1] In this connection, reference is often made to a letter written to the Emperor Trajan around AD 111 by Pliny the Younger (governor of the province of Asia Minor). In it he enquires about the punishment of Christians. He had arrested and tortured two female Christians he describes as *ministrae* (a Latin equivalent of 'deaconess').

Reasons for thinking Paul does not refer to Phoebe as a deacon(ess) include:

(i) The word *diakonos* is used in the New Testament on some thirty occasions. It usually refers in general to the service of an individual, not specifically to the role or office of a deacon. The statistics are telling: *apart from its use in Romans 16:1* the noun *diakonos* is used twenty times to refer to those who serve, another six times to a servant, but only three times to the 'office' of deacon. Thus, from the preponderant use, and in the absence of any clear indication otherwise, we can conclude from the purely statistical point of view, that the most likely translation of *diakonos* in Romans 16:1, is 'servant' not 'deacon.'

(ii) It is inappropriate to appeal to 1 Timothy 3:11. The ESV, for example, has the translation 'Their wives ...' in the text. The fact that Paul is discussing male deacons in verses 8-10, and returns to that discussion in verses 12-13, makes it unlikely that he pauses midstream to discuss a different group of people. Given the character of diaconal ministry and its sometimes sensitive nature, it seems more likely that the material relating to the wife of a deacon is an indication that she was occasionally associated with her husband in his service.

(iii) Since the pattern of thinking in the post-apostolic church cannot always be regarded as a safe guide to either the doctrine or practice of the apostolic church, it should not be granted any significant authority here.

(iv) It is sometimes argued that in its very nature the diaconal role involves 'authority.' Just as the elder must be able to 'manage his own household well' (1 Tim. 3:4), so also deacons need to be those who are 'managing their children and their own households well' (1 Tim. 3:12). The implication is that if one cannot 'manage' one's household it is unlikely one can 'manage' the affairs of the church. If so, implied in this qualification for the diaconate is the exercise of authority analogous to that exercised by a father in a family.

> This being the case, Paul's words in 1 Timothy 2:12 are relevant ('I do not permit a woman to teach or to exercise authority over a man'). Given these presuppositions Paul would not have thought of Phoebe as a 'deacon' but as a servant of the Lord's people in the church at Cenchreae.

Faced with these considerations, and responses that can be made to each of the points above, it is not difficult to see why there has been no unanimity on this question among orthodox and confessionally reformed churches.

It is worth reflecting here on the fact that sometimes in such debates we forget the principle that if a doctrine or practice not clearly stated in Scripture is to be universally required to be believed or practised in the churches, it must be demonstrated to be implied in Scripture by 'good *and necessary* consequence.' '*Good* consequence' may well fall short of being '*necessary* consequence.' For that to be established it is essential not only to demonstrate the consistency of an interpretation with the text of Scripture but also to demonstrate that no alternative interpretation is either grammatically, logically, or biblically coherent.[1]

The debate over this question cannot be settled in a work like this. But there are some principles embedded in Paul's teaching thus far that can help us. These include:

(i) Preserving church fellowship is important (15:5).

(ii) The kingdom of God is not a matter of deacons and or deaconesses. It is vital that we view any differences of viewpoint in the light of the central blessings of the gospel

[1] A striking illustration from a quite different issue illustrates the need for caution and grace in such discussions. In working through a number of 'case studies' to assess the biblical legitimacy or otherwise of remarriage after divorce, Professor John Murray concludes in one instance, 'We are not able to answer dogmatically one way or the other' (*Divorce* [Philadelphia: Presbyterian and Reformed Publishing Co., 1976], 115). Yet clearly a decision has to be taken 'one way or the other.' If it is true that the Bible does not answer every question and resolve every issue in a fallen world, then a measure of restraint and the exercise of the 'judgment of charity' is surely required. We see and know only 'in part' (1 Cor. 13:12), and for that reason some of our judgments will be provisional and therefore require the exercise of charity with respect to a different viewpoint. We should not place the same weight of emotion on every view we hold.

(cf. 14:17). This is so—as it was in chapters 14–15—because those who take different views on this issue both believe themselves to be following biblical teaching.

(iii) Nothing should be said or done that either minimises or demeans the loyalty to Christ of others committed to the same Scriptures and the same church (14:6-10).

Two other considerations are worth bearing in mind.

(i) It was already clear in the post-apostolic church, and should be no less so today, that it would be less than judicious to think that all diaconal ministry can be well and wisely engaged in exclusively by men.

(ii) 'Titles' and 'offices' are not so important as loving and sensitive service. It is of some interest that apart from Paul's instructions to Timothy, we know of only one church he established that undoubtedly had deacons—in Philippi (Phil. 1:1). We may assume that diaconal ministry did not ultimately depend on the 'office' of deacon in order to be exercised.

We must therefore avoid 'title neurosis.' In our time there has been a quantum acceleration of 'positions' and 'titles' in the secular business world. Today all must have a 'position' with a 'title.' Is it accidental that there has been a parallel increase in the number of positions, titles, and authority structures in many churches? By contrast the New Testament speaks of a variety of *gifts* but few *positions*. It is therefore important in relation to this issue to remember that the church is a family, not a corporation. In a family, structures are simple, striving for position is unseemly, and unity in love and respect are paramount. The further our church life strays from a familial character the more likely it is that pulses will race when 'position' is at stake. It is salutary to realize that in 1 Timothy 3:1 (ESV: 'If anyone aspires to the *office* of overseer he desires a noble task') the word 'office' is absent from the Greek text (which reads 'If anyone aspires to overseership ...').

ANDRONICUS AND JUNIA—AMONG THE APOSTLES?

Paul mentions Andronicus and Junia, fellow Jews who were 'in Christ' before he was. They were 'well known to the apostles' (verse 7 ESV). Other translations render these words 'of note *among the apostles*' (RSV), or even 'outstanding *among the apostles*' (NIV)—where the implication seems to be that they were themselves apostles.

From one point of view little hangs on the translation. The word 'apostle' (*apostolos*) has a range of meaning. It is the Greek-derived term that equates to the Latin-derived word 'missionary' (from the verb *mittere,* to send). In the New Testament 'apostle' usually refers to 'the twelve' and Paul—whose commissioning had come directly from the risen Christ. But on a few occasions it refers to those who have been commissioned by the churches they serve (*e.g.* 2 Cor. 8:23 where *apostoloi* is translated 'messengers'; Phil. 2:25 where the singular *apostolos* is used[1]). If Andronicus and Junia were 'apostles' it was in this latter sense.

Thus there could be no technical objection to calling a missionary from our church an 'apostle.' But given the confusion that exists over claims by individuals to be 'apostles' in a sense that at least rivals 'the twelve' and Paul, it seems wisest, as well as linguistically legitimate, to employ a different term (*e.g.* 'messengers'). Far from being special pleading, a moment's thought makes it clear that the same word does not always have the same meaning.

A MOTHER

The third person in this list whose presence is particularly intriguing is someone Paul does not name. We know her only by a family connection—the mother of Rufus, 'who has been a mother to me as well' (verse 13). This is perhaps the most beautiful description given to anyone in Paul's lengthy list. He had known her for some time. She had not only been a help to him (like Phoebe) but a 'mother' to him.

A clue to her identity is the reference to her son, Rufus, who is described as 'chosen in the Lord.' Since all Christians are equally 'chosen in the Lord' (Eph. 1:4), why does Paul say this specifically of Rufus but not of others? Clearly he assumes everyone in the church in Rome knows the reason, even although Rufus is apparently

[1] Interestingly the NIV (1984) translated the word as 'representative' in 2 Cor. 8:23 and 'messenger' in Phil. 2:25, which may suggest interpretive bias at Rom. 16:7 where 'outstanding among the apostles' has, to say the least, a certain ambiguity not present in the other two verses.

not a native Roman (Paul had never visited Rome, yet he knew his mother personally and well). There is something about him that is well-known (and not just because he either had ruddy cheeks or red hair—*rufus* is Latin for red or ruddy).

There is one other context in the New Testament where the name Rufus appears. Mark 15:21 records that our Lord's execution squad 'compelled a passer-by, Simon of Cyrene, who was coming in from the country, *the father of Alexander and Rufus*, to carry his cross.' Clearly Mark knew who these two men were (his Gospel was probably written when he was in Rome). The jigsaw puzzle pieces here thus seem to fall into place in a profoundly moving way. Hidden away in the fellowship of the Roman churches were a mother whose husband, and a son whose father, had one day arrived home to tell his family how he had been compelled to take up the cross of Jesus of Nazareth and become his crucifer, carrying it to his place of execution. It seems that he had carried the cross in the deeper New Testament sense by becoming a disciple (Matt. 16:24) and was in turn followed by his wife and sons.

TRUE FELLOWSHIP

So these verses have more interest than might appear at first sight. They abound in life. When we hear the hints Paul gives of the qualities, the commitment, and the loyal service of these believers it seems only natural that he would want to greet them.

There is one further noteworthy feature in what Paul is doing. Each of the Christians listening to his letter being read would hear the loving comments Paul made about them but also what he said about their fellow members! Was that a deliberate strategy on Paul's part? He was so generous, so catholic-spirited. Whether consciously or not he was promoting among them the mutual esteem and affection that would cement their harmony. The whole section wonderfully illustrates his pastoral instincts. It is as if he is saying, 'Brothers and sisters in Rome, do you realize the gifts God has graciously given to you in one another? Do you have any sense of your privileges as a church?'

It is no wonder, then, that Paul now also urges these Christians to 'Greet one another with a holy kiss' (verse 16)! True, he is addressing people living in an ancient culture. J. B. Phillips's paraphrase 'Give each other a hearty handshake all round'[1] may seem a somewhat tame dynamic equivalent, but it is a great deal better than a stoic acknowledgement of others in our church. And 'hearty' surely expresses real affection. 'Welcome' is Paul's watchword (14:1; 15:7). There should be no reluctance, no tardiness in our expressions of brotherly and sisterly love for one another in the church family.

In conveying his greetings, Paul feels he can speak for 'all the churches of Christ.' They share a common affection for the believers who live at the heart of the empire where Caesar claims to be Lord (verse 16b).

There are surely lessons for us to learn from the way Paul shares these details of the character, service, and devotion of his fellow believers in Rome. It would do us all much good to sit down beside other members of our church and ask the question—and teach our children to ask it too—'How did you get here?' so that we learn to grow in appreciation for the rich blessings Jesus Christ has graciously embedded in our church family.

One last detail is worth reflecting on here. Paul greets more than two dozen individuals by name. We can add to that number the following: the *church* in the house of Priscilla and Aquila (verse 5), the *family* of Aristobulus (verse 10) and of Narcissus (verse 11), the *mother* of Rufus (verse 13), the *brothers* who are with Asyncritus and his fellows (verse 14), and the *saints* who are with Philologus, plus the *sister* of Nereus (verse 15).

The list of greetings is impressive. That notwithstanding, if this represented the total membership of the church in Rome—even if we were to maximize the number of family members and individuals—it was still a small community, a tiny minority in a city whose population may have been pressing up towards a million.

And over this little flock a storm cloud of persecution was already gathering in the person of Nero.

Yet, looking back through two thousand years of church history, we are left in no doubt that Jesus' prophecy-promise was beginning to be fulfilled, 'I will build my church, and the gates of hell shall not prevail against it' (Matt. 16:18). The dream of another tyrant emperor—King Nebuchadnezzar—was coming to pass: the stone

[1] J. B. Phillips, *New Testament in Modern English*, 339.

cut from a mountain by no human hand, the kingdom of God, would prove stronger and more permanent than all the kingdoms of man (Dan. 2:31-45).

44

Until We Meet in Rome

I appeal to you, brothers, to watch out for those who cause
divisions and create obstacles contrary to the doctrine that you
have been taught; avoid them. 18 *For such persons do not serve*
our Lord Christ, but their own appetites, and by smooth talk
and flattery they deceive the hearts of the naïve. 19 *For your*
obedience is known to all, so that I rejoice over you, but I want
you to be wise as to what is good and innocent as to what is evil.
20 *The God of peace will soon crush Satan under your feet. The*
grace of our Lord Jesus Christ be with you.
21 *Timothy, my fellow worker, greets you; so do Lucius and*
Jason and Sosipater, my kinsmen.
22 *I Tertius, who wrote this letter, greet you in the Lord.*
23 *Gaius, who is host to me and to the whole church, greets you.*
Erastus, the city treasurer, and our brother Quartus, greet you.
25 *Now to him who is able to strengthen you according to*
my gospel and the preaching of Jesus Christ, according to the
revelation of the mystery that was kept secret for long ages
26 *but has now been disclosed and through the prophetic writings*
has been made known to all nations, according to the command of
the eternal God, to bring about the obedience of faith— 27 *to the*
only wise God be glory forevermore through Jesus Christ! Amen.
(Rom.16:17-27)

Paul's warm and generous words to the believers in Rome in 16:3-16 might well lead us to expect that his letter would conclude immediately with the personal greetings from his colleagues we find in verses 21-23 and the magnificent doxology of verses 25-27. But before we come to them we encounter in verses 17-20 a final appeal and a sharp warning.

These words may seem puzzling as well as jarring—a shock after the warm emotions stimulated by the previous verses. But this is not unique in Paul's letters (2 Cor. 10:1ff.; Phil. 3:2 are other examples). And it is readily explicable: the value of the fellowship Christ has established in Rome is so great that it must at all costs be guarded against attack. Paul never loses sight of the aggressiveness of the gates of hell (Matt. 16:18; cf. 2 Cor. 2:11; Eph. 6:10ff.). Any attack on the unity of the church in Rome seeks to damage God's (and Paul's) missionary purposes and attempts to hinder the spread of the gospel.

WATCH OUT!

How, then, does Paul counsel the church? 'Watch out for those who cause divisions and create obstacles contrary to the doctrine that you have been taught; avoid them' (verse 17). 'Look out! Keep your eyes open! Stand back!' Anticipation of the enemy is half the battle. Paul indicates both what to watch out for and what to do in response. Once again we sense that his emotions are heightened as he appeals to his readers as 'brothers' (verse 17).

Question: What do we need to guard against in the church? Or against *whom* do we need to protect the church?

Answer: Those who (i) 'cause divisions' and (ii) 'create obstacles contrary to the doctrine you have been taught.' Paul uses the same term 'divisions' (*dichostasia*) in his list of 'the works of the flesh' (Gal. 5:20); he had referred to 'obstacles' (*skandala*) already in this letter (11:9; 14:13).

We know that Paul believed some 'divisions' were inevitable if genuine believers were to be distinguished from false ones (1 Cor. 11:19). Here he is thinking about people whose spirit or teaching (and usually both) communicates a message and an atmosphere that alienates Christians from each other. They create 'obstacles' (stumbling blocks) that are 'contrary to the doctrine you have been taught.'

Paul may have in mind the same group about whom he would later write in Philippians 3:2 ('Look out for the dogs'—the 'Judaizers' who dogged his steps throughout his ministry). Their appearance in Rome would have the potential to destroy everything Paul had been seeking to build up through his letter. Perhaps they had already reached Rome ahead of the apostle. Or perhaps he knew from experience that if he did reach Rome they would find a way of sending their emissaries there too.

BAD FRUIT

The New Testament gives us litmus tests to help us identify destructive influences and 'influencers.' We learn to recognize them 'by their fruits' (Matt. 7:16). Paul indicates several of these tell-tale signs here:

(i) *Teaching that runs contrary to 'the doctrine that you have been taught.'* Here Paul indicates the need to become familiar with the teaching of the apostles (now given to us in the New Testament). Bank tellers in the past were trained to recognize forged banknotes not by being shown every conceivable forgery but by developing a familiarity with genuine notes. We similarly best grow in our ability to deal with false teaching not by amassing a library of books on heresies but by developing a solid understanding of biblical truth and growing in discernment.

(ii) *A spirit of divisiveness rather than one that promotes mutual affection.* We need to learn to discern a person's spirit as well as their words. Preachers, teachers, and social media 'influencers' are not just words on a page, or sound waves transmitted through the air. They possess, express, and then create an 'atmosphere' (Christlike or otherwise) by the way they speak and write as well as by the content of what they say.

Paul's goal was always to build up (2 Cor. 13:10). Since he is concerned here about divisiveness, we need to 'watch out for' the sinister tendency in preachers, teachers, or 'influencers' who' pull down' but never seem to 'build up.' Such men (and women) gather 'followers' like themselves by unremittingly creating a spirit of alienation. They stimulate strife and division among believers rather than heal it. Where a gap opens up they drive in a wedge. Some who attract 'followers' on social media seem to have an almost pathologically critical disposition towards others. How much we need to grow in our sensitivity to both the context and the atmosphere of New Testament teaching, and especially in our knowledge of the Lord Jesus himself!

This last growth point is related to a third hallmark of destructive influencers:

(iii) *A lack of love for the Lord Jesus Christ himself.* Paul warns against 'persons who do not serve our Lord Christ' (verse 18). Here we need to have three questions in mind. Not only, 'Is what is being said or taught consistent with apostolic teaching?' Additionally, 'Is there something omitted?' But also 'Is this person acting, speaking, and communicating with an evident love for the Lord Jesus and a desire to serve him by serving his people? Or is his or her concern domination?' People with gifts can use and abuse us rather than serve us. True service always echoes the mindset of the apostle Paul: 'what we proclaim is not ourselves, but Jesus Christ as Lord, *with ourselves as your servants for Jesus' sake*' (2 Cor. 4:5). We need to be on our guard against any 'ministry' that exudes self rather than Christ and that intimidates or dominates us rather than humbly serving us.

DISCERNMENT

The Greek philosopher Aristotle (384–322 BC) suggested that there were three analytical categories by which we can assess spoken communication, or 'rhetoric': *logos* (is what is said well-expressed and logically coherent?); *pathos* (are the emotions, the affections expressed, appropriate to what is being said?); and *ethos* (is there consistency between the speaker's own character and life-style and what he or she is saying?).

Communication theories have developed considerably since Aristotle's day, but his categories remain valuable. They reflect the basic elements of our communication with one another as the image of God. He has made us as rational, moral, and affectional people.

We can see, therefore, that what Paul is driving at (verse 18) is the importance not only of detecting false words (*logos*) but also a false spirit that comes to expression in the life of the speaker (*ethos*) and the way he expresses his message (*pathos*). These—*ethos* and *pathos*—may be more elusive elements, and more difficult to discern. But this is precisely Paul's point. It is the subtle nature of these elements that enables false teachers to '*deceive* the hearts of the naïve' (verse 18).

What should we look out for as red alerts? We need to ask

(i) Does this person's motivation and interest (and perhaps even his or her speech) seem to have a self-focus? Does it seem to feed their desires ('appetites') rather than feed me from the riches of Christ (verse 18a)?

And then we need to ask,

(ii) What is the approach of this person to me and the effect of what they say on me? If the answer is 'smooth talk and flattery,' beware deception (verse 18b).

Jesus was not naïve! There were many people in Jerusalem who 'believed in his name when they saw the signs that he was doing. But Jesus on his part did not entrust himself to them, because he knew all people ... for he himself knew what was in man' (John 2:23-25). Of course, we are not Jesus; we do not have perfect discernment. But we can learn from his example. He could tell the difference between those who trusted, loved, and served him because of who he was and those who 'believed' only because they were drawn to his 'effects.' He did not entrust himself to those he knew were untrustworthy in their relationship to him. Similarly the Christians in Rome must not be 'naïve,' says Paul.

The sharpness of this interjection of warning signs is rounded off in a way that illustrates that Paul himself is a teacher who is to be trusted. From the beginning of this letter his goal has been to serve, protect, and encourage. Notice especially his spirit of encouragement: the Lord Jesus Christ has given much to the church in Rome and has done much in them and through them. How heartening for this little flock to hear, 'your obedience is known to all' (verse 19). What an encouragement to these groups of believers numbered in dozens rather than thousands—they were by no means alone in the empire; they were appreciated everywhere!

No wonder Paul adds, 'I rejoice over you.' That is why 'I want you to be wise as to what is good and innocent as to what is evil' (verse 19). No doubt the Corinthians sitting in the room with him would remember how he had written similarly to them: 'Brothers, do not be children in your thinking. Be infants in evil, but in your thinking be mature' (1 Cor. 14:20).

Here, then, in Paul's ministry, there is *logos*, *pathos*, and *ethos* of the highest and most gracious kind.

PROMISE AND BLESSING

Warnings that are intended to protect can sometimes alarm sensitive souls. We may feel inadequately equipped to discern either the erroneous words or deceptive spirits of people who are more likely to mar the church than to make it healthy. It is a small step from feeling inadequate to becoming pessimistic. But Paul concludes this warning passage with a promise and a blessing.

First the promise: 'The God of peace will soon crush Satan under your feet.' The unspoken implication here is that behind every influence that seeks to mar the church stands the evil one. Paul does not intensify his warning by explaining this as fully as he does later to the Ephesians (cf. Eph. 6:10-18). His concern is simply to point the Roman church in the right direction and to encourage them. They will not be left to their own resources to defend their church. God is 'the God of peace' who (Paul had reassured them in 15:33) would be with them. He will guard them. And he will do this 'soon'—that is, exactly when it is appropriate and needful.

Paul's words express a striking view of God: he is the Peaceful Satan-Crusher! This description echoes the programmatic prophecy in Genesis 3:15 whose fulfilment constitutes the Bible's plot-line. There is perpetual conflict between the seed of the serpent and the seed of the woman. Christ, the ultimate seed of the woman, has crushed the head of the serpent himself, even as his own heel has been crushed in the process. Defeated and 'furious,' the serpent (now grown into a dragon) continues 'to make war on the rest of her offspring' (Rev. 12:17)—including the church in Rome. But Christ will keep his promise to build his church, satanic stratagems notwithstanding. He will defend his people and crush Satan under the feet of these small companies of Christ's followers. He did so then; he has often done so since; he is doing it today throughout the world; he will do it again until the day when John's vision will have come to pass of 'the devil ... thrown into the lake of fire and sulphur ... forever and ever' (Rev. 20:10).

Paul's warning note should be heeded. We too often tend to analyze opposition, divisions, and personal alienations in the church only at the horizontal level. Here is a helpful reminder that in the last analysis 'we do not wrestle against flesh and blood, but against the rulers, against the authorities, against the cosmic powers over this present darkness, against the spiritual forces of evil in the heavenly places' (Eph. 6:12). We must always remember to ask, Has an enemy done this? (Matt. 13:28).

Then, secondly, Paul adds the blessing—'Now receive the benediction: "The grace of our Lord Jesus Christ be with you."' His grace is sufficient (2 Cor. 12:9)—that is, for the present, all we need. And it is ours.

LOOKING ROUND THE ROOM

The Letter to the Romans comes from Paul alone (1:1); but he is not on his own. There are others with him, some of them—whom he mentions by name—were probably present with him as he now comes to the end of his letter. If so these three verses (21-23) present an attractive picture.

Imagine, if you will, the scene. Paul is perhaps conscious that his letter will be finished in a few more sentences. Dictating Romans has been a marathon. He glances round the room. Is he tired from his mental exertions, or exhilarated by the wonder of the gospel he has described? Or both? Tertius, his scribe is now on the last page. The task is now almost completed.

And—so great has been his concentration of thought—perhaps only now does Paul give his attention to the others who are with him. His eyes rest on Timothy, his 'beloved child' (2 Tim. 1:2). Does he say something like, 'Will I give them your greetings?' Beside Timothy sit Lucius, Jason, and Sosipater. He adds their greetings as well—and slips in the fact that they too are Jewish Christians—perhaps a final indication of his affection for the believers in Rome who share a Jewish background (verse 21).

Now Paul glances over to the writing table where Tertius sits. Was he a slave? Yes, he was a brother in Christ; but perhaps he was conscious that he belonged to a different class of society from someone like Gaius in whose capacious home they sat, or 'Erastus the city treasurer' (verse 23). Did they exchange words, or was the look on Tertius's face enough for Paul to understand how he felt and nod his head, gesticulate, and mouth the words, 'You send your greetings too, Tertius, and tell them you actually wrote the letter!' Perhaps he even said it out loud, just to make sure. And so we have the only words in the letter that are not Paul's but come from the person who actually wrote Romans: 'I Tertius, who wrote this letter, greet you in the Lord' (verse 22).

Think of him for another moment. He does not have a great personal family name, just a number (*tertius* is Latin for *third*). He is an otherwise unknown Christian brother, a one-verse figure, a mere sentence in the entire Bible, and in all likelihood a slave. And yet he wrote the most significant letter in world history. Can you imagine meeting him in the future resurrection? 'You're Tertius! You're *that* Tertius? Amazing! Thank you so much for your service.'

They were all sitting in the home of Gaius. He is presumably the same person Paul remembered he had baptized (1 Cor. 1:14), and (since like ourselves people had more than one name) he may be the person who is referred to in Acts 18:7 as Titius Justus, Paul's original host in Corinth. If so he is still the same open-hearted and open-homed man. His kindness in hosting Paul was ongoing, and his home was probably the meeting place for a house church in Corinth. In fact he is 'host ... to the whole church' (verse 23) which may suggest that he welcomed any fellow believer from any church who passed through the city.

And then there is Erastus. He held the responsible position of being 'the city treasurer' (verse 23), and was probably therefore a relatively wealthy individual, although he may also have been a freedman, as 'civil servants' often were in the Roman Empire—its efficiency largely depended on them.

Finally Paul comes to Quartus, about whom we know nothing. His name is Latin for 'fourth,' and it is tempting to think he was the younger brother of Tertius. We do not know. But we do know that to Paul he was 'our brother.'

So now, as Tertius looks over again to Paul, the last words of this great epistle are dictated. They are not in the form of a benediction (as verse 20 was) but are a doxology. The last words are for God, not for man. But they are about the God who has given the gospel to man. They form a fitting conclusion to what Paul again describes as 'my gospel.' It is, ultimately, 'the gospel of God' (1:1).

Thus the closing words of Romans not only conclude the whole letter but also echo the contents of the preceding chapters. They express Paul's own response to his gospel. In turn they model the only appropriate response. Preachers should take note and imitate.

The 'gospel of God' is the gospel of the only God, the God who is 'all wise' (verse 27). His ways are perfect even when he works mysteriously in history. Only such a God could devise the way of redemption he has provided in Christ. For this is the God 'who did not spare his own Son but gave him up for us all' (8:32). He is the very Saviour who has been preached to us in this letter in which Paul has explained 'the mystery that was kept secret for long ages' but has 'now been disclosed through the prophetic writings' (*i.e.* the Old Testament, verse 26). Salvation, the righteousness of God for those who believe in Christ, has come 'apart from the law' and yet its truth was already witnessed to by both 'the Law and the Prophets' (3:21).

Now, in this letter to the Romans, this gospel, in which the power of God's saving righteousness has been revealed, is being proclaimed 'to all nations'—to Jew and Gentile alike (1:16-17). Nor is this Paul's own idea; it is done by the 'command of the eternal God' (verse 26) who set Paul apart for his gospel (1:1). And the gospel's goal has also been Paul's goal: 'to bring about the obedience of faith' for the sake of his name among 'all nations'—including the Christians in Rome (verse 26; cf. 1:5-6).

The Letter to the Romans thus contains Paul's gospel. In it he has truly imparted a spiritual gift to us (1:11): Salvation is provided in Jesus Christ. It is all of the Father's grace; it is all ours in union with the Lord Jesus his Son; it is all made effectual in our lives through the Spirit. From him and through him and to him are all things (11:36). In this gospel our strength is to be found and for it our praise will eternally be given.

Therefore we surely want to echo Paul's closing words (verse 27):

> To the only wise God be glory forever more through Jesus Christ! Amen.

Amen, and amen.

Group Study Guide

SCHEME FOR GROUP BIBLE STUDY

(Covers 26 weeks; before each study read the passage indicated and the chapters from this book listed below)

STUDY	PASSAGE	CHAPTERS
1	1:1-17	1–3
2	1:18-32	4–5
3	2:1-29	6–8
4	3:1-31	9–11
5	4:1-25	12–13
6	5:1-11	14–15
7	5:12-21	16–17
8	6:1-23	18–19
9	7:1-12	20
10	7:13-25	21
11	8:1-11	22
12	8:12-30	23–24
13	8:31-39	25
14	9:1-5	26
15	9:6-33	27–28
16	10:1-21	29
17	11:1-24	30
18	11:25-36	31
19	12:1-8	32–33
20	12:9-21	34

21	13:1-7	35
22	13:8-14	36
23	14:1–15:7	37–39
24	15:8-33	40–42
25	16:1-16	43
26	16:17-27	44

This Study Guide has been prepared for group Bible study, but it can also be used individually. Those who use it on their own may find it helpful to keep a note of their responses in a notebook.

The way in which group Bible studies are led can greatly enhance their value. A well-conducted study will appear as though it has been easy to lead, but that is usually because the leader has worked hard and planned well. Clear aims are essential.

AIMS

In all Bible study, individual or corporate, we have several aims:

1. To gain an understanding of the original meaning of the particular passage of Scripture;
2. To apply this to ourselves and our own situation;
3. To develop some specific ways of putting the biblical teaching into practice.

2 Timothy 3:16-17 provides a helpful structure. Paul says that Scripture is useful for:

(i) teaching us;
(ii) rebuking us;
(iii) correcting, or changing us;
(iv) training us in righteousness.

Consequently, in studying any passage of Scripture, we should always have in mind these questions:

What does this passage teach us (about God, ourselves, etc.)?
Does it rebuke us in some way?
How can its teaching transform us?
What equipment does it give us for serving Christ?

In fact, these four questions alone would provide a safe guide in any Bible study.

PRINCIPLES

In group Bible study we meet in order to learn about God's word and ways 'with all the saints' (Eph. 3:18). But our own experience, as well as Scripture, tells us that the saints are not always what they are called to be in every situation—including group Bible study! Leaders ordinarily have to work hard and prepare well if the work of the group is to be spiritually profitable. The following guidelines for leaders may help to make this a reality.

Preparation:

1. Study and understand the passage yourself. The better prepared and more sure of the direction of the study you are, the more likely it is that the group will have a beneficial and enjoyable study. Ask: What are the main things this passage is saying? How can this be made clear? This is not the same question as the more common 'What does this passage "say to you"?,' which expects a reaction rather than an exposition of the passage. Be clear about that distinction yourself, and work at making it clear in the group study.

2. On the basis of your own study form a clear idea *before* the group meets of (i) the main theme(s) of the passage which should be opened out for discussion, and (ii) some general conclusions the group ought to reach as a result of the study. Here the questions which arise from 2 Timothy 3:16-17 should act as our guide.

3. The guidelines and questions which follow may help to provide a general framework for each discussion; leaders should use them as starting places which can be further developed. It is usually helpful to have a specific goal or theme in mind for group discussion, and one is suggested for each study. But even more important than tracing a single theme is understanding the teaching and the implications of the passage.

Leading the Group:

1. Announce the passage and theme for the study, and begin with prayer. In group studies it may be helpful to invite a different person to lead in prayer each time you meet.

2. Introduce the passage and theme, briefly reminding people of its outline and highlighting the content of each subsidiary section.

3. Lead the group through the discussion questions. Use

your own if you are comfortable in doing so; those provided may be used, developing them with your own points. As discussion proceeds, continue to encourage the group first of all to discuss the significance of the passage (teaching) and only then its application (meaning for us). It may be helpful to write important points and applications on a board by way of summary as well as visual aid.

4. At the end of each meeting, remind members of the group of their assignments for the next meeting, and encourage them to come prepared. Be sufficiently prepared as the leader to give specific assignments to individuals, or even couples or groups, to come with specific contributions.

5. Remember that you are the leader of the group! Encourage clear contributions, and do not be embarrassed to ask someone to explain what they have said more fully or to help them to do so ('Do you mean … ?').

Most groups include the 'over-talkative,' the 'over-silent' and the 'red-herring raisers'! Leaders must control the first, encourage the second and redirect the third! Each leader will develop his or her own most natural way of doing that; but it will be helpful to think out what that is before the occasion arises! The first two groups can be helped by some judicious direction of questions to specific individuals or even groups (for example, 'Jane, you know something about this from personal experience …'); the third by redirecting the discussion to the passage itself ('That is an interesting point, but isn't it true that this passage really concentrates on … ?'). It may be helpful to break the group up into smaller groups sometimes, giving each subgroup specific points to discuss and to report back on. A wise arranging of these smaller groups may also help each member to participate.

More important than any techniques we may develop is the help of the Spirit enabling us to understand and to apply the Scriptures. Have and encourage a humble, prayerful spirit.

6. Keep faith with the schedule; it is better that some of the group wish the study could have been longer than that others are inconvenienced by it stretching beyond the time limits set.

7. Close in prayer. As time permits, spend the closing minutes in corporate prayer, encouraging the group to apply what they have learned in praise and thanks, intercession and petition.

STUDY 1: ROMANS 1:1-17

Romans 1:1-7

AIM: To understand the content of the gospel of Christ and our witness to it.

1. Paul describes the gospel as 'the gospel of God.' What does he mean by this expression, and how important is it?

2. What aspects of the person of the Lord Jesus Christ does Paul emphasize in verses 3-4? Why do you think he does so?

3. Are there lessons we can learn about our evangelism from what Paul says in verses 5-6?

4. In verse 7 how does Paul model a Christian attitude to other believers?

Romans 1:8-15

AIM: To reflect on and be challenged to use our spiritual gifts well.

1. Paul encourages believers to imitate him (Phil. 3:17). What features in Paul's words in verse 9 are worthy of imitation?

2. Should we all think of our own particular spiritual gifts the way Paul thought about his? What would that look like in our church if we did?

3. Is there enough mutual encouragement in our church family? Is that always our goal in using the spiritual gifts we have received? Are there false goals at which we sometimes aim?

4. Paul felt a tremendous sense of obligation. What was it? Do we have the same or similar obligations?

Romans 1:16-17

AIM: To learn why we do not need to be ashamed of the gospel.

1. What might have caused someone like the apostle Paul to be 'ashamed of the gospel'?

2. Are there situations or people in particular that tend to make you 'ashamed'?

3. In Romans 1:16-17 Paul tells us the reasons he is not ashamed of the gospel. Should we have the same reasons? Are there others?

4. In these verses and throughout Romans Paul teaches a great deal about his own Jewish people. Do we have the same concern for them? Should we—why or why not?

STUDY 2: ROMANS 1:18-32

Romans 1:18-23

AIM: To grow in our ability to understand the people to whom we are called to take the gospel.

1. Why do you think Paul does not point people to Christ directly in these verses? He does not mention the Lord Jesus until 2:16. Is there anything we should learn from this?

2. Paul says unbelievers possess the knowledge of God. What kind of knowledge?

3. In what ways do people you know or work with 'suppress the truth' (verse 18)? What do we need to do to help them?

4. What is it that 'can be known about God'?

5. In what ways do people today illustrate verses 22-23?

Romans 1:24-32

AIM: To apply Paul's teaching in the first century to our own times.

1. In what ways, if any, do you think these verses are evidenced in our own society?

2. How can we explain to non-Christians the teaching Paul is giving here?

3. Many people (and their governments) today believe that what Paul calls here 'unnatural' is actually 'natural' and even 'normal.' Why should we believe Paul? What are the roots of this thinking?

4. Reflecting on verses 28-32, what do you think Paul means by a 'debased mind'? How does it manifest itself?

5. Does this dark passage help us in our witness to non-Christians? If so, how?

STUDY 3: ROMANS 2:1-29

Romans 2:1-11

AIM: To reflect on the judgment of God.

1. In 2:1 Paul indicates the inconsistency of those who judge. In what ways does this principle of the inconsistency of sinners help us to undermine the thinking of contemporary secularism?

2. How does Paul penetrate the bland assumption people make that they are 'OK' with God?

3. What does Paul mean when he says that 'God's kindness is meant to lead ... to repentance'? What implications and applications can we draw from this principle? How should we reflect God's kindness in our witness?

4. How would you help someone who thought that in verses 6-11 Paul is teaching us that we are justified by living a good life?

Romans 2:12-16

AIM: To consider principles of divine judgment.

1. What principles of God's judgment does Paul spell out in these verses?

2. How would you respond to someone who said that God's judgment was unfair?

3. In what ways does Paul's teaching that 'the work of the law is written on their hearts' give us a 'point of contact' with non-Christians? How does this help us to show unbelievers that they actually 'know' what they deny they know?

4. What do you think Paul has in mind when he speaks about God judging 'the secrets of men by Christ Jesus' (verse 16)?

Romans 2:17-29

AIM: To study Paul's analysis of the mistaken thinking of his own people.

1. What privileges did Paul's kinsmen believe they had?

2. What charge did he level against them? What do you think was the root of their problem?

3. Do you think that Paul's assessment in verse 24 of the impact on others of his own people whom he has described in verses 17-23 can be levelled against Christians? If so what is to be done?

4. Why did Paul think that being circumcised was not the same thing as being a real or true Jew?

STUDY 4: ROMANS 3:1-31

Romans 3:1-20

AIM: To reflect on Paul's teaching on human sinfulness.

1. Paul was accused of demeaning the privileges Jews believed God had given them. How does he respond to this charge?

2. Verses 5 and 7 are in some ways 'trick' questions designed to show that Paul's teaching is false. How does he respond to them? Do we encounter similar types of questions, and how do we respond?

3. Why do you think Paul uses so many Old Testament quotations in verses 10-18 to make his point?

4. How important is Paul's teaching on 'total' and 'universal'

depravity? What are some of the consequences of neglecting or rejecting this doctrine?

Romans 3:21-22

AIM: To revisit Paul's basic theme announced in Romans 1:16-17.

1. Does Paul simply repeat here what he had said in 1:16-17, or are there added details?

2. How would you explain to a new Christian what 'the Law and the Prophets' means?

3. How would you show from the Old Testament that Paul's teaching here is accurate?

4. Do the Law and the Prophets also bear witness to the fact that God's righteousness in Christ is 'for all who believe' and that 'there is no distinction'?

Romans 3:23-31

AIM: To grow in appreciation for what lies at the heart of the gospel.

1. How significant is it that Paul describes sinners as falling 'short of the glory of God' (verse 23)?

2. How would you explain the meaning of the big words in verses 24-25 to a new Christian? And how would you help them to understand the importance of the realities they describe and the effect they have on our Christian lives?

3. How does the gospel silence boasting (verses 27-28)?

4. What does Paul mean in verses 29-30?

5. Paul will later explain how his teaching upholds the law. Can you suggest from what he has already said what his response will be?

STUDY 5: ROMANS 4:1-25

Romans 4:1-12

AIM: To reflect on the ways Paul uses the Old Testament to confirm the gospel.

1. How would you show from the life of Abraham that the way of salvation in the Old Testament and the New Testament is one and the same?

2. How were Old Testament saints meant to understand the significance of circumcision? And how was it related to justification?

3. Paul describes only circumcision as a sign that served as a seal. But can those words be applied to other rites and symbols in the Bible? If so, to which ones?

4. How should we connect what Paul says here about circumcision (verses 11-12) to the way he relates circumcision and baptism in Christ in Colossians 2:11-12? How do these two rites shed light on each other?

5. What do you think it means to 'walk in the footsteps of Abraham'?

Romans 4:13-25

AIM: To gain a better understanding of grace and faith.

1. In what sense was Abraham to be 'heir of the world'? Does that apply to all believers?

2. How would you explain the word 'grace' to a new Christian? How is the grace-way the guaranteed-way? And how does Paul link grace and faith?

3. What does Paul mean by 'hope' and by saying that Abraham 'in hope believed against hope' (verse 18)? Do we ever do that? If so, how?

4. While the words spoken about Abraham apply to us (verse 23), is there any difference between Abraham's faith and our faith?

STUDY 6: ROMANS 5:1-11

Romans 5:1-5

AIM: To grow in our appreciation of the privileges of justification.

1. We often speak about having 'peace with God,' but what does it mean? What is the difference, and what is the relationship, between having peace with God and our feelings of peace?

2. What privileges flow from justification, and in what ways do we experience them in the Christian life?

3. How is it possible for us to 'rejoice in our sufferings'? Do you know anyone who does?

4. We often speak about 'character'; but what does Paul mean by 'character,' and how is it developed in us? Do some Christians lack 'character'? How did God create 'character' in Paul?

Romans 5:6-11

AIM: To meditate on the richness of God's love.

1. How does Paul describe those for whom Christ died (verses 8-10)? How do these descriptions apply to us? What difference do you think Paul expected this teaching would make to the Christians in Rome, and to ourselves?

2. How would you describe the greatness of the love of Christ?

3. Do we use Paul's 'much more' way of thinking (verses 9-10)? What is it supposed to produce?

4. What does it mean to 'rejoice in God'? Is it true we don't do this enough? What will enable us to do it more?

STUDY 7: ROMANS 5:12-21

Romans 5:12-14

AIM: To understand the analogy between Adam and Christ.

1. In verse 14 Paul describes Adam as 'a type of the one who was to come.' How does this help us to understand the teaching of this whole section?

2. What are the implications of Adam being our 'representative'?

3. How would you answer the question, 'Is this a fair arrangement on God's part?'?

Romans 5:15-21

AIM: To appreciate the greatness of Christ's work.

1. In what ways are Adam and Christ similar, and in what ways different?

2. How does Paul's teaching here help us to understand the human condition and predicament?

3. What are the practical implications of Paul's emphasis on the 'much more' of grace?

STUDY 8: ROMANS 6:1-23

Romans 6:1-14

AIM: To reflect on what Paul means by teaching that we have died to sin and been raised to new life.

1. How would you explain to a new Christian why the question in verse 1 arises and how Paul responds by his teaching on our union with Christ?

2. In what ways does our union with Christ in his death and resurrection transform our sense of who we are as believers?

3. What practical differences in our lives should Paul's teaching make?

4. How do we present ourselves to God (verse 13)?

5. Why do you think theologians have believed this passage is so significant?

Romans 6:15-23

AIM: To consider what it means to be set free from sin for the service of Christ.

1. How do these verses help us to understand what Paul meant by saying we are 'not under law but under grace' (verse 14)?

2. What does it mean that we have become 'slaves' of Christ?

3. What most impresses you when you compare what you were by nature with what you have become by grace?

4. In what ways are we 'set free from sin' (verse 22)? What are the effects of this freedom?

STUDY 9: ROMANS 7:1-12

Romans 7:1-12

AIM: To understand more fully the nature of our relationship to the law.

1. A fellow Christian says to you, 'I am not under law but under grace' (6:14). How do you react and respond?

2. If the law is not 'sin' (verse 7), how would you describe its nature and function?

3. What did Paul mean by saying he was 'alive apart from the law' but then 'died' (verse 9)? Was that unique to his experience?

4. Put into your own words the meaning of verse 12. What effect does Paul's description have on our view and use of the law?

STUDY 10: ROMANS 7:13-25

Romans 7:13-25

AIM: To see how the law functions in the Christian life.

1. How does Paul describe the effects of seeing our life in the light of the law?

2. Augustine of Hippo once said that he had become a 'problem' or puzzle to himself. That seems to agree with Paul's words in verse 15. Is that something the Christian experiences?

3. How should we understand the distinction Paul makes in verse 17 between 'I' and 'sin'?

4. Can a Christian say the words of verse 18?

5. How should we understand the perspective from which Paul is speaking in these verses?

STUDY 11: ROMANS 8:1-11

Romans 8:1-11

AIM: To appreciate what it means that in Christ there is no condemnation.

1. How is it that we are set free from condemnation?

2. How is the law 'weakened' (verse 3)?

3. How would you explain verses 1-4 and their importance to a new Christian?

4. What is involved in walking according to the Spirit?

5. What does Paul teach us about the Holy Spirit in verses 9-13?

STUDY 12: ROMANS 8:12-30

Romans 8:12-17

AIM: To learn how to deal with indwelling sin in the light of our adoption into God's family.

1. What do we mean by 'the mortification of sin'?

2. What motives does Paul give us to put sin to death?

3. Calvin wrote that 'the Spirit of adoption' is the 'first title' of the Holy Spirit. Why do you think he said that?

4. What are the privileges of adoption implied in these verses?

Romans 8:18-30

AIM: To understand better the nature of the Christian life in the present age.

1. How can Paul say what he does in verse 18? Should we be able to say this? Can we?

2. How do verses 19-22 give us a different view of the created order from the views generally held by non-Christians?

3. In what ways does the teaching of verses 23-25 affect our Christian life?

4. Do you 'groan inwardly' as you 'wait eagerly'? If so, why? Does this agree with what Paul says here?

5. How does Paul describe God's goal for Christians and how should that affect the way we think about the Christian life? How does he achieve this goal?

STUDY 13: ROMANS 8:31-39

Romans 8:31-39

AIM: To appreciate the assurance and security the message of the gospel gives us.

1. In what ways do these verses suggest that Christians will experience many different kinds of pressure and opposition?

2. What significance is there in the way Paul uses the personal interrogative 'who' rather than 'what'?

3. How would you explain the gospel to someone from Romans 8:32?

4. Do we think enough about the present ministry of Christ—for example in his intercession?

5. How can we make our own the assurance Paul expresses in these verses?

STUDY 14: ROMANS 9:1-5

Romans 9:1-5

AIM: To reflect on the pain experienced by Paul about his own people and its implications.

1. What do you think helps to explain the apparently sudden transition in mood and atmosphere from Romans 8:39 to Romans 9:1-5?

2. Is Paul's pain unique to him? Or unique to apostles? Is there any sense in which we should share it, either in general or even in particular for the Jewish people?

3. Paul was accused of denying that God had been gracious to the Jewish people. How does he prove the reverse here?

4. Is Paul's statement in verse 3 something that should be true of all of us, or is it unique to Paul as an apostle who was Jewish?

5. Does the doctrine of the deity of Christ depend on Romans 9:5? What other passages point to it?

STUDY 15: ROMANS 9:6-33

Romans 9:6-18

AIM: To learn how how Paul defends the faithfulness of God and the reliability of his word.

1. What is the problem Paul is responding to in verse 6? Is it a problem to you, or to others you know?

2. How does Paul show that not all Israel's descendants belonged to the 'true' Israel of God?

3. Why do you think he used the illustrations to which he appeals in verse 9, and verses 10-12?

4. What question does this raise, and how does he answer it?

5. How would you express to another Christian what Paul says in verse 18?

Romans 9:19-33

AIM: To study the way Paul speaks about both divine sovereignty and human responsibility.

1. Is Paul's response in verse 19 satisfactory? Why does he respond in this way? Is there anything for us to learn from his response?

2. How is the character of God revealed in what Paul says here about divine election?

3. How has God shown his mercy in history?

4. How would you describe and explain to a young Christian what Paul says here about the relation between divine sovereignty and human responsibility?

STUDY 16: ROMANS 10:1-21

Romans 10:1-21

AIM: To grow in our appreciation of the gospel and how it reaches people.

1. Where did Paul think his Jewish kinsmen had gone wrong?

2. How does Paul use the Old Testament to contrast the way of works and the way of faith?

3. Trace the pattern God uses in verses 13-17 in the way we are brought to faith and reflect on how the pattern functions today.

4. How does Paul show that the situation he saw in his ministry was already foreshadowed in the Old Testament?

STUDY 17: ROMANS 11:1-24

Romans 11:1-24

AIM: To explore God's ways with and purposes for both Jew and Gentile.

1. How does Paul answer the question, 'Has God rejected his people?' (verse 1)?

2. How do these verses emphasize human responsibility?

3. What is the significance of the question in verse 11? How does Paul answer it?

4. Why do you think Paul addresses the Gentiles in particular in verses 13ff.?

STUDY 18: ROMANS 11:25-36

Romans 11:25-36

AIM: To reflect on the 'mystery' Paul unveils and his (and our) response.

1. What is the 'mystery' Paul is speaking about here? How does he explain it?

2. What is Paul's final conclusion?

3. On the assumption that 2 Timothy 3:16-17 applies also to these verses, how is Paul's teaching here 'profitable for teaching … reproof … correction, and for training in righteousness'?

4. What do we learn about the character of God from verses 33-36?

5. How does the knowledge of verse 36 make a difference to our lives?

6. As an exercise for reflection, can you write a hymn on the basis of these verses?

STUDY 19: ROMANS 12:1-8

Romans 12:1-2

AIM: To sense the nature and importance of consecration.

1. How important is the word 'therefore' in living the Christian life?

2. What does Paul mean when he speaks about 'the mercies of God' (verse 1)? How does it provide a basis, a motive and an encouragement for our consecration?

3. The ESV translation refers to us presenting our 'bodies as a living sacrifice.' How do we do that?

4. How important is the mind in the Christian life? How is it renewed?

5. What do you think Christian non-conformity to the world looks like today?

Romans 12:3-8

AIM: To appreciate what it means for the church to be a body.

1. How can we learn not to think more highly of ourselves than we should? What is a 'sober assessment' of ourselves?

2. How important is it that we recognize we have different gifts?

3. Can you describe the ways the different gifts Paul mentions here are employed in your church family?

4. Why do you think Paul used the picture of the body here?

STUDY 20: ROMANS 12:9-21

Romans 12:9-21

AIM: To recognize the ways in which consecration to Christ is worked out in practical details.

1. Put in your own words what the different exhortations in verses 9-13 might mean in your own life.

2. What will help us to bless those who oppose us and our Christian faith?

3. What are some of the ways the exhortations in verses 14-21 were illustrated in the life of the Lord Jesus?

4. How can I learn not to be wise in my own sight?

STUDY 21: ROMANS 13:1-7

Romans 13:1-7

AIM: To understand the basic biblical view of the state.

1. What is the 'normal' attitude of the Christian believer to the state? Is there a danger in not having that attitude?

2. How do we as Christians show respect to the state in our actions, words, and attitudes?

3. Are there times when we should not be subject to the state? If so, how would you show this from biblical teaching?

4. Does the church do enough to help its members fulfil their responsibilities as Christian citizens?

STUDY 22: ROMANS 13:8-14

Romans 13:8-14

AIM: To grow in our appreciation of the relationship between law and love.

1. Is love a spontaneous emotion or something else—so that it can be 'owed' to someone else?

2. How is it that love is the fulfilment of the law? How do Paul's words help us to understand the nature and purpose of God's law?

3. Why are verses 11-12 motives for holiness?

4. How would you describe 'the armour of light' (verse 12)?

5. What other passages in Scripture might help us to explain verses 13-14?

STUDY 23: ROMANS 14:1–15:7

Romans 14:1-12

AIM: To study biblical principles for dealing with differences in the church family.

1. What does it mean in the context Paul is addressing to be 'weak in faith'?

2. What causes one Christian to despise another one (verse 2)? What has gone wrong when that happens?

3. How can we distinguish between having genuine spiritual discernment and passing judgment on someone?

4. Can you think of applications of Paul's teaching here that are relevant today?

5. What principles does Paul teach us here to help us maintain fellowship when we disagree?

Romans 14:13-23

AIM: To reflect on self-discipline in the way we respond to fellow Christians.

1. Should we have a commitment not to pass judgment on other church members in the vows we take when joining a church?

2. We sometimes speak about having the courage to practise our convictions. But what is involved in having the courage not to practise them?

3. Why does Paul make the basis of his thinking what he says in verse 17?

4. What does it mean to keep your faith between yourself and God?

5. Should a Christian ever act contrary to conscience? Explain why or why not.

Romans 15:1-7

AIM: To see the importance of Christ's example.

1. Why does Paul place the responsibility to have forbearance on the 'strong'?

2. What is the difference between pleasing our neighbour and being a man-pleaser?

3. Sometimes Christians say the first question we should ask about what we should do is WWJD (What would Jesus do?). Is this always right? Is it always helpful?

4. What can we learn from verse 4 about the way we read the Old Testament?

5. How are truth and harmony or peace to be related to each other?

STUDY 24: ROMANS 15:8-33

Romans 15:8-13

AIM: To study how the hope of the Old Testament has been fulfilled.

1. What does Paul mean when he says that Christ was a 'servant to the circumcised'?

2. Why did Christ become such a servant?

3. What do verses 9-12 tell us about Paul's knowledge of and understanding of the Old Testament?

4. How does 'the God of hope' enable us to 'abound in hope'? Is there a difference between being 'hopeful' and being able to 'abound in hope'?

Romans 15:14-21

AIM: To learn from Paul's example of Christian service.

1. Considering what Paul has already taught the Romans, does what he says in verses 14-15 come as a surprise?

2. Looking back through Romans, on what points do you think Paul has 'written very boldly' (verse 15)?

3. What is the significance of Paul's description of his ministry in verse 16? Can we apply this today to our own various ministries in the church?

4. Is it legitimate for the Christian to have pride? If so, how, and what does it look and sound like?

5. How does Paul relate the sovereignty and the grace of God to his own hard work in verse 17-18? What can we learn from this?

Romans 15:22-33

AIM: To consider the significance of 'The Collection.'

1. Are all hindrances in the Christian life evil and from Satan (as in 1 Thess. 2:18)? How can we tell the difference between Satan hindering and God directing—as for example in Acts 16:6-10?

2. Are there principles that help us to realize when it is the Lord's will for us to move to another place, or sphere of service?

3. Paul had a burden that the churches he had planted should take up a special collection for the Jews in Jerusalem. Can we learn something from this—and if so, what?

4. What is the love of the Spirit, and why is it important?

5. What would be required in us for people to feel refreshed by being in our presence (verse 32)?

STUDY 25: ROMANS 16:1-16

Romans 16:1-16

AIM: To reflect on the privilege of having Christian friends.

1. What does this whole passage teach us about the importance of friends to the apostle Paul—and to ourselves?

2. Taking Paul's expressions one by one, think of Christians you know who fit his descriptions:

(i) fellow worker;

(ii) neck-risker;

(iii) hard worker;

(iv) beloved in the Lord;

(v) approved in Christ.

3. What would be needed in your life to make all of these descriptions fit you?

STUDY 26: ROMANS 16:17-27

Romans 16:17-27

AIM: To appreciate the practical advice with which Paul ends Romans and his closing doxology.

1. What are the characteristic features of people who cause divisions in the church?

2. How can we guard against being deceived ourselves?

3. What do you think it means to be 'wise' to what is good, but 'innocent' to what is evil? How can this be true of us?

4. Why do you think Paul refers to Satan here (verse 20)?

5. Rearrange what Paul says in verses 25-27 in chronological sequence. How does this lead Paul to his closing doxology?

6. How does this lead Paul (and us) to say 'to the only wise God be glory forevermore through Jesus Christ. Amen' (verse 27)?

For Further Reading

The following commentaries will be found helpful for further study of Romans:

William Hendriksen, *Exposition of Paul's Epistle to the Romans* (Edinburgh: Banner of Truth Trust, 1980, 1981).

Douglas J. Moo, *The Epistle to the Romans* (Grand Rapids: William B. Eerdmans, 1996).

Leon Morris, *The Epistle to the Romans* (Grand Rapids: William B. Eerdmans, 1988).

John Murray, *The Epistle to the Romans* (London: Marshall, Morgan & Scott, 1967).

John R. W. Stott, *Romans: God's Good News for the World* (Leicester: Inter-Varsity Press, 1994).

Other Books by Sinclair B. Ferguson published by the Trust

Child in the Manger: The True Meaning of Christmas, small clothbound, 216pp.

Children of the Living God, Delighting in the Father's Love, small paperback, 144pp.

Christian Life: A Doctrinal Introduction, large paperback,

Deserted by God: Hope for All who Do Not Sense the Lord's Sustaining Presence during Life's Most Troublesome Times, large paperback, 182pp.

Devoted to God: Blueprints for Sanctification, large paperback, 296pp.

Devoted to God's Church: Core Values for Christian Fellowship, large paperback, 200pp.

Discovering God's Will, small paperback, 128pp.

From the Mouth of God: Trusting, Reading and Applying the Bible, large paperback, 224pp.

Grow in Grace, small paperback, 160pp.

Healthy Christian Growth, booklet, 32pp.

Heart for God, small paperback, 144pp.

Heroes of the Faith (for children): Ignatius of Antioch, Irenaeus of Lyons, Polycarp of Symrna, hardback, 120pp.

Icthus: Jesus Christ, God's Son, the Saviour, large paperback, 184pp.

John Owen on the Christian Life, large clothbound, 316pp.

Let's Study Ephesians, large paperback, 224pp.

Let's Study James, large paperback, 160pp.

Let's Study Mark, large paperback, 328pp.

Let's Study Philippians, large paperback, 154pp.

Man Overboard! The Story of Jonah, large paperback, 112pp.

Maturity: Growing Up and Going On in the Christian Life, large paperback, 244pp.

Pundit's Folly: Chronicles of an Empty Life, small paperback, 104pp.

Read Any Good Books?, booklet, 32pp.

Sermon on the Mount: Kingdom Life in a Fallen World, small paperback, 184pp.

Some Pastors and Teachers: Reflecting a Biblical Vision of What Every Minister is Called to Be, large clothbound, 824pp.

Welcome to the Library: Introducing the Puritan Classics, booklet, 32pp.

Wisdom Everywhere: Introducing the Treasures of John Owen, booklet, 32pp.

BANNER *of* TRUTH

The Banner of Truth Trust originated in 1957 in London. The founders believed that much of the best literature of historic Christianity had been allowed to fall into oblivion and that, under God, its recovery could well lead not only to a strengthening of the church, but to true revival.

Interdenominational in vision, this publishing work is now international, and our lists include a number of contemporary authors, together with classics from the past. The translation of these books into many languages is encouraged.

A monthly magazine, *The Banner of Truth*, is also published, and further information about this, and all our other publications, may be found on our website, banneroftruth.org, or by contacting the offices below:

Head Office:
3 Murrayfield Road
Edinburgh
EH12 6EL
United Kingdom

Email: info@banneroftruth.co.uk

North America Office:
610 Alexander Spring Road
Carlisle, PA 17015
United States of America

Email: info@banneroftruth.org